The Daily T

Guide

EVERYDAY
LAW

The Daily Telegraph

Guide to
EVERYDAY
LAW

Aviva Golden

HarperCollins*Publishers*

HarperCollins*Publishers*
P.O. Box, Glasgow G4 ONB

First published 1994

Reprint 9 8 7 6 5 4 3 2 1

ISBN 0 00 470142 9

A catalogue record for this book is
available from the British Library

Photoset by Rowland Phototypesetting Ltd
Bury St Edmunds, Suffolk
Printed in Great Britain by
HarperCollinsManufacturing Glasgow

Contents

Acknowledgments

In the preparation of this book I received assistance from several people. In particular I would like to thank the following: Jean Campbell, BA, LLM, who contributed three chapters (chapter 4, *Death – Before and After*, chapter 6, *Goods and Services* and chapter 11, *Accidents*); Lisbeth Grayson, my administrative assistant, who compiled the directories; Ann Hand, LLB, Hons, the indexer who also provided the update to chapter 10, *Motoring*; Hirsh Jacobson, BSc, researcher; and Marina Milmo, solicitor, teacher of French Law and adviser to the Islington Legal Advice Centre, consultant editor.

I am also grateful to those who read chapters of the book at various stages of work in progress: Leslie Blake, LLM, AKC, barrister, lecturer in law, Department of Linguistic and International Studies, University of Surrey – *Landlords and their Tenants* (chapter 5) and *Countryside* (chapter 9); Suzanne Davies, solicitor – *Goods and Services* (chapter 6); Professor Roger Fisher, Faculty of Design and the Built Environment, University of East London – *Neighbours* (chapter 8); Susan Krikler, family law barrister – *Setting up Home* (chapter 1), *Divorce* (chapter 2) and *Children* (chapter 3); Carol Kohll, solicitor – *Death – Before and After* (chapter 4); Rosalind Malcolm, LLB, barrister, lecturer in law, Department of Linguistic and International Studies, University of Surrey; *Coutryside* (chapter 9) and Marina Milmo – *The Legal System* (chapter 12).

I would also like to thank Christopher Riches of HarperCollins and Marilyn Warnick of Telegraph Books who gave the project their enthusiastic backing, as well as Monica Thorp of HarperCollins for editing the text so thoroughly.

Finally I should like to give special thanks to Eileen O'Grady, barrister and law reporter, for her encouragement and support.

The tables in the *Motoring* chapter are reproduced with the permission of the Controller of Her Majesty's Stationery Office; those on pages 303, 316 and 323 are from the Highway Code and that on page 314 is from the Road Traffic Act 1991. The law's view of stages of growing up, at the end of the *Children* chapter, is based on information in the booklet *At what age can I . . . ?*, published by the Children's Legal Centre.

Author's note

Please note that the law in this book is applicable to England and Wales only. I have endeavoured to state the law at the date of going to press. However, this can only present a snapshot of a moving image. With every day that passes, the law undergoes subtle – and sometimes dramatic – changes both in the courts of law and in Parliament.

The examples in the text are there to illustrate a principle. They do not point to a conclusion or outcome in any specific case and are not a substitute for a full consideration of all the relevant facts and law in any given situation.

The directories

At the end of each chapter from chapter 3 onwards, you will find a directory of relevant organizations. The directory in chapter 3 is a combined one for all the first three chapters. We have endeavoured to ensure that names and addresses are correct at the time of going to press. If any organization would like to be considered for inclusion in one or other of the directories in future editions of the book, a letter should be sent to the Reference Department, HarperCollins Publishers, PO Box, Glasgow G4 0NB.

Readers are asked to note that some organizations give advice only to their own paid-up members; some organizations provide information but do not offer advice or handle complaints; some organizations respond to written queries only and cannot answer over the telephone.

As far as the religious organizations are concerned, for detailed information on the requirements of any particular faith we advise you to contact someone connected with that faith.

Do note that some religious organizations are faith-led and offer advice only to their own adherents.

Aviva Golden
November 1994

1. SETTING UP HOME

MARRIAGE AND COHABITATION

According to the law of England, marriage is 'the voluntary union for life of one man and one woman to the exclusion of all others.' However, the law today encompasses a reality in which much has changed in family life. While marriage in this country must still comprise a voluntary union between one man and one woman, the statistics of today's England speak for themselves: more than a million couples each year choose to live together rather than to marry; one in three children today is born to unmarried parents; and even among those couples who do get married, one in every three of them will seek a divorce.

Again, nothing could seem more basic than the concept of parenthood itself – from both the biological and the social points of view. Yet, today, when we talk in terms of a child's 'natural' parents, we must also consider the legal implications of artificial insemination, *in vitro* fertilization, 'virgin' birth and surrogate motherhood.

Thus family law has to take account of rapid and dramatic shifts in our established patterns of family life. Of course, this is far easier said than done. The issues raised are highly charged and very complex. How far must the law adapt to these changing patterns? Or rather, to what extent should it impose its own pattern of what is 'desirable' in family life? Can conflicting ideologies over family values be bridged at all? Are the courts the right place in which to try to build these bridges?

No wonder then that profound difficulties arise – for those who have to make the laws, for those who have to implement them, and for those who have to turn to the courts for assistance. No wonder, too, that the law can sometimes appear helpless in the face of these problems, which it has to confront and endeavour to settle, on a daily basis.

◆ **Note:** A DIRECTORY of organizations and other bodies which provide support or information on all aspects of family law can be found at the end of Chapter 3.

This chapter looks at

- who can get married
- the engagement
- marriage formalities
- effects of marriage
- cohabitation
- agreements

1. Who can get married?

1.1 Determining who is a 'single' person

The law stipulates that in order to marry, every person must

(a) be unmarried (for definition of a single person see section 1.1.1 below);
(b) be over the age of 16;

(c) want to marry someone of the opposite sex;

(d) not be closely related to their future spouse;

(e) agree to the marriage (i.e. it must be a 'voluntary union').

1.1.1 An unmarried person

Every marriage in this country must be a monogamous union, i.e. it must be between two single persons. The law regards you as a single person if

(a) you have never been married at all or

(b) you have been married before but that marriage has

      i. been dissolved (through recognized divorce proceedings);

      ii. ended with the death of your spouse; or

      iii. been annulled (as void).

1.1.2 Someone who has been through a recognized divorce

A divorce is recognized in this country if it is obtained in a civil court according to the law of England. Thus divorces which are obtained in England in purely religious proceedings are not recognized.

You and your husband are Orthodox Jews who have always lived in London. You have agreed to his request for a divorce and have obtained a divorce according to Jewish law (a get*). You are told that you have to go through civil divorce proceedings if you wish to remarry here.*

That is correct. A *get* on its own would not entitle you to remarry under the laws of England.

Divorces obtained abroad are recognized provided

(a) the parties are domiciled there; and

(b) they are proper proceedings recognized under the law of the country where the divorce proceedings took place. The proceedings can be religious or civil provided that they are formally held and proceed under set rules.

1.1.3 A widow or widower (including presumption of a former spouse's death)

There may be difficulties if you need to establish the death or disappearance of a former spouse before you can remarry. To assist in such cases, the law 'presumes' that a spouse is dead if all contact has been lost with him or her for seven years and you have no reason to believe that he or she is alive.

Your husband left you several years ago to live abroad. You have never heard from him and all your endeavours to trace him have failed. Someone has suggested that your husband may even be dead. You now want to remarry. What can you do?

If your husband has not been heard from for seven years you can petition the courts to dissolve your first marriage on the grounds that he is 'presumed to be dead'. If he has been out of touch for less than seven years, you would have to show positive evidence as to why you think he may be dead. In any event, you might have grounds for divorce on the basis of a five-year separation (see chapter on *Divorce*), if he has been away for that long.

1.1.4 Someone whose previous marriage has been annulled

You are also in law a single person if your previous marriage has been annulled (see section 1.3 below).

1.1.5 The question of polygamy

Difficulties can arise in our multi-ethnic society where some groups accept polygamous unions which are not accepted by the law of England. For example, you might marry a foreigner in this country and then discover that he already has a legal wife, since under the laws of his own country, it is legal for a man to be married to more than one woman. As far as your own marriage is concerned, it is void in English law.

In certain circumstances, however, the courts will recognize a polygamous union, entered into abroad, according to the law of *both* parties' domicile.

1.1.6 Summary

Anyone who has been married once before cannot remarry in this country until the law regards him or her as single once again. In other words, monogamy is still the guiding principle of the institution of marriage according to the law of England – for the purposes of marrying here.

1.2 Other necessary qualifications to meet

In addition to insisting that marriage can only take place between two single people, the law insists on several other necessary criteria before two people can marry.

1.2.1 Age requirements

You must meet the age requirements:

- Any single person can get married over the age of 18
- If you are aged between 16 and 18, you must obtain parental consent
- A marriage where one of the persons is under the age of 16 is absolutely void.

If someone marries between the ages of 16 and 18 without parental consent, their marriage is voidable (for the difference between 'void' and 'voidable' marriages, see sections 1.3.1 and 1.3.2 below).

Who must consent to a marriage of a child aged 16 to 18?

- The parents or
- The guardian or
- The court

You are 17 years old and are desperate to marry the man of your choice. However, your parents thoroughly disapprove of him and refuse to consent to the marriage. You are so determined that you make a false statement to the superintendent registrar that you are 18 in order to get a licence (see section 3.2.1(d)). Three weeks later you get married. Now your parents state that your marriage is void. What is your position?

Your false statement has not invalidated your marriage (see section 1.3 below). However, giving false information to the superintendent registrar of marriages is a serious criminal offence.

The sensible alternative would have been to apply to court to ask its permission to marry. The court can dispense with parental consent and give its own consent to your marriage if you can persuade the magistrates that your parents, by withholding their consent, are acting unreasonably.

You are 17 and wish to get married. You live with your mother, who divorced your father when you were ten. She is quite agreeable to your proposed marriage. You received occasional visits from your father for the first couple of years after your parents' divorce, but he has been out of touch with you since. Do you need his permission too?

The law on this issue is not clear; if your mother has sole parental responsibility for you only her consent would be necessary. If your father and mother have joint parental responsibility then you might have to seek your father's permission (for Parental Responsibility see chapter on *Children*).

In any event, you could apply to a magistrates' court to dispense with your father's consent.

1.2.2 Intention to marry someone of the opposite sex

The law specifies that the parties must be male and female, 'one man and one woman'. So there cannot be a legal marriage of a couple who are homosexual.

Problems also arise with transsexuals who wish to marry. As far as the law is concerned every person's sex is determined at birth and as entered on their birth certificate. Thus even if a person has undergone a sex change, there cannot be a valid marriage to someone of the opposite sex in this country. The issue has even been taken to the European Court of Human Rights. It ruled that English law is entitled to use biological criteria for determining a person's sex. 'An attachment to the traditional concept of marriage' was sufficient reason to maintain the present position, the court ruled. However, the court also stated that the law should be kept under review.

1.2.3 No marriage can take place between close relations

How is relationship defined?

There are many degrees of relationship in which intermarriage is forbidden by law. These relationships are usually grouped into two categories:

(a) blood relations (consanguinity)
(b) non-blood relations but where the relationship is so close that a ban on intermarriage is still imposed (affinity).

◆ **Note:** an adopted child is generally treated in law as a blood relative.

(a) Consanguinity

A man cannot marry	A woman cannot marry
his daughter	her son
his mother	her father
his sister	her brother
his niece	her nephew
his granddaughter	her grandson
his adopted daughter	her adopted son

(b) Affinity

In general a man or woman cannot marry

- a stepchild
- a son- or daughter-in-law

However, in the affinity category, the prohibitions on intermarriage are not always absolute.

After the sudden death of your wife, you found it difficult to cope with your job as well as having to look after your two small children. Your wife's sister, who is a divorcee, came to live in your house to assist you with the housekeeping. You have now fallen in love with her and you both decide that you would like to get married. What is the position?

An Act of Parliament allows brothers-in-law and sisters-in-law to marry.

So marriages in the affinity category can be allowed in certain, tightly-circumscribed circumstances: for example, a step-parent can marry a step-child – provided only that

- the step-child has not been brought up as a 'child of the family' and
- is over 21.

1.2.4 The marriage must be voluntary

Where a person has gone through a ceremony of marriage because of coercion, the law holds that that person has not given proper consent to the marriage. Among certain ethnic and religious groups, it is common practice for the parents to arrange marriages for their children. Is an arranged marriage regarded as a 'voluntary union'?

In general, the law does not interfere with arranged marriages. However, the issue can become a problem when there is a conflict between the wishes of the parents and those of the child. If the conflict is grave, the courts may be called upon to assess the point at which parental and social pressures overstep an acceptable limit and become unacceptable duress. The courts have found instances of duress where there is

- a threat of injury to life or liberty or
- a child is threatened with expulsion from home and community.

1.3 Marriages which can be annulled

1.3.1 Void marriages

Certain marriages are regarded in law as absolutely void. In other words, the marriage – in the eyes of the law – has never taken place at all.

Marriages are absolutely void where

- one of the parties is under the age of 16
- the parties are closely related (see section 1.2.3 above)
- one of the parties is not a single person, i.e. the marriage is bigamous or polygamous (see section 1.1.5 above)
- the parties are regarded in law as being of the same sex (see section 1.2.2 above).

1.3.2 When are proceedings for annulment instituted – voidable marriages

Certain marriages are regarded in law as valid until they are annulled. These are 'voidable' marriages and, in the eyes of the law, they can be annulled on the petition of either party.

On the whole these proceedings are rarely used. However, they are retained to meet the needs of those who have objection to divorce proceedings and who have grounds for annulment.

1.3.3 Grounds for annulment

In order for a court to annul a voidable marriage, a person would have to show one of the following grounds:

(a) the marriage has not been consummated;
(b) the husband or wife had not understood the nature of the ceremony; in other words, he or she got married through a mistake (such as not knowing that it was a ceremony of marriage);
(c) the marriage was to someone of unsound mind;
(d) the marriage was to someone with VD.

2. The engagement

2.1 Breach of promise?

Today an engagement is not a precondition of a marriage although couples often do make a public, formal announcement of their engagement.

At one time, an engagement was considered a binding legal contract. If you broke off an engagement, you could be sued by your ex-fiancé(e) for 'breach of promise' to marry. Today this is no longer so.

Thus whatever heartache their decision to part entails, an engaged couple are absolutely free to change their minds if they decide not to marry after all. They need not fear a court action!

> You lived abroad and became engaged to your fiancé in a foreign country where engagement is regarded as a binding legal agreement. You both now live in England. After a time, you decide to break off the engagement. Your ex-fiancé threatens to sue you. What is your position?

> An agreement to marry is not legally enforceable in the English courts – wherever the engagement took place. It might still be actionable abroad.

2.2 Problems if an engagement falls through

Although there is no action for breach of promise, legal disputes do arise between an engaged couple who decide to part. These disputes usually concern property and gifts.

2.2.1 The engagement ring

Certain clear rules of law govern the question of the return of an engagement ring. It is regarded as an outright gift – unless it can be shown to be a family heirloom.

> Your fiancé has given you a very expensive engagement ring but the engagement has since been broken off by mutual agreement. Are you under a legal obligation to return the ring?

> The answer is that an engagement ring is presumed to be an absolute gift so that there is no obligation to return it. The same rule applies to birthday or Christmas gifts which your fiancé may have given to you – or you to him.

> Your fiancé has given you a very valuable engagement ring which is a family heirloom, having once belonged to his great grandmother. The engagement is broken off by mutual agreement. Are you under a legal obligation to return the ring?

Again the presumption is that an engagement ring is intended to be an outright gift. However, where your fiancé can show — as in this case — that the ring is intended to remain in his family, you may be obliged by law to return it.

2.2.2 Other expenses

Weddings today can be very expensive and involve an outlay of thousands of pounds. What is the position if the wedding is cancelled? In addition, the couple may have gone to the trouble and expense of putting a down-payment on a flat or house. What happens to their deposit if they decide to call the whole thing off?

In each case, the question will turn on the contract into which the parties have entered.

You have each put down money on the asking price of a flat where you were intending to live after your marriage. A great deal of expense has been incurred for your forthcoming wedding. The bride's father has hired the hall and paid a deposit to the caterers and the band; the groom's family have paid for a honeymoon in the West Indies. Family and friends have already sent gifts. The wedding is called off and you blame each other. What is the position?

(a) The wedding expenses

With regard to the expenses incurred for the wedding, such as the deposit on the hall or the catering costs, the money may well be lost.

Recovery of the money would depend on the terms of the contract on making the arrangements. It would always be prudent to ask, specifically, in dealing with caterers and others, what would happen in the event of a cancellation.

Can you obtain insurance cover against calling off the party?

In the scenario above, the wedding was entirely called off. Insurers are unlikely to cover a change of heart. However, in other circumstances, a bride or groom may fall ill, have to cancel arrangements, and not be able to fix another date for their planned wedding for many months. Enquiries should be made from certain specialist insurers who have policies which carry cover against cancellation of wedding arrangements in these circumstances.

(b) The honeymoon

With regard to the cancelled honeymoon, most people take out insurance to cover the sudden curtailment of holiday plans. Such policies usually deal with illness or bereavement.

(c) Property

With regard to the question of the flat, rights to it are governed by the law of property, as well as by statute. The Matrimonial Proceedings Act 1970 states that the same rules apply to interests in property between formally engaged couples as between husband and wife.
On the face of it, each partner should be entitled to a share in the property equivalent to the sum of money which has been expended on it. But other factors will come into account, such as the name or names in which the down-payment was made, any arrangements for a mortgage, and whether contracts on the flat have been exchanged with the seller.

7

◆ **Note:** In spite of the provisions of the Act, the courts do not have the same extensive powers to make arrangements for the sharing out of the property of an engaged couple, who then break up, as they have on that of a married couple who decide on a divorce.

In any transaction where there is an intention to purchase property jointly, **both parties must seek legal advice**.

(d) Wedding gifts

Last but not least – what about the expenses of other people? For example, guests might have spent money on gifts which they have already despatched only to learn that the wedding is cancelled.

The couple are obliged to return wedding gifts already received to their senders. The law implies a condition that the presents were sent in the event of a marriage taking place; that condition having failed, the guests are entitled to the return of their gifts.

3. Marriage formalities

For a marriage to be valid, a licence and a formal ceremony are necessary.

3.1 The preliminaries

3.1.1 Simplifying the law?

The preliminary formalities necessary before a couple can get married are surprisingly complicated. They are also outmoded. Many of the rules which regulate these preliminaries were first formulated in the eighteenth century and were primarily designed to protect wealthy heiresses from making clandestine – and unsuitable – marriages.

Law Commission Papers in 1973 and 1990 recommended simplifying the law so that everyone could readily understand the rules and regulations which govern the ceremonial aspects of marriage. Changes have only been enacted in relation to premises to be approved by local authorities for civil marriages (see section 3.4.3 below).

3.1.2 Who can give authorization for a marriage?

Authority to license marriages is given to priests of the Anglican church and to civil officials (the superintendent registrar of marriages of each district). Every couple, therefore, must first obtain either religious or civil authorization to marry, or publish banns in an Anglican church before they can go through a wedding ceremony.

3.2 Religious ceremonies

Religious ceremonies are categorized according to whether they are solemnized by

- the Anglican Church including the Church in Wales, or
- Jews or Quakers (for whom special rules apply under the Marriage Act 1949) or
- some other recognized religion.

We live in a multi-denominational, multi-ethnic society. The fact that different rules apply to different religious groups has increased the pressure for change in these rules.

3.2.1 Church of England: licence to marry

One in two of all religious marriage ceremonies take place in the Church of England.

There are four ways to effect the necessary preliminaries for an Anglican marriage. Only one of these may be used. Thus in order to obtain consent to get married in the Church of England, you must either

- publish banns

or obtain one of the following:

- a common ecclesiastical licence
- a 'special' licence, also from the ecclesiastical authorities
- a superintendent registrar's certificate from the civil authorities.

(a) Publishing banns

The banns, i.e. the declaration of the names of the couple who intend to marry, have to be read aloud ('published') in the church of the parish where the couple are resident. If they are resident in different parishes, the banns must be read in each parish church, in one or other of which the ceremony must take place.

You and your husband-to-be live and work in the same parish in London. However, you decide you want to get married in a church in the village where your mother-in-law lives as she is not very mobile. Where should the banns be read?

In this case, the banns will have to be read in the church in which you intend to get married as well as in the church of the parish in which you are resident.

The priest needs seven days' notice in writing from both parties before he can read the banns. He has to read them in 'an audible manner' in his church on three successive Sundays.

If there is no objection from a member of the congregation, the marriage can take place at any time up to three months after the third reading of the banns.

Any objection to the marriage must be voiced publicly in church by a member of the congregation after the banns are read. The banns are then void.

The purpose of the banns is clearly intended to ensure publicity for the intended marriage. Provided, therefore, that you do not intend to conceal your identity, you can publish the banns under a name by which you are generally known.

You are known as Miss Roberts after the name of your stepfather although the name on your birth certificate is Smith (your father's name). You publish your banns under the name of Roberts. Are they still valid?

The answer is 'yes', provided there has been no attempt to conceal your identity.

(b) Common licence

This dispenses with the banns and is granted by the bishop of the diocese. You must make a sworn statement in writing [an *affidavit*] that there is no impediment to the marriage, that any necessary parental consent has been given (see section 1.2.1 above), and that you have resided in the parish for 15 days.

Once granted, the licence to marry takes immediate effect and remains valid for three months. It must specify the church or chapel in which the wedding is to take place. In general the church authorities advise this procedure for a marriage between a foreign person and a British subject or between two foreigners who wish to get married in a church of the Church of England.

(c) Special licence

This is issued by the Archbishop of Canterbury and enables a marriage to take place at any time or place. It also dispenses with the residence period of 15 days. It might be applied for if, for example, one of the couple was seriously ill. To get such a licence, a sworn statement is required with the same particulars as above.

◆ **Note:** Addresses for the issue of common licence and special licence by the ecclesiastical authorities are found in the DIRECTORY at the end of Chapter 3. You are advised to approach the Vicar-General (see Directory).

(d) Superintendent registrar's certificate

It is usual for a wedding in the Church of England to take place after publication of the banns or after obtaining a licence from the church authorities (above). However, an Anglican wedding can take place after a superintendent registrar's certificate to marry has been obtained.

The procedure is as follows:

The parties must give their notice to the superintendent registrar of the district in which they must have resided for at least seven days before giving notice.

They must make a solemn declaration (not an affidavit) that

- there are no lawful impediments to their union
- they meet the residential requirement

and (in the case of persons between 16 and 18) that

- their parents have consented.

If the parties live in different districts, then notice must be given in each district.

The notice, written into the notice book, is displayed in the superintendent registrar's office for at least 21 days. At the end of that period – provided there has been no objection – the superintendent registrar's certificate is issued. The marriage can take place in a church in the superintendent registrar's district. The consent of the minister of the church must be obtained.

3.2.2 Divorced persons who wish to remarry in the Church of England

The Anglican Church regards marriage as a union for life. As a result, where either party to a marriage is a divorced person, a remarriage generally cannot be solemnized in a Church of England church. This rule does not apply to marriages which have been annulled.

You have recently decided to get married for a second time, having been divorced from your first husband. You attend church regularly. You obtain a superintendent registrar's certificate and approach your minister to ask whether he would solemnize your marriage. He refuses. Can you prevail upon him to change his mind?

The answer is 'no'. He is not obliged to solemnize the marriage of a person whose first spouse is still alive. He can also refuse to permit your marriage to be solemnized in his church by any other person standing in for him. However the minister may well be prepared to bless the union in his church after a civil ceremony.

3.2.3 Need to observe other rules

Other stipulations to a Church of England wedding are also laid down by law:

an Anglican wedding must take place

- in an unlocked church
- between the hours of 8 am and 6 pm
- with two witnesses present during the ceremony

(see section 3.5 below for the application of these rules to other wedding ceremonies – religious and civil).

3.3 Other denominations and religions

If you belong to a denomination or religion other than Church of England you must first obtain permission (either certificate or licence) from the civil authorities in order to marry.

There are four ways of meeting the civil requirements; only one of these need be used:

- a superintendent registrar's certificate (see section 3.2.1(d) above).
- a superintendent registrar's certificate with a licence. This has a residence requirement of 15 days for one of the parties only; it is not displayed but the parties must make the same declarations as to age, etc. The marriage can then take place after one clear day.

For those seriously ill or otherwise confined, special provisions apply

- under the Marriage Act 1983 and
- under the Marriage (Registrar General's Licence) Act 1970.

3.3.1 Formalities: Jews and Quakers

Weddings for Jews and Quakers can take place anywhere and at any time under the Marriage Act according to their own practices. The marriage is solemnized by a person designated for the purpose after the issue of a civil licence.

3.3.2 Formalities: other denominations and religions

(a) Civil certificate and registered building

In addition to the need to obtain a civil certificate (see section 3.2.1(d) above), marriages for denominations and religions other than Jewish or Quaker must take place in a registered building or chapel.

(b) Solemn declaration according to civil procedure

Not only is a civil licence required, but at some stage of the proceedings, the person designated to officiate at the ceremony must use the same form of words as is used in a civil ceremony (see *Solemn Declaration* section 3.4.1 below).

3.3.3 Possible source of friction

It is clear that different rules apply to different religious groups and denominations. Legislation in an area as sensitive as marriage can cause resentment among groups who are not accorded the same treatment in law.

3.4 Civil ceremonies

The General Register Office issues a form, Form 357, which provides notes on the legal requirements of getting married. The fees payable are set out in Form 357A.

3.4.1 Solemn declaration

Marriages in a register office (as well as marriages of faiths other than Anglican, Jewish or Quaker) require a solemn declaration from both bride and groom according to the civil form

- that they know of no impediment to their union
- that they call upon those present to witness that they take each other as lawful wedded wife and husband.

The two witnesses present then sign the register; this is a requirement in all cases (see section 3.5.1 below).

3.4.2 Presence of registrars

The superintendent registrar and the registrar must both be present at a civil wedding, which currently takes place in a register office (except in the very unusual circumstances where someone is seriously ill or otherwise confined (see, however, sections 3.4.3 below).

3.4.3 Choosing your venue

The premises in which a superintendent registrar can marry a couple by civil procedure are confined to municipal buildings designated for this purpose. However, changes to this stipulation will be made under the 1994 Marriage Act (see also section 3.6 below).

Under this act local authorities will be able to 'approve' premises for the solemnization of marriages. Parliamentary regulations will be passed which will cover such matters as

- kinds of premises to be approved
- procedures for applying for approval
- conditions and fees which a local authority may impose
- keeping of registers of approved premises.

3.5 Other rules: religious and civil ceremonies

The rules concerning witnesses to the ceremony of marriage, the buildings in which such ceremonies can take place, and the hours during which they can take place, were drawn up to ensure that marriages cannot take place in secret.

3.5.1 Witnesses

All marriages – without exception, be they religious or civil, require two witnesses to the ceremony. The witnesses need not know the couple.

3.5.2 Buildings

All marriages, except those according to the practices of Jews and Quakers, must take place in a building registered for that purpose. Where someone is so sick as to be housebound, then special procedures are allowed for (see sections 3.2.1(c) and 3.3 above).

3.5.3 Hours

All marriages, again those of Jews and Quakers excepted, have to take place between the hours of 8 am and 6 pm.

3.5.4 The marriage certificate

After every ceremony, civil or religious, the marriage is entered on the marriage register and signed by two witnesses. The couple are entitled to a copy of the certificate. Extra copies, if required, can be obtained from the register office.

3.6 Proposals for change

(a) Simplifying licence procedures

Two Law Commission Papers have suggested that licence procedures should be simplified in the public interest. It has been suggested that there should be one form of certificate, plus one other procedure for cases of real urgency.

(b) Civil wedding package

The 1990 White Paper proposed that, for those who want it, a civil marriage ceremony should offer more glamour. While local authorities should continue to solemnize marriage in 'standard' ceremonies, they should also be able to use notable public buildings for venues. These proposals have now been enacted in the Marriage Act 1994 but have still to come into force. Marriages in approved premises will still require the standard form of words as used in all civil marriages, and the presence of two witnesses, plus that of the superintendent registrar and the registrar of the district.

3.7 Marrying abroad

In this section, we are not dealing with persons who marry abroad because one or other spouse is a foreign person or lives abroad. We are dealing, instead, with English persons, domiciled here, who choose to marry abroad. Certain problems can arise if your wedding takes place abroad – the most important being that you can find yourself bound by the laws of the country in which you have got married (see section 3.7.1 below).

> *You are planning your wedding and have read in a magazine that you can get married abroad. The idea of getting married in an exotic location really appeals to you and you want to find out more about it. You wish to know whether there are any legal snags of which you should be aware.*

> Specialist travel agencies publish brochures which arrange for wedding ceremonies in a host of countries from the Far East to the Mid-West of the United States. The brochures are usually very detailed and are quite specific as to the documentation required for each country, as well as for residence requirements.

With regard to the legal issues, a marriage that is valid by the laws of the country in which it has taken place is regarded, generally speaking, as a legally binding and valid marriage in this country.

3.7.1 Problems which might arise

If both parties are domiciled in England, the marriage also has to be valid by the law of your domicile, i.e. England. For example, a marriage would be invalid here if one of the parties was under-age or the couple were too closely related to each other. Such a marriage could be a valid marriage in the country in which it took place, but it would not be regarded as valid here.

Another question also arises. Would you be bound by the laws of the country in which the wedding ceremony has taken place? For example, you might choose to have a wedding ceremony abroad and only subsequently discover that, according to that country's marriage laws, a husband can administer (i.e. take charge of) his wife's property. That could land you in a very awkward situation.

◆ **Note:** It is essential to seek legal advice on these issues. To make absolutely sure that your marriage would be governed – for all future purposes – by the laws of England, you might have to arrange to go through a civil ceremony in the British Embassy in the country which you have chosen for your wedding venue.

4. Effects of marriage

4.1 The effects

'Being married' confers a definite legal status on both husband and wife. This status affects many aspects of their lives and can last for the rest of their lives. It confers rights and duties on them both, stemming from their 'common home and common life'. Moreover, the change in their legal status takes place from the moment that they marry.

At one stage, a husband and wife were even regarded as one person in law. That person was the husband! A wife's legal personality was said to have 'merged' into his.

Over the past hundred years, there have been significant changes to the law in an endeavour to free wives from this legal doctrine. It has been described recently in the House of Lords as anachronistic and offensive. A wife is no longer her husband's chattel and a marriage should be regarded in law as a partnership of equals.

In general, questions of status, rights and duties concern the following:

4.1.1 Duty to live together

Husband and wife have a duty to live together. Of course, they are free to leave if the marriage proves unhappy. However, if one spouse leaves the other for good, this can be a fact in showing that the marriage has irretrievably broken down (see chapter on *Divorce*).

4.1.2 Duty to maintain

Spouses have a duty to maintain one another. Again it is usually only on divorce that this element of marriage takes on legal significance. Its significance is great, however. Along with responsibility for caring for their children, the duty to maintain one another can survive even the breakup of a marriage. It also can lead to protracted legal battles on divorce when all other issues between the couple have been settled.

4.1.3 Sexual relationship

Husband and wife are expected to have sexual relations. Failure to consummate a marriage can be grounds for annulment (see section 1.3.3 above).

◆ **Take note:** The sexual act must be voluntary and the wife must consent to it. A husband can be charged with rape if he forces himself on his unwilling wife.

4.1.4 Fidelity

Husband and wife are expected to be faithful to one another; adultery is still a main fact in showing the irretrievable breakdown of a marriage (see chapter on *Divorce*).

4.1.5 Common surname?

The wife can take her husband's surname but she is not under a legal duty to do so. A wife's right to use her husband's surname survives his death and even a divorce from him. It is unusual for the husband to take his wife's name though he can do so if he wishes. Occasionally, couples adopt both surnames.

If a wife does change her name to her husband's surname, she can do so informally, simply by using his name. However, married women have to inform institutions, such as banks or building societies, of their change of name and could expect to be asked to produce their marriage certificates.

> *You intend to take your husband's name from the day that you get married. You have made plans to spend the honeymoon abroad. Can you apply for a passport in your married name before the wedding day?*

> The answer is 'yes'. You can apply for a British passport which can be *postdated* with your married name. In order to make the application, you have to get two forms from the Passport Office: Forms PD2 and PD3. The Passport Office also issues an explanatory leaflet (ask for leaflet PD1).

Interestingly enough, if you apply for a British visitor's passport from the post office, it cannot be postdated in your married name.

4.1.6 Joint assets

Matrimonial property such as the matrimonial home, as well as family income, become an 'asset' of the marriage. Again, in general, the issue arises on marriage breakdown and divorce proceedings. The courts have very extensive powers to intervene in a dispute to redistribute the assets between husband and wife in a manner that the judges think is 'fair and reasonable'.

(a) The matrimonial home

In particular, irrespective of questions of whether she owns or part-owns the family home, a wife has the right to *occupy* the matrimonial home under the Matrimonial Homes Act 1973.

(These issues are discussed in greater detail in the chapter on *Divorce*.)

(b) Pledging the matrimonial home

Over the last ten years, there have been a number of cases which have involved a husband who has persuaded his wife to pledge the matrimonial home with his bank against his business debts.

Your husband has run into financial difficulties in his business. He has asked you to come to the bank with him to sign a guarantee to the bank for extra funds for his business. The bank has asked that your family house, which you own jointly with your husband, should be given as collateral for the loan and has prepared forms for you to sign to that effect. You are reluctant to sign but are very anxious not to let your husband down.

You must take legal advice. The courts have taken a protective attitude towards married women in these circumstances. They have recognized that while the pattern of family life has changed and that some women can exert their independence, others are vulnerable to their husband's influence.

The overriding consideration for the courts is whether a woman who appears to be acting in a way which is to her manifest disadvantage, is given an opportunity to exercise an independent judgment before committing herself to giving their home as collateral for her husband's debts. Where banks or other lenders have reason to think that a husband has prevailed upon his wife through emotional pressure into pledging the matrimonial home,they are under a duty to:

- have an interview alone with the wife
- explain to her what acting as a surety entails
- warn her of the risks to their property
- tell her to seek independent advice.

4.1.7 Common parenthood

Husband and wife automatically acquire parental responsibility for the children of their marriage. This aspect will be discussed more fully in the chapter on *Children*, but it is worth noting that parental responsibility covers such basic concerns as decisions over the children's religion, education, consent to marriage etc.

If the parents separate, of course, the courts can be asked to alter the relationship between parent and child: for example, the courts can determine the question of how much contact a divorced father or mother should have with their children although both will be expected to continue to share parental responsibility. The obligation to maintain their children survives a marriage breakdown.

4.1.8 Tax position of husband/wife

In 1990, the tax laws were changed so that husband and wife now have separate tax identities. Instead of the married man's allowance, there is now a married couple's allowance which is transferable between the spouses.

Until 1990, husband and wife had been taxed as one person, *unless* the wife opted to have her earnings separately taxed; even then, her unearned income was still treated as the income of her husband.

Gifts between husband and wife are not liable to capital gains tax.

4.1.9 Questions arising on spouse's death

The death of a spouse raises many questions concerning married status. These issues are discussed in detail in Chapter 4, *Death – Before and After*. It is just worth noting the following at this stage:

(a) Pensions

If you are a married woman, you will be entitled to a widow's pension on the death of your husband.

(b) Position under will

If you inherit under your spouse's will, you are entitled to take your share of the estate free of inheritance tax.

(c) Intestacy

If your spouse dies without a will, the position of the surviving spouse is well protected by law. He or she will be entitled to the major share of the estate, if not all of it. As most people do not make wills, this safeguard for provision of the surviving spouse under the intestacy rules is of considerable importance.

4.2 Marital confidences

Secrets, and other confidences of married life shared between husband and wife, are protected by law. In an era of 'kiss and tell' journalism, the legal principle of protecting husband–wife confidentiality cannot be over-emphasized. A divorced spouse has even been able to get an injunction to stop publication of marital secrets.

4.3 Questions of nationality

In general, issues of nationality have become so difficult that if you are in any doubt as to your status or that of your spouse, you would be well advised to seek legal advice. A UK resident is allowed to bring his or her spouse into this country after receiving clearance to do so. A UK resident is also entitled to bring his fiancée or her fiancé into this country.

4.3.1 Marriages of convenience

There has been a systematic tightening up of this rule in order to prevent bogus 'marriages of convenience' to UK residents, where such marriages are intended to get round stringent immigration laws. In order to issue you with an entry clearance certificate to enter the UK as an affianced person or as a spouse, the immigration authorities will want to be sure that

(a) your 'primary purpose' is to get married, or, to put it negatively, it is not your primary purpose to enter the UK; and

(b) that you and your spouse intend to live together as man and wife. In other words, you are not going to part immediately after the ceremony;

(c) if the couple are not already married, the marriage will take place within six months.

You also have to show that you 'intend to settle' in the UK. However, once the primary purpose tests have been satisfied, the need to show an intention to settle in the UK has been liberally interpreted by the courts.

You live in the UK. Your fiancée lives abroad and she has been refused entry clearance because she has told the authorities that she does not know whether she intends to settle in the UK. She is certain that she wants to come to England to marry you but you are both undecided about your long-term plans. She has been told by the consular authorities that she is not eligible either as a visitor or as a fiancée entering for marriage and settlement. Is that correct?

Your fiancée has satisfied the primary purpose tests of (a) wanting to enter the UK in order to get married and (b) of her intention of making a genuine marriage. She does not have to show that she intends to take up permanent residence in the UK as well. Her intention to settle here for a limited period will suffice.

5. Cohabitation

5.1 The legal effects

Despite the common misconception, there is no such thing as a 'common law marriage'. Either one is legally married or one is not. Of course, many cohabiting couples do regard themselves as married to all intents and purposes – and look on the absence of legal formalities as a mere detail. However, in the eyes of the law, a cohabiting couple is regarded, in almost all respects, as two single people. About a million couples cohabit and many of them have children. The fact that they are considered as two single individuals – as far as the law is concerned – entails certain clear consequences.

5.1.1 No legal duties

Whether or not they are married, couples still care for one another, support one another and are faithful to each other. However, in the case of a cohabiting couple, these duties are not legal ones. Hence, if they separate, the law does not impose duties upon them – except where there are children involved (see section 5.1.1(b) below).

(a) No duty to cohabit

Either partner can leave the other at any time to marry someone else, without having to go through any formal legal procedures whatsoever in order to separate.

(b) No duty to maintain

There is no duty to maintain one another. Thus, there are no proper legal structures, in the event of a breakup of the relationship, whereby the courts can adjust the assets of the partnership to take care of a partner hard hit financially by the separation. This is in striking contrast to the position of married couples in the event of their divorce (see chapter on *Divorce*). However, the position with regard to the children of the relationship is different; an obligation to maintain the children is legally enforceable (see immediately below). Under the Child Support Act (see chapter on *Children*, section 1.1.1(b)) an element of maintenance is calculated for the person with care of the child. This is not intended to be the same as maintenance for a divorced spouse.

5.1.2 Effect on children

At present, parental responsibility for a child whose parents are not married to each other is given to the mother.

However, since the passing of the Children Act 1989, greater emphasis is laid on the notion of parenthood. The position of the unmarried father is thus improved by law. Mother and father can enter into a 'parental responsibility agreement' which would place them in a similar position to that of married parents to share fully the responsibility for their children.

> *You are living happily with your partner and you are shortly expecting your first child. You would like him to share parental responsibility with you. How can this be arranged?*

The steps entail a formal declaration on a prescribed form, in front of witnesses. The form must then be registered at the High Court (see chapter on *Children*, section 2.3.1, for details).

(a) Duty to maintain

If a couple do have children and then separate, the 'absent' parent, often the father, is under a legal duty to maintain the children until they reach the age of 17 (see chapter on *Children*).

5.1.3 Effect on assets

There are cases where the courts have established that one partner is to be given a share in assets which a couple own together. However, this share is based on the concrete facts of the couple's individual contributions. For example, a partner would be entitled to share in the assets where he or she has contributed to the purchase of a car, paid money into a joint bank account, put down a deposit on a house or flat, or helped to pay off the mortgage. So if you do have a financial share in the bank account, car, or house along with your boyfriend or girlfriend, that share is *not* based on a question of what is 'fair' or 'right' or 'just' when you split up. It depends on your own financial contribution.

▶ **Remember:** although these rules generally work against women, it can occasionally be a man who is disadvantaged.

> *You are a successful businesswoman who recently met a man who had been made redundant. He moves into your house and puts a great deal of work and time into improvements to it. The relationship deteriorates and when he leaves, he claims an interest in your home on the strength of the labour that he expended on it. What is your position?*

> A man who does work on a cohabitee's property without any clear financial basis on which the work was done, does so at his own risk.

In the same way, where a woman contends that she has looked after the children or redecorated the home, the courts have not found that this alone entitles her to an interest in the home she shared with her boyfriend.

▶ **Most important:** in the event of a split-up, the courts do not have the same wide powers to deal fairly with the couple's house or flat. Sometimes the judges have had to resort to legal doctrines which were never intended to fit such situations and will try to find a 'trust' in favour of one partner who has put a lot of hard work into a property. On the whole, though, this is poor protection.

Certain countries have passed legislation to deal with property disputes in what they call *de facto* relationships. We have no such laws in England.

◆ **Note:** a live-in partner has no right to occupy the family home under the Matrimonial Homes Act 1973 (*cf.* the position of the wife, see section 4.1.6(a) above; and see chapter on *Divorce*).

> *Your boyfriend persuaded you to move into his flat. You agreed to pay half the mortgage instalments and you did so until the birth of your first child when you stopped working. After that, you looked after the baby, did the housework, and spent a great deal of time on doing up the flat. Your boyfriend now insists that you and the baby must leave the flat which, he says, he intends to sell. He is quite agreeable to pay maintenance for his child. Can you insist on staying on in the flat?*

> (a) You have no automatic rights of *occupation* under law. In order to assert any rights of *ownership*, you would have to show that when you moved in and agreed to pay your share of the mortgage instalments, your name was entered on the title deeds as joint owner.

(b) Alternatively, you would have to show that your solicitor drew up a trust deed in which your boyfriend declared that he held a share of the property in trust for you.

(c) Otherwise you have the task of persuading the court to imply a trust in your favour.

(d) Your solicitor should establish whether the property is registered with the Land Registry and enter a caution to warn an intending buyer that there is a conflict over your property rights.

(e) Under the Children Act 1989, the court has been given power to make a property transfer 'on behalf of a child'. It remains to be seen whether this power will be used in favour of an unmarried mother.

5.1.4 Tax position

The tax position of a married woman has been altered so that her position now much more closely resembles that of a single woman (see section 4.1.8 above). However, there are still important differences between the taxation position of a cohabiting couple and that of a married couple:

- they cannot take advantage of the taxation rules between husband and wife that ensure that gifts between husband and wife are free of capital gains tax;
- they cannot take advantage of the fact that on the death of a spouse, the other spouse inherits free of inheritance tax;
- they cannot take advantage of the fact that if one partner in a marriage stops working or is made redundant, he or she can transfer mortgage relief to the other.

5.1.5 Effect on intestacy

As we shall see in Chapter 4, most people do not make wills. So it is very important to note that when a husband or wife dies, leaving no will, the other spouse is entitled *as of right* under the provisions of the intestacy rules to receive something from the estate. When you are not married, however, your position is very different (see chapter on *Death – Before and After*).

(a) Pensions

Neither a widow's pension nor a widowed mother's allowance is available to the surviving partner of a cohabiting couple – no matter how longstanding the relationship.

You and your partner have been together for several years. You are an employee of a multinational firm. You belong to a company pension scheme and would like to ensure that your partner will benefit from it. What can you do?

You would have to sort out the position with regard to nominating your partner as beneficiary of an employee pension scheme. A spouse benefits automatically from these schemes but a cohabitee does not. Whether or not the trustees of the scheme will accept your nomination is a matter that you would have to ensure. It is also very important to check the terms of a private pension scheme.

(b) Wills

Persons who live together are advised to make wills to ensure that their partner will receive under their estate. If the relationship breaks down, a will would then have to be formally revoked. In cases of divorce, a will is automatically revoked (see chapter on *Death – Before and After*).

(c) Intestacy

A surviving partner can claim against the estate of his or her deceased co-habitee, if it can be shown that immediately before the death, that partner was maintaining the other, i.e. was 'making a substantial contribution towards his or her maintenance in money or money's worth'. In other words, survivors have to show that they have been dependants.

> *You have been living with a 54-year-old divorced man for several years. You were talking of getting married but have never got round to formalizing the relationship. You also have heard your partner talking of making a will but you do not know if he ever got round to it. Your partner has recently died of a sudden heart attack. You live in his house and you learn from the solicitor, appointed by your partner's children, that they want the house sold. What are your rights, if any?*

> You may be able to establish some rights if you make a claim under the Inheritance (Provision for Family and Dependants) Act 1975. You would need to consult your own solicitor and would have to establish that you have not received 'reasonable financial provision' from his estate. (See also chapter on *Death – Before and After*.)

5.1.6 Nationality issues

A cohabitee has no rights to bring a foreign partner into this country.

5.1.7 Confidentiality

As we have seen, the law imposes a duty of confidentiality on husband and wife. The question is whether this principle would include live-in partners or other friends to whom secrets have been told in confidence.

> *You tell a very close friend of your sexual problems in your relationship with your live-in girlfriend. You make it clear to her that the information is imparted only in the strictest confidence. Soon afterwards, you hear from someone else that your friend is intent on selling the information to a newspaper. Can you stop publication?*

> In a similar example, the court stated that there was a case against someone who tried to sell information to a newspaper, as well as a case against the paper's editors. The information, the court stated, had been received on the basis of confidentiality which ought to be protected.

5.2 Surnames

There is nothing in law to stop you taking your partner's surname, either informally or by deed poll. However, even if you call yourself by your partner's surname and refer to yourself as a 'Common Law Wife' or a 'Common Law Husband', the term has no meaning in law.

5.3 Where the law treats cohabitees as husband and wife

Having outlined the differences in how the law regards husband and wife from how it regards a cohabiting couple, it is important to note that

(a) victims of domestic violence are entitled to protection under the law, whether or not the couple are married; the procedure may be different in certain instances, however (see chapter on *Divorce*, section 9).

(b) with regard to secure tenancies, a couple who 'live together as husband and wife' are entitled to security of tenure under council housing as are husband and wife (see Chapter on *Landlords and their Tenants*);

(c) certain social security benefits are available for live-in couples, as well as for parents and children, irrespective of marital status;

(d) most importantly, as we have seen, a duty to maintain the children of the relationship is imposed – irrespective of marriage, divorce, cohabitation or relationship breakdown.

(e) Cohabitees who pledge their home to secure the debts of a partner are as vulnerable to emotional pressure as spouses. So when they act as sureties, they must be given the same safeguards as a wife in similar circumstances (see section 4.1.6(b) above).

(f) Under the Fatal Accidents Act, dependent cohabitees, who have lived with their partner for two years, may be entitled to damages on his or her death (see chapter on *Accidents*, section 11.5).

6. Agreements

Certain countries have enacted legislation to deal with property and other matters which concern a cohabiting couple who then split up. As there are no such laws in this country, the question then arises whether cohabitees should enter into their own agreement to protect themselves in the event of a breakdown in their relationship. At the same time, some have argued that even couples who are in fact contemplating marriage or are already married should enter into contracts or agreements to avoid possible litigation at a later stage.

6.1 Contracts between married couples

At common law, a husband 'administered' his wife's property. In effect, a woman no longer owned property once she married. This effect of marriage was removed in 1882 by the Married Women's Property Act. Today, property which a woman owns before she marries remains her property during the subsistence of the marriage. If she divorces, the issue turns on whether or not the property has become an 'asset' of the marriage. For example, if a woman inherits a house from her mother, this is not an asset of the marriage and cannot be used by the court in its powers to divide up the couple's assets on a divorce (although it could be taken into account in assessing a wife's needs). If, however, a woman or man buy a property together before they marry with a view to using it as their home, it will become an asset at the court's disposal in the event of a divorce (see chapter on *Divorce*).

In view of the court's wide powers to share out the family assets, few couples enter into agreement on what would happen in the event of a divorce between them. Certain of the legal difficulties of such agreements are also dealt with in section 6.2 below.

6.2 Cohabitation agreements

When an unmarried couple part, as we have seen, the courts do not have power to adjust their assets. Should the couple enter into an agreement to pre-empt a situation which could arise in the event of the breakdown of their relationship?

With regard to cohabitation agreements, there are immediate problems under the law of contract. In brief, when parties enter into a contract, both sides have to offer something towards the contract. For example, an employee will offer his labour and the employer will offer a monthly salary. The 'something' that each side offers is called the 'consideration' for the contract. In an agreement to cohabit, it would be difficult to define the consideration, other than on the basis of a sexual relationship, which the law may not accept as a valid contractual basis.

Marriage, on the other hand, paradoxically enough is described in law (among other things) as a 'contract'. It is a contract with so many peculiar features that the label tends to mislead rather than to illuminate the true position of husband and wife. Which other contract, for example, is intended to last a lifetime?

6.3 Problems with agreements

A crucial argument against cohabitation agreements or agreements between husband and wife does not stem from problems to do with definition, however. A critical issue is that circumstances change so dramatically in people's lives that few of the issues which the couple decide upon beforehand might assist them in a crisis.

How could one draw up an agreement to cover all contingencies? One or other partner might become unemployed or sick; they may have children; an elderly relative might move in. It is difficult enough to handle such events after they take place. To try to pre-empt them with a binding legal document before such events even occur could complicate matters rather than simplify them.

Indeed, rather than involving lawyers in drawing up agreements or contracts for those setting up home, the emphasis today lies in a different direction altogether. Concerted efforts are being made, by the legislators and the legislated alike, to take family law out of the domain of the courts as much as possible. These efforts have the support of many members of the legal profession, too, who feel that the courts are ill-equipped, as well as being under-funded, to deal with questions of such immediate social and personal concern.

The focus is presently on mediation – with the assistance of lawyers as a last resort (see chapter on *Divorce*). It is increasingly felt that people must be helped to resolve their own difficulties as much as possible rather than have solutions imposed upon them.

(See also the DIRECTORY at the end of Chapter 3 for more details of organizations which provide information or assistance.)

2. DIVORCE AND SEPARATION

By the end of the 1960s, it was felt that it was no longer in the public interest to try to keep alive marriages which were dead to all intents and purposes. The modern divorce law was thus introduced. For the first time, 'irretrievable breakdown' became the sole ground of divorce. In the event, the law emerged as a somewhat uneasy compromise. While it stated that irretrievable breakdown was the only ground for divorce, it also perpetuated some requirements from earlier divorce legislation (see section 1.3.1 below for the 'five facts' which have to be shown).

Until the recognition of irretrievable breakdown, the law had insisted upon an 'innocent' party and a 'guilty' party in divorce proceedings. A 'guilty' spouse could not petition for a divorce; an 'innocent party', on the other hand, could only obtain a divorce after proving to the court that a 'matrimonial offence' (such as adultery or desertion) had been committed against him or her.

Since the introduction of the present law which governs divorce, the number of divorces has risen dramatically. At present one in three couples divorces in Britain – the highest rate in Europe.

Today the law of divorce is again under consideration. As always, the conflicts in the debate cannot be easily reconciled. If society respects the institution of marriage, should the law try to preserve it? If so, how? Is there any purpose served by keeping people locked into marriages which they do not want? Should the law encourage reconciliation between warring spouses? Or, rather, should it endeavour to make their parting as painless and as 'conciliatory' as possible? Should, indeed, these issues be taken out of the hands of the lawyers and judges so that the process becomes a non-judicial one? To what extent should conciliation services be employed in – rather than out of – the courts? (For fresh proposals on divorce law, see section 4 below.)

In relation to children of separating spouses, dramatic changes in the law are already in force. Under the Children Act 1989, parents in divorce proceedings are actively encouraged to take matters into their own hands and make their own decisions regarding their children's future. The courts' interventionist role has been confined (see section 5 below).

Another striking change is that maintenance applications for children made after April 1 1993 are also no longer a matter for the courts. Under the Child Support Act, a government agency assesses and determines such applications for maintenance according to a set formula (see chapter on *Children*, section 1.1). The courts will only deal with maintenance matters in certain clearly defined circumstances (see section 5 below).

How these and other projected major changes will work in practice is unknown as yet. The hope is that they will lead to less litigation and to less heartache. There is no certainty that they will.

In this chapter we look at

- seeking a divorce
- seeking an amicable solution – reconciliation and mediation
- procedure – an outline
- changes to the law?
- the children of the marriage
- sorting out family assets on divorce
- the court orders: maintenance
- when co-habitees split up
- domestic violence.

1. Seeking a divorce

1.1 Is there 'irretrievable breakdown'?

Husbands and wives, as we have seen in Chapter 1, have many obligations to one another. In particular they are expected to live together and to support one another.

An absolute decree of divorce makes the couple into two single persons again for all legal purposes. They are, of course, then free to remarry. Most of their mutual obligations fall away.

However, their obligation to support one another remains despite a divorce. Hence the number of factors which the court must take into account in trying to distribute the family assets. (For the issue of imposing a 'clean break' between the couple, see section 6.4 below.)

Another primary obligation remains unalterable. Where husband and wife have children, they are both responsible, as father and mother, for their children until these reach the age of maturity (usually 18).

1.2 Jurisdiction

The first issue, for any couple who wish to divorce, is to establish whether the court has jurisdiction to hear their case. In other words, the question is: can they bring divorce proceedings?

If a husband or wife wishes to divorce the other spouse, he or she must

(a) have been married for a minimum of a year; and
(b) be domiciled in this country, i.e. England is regarded as their home. Alternatively, they must have been resident in England for one year before the date on which proceedings are brought.

1.2.1 The marriage must have lasted for a minimum of a year

No petition for divorce can be presented to the courts before the expiry of one year from the date of the marriage. This is an absolute bar.

In some difficult situations this one-year bar can cause problems.

Three months ago, you married a woman 20 years younger than yourself. You find that not only are your personalities totally incompatible but she is having affairs with other men and bringing them into your house. One of her boyfriends threatened you when you protested at his presence in your own home. You feel that a year is a long time to wait in the circumstances. You wonder what you can do?

You can petition for judicial separation within the year (see *Judicial separation*, section 1.4 below). Otherwise you must wait for the first year of marriage to elapse before you can petition for divorce. However, when you are able to present the petition at the end of your first year of marriage, it can be based on events occurring in the course of that year.

Where there is violence in the home, or the threat of violence, you can apply immediately to court for an order to exclude the other spouse (see *Domestic violence* section 9 below).

1.2.2 Living in the UK

Generally speaking, you must be domiciled in this country to petition for divorce, i.e. you must regard England as your home. However, you can also petition for divorce in this country if you are 'ordinarily resident' here.

> *You are an English woman who married your French husband in France two years ago. He has been working as an engineer in England on the Channel Tunnel for more than a year. You wish to petition for divorce in England. Your husband says that he does not have to face divorce proceedings here as he is domiciled in France. He also says that although he has been living in England for more than a year, he has been back to France on holiday.*

(1) Even if you and your spouse have been living in England for business reasons you are ordinarily resident here for the purposes of divorce proceedings – provided you have lived here for one year preceding the petition.
(2) Short absences abroad during the year for holidays or business trips do not count against a year's ordinary residence.

1.2.3 When can a court refuse to hear divorce proceedings because of domicile or residence issues?

A court can order a halt to proceedings for divorce in England if it would be better for the case to be heard in another country. The usual test which the courts apply is to decide 'with which country the parties are most closely associated'. For example, in the scenario above, if husband and wife were both French and living temporarily in England, a court here might decide that it would be better if divorce proceedings take place in France.

1.3 Grounds for divorce

There is only one ground for granting a decree: the marriage must have broken down irretrievably (Matrimonial Causes Act 1973). Ostensibly, therefore, a divorce is no longer based on a matrimonial 'offence'.

◆ **Note:** The spouse who asks for a divorce is the *petitioner*; the other spouse is the *respondent*.

1.3.1 The five facts

However, the court must be satisfied that the marriage has broken down irretrievably and that there is evidence of one or more of the following five facts:

- that the respondent has committed adultery and the petitioner finds it intolerable to live with the respondent (see section 1.3.1(a));
- that the respondent has behaved in such a way that the petitioner cannot reasonably be expected to live with the respondent (see section 1.3.1(b));
- that the respondent has deserted the petitioner for a continuous period of at least two years immediately preceding the presentation of the petition (see section 1.3.1(c));

- that the parties to the marriage have lived apart for a continuous period of at least two years immediately preceding the presentation of the petition and the respondent consents to a decree being granted (i.e. two years' separation plus consent of the other spouse). This is known as the 'no fault' ground (see section 1.3.1(d));
- that the parties to the marriage have lived apart for a continuous period of at least five years immediately preceding the presentation of the petition (see section 1.3.1(e)).

Statistics show that about 70 per cent of divorces are awarded on the grounds of unreasonable behaviour and adultery (the classic matrimonial offences). About 18 to 25 per cent of all divorces are on the basis of a fact of 'no fault', i.e. that the couple have been separated for two years and both partners consent to the divorce.

So despite the fact that there is only one ground for divorce, i.e. irretrievable breakdown, the law lays down two separate requirements: irretrievable breakdown and one of the five facts as evidence of the breakdown. Thus, without necessarily intending to, the law lays stress on the unhappiest aspects of a marriage. It requires the parties to cite them as one of the five facts in their petitions for divorce in order to give the petitions credibility to their divorce proceedings.

(a) Adultery plus intolerability

Adultery is defined as heterosexual sex between one spouse of the marriage and some other person who is not the other spouse. There must be penetration, so 'heavy petting' does not constitute adultery. Because the law specifies a heterosexual act, a gay or lesbian sexual act cannot constitute adultery.

> *You are a married man and you learn from your wife that she is involved in a lesbian relationship. You both feel that the marriage has irretrievably broken down and agree that you should petition her for an undefended divorce.*

> You cannot base the petition on adultery because your wife's relationship with someone outside the marriage is not a heterosexual one. However, you could petition on some other ground, for instance, two years' separation with consent if you leave home, or on the 'unreasonable behaviour' ground (see sections 1.3.1(d) and 1.3.1(b) below).

To prove adultery, an admission by the respondent and co-respondent or circumstantial evidence generally suffices. The courts do not inquire into the evidence closely in undefended petitions.

The co-respondent need not be named in the petition.

> *Your wife has committed adultery with the husband of a close family friend. You do not want to name him as co-respondent because of the unhappiness it will cause his family. You are told that because you know the identity of the co-respondent, his name must be given in the divorce petition.*

> This is no longer the case; even where the co-respondent's name is known, it does not have to be cited.

Evidence of fathering a child outside the marriage would be certain proof of adultery. However, the court will only order blood tests to establish paternity in circumscribed cases. These do not include someone's wish to prove adultery in divorce proceedings.

> *An unmarried woman who works in your husband's business is about to have a baby. You have been suspicious for some time that there is a relationship between your husband and this woman. You think that he could be the father of her child. You would like to have DNA testing done when the baby is born in order to ascertain whether your suspicions are correct.*

A court will not order blood tests to establish adultery.

'Intolerability' is an additional factor required in a petition alleging adultery. It was introduced because it was felt that an occasional 'fling' should not be sufficient to bring marriages to an end. There had to be something more: so the petitioner must not only prove adultery but must also show that he or she can no longer live with the other spouse. The two requirements are separate so that the 'intolerability' need not be linked to the adultery.

> *Your husband, whom you married five years ago, admitted that he committed adultery with a woman called Jane. After a few weeks' separation, he has returned home, saying that the affair is quite over. You wish to rebuild your marriage. However, since his return, your husband has been telephoning another woman called Mary and has gone out at night without telling you where he is going. You find his behaviour intolerable even though he assures you that he and Mary are not having an adulterous relationship.*

You would be entitled to petition for divorce. Even though his adulterous affair with Jane is over, his past affair and present behaviour satisfy together the requirements of the law.

(b) Behaviour

This ground is pleaded where one spouse has behaved in such a way that the other cannot reasonably be expected to live with him or her – taking into account all the circumstances as well as the personalities of the parties.

There has been a range of case law on the subject of 'behaviour' and whether the other spouse could reasonably be expected to put up with it. The courts have examined instances of where one spouse was emotionally or sexually unresponsive; where one partner was financially irresponsible; where a husband treated his wife like a child.

▶ **Take care:** one set of circumstances cannot automatically be applied to another case in a divorce petition: every case, as every unhappy family, has its own particularity.

A court is not supposed to 'rubber stamp' divorce petitions. On the other hand, it does not wish to make pointless inquiries into conduct once one spouse has declared that the marriage is at an end. In all such cases it is a matter of fact and degree. A course of conduct made up of a number of incidents is often cited on this ground.

> *Three years ago you married a man many years older than yourself. He has subjected everything you do at home to a constant stream of criticism. You live in an atmosphere of disapproval which is profoundly undermining. You would like to petition for divorce but cannot bring any grave allegation against your husband such as violent behaviour. You also do not think he would consent to a divorce.*

In the circumstances, the court is likely to view your petition sympathetically on the grounds of your husband's behaviour.

Your wife has petitioned for a divorce on the ground that the marriage has irretrievably broken down. The fact which she alleged in her petition concerned your behaviour. She stated that she could not reasonably be expected to live with you. She alleged that your enthusiasm for DIY interfered with your life together and caused you to neglect her. You feel that her allegations are trivial. You wonder how closely the court is likely to inquire into the reasons for the failure of your marriage.

A petition based on behaviour should be able to substantiate its claims, and a court is expected to consider the issues involved.

However, in certain circumstances, the courts have accepted that a series of seemingly trivial acts can add up to unreasonable behaviour.

(c) Desertion

The petitioner must show that he or she has been deserted for a continuous period of at least two years immediately preceding the presentation of the petition.

(1) There must be a clear evidence of a separation.

♦ **Note:** Separation means two separate households; it does not necessarily mean that each spouse lives under a separate roof. For example, if a couple cannot afford separate accommodation, they may continue to live in the same premises but to lead quite separate lives.

(2) There must be a clear intention to desert the other spouse; for example, if a separation is involuntary through imprisonment or because of an overseas posting, the necessary intention to desert is missing.

(3) The petitioner does not consent to the desertion. This distinguishes desertion from the 'no fault' ground of two years' separation with consent.

(4) There must have been no just cause for the desertion. In other words, if a husband or wife petitions for divorce on the ground of desertion, the court will wish to establish whether it was their own behaviour which caused the other spouse to leave home.

Your wife has become extremely suspicious of you and is convinced that you are committing adultery although this is not the case. She spies on you at every opportunity, listens in to your phone calls, and rummages through your briefcase and your clothing. You are beginning to find her behaviour impossible to tolerate and are thinking of leaving home. You would like to know whether you would be deserting your wife in these circumstances.

It may well be that a court would find that you were being driven from your home by her behaviour, in which case your wife would be the 'deserting' spouse.

(5) There must be satisfactory financial provision for the deserted spouse.

(d) Separation for two years with consent

This is the closest that the law approaches to a divorce by mutual consent.

Either spouse can apply after they have lived apart for a continuous period of at least two years immediately preceding the presentation of the petition. The petitioner must show that the respondent consents to a decree being granted.

Consent entails

- proper information

- proper documentation
- proper procedure

You have lived abroad for three years and have received a form from your wife's solicitors in England asking you to acknowledge 'service' of her petition for divorce. You write back on your own notepaper acknowledging the receipt of this letter. You wonder if you have now 'consented' to the divorce.

The court will refuse to accept that this is specific consent. A proper procedure must be followed and you must acknowledge service of the petition on a prescribed form (see section 3.1.1 below).

(e) Separation for five years

Once husband and wife have lived apart for a continuous period of five years, a petitioner can be granted a divorce without having to show that the other spouse consents to it.

However, there is a proviso that, if the financial arrangements are not reasonable, the respondent can raise an objection.

1.4 Judicial separation

There are about 2,000 petitions a year for judicial separation. These are based on the same five facts as are necessary for a petition for divorce but there is no need to show irretrievable breakdown of the marriage.

There is no need to wait for one year to elapse to petition for judicial separation as is the case with divorce. The effect of judicial separation is to end the duty of husband and wife to cohabit with one another.

It does not end the marriage. Where there are religious objections to divorce, a decree of judicial separation can be an alternative.

◆ **Note:** The provisions for financial arrangements between spouses (see section 6 below) apply to judicial separations in the same way as they apply on divorce.

If there is a formal separation agreement or a decree of judicial separation there cannot be desertion. The duty to cohabit has in fact been legally terminated by such a decree. If there is no duty to cohabit, there can be no desertion.

2. Seeking an amicable parting

2.1 Reconciliation

In all the provisions of the law relating to the five 'facts' which have to be shown in addition to irretrievable breakdown, there are in-built reconciliation provisions. In effect, these provisions allow for a period of up to six months in which the parties can make an attempt at reconciliation. If in the event, the reconciliation fails, the six-month reconciliation period of grace will not jeopardize their legal position in subsequent divorce proceedings.

The reconciliation provisions apply for a single period of up to six months or for periods which do not total more than six months.

Your wife has told you that she is in love with another man. You persuade her that she should give the marriage another try – particularly for the sake of the children. You then live together for three months but she says that she cannot continue in the marriage. She leaves home. Again you prevail on her to return but this time she only stays for a few weeks.

The fact that you have lived with your wife on and off for a period of less than six months – since you learned of her adultery – does not affect your legal position if divorce proceedings ensue. In earlier times, once a man took a wife back (and vice versa) after learning of adultery, he was considered to have 'condoned' the adultery and so lost the right to petition for a divorce.

In addition a solicitor acting for a petitioner has to certify that he or she

- has discussed the possibility of reconciliation; and
- has made sure the parties know where they can seek guidance if they sincerely desire reconciliation.

The court can also adjourn proceedings to give the parties further time to decide whether they genuinely wish to make another attempt at sustaining their marriage.

◆ **Note:** a list of organizations which provide marriage counselling as well as mediation and conciliation services is found at the end of Chapter 3 under DIRECTORY.

The matters discussed above under the term 'reconciliation' concern an attempt by both spouses to live together again as husband and wife.

2.2 Conciliation and mediation services

Conciliation, on the other hand, is directed towards different goals. It is intended to make parting easier. A conciliator's role is to sort out some of the difficulties between spouses who have made a firm decision to divorce. Conciliation may take place out of court or in court.

In-court conciliation, obviously, only arises once litigation has begun. In particular, it is available where difficulties centre on the future of the children of the marriage. There is usually a pre-trial review of the issues which the couple are unable to settle for themselves. Both the district judge and the court welfare officer are involved. Their task is to narrow the areas of dispute between the couple.

2.2.1 Out-of-court conciliation and mediation

This is intended to assist the parties in reaching a negotiated agreement at the stage before they approach the courts. A neutral conciliator – usually a social worker trained for the purpose – acts as go-between. The areas of dispute often range beyond the children's needs to cover financial settlement as well.

Specially trained lawyers can also be used by the parties to assist them in reaching an agreement. This is more akin to an arbitration process, and is also known as *alternative dispute resolution*.

Research is being done into the effectiveness of these various methods of settling fraught and sometimes tragic disputes between couples. Alternative dispute resolution is intended to sidestep the adversarial approach of legal proceedings or, at the very least, to make these less acrimonious.

2.2.2 'First stop' family advice centres?

In proposals to be put forward for reforms to the divorce laws, 'first-stop' family advice centres are being advocated (*The Way Forward*, issued by the Lord Chancellor, December 1993). Such centres, to be set up nationally, would refer couples to counselling, to child guidance or to solicitors – as the case may warrant – after an initial diagnostic visit.

3. Divorce procedure: an outline

In undefended petitions both spouses accept that the divorce will go ahead; in defended divorces one spouse resists the petition and seeks to raise a defence against it (see section 3.2 below).

3.1 Special procedure: undefended divorces

A special procedure was introduced to deal with undefended divorce petitions. The statistics show that this procedure is the normal practice. There were just under 180,000 petitions for divorce in 1991, of which about 155,000 were finalized (in the language of the law 'made absolute'). None of these was defended or contested by the other spouse. Of the defended divorces, only 153 cases were listed for trial, 82 of which proceeded to a full trial. Presumably the other cases were settled out of court.

There have been consistent calls for reform to this procedure (see section 4 below).

3.1.1 Standard forms

The procedure follows a set pattern. There are standard forms available from law stationers, the courts and HMSO.

(a) The petition must be filled in;
(b) it must enclose a statement of the arrangements for the children;
(c) it must be sent to the registrar of the divorce county court;
(d) there must be sufficient copies for the other parties (e.g. a named co-respondent);
(e) the respondent will receive his or her copy from the court;
(f) so will any other of the parties involved;
(g) the respondent must acknowledge service (also on a prescribed form);
(h) the respondent must make clear that he or she has no intention to defend;
(i) the documents are examined by an official of the court (the divorce registrar);
(j) s/he then certifies that the facts of the case are proved;
(k) the judge pronounces the decree nisi in open court;
(l) the decree is made absolute on application by the petitioner.

3.1.2 Legal aid

Help with the form-filling entailed in undefended divorce procedure can be available from certain solicitors under a scheme known as the *Green Form Scheme* (see also chapter on *The Legal System* on meeting the legal aid requirements). Solicitors are available to give three hours of their time to assist in presenting the forms. Legal aid only applies to actual court proceedings. It is therefore not available in undefended divorces. However legal aid is available for actual disputes relating to children and financial and property matters (known as 'ancillary relief').

3.2 Defended divorces

The respondent who intends to defend a divorce petition must file an answer to the allegations.

Among other matters which can be raised is the issue of financial hardship. For example a court is not allowed to make an order in cases of desertion, if no adequate provision is made for the deserted spouse (see section 1.3.1 above).

3.3 Decree nisi and decree absolute

A decree nisi is pronounced in open court. A decree absolute follows after an interval of six weeks.

4. Changes to the law?

The present state of divorce law is seen as unsatisfactory. This applies both to the substantive law, i.e. the actual basis on which divorce is granted, and to the present 'special procedure'. The debate over how to reform the law is intense in view of public concern over one-parent families and the breakdown of the family.

4.1 Proposals

These proposals are under discussion for possible changes to the law:

- divorce will be obtained on the ground of 'irretrievable breakdown' of the marriage;
- there will be no need to prove any of the five facts; however, the couple must show that there has been a period of reflection and consideration of the practical arrangements;
- the period will last one year;
- the couple do not have to be separated during this period;
- the period of a year will date from when one or both of the spouses files a sworn statement to the court that in his or her belief the marriage has broken down;
- conciliation will be available. It is now suggested that the couple will be bound to make use of a family advice centre as their first port of call. They will then be directed to conciliation, mediation, counselling or to lawyers as their needs dictate (see section 2.2 above).

5. Children

It is the duty of the court to have regard to all the circumstances in a divorce petition, and the *first consideration* must be the welfare of any child of the family under the age of eighteen.

5.1 The Children Act 1989

Children of parents who live in amity do not need the law's guidance. The underlying intention of the new Children Act 1989 is that even when there is marital breakdown, the law should not be called on to intervene. Parents should continue to care for and to have responsibility for their children until they reach the age of 18. As far as possible parents should make their own decisions. Thus the new Act is intended to minimize the court's role. It can only intervene if it decides that to make an order for a child would be better than to make no order at all.

Even the terminology has changed. Orders for children no longer refer to 'access', 'custody', and 'care and control'. These terms were seen as objectionable: for example, the connotation of someone 'in custody' was felt to be wholly inappropriate to the relationship between parent and child.

The new orders are

- residence orders
- contact orders
- specific issue orders
- prohibited steps orders.

(These orders are discussed in detail in the chapter on *Children*, section 3.1.2)

5.1.1 Financial relief under the Matrimonial Causes Act 1973

In the next section, we shall deal with the orders which are available to the court to distribute the family assets on a divorce. These orders are available for the benefit of the children of the family too. The orders last until a child's eighteenth birthday. For children over 18, provision is made where a child is receiving further education or there are other circumstances which warrant special provision, e.g. disability. In deciding whether to grant an order and, if so, for how much, the court takes into account all the circumstances, including

(a) income, earning capacity and property and other financial resources, including those available in the foreseeable future, of the child;
(b) the parents' financial needs;
(c) the child's financial needs;
(d) any physical or mental disability of the child;
(e) the manner in which the child was being or was expected to be educated or trained.

5.1.2 Financial relief under the Children Act

Under the Children Act wide-ranging powers are given to the court for orders which can be made for the benefit of a child. Orders can be made for periodical payments, lump sums, and transfers of property. The powers under this Act, unlike those under section 5.1.1 above, do not depend upon divorce proceedings. They are thus available to children of unmarried parents. Day-to-day maintenance is now determined under the Child Support Act.

5.2 Child Support Act

The Child Support Act 1991 has taken away jurisdiction from the courts to decide on questions of financial support for children to a large extent. The courts will only be called upon to decide such issues in limited circumstances, for example when there are special grounds or when a parent seeks 'topping up' of the maintenance awarded under the Act (see section 5.2.1 below).

Under the Child Support Act, which came into force in April 1993, children's maintenance is assessed by a Child Support Agency (CSA). (See chapter on *Children*, section 1.1.)

◆ **Note:** it is difficult to foretell how such major changes to the law will work out in practice. Some predict a much fairer system in that the divorce 'lottery' will no longer operate. On the other hand, others who work in the field predict that the new formula will work out unfairly as it gives the parties themselves little scope for negotiation.

For example, the courts now can make a transfer of property order to one party, usually a mother caring for children, and reduce the maintenance a father would have to pay to her on behalf of the children (see section 7 below). If a property transfer is made, this is a factor which is not taken into account in the assessment of maintenance payments. Time – and no doubt many expensive and long-drawn-out court actions – will tell how the new dispensation will work out in practice.

5.2.2 The court's jurisdiction

Thus the courts will no longer make orders for maintenance for children in divorce proceedings except where

- they exceed the amount assessed by the agency, or
- there are special grounds put forward such as educational needs.

In addition

- the court will still have jurisdiction to make orders for step-children and other 'children of the family' (see section 5.2.3 below);
- the court will still make orders for lump sum and property adjustment orders for children;
- the court will make orders for disabled children.

It is important to realise that two regimes will exist until there is a gradual phasing in of all maintenance applications under the CSA.

5.2.3 Step-children

Financial Orders are still to be made by the courts for the 'children of the family'.

You are a wealthy woman who married some years ago. Your husband had two children by his former marriage and you have effectively brought them up. You are now in the middle of rather acrimonious divorce proceedings and your husband states that you have assumed responsibility for his children so he will be applying for a financial order against you on his children's behalf. You wonder what your legal position is.

The court must weigh up whether you in fact assumed responsibility for the children's maintenance. If you did, the court must establish the extent to which you were responsible for them, and for how long you met that responsibility. It will then take into account their father's liability to maintain them. If it does make an order, it must state that you are not the children's mother.

5.2.4 Who can apply

Any person with whom a child is resident under a residence order can apply to court for maintenance (see chapter on *Children*, section 3.1.2, for a residence order).

Your wife left you and your two children to live in another town. You are unable to care for the children and continue to work so, as a result, they both live in your parents' house, i.e. with their grandparents. Costs of their keep are mounting and your parents would like some additional support from your wife.

If the children are living with their grandparents under a residence order, then the grandparents can apply to court for financial provision.

6. Sorting out family assets on divorce

6.1. Duty to support continues

The duty of husband and wife to support one another and for both to maintain their children continues despite a divorce. Thus even in un-defended petitions, quite separate proceedings can and do take place over maintenance and the family home.

6.1.1 Need to sort out amicable arrangement

While each spouse should receive independent legal advice where necessary to guard their interests, the parties' main endeavour should be to sort out their financial affairs as amicably as possible. The costs of litigating over 'who gets what' can eat up family assets very effectively. In that case, the whole family may lose more than any individual family member is likely to gain from a protracted dispute.

(See DIRECTORY for mediation organizations which assist in trying to mitigate acrimonious disputes over property and related matters on divorce.)

6.1.2 The Child Support Act

As we have seen (section 5.2 above), the Child Support Act 1991 came into operation in April 1993. We do not yet know the effect it will have on long-term financial arrangements which a court is likely to make on a divorce.

6.1.3 Tax and divorce

A very important factor is the parties' tax position on divorce. Specialist advice should always be sought.

6.2 What are the assets of a marriage?

On the breakdown of a marriage, everything which has been earned or owned during the marriage is considered part of the assets of the marriage. These can all be redistributed on divorce. Assets can include present and future earnings; savings; the family car; holiday cottage or boat; expectations under a will in certain circumstances; and even the family pet!

The emphasis is on 'family' assets. So property owned by either spouse before the marriage was contemplated remains his or her property exclusively. It cannot be dealt with by the courts although it will be a factor in assessing need.

However, if one or other spouse buys a home – or acquires some other asset – before marrying with a view to living in it or using it together, then it too becomes a 'family asset' on divorce.

6.3 Court's wide powers

The court has very wide powers indeed to redistribute the family assets (see section 6.7 below). Its task is to try to reach a fair and just division in all the circumstances of each individual case.

- The circumstances of each case are to be taken into account so that every case is dealt with individually on its merits;
- past cases are not necessarily a guide to present decisions;
- children come first in any financial arrangements on divorce (see section 5 above).

6.4 A clean break

The duty of husband and wife to support one another does not end on divorce. In principle, their duty to maintain remains. However there have been inroads on this principle.

In particular the court must consider whether it would not be better to impose a clean break on the couple. This is seen as a desirable alternative to long-term support. Today the court has the power to impose a clean break in divorce proceedings – whether or not husband or wife wants it. It is obligatory for the courts to consider the question of ending one spouse's financial dependence on the other, once the marriage itself has come to an end.

6.4.1 Difficulties in practice

Obviously, the principle is easier to state on paper than implement in practice. Circumstances vary so much from household to household that it is difficult to lay down anything except the most broad of rules.

- If the marriage has been short-lived
- if the parties to it are still young, and
- if there are no children involved

the courts will generally want to see a clean break between the parties.

You are a 25-year-old woman, married to a wealthy man. The marriage lasted only eighteen months and you have not had any children. You kept on your flat which you owned before you married, and rented it out. In your application for ancillary relief to your divorce petition, you have asked for secured payments as you do not need a lump sum to purchase accommodation. Your lawyer has told you that the court can impose a clean break whether or not you have asked for it and whether or not you would consent to it. You want to know if this is correct.

The answer is 'yes'. The courts now have the power to impose a clean break even if one of the parties is unwilling to accept it.

Generally, it is fair to say that the clean break principle has been more honoured in its breach than in its observance. For example, the courts have stated that a settlement of the matrimonial home on the wife until the children reach the age of 18 does not offend against the clean break principle.

6.5 The one-third rule

In very general terms, if a clean break is not ordered, the court calculates on the basis of the 'one-third rule', i.e. the wife gets one third of the combined income – exclusive of maintenance for the children.

◆ **Do take note:** this is not an invariable rule but just a rule of thumb for starting calculations in each case.

6.6 The role of the welfare state

State benefits have been an ever-increasing factor in assessing financial arrangements. The social security legislation is outside the scope of this book, but its importance in overall terms cannot be over-emphasized.

Thus the legal principle which underlies financial arrangements on divorce is that spouses are expected to maintain one another and both are expected to maintain their children. This principle applies as much to feckless or devious spouses as to responsible and caring ones. However, there is no doubt that while the courts accept that the burden of maintenance should not be taken out of individual hands and placed on the state, they also must accept that – in practice – this is what often happens. Fierce debate rages – particularly in today's economic climate – on the extent to which the benefit system is seen as a factor in family disintegration.

The Child Support Act (see section 5.2 above) is indicative of a change of policy to make parents rather than the state bear the burden of supporting children in family breakdown.

6.7 Factors which the court takes into account in making its orders

6.7.1 Income, earning capacity, property and other financial resources of each party to the marriage – what they have and what they may expect

This is the totality of the family's available resources. Calculations are based on wage slips of gross income less other contributions such as NIC, superannuation, and trade union dues. The court will assess a couple's true income and will look beyond what the parties may say about their position in order to establish precise figures.

> *You allege that the salary statements of your wife, who is suing you for divorce, give an inadequate idea of her true income. She receives a company car, free travel and travel insurance, belongs to a BUPA scheme paid for her by her employers, and is given cash bonuses. You also understand that she is due for a substantial salary increase.*

These are legitimate matters to be taken into account in assessing her income and earning capacity.

Other matters to be taken into account would be expectations under a will or a family settlement. While the courts have taken these matters into account in the past, they will always be circumspect about them. Evidence which would be an invasion of privacy will not be allowed.

> *Your husband is the only son of an 85-year-old mother. She is a woman of considerable means and you understand that he is to be her sole heir. You would like to receive evidence of her will.*

The court will not order a relative to give evidence in these circumstances. However, this does not mean that your husband's expectations on his mother's death will necessarily be ignored in the court's assessment.

6.7.2 Financial needs, obligations and responsibilities; now or in the near future

This covers all outgoings such as food, fuel, clothing etc. If either spouse has set up home with another partner or intends to remarry, then that second family's needs will also be an important factor in the computation.

6.7.3 Standard of living before breakdown of marriage

The parties are not expected to be put in the position that they would have been in if the marriage had survived. Two separate households cannot cost the same as one. In the case of very wealthy people, however, an adjustment might be made to approximate the standard of living which would have been expected had the marriage survived.

6.7.4 Age of each party and duration of the marriage

The court has to take into account factors such as how old the parties are; for example, a young person may need less support than an elderly one. The duration of the marriage is also relevant. A very short union might well lead to the imposition of a clean break where there are no children involved. Of course, a short marriage might have been preceded by a long period of cohabitation.

> *Your wife and yourself cohabited for five years before marrying but thereafter soon split up. She says that the period of cohabitation is to be taken into account in assessing the duration of the marriage.*

The court has a duty to consider all the circumstances of the marriage. So the meaningfulness of a period of cohabitation will be assessed in terms of the actual situation at the time. e.g. whether before you got married you had children together or bought a house together etc.

6.7.5 Physical or mental disability

If either spouse suffers from a disability or serious illness, this will obviously be a factor in assessing the proportionate shares in the division of a family's assets on divorce.

6.7.6 Contributions to the welfare of the family including any contribution by looking after the home or caring for the family

(a) Wide interpretation of 'contribution'

It is important to note that *contribution* under this heading includes looking after home and/or children. It does not exclude other contributions, for example to a family business.

> You and your husband came to this country as poor immigrants from Eastern Europe. You both decided to set up a small bakery business on money which your husband borrowed from a bank. It involved your working unsocial hours together with him for several years. The business is now a flourishing chain of cafés and patisseries.

The court is very likely to hold that you are entitled to some share of the assets in the business for your contribution to its exceptional success.

However, moral support alone might not be enough to gain a share of a business!

(b) 'Contribution' of both spouses to home and children

This heading of 'contribution to family welfare' is generally seen as intended to protect a wife on divorce. It can assist a husband too, however.

> You married a well-to-do woman whose family provided you with the matrimonial home. However, during the course of the marriage, you worked hard as a commercial traveller and made strenuous efforts to keep the family together. You feel that your endeavours are entitled to credit when it comes to assessing shares in the house which you and your wife have agreed to sell.

The court is likely to give a sympathetic hearing to your case for your contribution to be taken into account.

6.7.7 The conduct of each of the parties if, in the opinion of the court, it would be unfair to disregard it

In settling financial claims, the courts do not want to investigate the relative behaviour of spouses. An allocation on this ground, it is felt, would mean inquiring into guilt or blame for failed marriages. This in turn would lead to the court imposing financial penalties for supposed misbehaviour in the course of an unhappy marriage. However, there may be cases where it would affront a sense of justice for an award to be made to one spouse at the expense of the other.

The legal phrase is that conduct must be 'obvious and gross' before a spouse should be deprived of financial provision. Cases where conduct has been taken into account include physical violence, the dissipation of family assets, and dishonesty.

6.7.8 The value of any benefit e.g. a pension, which that party will lose the chance of acquiring

The question of pension rights is a very vexed one. Pensions can represent a considerable aspect of family investment in the long term. For a couple who divorce late in life, the value of lost pension rights for one of the spouses can mean the difference between relative comfort and penury. Moreover, a woman can lose the prospect of her widow's pension once she is a divorcee.

At the same time, there are great difficulties in trying to put an *actual* value in today's terms on the projected value of future pension rights, which can depend on so many incalculable factors.

The whole area of pension rights on divorce is currently under review and legislation on the matter is expected shortly. In May 1993, the court allowed a wife a share of her husband's pension on divorce. However, the decision applied only to a small self-administered pension scheme. It is the division of pensions in schemes in large firms with which the legislation will have to deal.

The Institute of Pension Management produced a report in which proposals were put forward as means of allocating pensions on divorce.

7. The court orders

7.1 Immediate action

The court has the power to order one party to a divorce to pay to the other reasonable sums at any time after the filing of a divorce petition. These orders can begin immediately. They are known as 'orders pending suit'.

> *Your husband has filed for a divorce and you have been served with papers. You are very concerned that he should keep up the payments for your son's university education while long-term arrangements are made.*

The court can make an order which will take immediate effect until the divorce is finalized. For example, it can order monthly payments for your son's benefit if it feels that is necessary in all the circumstances of the case.

7.2 Court orders: money payments

7.2.1 Periodical payments

Periodical payments are regular sums usually ordered to be paid on a monthly basis. These can be secured or unsecured. Problems can arise in enforcing unsecured payments.

7.2.2 Secured periodical payments

The court has the power to take steps in advance to ensure that a spouse will receive the payments it orders. Of course, this would only be applicable where there are capital assets which can be charged, such as an ex-spouse's home, or where there are income-producing assets, such as a savings account, or shares.

You have petitioned for a divorce and your husband has been required to pay you a monthly sum in maintenance. You understand that he is now talking of going to Australia to make a fresh start and you are concerned that you may not be able to secure the maintenance ordered. What can you do?

You can approach the court to ask that the maintenance payments be secured on your husband's assets. Alternatively, you can ask for a lump sum instead of regular payments.

A secured charge can be limited in time and the property or assets charged can revert – free of the charge – to the person against whom the order was made, or to his estate.

You received £5,000 per annum as a secured periodical payment from your ex-spouse. You now hear that he has died. You would like to know what your position is.

It will depend on the terms of the order. Orders such as these may only last for as long as either you or your husband are alive. It might survive your husband's death. If you are likely to lose the benefit of the order, you might be able to make a claim out of his estate under the Family Provision legislation (see chapter on *Death – Before and After*, section 8.4).

◆ **Note:** a husband's life can be insured to protect these sums.

7.2.3 Lump sum

A lump sum is used

- to transfer the matrimonial home to one or other spouse (see section 7.3 below)
- to replace periodical payments;
- to compensate for the loss of the home;
- where enforcement is going to be difficult (e.g. where an ex-spouse may emigrate or dissipate the assets).

It is self-evident that an order for a lump sum will only be available where there are assets to meet it.

You have a flourishing photography business which you run from home. Your wife is suing you for divorce and is asking for a lump sum to compensate her for the fact that she has to find alternative accommodation. The only way you can meet her demand is to sell your house which will put you out of both home and business.

The court will not put you in a position where you stand to lose your home and jeopardize your business. However, it will enquire whether it could reasonably expect that you might be able to raise a loan to pay a lump sum which would assist your wife in finding accommodation.

7.2.4 When do orders for maintenance cease?

Orders for maintenance generally cease on the remarriage of the spouse who receives them or on his or her death. They also cease on the death of the spouse who is making the payments except in certain cases of secured payments (see section 7.2.2 above).

7.3 Court orders: the family home

This is usually the family's greatest asset in financial terms. Even more important, it provides a roof over the family's head. Children's interests, as we have seen, generally take priority. So a decision on who will have the family home – whether in the short or long term – must always take account of children's needs.

These orders must not be viewed in isolation from questions of financial relief dealt with above. For example, a court can reduce or terminate monthly payments to make up for the capital involved in a transfer of the matrimonial home from one spouse to another.

Moreover, these orders cannot be viewed in isolation from the general economic climate. Since the collapse of the property market in the late 1980s, couples sometimes owe more on their homes than their houses are worth at today's prices. This is an unprecedented situation. Once the family's 'greatest financial asset' becomes a millstone, it is exceedingly difficult for the courts to achieve equitable solutions.

7.3.1 A necessary precaution

▶ **Important:** a spouse in divorce proceedings should take immediate steps to protect his or her rights of occupation (see section 7.3.3 below). Do seek legal advice on this.

7.3.2 Who owns the family home?

To answer this question, one must look at the title deeds. Usually property is registered in the names of both husband and wife so that they own it jointly; otherwise it will be registered in the name of one of the spouses only.

However, whoever owns it, the court can make an order with regard to the matrimonial home. In an endeavour to ensure fairness to the family as a whole, it can transfer the whole of the property to a spouse, particularly a mother with young children, usually on certain stringent conditions. The court can order an outright sale, or it can postpone a sale so that the capital is tied up for years (see section 7.3.4 below).

7.3.3 Who can live in it?

In general, rights of occupation are registered as a notice in the Land Registry or as a land charge on the title deeds to property. This gives a right of occupation in law under the Matrimonial Homes Act 1983 – irrespective of ownership.

The court will then deal with the question of the long-term disposition of the matrimonial home.

7.3.4 The orders available to the court

As we have seen, a house in today's market is a fluctuating asset. This makes long-term solutions by the court, as much as by the parties themselves, particularly difficult.

The court, as we know, has the widest discretion in sorting out the assets of the family. With regard to the family home, there are usually three types of order:

- immediate sale and division of proceeds
- transfer of house into the sole name of one spouse
- postponement of the sale of the house till a later stage.

(a) Postponement of sale until children grow up

The courts can order that the matrimonial home should be occupied by the spouse who has the children living with him or her. It could then be sold when the youngest child turns 17.

While this was at one time seen as a satisfactory solution to housing needs, it is now realized that it can be a recipe for problems at a later stage.

> *Your wife was granted an order by the court that she should remain in the house after divorce until the youngest child was 17. The children were then 12, 9 and 7. Ten years have passed and your youngest child is now about to leave home. You are in a quandary as the house has fallen in value considerably over the past three years, your ex-wife is in her mid-fifties and depressed at the prospect of the last of her children leaving home. She also does not wish to move. On the other hand, you need some capital at this stage of your life. Can she ask the court to vary the order?*

In general, orders which have dealt with property are final. It would be helpful if you could work out some arrangement between you on the best way of dealing with the problem of the house e.g. your wife could perhaps raise money to buy out your share. Do ensure that you both take separate legal and accountancy advice.

(b) Postponement of sale until wife's circumstances change

There is another type of order which the courts use in postponing sale of the house on divorce proceedings. One spouse can have the use of the home (with the children) until such a time as he or she remarries, cohabits with someone else, or dies – whichever is the soonest. Then it must be sold and the proceeds divided up.

Again, this solution may create as many problems as it solves.

> *Your husband divorced you. You are presently living in the home with your two small children of the marriage. The court has ordered that you are to live there until you remarry or cohabit with someone else. The children are receiving maintenance from your ex-husband. You have recently met another man and have formed a deep relationship with him. He is very attached to the children and you want him to move in with you. You cannot move into his accommodation as it is unsuitable for a family. You are fearful of losing either your boyfriend or your home. You would like some advice.*

Perhaps you and your boyfriend could raise the capital to buy out your ex-husband's share of the home. Alternatively, you may be able to ask the court to vary the order to work out some compensatory arrangement for his share of the capital asset.

▶ **Remember:** The court will certainly take into account the pooling of resources on your cohabitation.

7.3.5 Rented accommodation

A tenancy is just as much a property right as outright home ownership.

(a) The private sector

Under the Matrimonial Homes Act 1983, the spouse of a secure tenant has rights of occupation as long as the marriage subsists. It also allows for a transfer of the tenancy from one spouse to another on a divorce, provided that the tenancy can be transferred. In other words, it cannot override a tenancy agreement. For example, if the husband is the sole tenant and he leaves a flat in private rented accommodation, a landlord cannot be forced by the courts to accept his wife in his stead – unless she has security of tenure in her own right or the landlord has accepted her presence as tenant by taking rent from her (see also chapter on *Landlords and their Tenants*).

(b) The public sector

A tenancy of a council house can be transferred by the council. It will do so only if a court order has been made on a divorce or judicial separation (see also chapter on *Landlords and their Tenants*).

◆ **Do note:** This area of law is extremely complex: If there is any change in your married circumstances which could jeopardize your position in a rented house or flat, do seek proper advice.

7.4 Court orders: thwarting them?

7.4.1 Can you dispose of the family assets?

Some people would rather dispose of their assets than have to hand them over to an estranged husband or wife. Of course, if they were allowed to do so, many orders in divorce proceedings would not be worth the paper they are written on.

So the court has power to prevent a disposal of assets – either as a pre-emptive measure or even after a transaction has taken place, if it can be shown that the transaction was clearly intended to thwart an order in matrimonial proceedings.

(a) Pre-emptive measures

You learn that your wife intends to set up an elaborate trust fund which would in effect strip her of all her assets prior to your divorce. You wonder what you can do?

You can ask for an injunction to freeze her assets pending settlement.

(b) Setting aside transactions which have already taken place

The court can even order that a transaction be set aside after it has taken place provided a claimant can show that it would directly affect the relief he or she might expect.

An off-shore company has been set up by your ex-husband who has transferred all his private shareholdings into the new company.

If you can show that you would be entitled to financial provision from those particular shareholdings or that the setting up of the company would otherwise affect what you were entitled to receive, you could ask for the transaction to be set aside. Of course, the more complicated the transaction, such as the one in this case, involving a corporate structure and an off-shore base, the more difficult it may be to enforce any order you may obtain from the court.

7.5 Court orders: enforcing them?

All court orders are only as good as the court's methods of enforcing them. If orders which are handed down by the judges are going to be flouted or ignored, they are of little help to those who asked for them.

In theory the judges' powers are wide-ranging.

7.5.1 The attachment of a maintenance order to earnings

For maintenance payments, the courts can attach an order to earnings.

This involves applying to court and swearing a written statement (an *affidavit*) giving the amounts of payment in arrears. The courts will not generally enforce arrears more than a year old.

The order is then 'attached' to the ex-spouse's earnings and payments are deducted by his (or her) employer. To state the obvious, such an order is only effective against someone in employment. In any event, the courts will never make an order which will leave the other side so out-of-pocket as to reach subsistence level. The protected earnings rate, which is the basic level, is calculated on income support and other benefits and includes other long-term outgoings such as rent.

7.5.2 The sending in of bailiffs to seize goods

A *warrant of execution*, as this is called, also follows on application to court and the signing of an affidavit setting out the arrears of maintenance. In practice, of course, goods seized fetch little on forced sale and it is the threat of seizure, rather than the actuality, which is hoped to be effective.

In practice maintenance payments are often made over to the DSS.

◆ **Note:** enforcement procedure by the courts is currently under review by the Lord Chancellor.

8. When cohabitees split up

Despite the numbers of cohabiting couples, their status in law differs fundamentally from that of married couples (see also chapter on *Setting up Home*).

The law of divorce reflects certain profound legal assumptions about the marital relationship – in particular, a duty to maintain the other spouse. This duty survives even breakdown of the marriage – hence the detailed provisions on ancillary relief (see section 6 above).

In cohabitation, on the other hand, no such assumptions are made. As a result the courts do not have the powers to deal with family assets of a cohabiting couple who split up that they have when a married couple get divorced. In fact, of course, the situations of both couples may be identical in other ways: there may be children, there may be a deserted partner who needs somewhere to live. However, they are treated differently in law.

◆ **Do note:** the popular phrase 'a common law marriage' has no legal content.

8.1 Who owns the house?

The answer to this question is usually determined by the names on the title deeds.

Unlike its powers on divorce, the court has no power to make a property transfer order – unless there are children involved. Thus as between the couple themselves, legal ownership of the property is the definitive factor when they split up.

In dealing with property matters, legal advice must always be sought.

8.1.1 Joint ownership

If the property is in joint names, the usual division is on a fifty-fifty basis. With regard to the position of a person with whom a child of the family is resident, however, see section 8.1.5 below.

8.1.2 Title deeds in one name only

What happens if a cohabitee, whose name is not on the title deeds, wants to claim part-ownership or some other interest in the home? The task is made very difficult; the law presumes that whosoever has his or her name on the deeds is the owner.

Doctrines have been developed in order to mitigate the rigour of the law but these would apply as much to two friends who share a flat or house as to a couple who might have been living together for years as man and wife.

A cohabiting partner who wants to claim a share of a house which is in one name only must prove to the court's satisfaction

(a) that at the time the home was purchased there was an intention to benefit both parties;
(b) that the person making a claim also made a contribution to the purchase in money or money's worth;
(c) that he or she has lost out as a result of that action.

8.1.3 Who can live in the home?

There are no rights of occupation. This is in striking contrast to the position of a married spouse under the Matrimonial Homes Act (see section 7.3.3 above).

However, property transfer orders can now be made for children under the Children Act 1989 (see section 8.1.5 below).

8.1.4 Rented accommodation

(a) Where there is a sole tenant: the position is that there is only one lawful tenant. The landlord is not obliged to accept rent from the other partner, who has no right to stay on.
(b) Where the tenancy is in joint names, the position is much more complicated. A joint tenant can give a notice to quit which will bring the tenancy to an end. However, it must be a valid notice. Certain statutory tenants will be protected however (see chapter on *Landlords and their Tenants*).

8.1.5 Claims on behalf of children of cohabitees

Under the Children Act 1989, a parent can apply for a financial order for a child. The term 'parent' extends to parents who are not married to each other. There is a wide range of orders available including an order to make a lump sum or to transfer property. Thus an order can apply to a family home or to a local authority tenancy. The home – belonging to either parent – could be set up on trust for the parent with whom the child is living until the child's 18th birthday.

◆ **Note:** As yet there is no indication of how these powers under the Children Act will be used in the case of unmarried parents.

(a) Home ownership

However, under the Children Act 1989, claims can be made on behalf of children for a property transfer against the other parent for the benefit of a child.

There is a wide range of orders available under the Act which include the making of a lump sum or the transfer of property. A court can make a transfer of property order which can directly benefit the children of the family. In effect, this would give an indirect benefit to the other partner as well. Thus an unmarried parent may have rights of occupation, for example, conferred on him or her with regard to the family home.

> *You and your boyfriend live in a house which belongs to him. You have had two children together. He now wants to end the relationship and bring his new girlfriend into the house. You and the children have nowhere to go.*

Under the Children Act, the court can make property orders. It could, for instance, determine that the house should be held in trust for the benefit of the children until they reach the age of 18.

(b) Rented accommodation

In the case of local authority accommodation, a parent can apply for the transfer of the tenancy under the Children Act for the benefit of the child.

8.2 Maintenance

A cohabitee has no right to claim maintenance from his or her partner on separation. Obviously this too can lead to grave injustice when the couple may have been living as man and wife for many years and have brought up a family together.

8.2.1 Parent 'with care'

Maintenance must be paid for and on behalf of the children however. The question of applications for maintenance against an 'absent parent' under the Child Support Act 1991 is dealt with in the chapter on *Children* (see Chapter 3, section 1.1). Maintenance for the child includes an element for the person with care of that child.

9. Domestic violence

The question of how best to assist victims of domestic violence is receiving increasing attention from the authorities, welfare organizations, and women's groups. (Some of the organizations concerned to provide help for its victims are to be found in the DIRECTORY at the end of Chapter 3.) The police are setting up specialist units to deal with domestic disputes involving violence.

9.1 Unsatisfactory state of the law

Unfortunately, the laws governing the protection of victims of violence in domestic disputes are most unsatisfactory and extremely complicated. Among other matters, they turn on

- whether a couple is married or not, and
- which jurisdiction is invoked i.e. whether a person turns to a magistrates' court or a county court for assistance.

The Law Commission has produced a discussion paper in order to make the law on domestic violence more uniform and to streamline procedures. At the moment, the law is as outlined below (see section 9.2).

9.2 Immediate action

Persons who are being subjected to actual physical violence, or even the threat of it, should seek immediate protection from harm. They should

- call in the police if need be
- seek temporary shelter
- obtain an exclusion or non-molestation order immediately (see below, section 9.3).

These orders can be obtained in an emergency. They are available, if need be, without telling the other party. (These are then called *ex parte orders*.) Where there is a real need for protection in the face of imminent danger a judge or magistrate can issue an order out of hours or over weekends.

9.3 Orders dealing with domestic violence

There are two general orders:

- exclusion or ouster orders which forbid a partner or spouse to enter the home
- non-molestation orders which are intended to prevent harassment as well as violence.

9.3.1 Exclusion orders against a spouse

Applications for exclusion orders (or ouster orders) under the Matrimonial Homes Act 1983 apply to married couples only.

An exclusion order will

- terminate
- restrict or
- suspend

the other spouse's rights of occupation irrespective of who owns the house.

Because an exclusion order is so drastic, the courts will consider

- the conduct of the couple
- their needs and resources
- the needs of the children
- any other circumstances.

(a) The conduct of the couple

It will not make an order to give a couple a breathing space. The couple's conduct is viewed seriously.

You are a married woman. Your husband has never used violence against you. However, you find the tense atmosphere in your home intolerable and would like to know whether you can get an order to exclude your husband from the home – even for a limited time.

It is most unlikely that these circumstances would justify your application to court for an exclusion order. In the absence of physical violence, the court would probably want evidence that your husband's presence is causing you injury to your health – either physical or mental. Moreover an exclusion order will never be used as a means to effect a reconciliation.

(b) The couple's needs and resources

The court is certain to consider the question of alternative accommodation for either spouse.

(c) The needs of the children

It will consider where the children are living and with which parent. The needs of the children are not paramount and will not override every other consideration.

(d) Any other considerations.

The court may use an exclusion order pending divorce.

You have decided to petition your wife for divorce and have left her in the matrimonial home while you live in a rented studio flat. The house is in your sole name and you hope to sell it once the financial arrangements between yourself and your wife are sorted out. You now learn that your wife intends to sublet one entire floor of the house. You are anxious that you may have great difficulty in obtaining vacant possession for a sale at a later stage.

The court may well grant an exclusion order against your wife if it feels that she is trying to deal with the property so as to prejudice your rights in it. However, the court will weigh up all the other factors mentioned above, such as the needs of the children, if any, as well as the question of alternative accommodation for your wife.

9.3.2 Limitations

The Matrimonial Homes Act applies only to married couples; unmarried couples have to resort to other action (see section 9.4 below).

9.4 Orders under the Domestic Violence and Matrimonial Proceedings Act 1976

This Act applies to

- married couples

and to

- 'a man and a woman who are living with each other in the same household as husband and wife'.

It also gives the right to apply for

- a non-molestation order
- an exclusion order from the home.

Applications must be made to the county court.

9.5 Non-molestation orders

An exclusion order will not prevent your former spouse or partner harassing you outside your home. If you are being harassed in that way, you must apply for a non-molestation order. Molestation is conduct which 'involves such a degree of harassment as to call for intervention by the court'. There need be no violence or threat of violence involved.

You cohabited with a woman for several years but have recently parted from her. You are now living at your mother's house. Your former partner is very jealous of a new relationship you have formed with another woman and is becoming very difficult to deal with. She stands on the street corner near your mother's house and assails you with abuse as you pass; she follows you to work and embarrasses you in front of your colleagues.

In this case you could apply for a non-molestation order to the county court. However, a solicitor's letter to the effect that you intend applying for an order could help to alleviate the situation.

3. CHILDREN

At first glance, it would seem that the law has little to do with the upbringing of a child. Parents, after all, are nature's protectors of their children and have their well-being most at heart. How can parents' responsibilities be defined in legal terms? And when would it be necessary to think in such terms?

In fact, as we shall see, the law intervenes from the first day of a child's life. Moreover, throughout childhood, the law watches over the welfare of children at every turn. Children are regarded as vulnerable, as open to exploitation, in need of education, in need of protection from themselves and from others. Thus, as far as children's day-to-day lives are concerned, their activities are governed by a battery of legislation – not always appreciated by young persons themselves!

Only gradually does the law allow children to assume adult 'rights'. For example rules and regulations govern such matters as when a minor can marry, and the age at which he or she can open a bank account, leave school, or simply do a newspaper round. As we all know, even the films a child can watch are categorized according to age.

Thus, although we tend to think that a child 'becomes' an adult on his or her 18th birthday, growing up is a very complicated process as far as the law is concerned (see *The stages of growing up* on page 88).

With regard to the role of parents, the law generally steps in when things go wrong; for example, parents have a legal duty to protect their child; if they fail in that duty and their child is neglected, other authorities will take charge.

In the sphere of children's welfare, the law has made strenuous efforts to move with the times. A landmark piece of legislation, the Children Act 1989, came into force on 15 October 1991. The Act has been described as the most far-reaching and revolutionary change in the law concerning children, this century.

Along with new legislation, a general awareness has developed that children too have 'rights'. Children's views are heeded now in the courts when possible. No longer is it just a matter of the courts or others in authority deciding what is 'best' for the child.

In this chapter we look at

- parental responsibilities
- unmarried parents
- when parents split up
- when parents fail
- other parents
- education
- children and crime
- children's rights.

1. Parental responsibilities

Attitudes to parent/child relationships have changed. For many centuries the common law had assigned a legitimate child – for all legal purposes – to the father's sole authority. Now no longer has a married father absolute authority over his child. Parental responsibilities are shared equally between married mother and father (see section 1.2 below).

In the case of unmarried parents, the mother is entitled to all parental responsibilities in law unless the parents themselves or the courts decide that they should be shared between father and mother (section 2.3 below).

It is natural that the parental role diminishes with time. This process, too, is recognized by law. The courts are hesitant to enforce parental authority as children grow older. What starts with a right to control 'ends with little more than advice'.

Until very recently, the law spoke of 'parental rights' – now it refers to 'parental responsibilities'. This is more than a mere change of terms; it reflects a distinct shift in perception of the relationship between parent and child. The concept of 'rights' over your son or daughter is quite a different one from that of 'responsibility' for them. The change in terminology, reflecting the change in social attitudes, was introduced by the Children Act 1989.

1.1 Children Act 1989 and Child Support Act 1991

(a) The Children Act 1989

The Children Act 1989 was passed so that the law relating to children would be more in keeping with modern views. It was also intended to make uniform the multiplicity of laws governing the legal position of children. It was also hoped to ensure, as far as possible, that the courts' structure would be more 'family-friendly' (i.e. less adversarial!) and that trained personnel would deal with issues involving children and the law.

The central assumptions of the Children Act are that

- the welfare of children is the paramount and overriding factor in any decision which the courts take on their future;
- children are entitled to the love and care of both parents, irrespective of whether both parents live at home with them or not;
- delay in arrangements for children can have tragic consequences;
- parents who separate should decide for themselves as far as possible – without the court's intervention – on the best arrangements for their children;
- the courts should have a range of flexible orders at their disposal in dealing with children;
- proceedings should be simplified in everyone's interest;
- local authorities which deal with children at risk or in need must do so – as far as possible – in partnership with parents;
- the courts should only intervene after deciding that intervention would be more beneficial for the child than non-intervention.

The success or failure of the Act depends – as it is intended to – on the parents involved just as much as on the courts, welfare officers, social workers, lawyers and judges.

◆ **Note:** The Act makes sweeping and fundamental changes in both the private and public law aspect of child care.

(b) The Child Support Act 1991

As we have seen in the chapter on *Divorce*, parents are liable to maintain their children while they are minors. In cases of broken homes, that liability was imposed by the courts of law although in practice the State often had to bear the cost of maintaining children of lone parents.

The Child Support Act 1991 was brought in to change the whole approach to child maintenance. The courts were no longer to act as the collectors of children's maintenance; that task was now to be given to a new body – the Child Support Agency. It is run by the Department of Social Security with centres throughout the country.

(a) *The 'qualifying child'*
A child qualifies for maintenance under the Child Support Act if one of its parents does not live at home. In other words he or she has an absent parent.

(b) *The absent parent*
An 'absent parent' is the one who does not live with the child at home. The status of an absent parent does not depend on whether the parents are married.

(c) *The person with care*
The term applies to the person who has the daily care of the child.

◆ **Note:** although the absent parent is usually the father and the person with care is usually the mother, this need not always be the case.

(d) *The Act's wide ambit*
The Act was originally intended to apply to families on social security benefits. However, it has now been extended to apply to all families which have a qualifying child. This means that

- all new claims for maintenance from April 1993 will be dealt with by the CSA.
- parents who have already made arrangements for their children's maintenance will be liable to assessment under the Act.

The phasing in will be gradual and will take place over the next three years so that all children should be within its ambit by January 1997.

◆ **Note:** The Act applies where both parents are normally resident in the UK. The courts will deal with cases where an absent parent or a person with care lives abroad.

(a) *How the assessment is made*
Lone parents on social security benefits are sent an application form automatically. They have to fill in the form and, in particular, supply information so that an absent parent can be identified and traced. Refusal to supply the information will have to be justified by showing good reason – such as fear of violence.

A child support officer is entrusted with the task of making the assessment.

(f) *How the assessment is calculated*
The assessment is calculated according to a formula which takes into account

- the maintenance needed for the children
- the income available to each parent after their own personal expenses have been set off against their net income
- the assessable income then left after the set-off. It is from that assessable income that the maintenance requirement is taken.

(g) *Element of maintenance for carer*
The assessment includes an amount for the person who has care of the child based on income support rates. This particular provision has caused a great deal of resentment as it is seen as an 'adult' maintenance payment.

(h) *Appeals*
Periodic reviews are built in to the Act based on fresh information from the person with care or the absent parent. There can also be a review after a change of circumstances. If dissatisfied with a decision, an absent parent can apply for a review to a different child support officer.

There is a basic right of appeal to a Child Support Appeal Tribunal. There are 50 appeal tribunals throughout the country. The judge in charge has stated that payers and recipients will have an unfettered right to be heard (*The Times*, 21 October 1993).

(i) *Criticism of the Act*
The Act has evoked a great deal of public outcry with a fierce divide between opponents and proponents of its provisions.

The particular charges against the Act are:

- that longstanding agreements between ex-partners are being over-turned;
- that fathers who have started second families, bought second homes etc., are now finding themselves unable to finance commitments made before the Act came into force;
- that caring fathers are being penalized as 'soft targets' while feckless fathers, who are more difficult to track down, are not being dealt with.

(j) *Changes to the regulations*

These changes were introduced in February 1994. Among them are:

(a) the care allowance at the moment is £44. This amount will be reduced when the child reaches 11 and 14 respectively;

(b) an extra maintenance will be imposed where the absent parent pays for only one or two children and the assessable income is more than the amount needed for the maintenance requirement;

(c) safeguards are introduced to protect an absent parent's level of income;

(d) increases are to be introduced in stages.

1.2 Position of married parents

Where the parents of a child are married to each other, both mother and father share all parental responsibilities. Even if they subsequently divorce, so that their child lives with only one parent, the other parent still has continuing responsibility for the child.

1.3 The nature of parental responsibilities

1.3.1 When do they begin?

In general parental responsibilities begin at birth.

A pregnant woman is not responsible in law to her unborn child for her lifestyle; in other words, even if harm were to come to the foetus from her behaviour, she cannot be prevented from smoking or drinking too much, or from taking drugs. However, if she has a car accident because, for example, she drives negligently, and her baby is born handicapped as a result, the child could bring an action against her. That would be the responsibility of the insurers.

A father cannot take steps to prevent the mother of their child from terminating her pregnancy.

> *Your wife is pregnant but says that she does not want the child. She feels that she has good, legal grounds for an abortion. You are desperately keen to have the child and wish to prevent any harm coming to it. What can you do?*

You would not be able to stop the abortion in this case provided your wife could fulfil the legal/medical grounds for terminating her pregnancy; nor can an unmarried man stop his girlfriend from proceeding with an abortion.

1.3.2 Notice of birth

A notice of every birth must be given by a person in attendance at the birth, such as doctor or midwife, to the district Medical Officer of Health within 36 hours.

1.3.3 Registering the birth

The birth of every child must be registered within 42 days of birth with the Registrar of Births and Deaths of the sub-district in which the birth took place. Where parents are married, it is usually the father or mother who registers the birth.

Arrangements can be made to register a child even if you are no longer in the district in which the birth took place.

> *You leave the district where your baby was born. Do you need to go back to it in order to register the birth?*

The answer is 'no'. You need not return to the district in person. You could go to any registrar of births in England and Wales to give details. The mother or father, as well as the registrar, must sign a declaration. This is then sent to the registrar of the sub-district where the birth took place.

1.3.4 Naming a child

Parents give the child both surname and forename, usually for life. The custom, although not the law, in the case of the married parents, is that the child is given the father's surname. The names are registered at the time of the registration of the baby's birth. If the parents are married, both their names must be registered. (For the status of an unmarried mother with regard to registration, see section 2.2 below.)

(a) Can you change a child's name?

Changing a name on a birth certificate:

(a) *Forename*: if you wish to change your child's forename, this can be done within 12 months of the original registration, either on production of a baptismal certificate under the new name or on a form available from the registrar.

(b) *Surname*: if, in the case of married parents, the child is given the father's name, the mother cannot apply to have the child registered under her name unless with the father's consent. Over the years, the courts came to feel that a unilateral change of a child's name, for example to the name of a step-parent, was a serious matter. The new legislation reflects this view.

Under the Children Act 1989, a child's name cannot be changed without the consent of persons who have parental responsibility for the child – usually both mother and father.

If one of the persons with parental responsibility withholds consent, application will have to be made to court to give its consent. The court will scrutinize such an application very carefully indeed to see if it is in the child's best interests (see section 3 below on Orders available to the court).

> *You divorced your husband in December 1991 when your little girl was three and she came to live with you under a residence order from the court. The child has very regular contact with her father. You recently remarried and changed your name to that of your second husband. You are now expecting another baby. You would like your daughter to have the same surname as yourself as you think it will be easier for her to integrate into her new family. Can you do so at will?*

Under the Children Act, as we have seen, you cannot change your daughter's surname to that of your second husband without her father's consent or consent of the court. That was an automatic condition attached to the fact that the court allowed her to live with you under the residence order.

You thus have two choices. You could discuss it with her father and seek to persuade him that it is in your daughter's best interest to have the same name as her half-brother or sister. You can assure him that you do not wish to take this step in order to sever the relationship or weaken the links between him and his child.

If you cannot persuade him, you could apply to court for permission for the name change but you may find it difficult to persuade a judge that your reasons are sufficient.

1.3.5 Issue of birth certificate

After the birth has been registered, a short birth certificate is issued free of charge. It would suffice for most purposes (e.g. applying for a passport) but a full birth certificate, containing all the details of the register entry, is also available. This can be purchased at the time of registration or at any time afterwards, as can copies of the short birth certificate.

1.4 Other responsibilities

Notifying the authorities of the birth of your child, and registering his or her birth with the names you have chosen, are the very first formal steps to be taken. Other parental responsibilities are outlined below.

1.4.1 Duty to protect

There is a duty to protect a child from harm. This duty is enforced with criminal sanctions. A child is not to be ill-treated, neglected or abandoned, under the Children Act 1933. A parent is guilty of neglect if he or she fails to provide a child with adequate food, clothing, medical aid and lodging (see also section 7 below).

The 'home alone' case of a mother who left her two-year old daughter alone when she went to work is an extreme example of neglect under this heading. (See also section 7 below.)

◆ **Note:** this law is now 60 years out of date; there are calls to reform it.

It is also a criminal offence for anyone over the age of 16 to allow a young child in a room with an unguarded open fire or any other heating appliance liable to cause injury and an injury ensues.

(a) Duty on others who care for a child

If someone over the age of 16 wilfully neglects, assaults, ill-treats or abandons a child in his or her care, that too is a criminal offence.

This does not mean, however, that a young person under the age of 16 cannot look after a child.

> *You have put an advertisement in the local post office for a babysitter. You have received a reply from a fourteen-year-old school girl who seems level-headed and sensible. You have been told that no person under the age of 16 is allowed to babysit by law. Is that correct?*

The answer is 'no'. There is no specific age at which a person can be left alone in charge of a child. The law specifies, however, that if anyone over the age of 16, who has a child in his or her charge, wilfully neglects the child, that person is guilty of a criminal offence.

(b) Looking after children for profit

Many mothers today go out to work and leave their children with others to care for them. As far as possible, the law tries to ensure that childminders and those who run nursery schools are fit and proper people to take care of children. Anyone who looks after more than one child, for profit, for more than two hours per day, must be registered by a local authority under the Children Act 1989. The Act lays down regulations for vetting of persons and inspection of premises before registration. Names, addresses and other details are registered on computer with every local authority and a list is available for your area on request.

In a recent case a mother left her baby with a registered childminder. The baby suffered severe injury at the hands of the minder. The local authority officer had assured her that it was safe to leave her child with the minder although he was aware that there had been an earlier incident when another baby had suffered injury in the same woman's care. The court ruled that the local authority was liable to the mother because of its negligent assurances that her child would be safe. However, merely putting a name on a register did not – of itself – carry any assurances as to safe care.

1.4.2 Duty to maintain

The duty to maintain children does not depend upon the status of the parents. As we have seen (section 1.4.1 above) at the very least, a child must be fed, housed and clothed. This duty applies whether parents are married, whether they have been married and are now divorced, or whether they have never been married at all.

Under the Child Support Act 1991, each parent of a 'qualifying child' is responsible for maintaining him or her. A qualifying child has one or both parents absent from home. The Act stipulates how maintenance is to be assessed and also allows for appeals against assessment. Even if an unmarried father has no parental responsibility for his child, he still has a legal duty to maintain the child (see section 2 below, for the position of unmarried parents; see also chapter on *Divorce*).

1.4.3 Keeping discipline

Parents generally insist on certain behaviour from their children although in some families discipline will be much stricter than in others. The law states that parents can inflict 'lawful' punishment. The question, of course, is what is 'lawful'? It is important to note in this context how much society as a whole has moved away from accepting corporal punishment as the answer to a recalcitrant child.

> *You have recently remarried and there is a running conflict between your teenage daughter and her stepfather. He has lost his temper with her frequently and has lately begun to hit her too. She states that she will not be punished or hurt in this way and is going to complain to the police.*

If excessive force is used against a child by a parent or someone in the role of a parent, the child may invoke the criminal law of assault. It is all a matter of degree. There are various organizations and Help Lines available to contact – for parents, step-parents, and children who need assistance if there is a fraught situation (see DIRECTORY at the end of this chapter).

A parent's 'right' to punish his or her child cannot be passed on to another member of the family. In one case an older brother administered a beating to his younger brother and claimed that he did so on their father's behalf. The courts held that this was unlawful.

◆ **Note:** It is unlawful for a teacher to administer corporal punishment in a state school. It is also unlawful to administer 'degrading' punishment in an independent school (see *Education*, section 6 below).

It is only too clear that children are vulnerable to excessive punishment wherever they are.

Cases have occurred where children who have been taken into care, on the grounds of need or of being at risk – in other words, some of the most vulnerable of all children – have been subjected to unlawful punishments such as 'pindown' in local authority homes.

1.4.4 Medical treatment

(a) Allowing treatment

The general rule: Parents are entitled to give consent to medical treatment for their children up to the age of 16. A child over the age of 16 can consent to any surgical, medical or dental treatment without his or her parents' consent.

However, delicate and difficult problems have arisen.

(b) Refusing treatment

What if a parent refuses consent to treatment which the doctors consider necessary for the child's welfare? Parents may refuse on religious grounds or for some other reason – such as not wanting the doctors to inflict suffering on the child. In certain cases where a parent has refused to allow a blood transfusion for a sick child, the court has made the child a 'ward of court' (see *Other parents*, section 5.4 below) and given consent to treatment.

The conflict between doctor and parent can go the other way too – in a recent case, the mother wanted her child to remain on a life support system while the doctors felt it was not in the child's interests to continue treatment. The courts overrode the mother's views and left the ultimate decision to the doctors.

(c) Child's own choices

(i) What if a child is under 16 but wants to consult a doctor or consent to treatment without involving parents?

A landmark decision decided that

- where a child has sufficient understanding and intelligence and
- can understand the nature of the treatment being proposed, then he or she can consent to treatment.

The case concerned advice given by the (then) Department of Health and Social Security to doctors allowing them to advise on contraception for girls under 16 if the circumstances warranted it. Mrs Gillick, a mother of five daughters, all under 16, challenged the DHSS advice and her case went all the way to the House of Lords. The Law Lords decided that it would be most unusual for a doctor to advise a child on contraceptive matters without the knowledge and consent of her parents.

However, parents do not have an absolute veto on such matters. In certain circumstances, a doctor may be in a better position to judge issues of medical advice and treatment most conducive to a child's welfare. Further, a child who had sufficient understanding and maturity to grasp what was involved could give a valid consent. Understanding varied as to the complexity of the issues but did not turn on a fixed age.

◆ **Note:** The fact that doctors may be in a better position than parents to judge medical issues is applicable to boys under 16 as well as to girls.

(ii) What if a child wants to refuse treatment?

It would appear that in a life-threatening situation, a doctor can get the court's sanction to override the wishes of the child. This does not appear to be age-dependent; in a recent case an anorexic girl, aged over 16, was ordered to have treatment against her wishes.

(d) Non-parental consent

What if you are looking after children in their parents' absence and consent to medical treatment is needed?

Your sister has gone abroad on a motoring holiday and left her 15-year-old daughter in your charge. Your niece falls and breaks a leg in a school hockey match and needs surgery to reset it. The doctor asks you to sign a consent form.

In this case, the girl herself could consent if she is not too upset. As far as your position as aunt is concerned, the new Children Act specifically gives parental responsibility, which includes the right to consent to medical treatment, to people who have temporary charge of a child.

The situation might be different if you had to consent to elective treatment, i.e. treatment which a patient could choose to have or not, such as the removal of a tooth under anaesthetic. You would be advised in such circumstances to await the parents' return.

Again the age of the patient is a very material factor in elective treatment; a girl or boy of 15 might be able to consent whereas a much younger child would have to show that he or she clearly understood the issues involved in letting a doctor or dentist treat him or her.

1.4.5 Ensuring education

See section 6 below.

1.4.6 Emigration, nationality and passport matters

Parents can decide together to take the child out of the UK. However, a parent's right to act alone is limited. Where a child lives with one parent under a residence order, that parent can take a child abroad for a period of up to one month; for a longer period, every person with parental responsibility must give written consent. If they refuse, consent of the court must be obtained.

(a) Emigration

You have recently married for the second time and your second husband is Canadian. You would like to settle in Canada with him, taking your two children by your first marriage. Their father objects. What can you do?

If you cannot get the father's written consent, you would have to apply to court for an order to settle this specific issue ('a specific issue order', see section 3.1.2 below). The court would weigh the advantages to the children of a new life against the fact that they would lose touch with their natural father.

(b) Nationality and passport

A child born in the UK is automatically a British citizen provided that at the time of the birth one or both of the parents is a British citizen or is settled in the UK without time limit restriction. This applies where the parents are married. See section 2.6 below for the position of a child of an unmarried mother. Their child can be included on both parents' passports and can travel abroad with either parent. If the parents divorce, unless there is concern for the child's safety, a child can go abroad for up to one month with either parent on his or her passport.

In all cases, over the age of 16, a child must have his or her own passport.

A standard passport can be issued for a child in his own name at any age; this would be necessary if, for example, you work abroad but your child is being educated in the UK. A parent must consent on the application form for a passport for a child under the age of 18.

As far as a British visitor's passport is concerned, a child over the age of 16 must have his or her own. However, no child under the age of 8 can have his or her own visitor's passport.

1.4.7 Choosing religious upbringing

Parents are generally said to have the 'power' to determine their child's religious upbringing. Indeed such a right would seem to be self-evident along with all the other incidents of parenthood.

In today's pluralistic, secular society, parents may choose to bring their children up as non-believers.

◆ **Note:** there is a general requirement under the Education Acts that schools must provide religious education (see *Religious Education*, section 6.3.2 below).

As far as the law is concerned, religion as an issue in a child's upbringing also arises

- in cases of adoption
- in cases of fostering
- where there is conflict between the parents.

Although the courts have intervened where they feel that a child may be brainwashed by an undesirable set of beliefs, in general it is not the duty of the courts to sit in moral judgment on people's religious beliefs.

You discover that your ex-husband is taking your six-year old daughter to meetings of a revivalist sect on the weekends that he has access to her. You are very unhappy about it as you fear that the child is being indoctrinated with the sect's beliefs. You have talked to him about the problem but to no avail. He stoutly maintains that there is freedom of religion in this country. What can you do?

You would want to avoid the child becoming embroiled in a conflict in court over religion between two estranged parents although the courts have taken such matters up in the past. You might try to arrange for her father to have contact on days other than those on which meetings are being held.

If it were to go to court, you could seek a 'specific issue order' that the child should be brought up in your own religion – but you would have to persuade the judge that such an order would be better than no order at all and was in the child's best interests.

Alternatively, you could apply for an order which would prohibit her father from taking your daughter to the meetings (a 'prohibited steps order'). Again the court would weigh up the issues very carefully in your daughter's interests before making any order at all.

◆ **Note:** Where certain sects have been outlawed for dubious practices and beliefs, the courts will take a stronger view in protecting children against them.

1.4.8 Appointing guardians

See section 5.2 below.

1.4.9 Consenting to adoption

See section 5.1 below.

1.4.10 Consenting to marriage

- Marriages of children under the age of 16 are not allowed at all.
- Marriages of minors between the age of 16 and 18 need parental consent.
- Over-18-year-olds are free to marry without parental consent.

◆ **Note:** Issues of consent for the marriage of minors will be found in Chapter 1, *Setting up Home*, section 1.2.1.

1.5 When parental responsibility ends

Parents who have parental responsibility for their child cannot abrogate it. In other words, you cannot give up responsibility unilaterally for as long as the child is a minor.

A child attains majority at the age of 18. At that age parental responsibility formally ceases. Many court orders last until a child is 16 or 17. However, if a child is in further, full time education, a parent can be called upon to support his or her child beyond the age of 18.

The list at the end of the chapter (page 88) sets out the ages at which a child's activities are legally allowed (or proscribed). Apart from the 18-year threshold, parental responsibility will also cease

- when a minor marries
- when a minor is serving in the armed forces
- by court order.

1.6 Listening to a child's views

As we have seen, a most important feature of the Children Act is its emphasis on giving children their own voice. This is not age-dependent. Rather, the court's duty is to pay heed to the views of children provided that they have sufficient understanding and maturity to understand the issues at stake. Thus although parents still have responsibility for their children, a young person of sufficient understanding can put his or her views to the court in matters which affect their welfare or well-being. For example, they can ask the court to decide that

- an absent father should visit them
- a parent should pay for their full time education over the age of 18
- contact with their natural parents by adopted children should be resumed
- that life at home is so intolerable, a move into a boyfriend's family should be allowed.

All these instances have been heard in the courts recently.

2. Unmarried parents

In the case of parents who are not married to each other, the mother alone has legal responsibility for the child.

However, under the Children Act 1989, if an unmarried mother agrees, parental responsibility can now be shared by the father of her child.

2.1 Status of child

As far as the child is concerned, the law has moved steadily in the direction of equating the status of a legitimate and an illegitimate child. The stigma has been removed as far as illegitimate children's own rights in law are concerned. For example, if a parent of an illegitimate child dies and does not leave a will, the child can inherit under the laws of intestacy (see chapter on *Death–Before and After*).

2.2 Status of mother

However, the Children Act 1989 still draws a very clear distinction between the parental responsibility of married and unmarried parents. That very fact means that equal treatment is not quite accorded to a child whose parents are not married to each other. In particular the status of the mother is the cardinal indicator of the different approach of the law. All parental responsibility is given to the mother at the birth of the child if she is not married to the child's father. This position is not irrevocable, however (see *Status of father*, section 2.3 below).

- There is no obligation for an unmarried mother to register the father's name if she does not wish to. That part of the register can be left blank.
- If she does want to register the name of the father, this can be done at their joint request and they generally must both be present to sign the register.

(a) Birth certificate

The Registrar General issues an explanatory leaflet on the information which has to be supplied for registration of a baby's birth (Form 362). He also offers further advice and clarification in the case of unmarried parents.

> *When your daughter was born, you were not married to her father because he was married to another woman at the time. Your personal details on the birth certificate appear under your maiden name, in which your daughter was also registered. Since then your boyfriend has divorced his wife and you intend to marry each other soon. You would both like to alter the birth certificate so that you and your daughter are registered in her father's name.*

Once you are married to the father of your child, you can apply at any time to have the birth certificate re-registered in your married name. Your daughter's surname can also be altered to that of her father. You would have to produce her original birth certificate, your marriage certificate, and a form (LA1) for authorization to the Registrar General.

(b) Father's declaration of paternity

Special rules apply if the unmarried father cannot be present to register the birth.

> *Your boyfriend is a serviceman who is about to be sent abroad shortly before you are to give birth to his child. It is unlikely therefore that he will be able to be present to sign the register with you. Both of you are very concerned that his name should appear on the register. What can you do?*

Your boyfriend must sign a special statutory declaration of paternity (the form is available from the local registry office) before he leaves for abroad. The signing of the form must be witnessed by a solicitor, JP, or notary public.

(c) Changing a child's name

Under the Children Act persons with parental responsibility for a child must consent in writing to any change of surname of the child. If that cannot be obtained, consent of the court must be granted. The long-term interests of the child are always the court's primary consideration.

> *Your 14-year old son by a former liaison lives with you. You have recently married and want to change your son's surname to that of his stepfather. His natural father has not seen his son for many years and his consent is, in any event, unnecessary as he never assumed parental responsibility for the boy. However, your son, who is entering into a rebellious phase, objects to the change of name plan. Can you insist?*

The answer is 'no'. Under the Children Act 1989, a child of 'sufficient understanding' is entitled to object to a change of name. He can even seek the court's assistance in prohibiting you from taking such a step.

2.3 Status of father

The position of an unmarried father is not quite the same as that of a married father, as we have seen. However, his position has been strengthened by recent legislation as well as by the attitude of the courts.

- He can assume parental responsibility with the mother's consent
- if the mother does not consent, an unmarried father can apply to court and ask for a parental responsibility order so that he then has a right to be involved in all major matters concerning his child.

So although the position of an unmarried father has improved under the Act, he still does not have the same status in law as a married father unless he takes steps to acquire it.

2.3.1 Acting with the mother's consent

Under the Children Act 1989, if an unmarried mother agrees, parental responsibility can now be shared by both parents.

Your girlfriend is expecting your first child. You have been living together for some years and have a happy, stable relationship. Although you are not married, you would like your relationship with your child to approximate to that of a married father as much as possible. What can you do?

You can sign a Parental Responsibility Agreement with the mother's consent.

Certain formalities have to be observed with regard to signing a parental responsibility form.

(a) The parental responsibility agreement

Under section 4 of the Children Act 1989, where mother and father agree, they can enter into a Parental Responsibility Agreement. The Agreement has to be in this prescribed form (obtainable from Law Stationers). The form must include details of both parents, who must declare that they both agree that the father should have parental responsibility for the child.

The form must be signed by each parent in the presence of a witness. The Agreement is legally binding on both mother and father so legal advice is urged before signing.

The Agreement must then be filed with two copies at the Principal Registry of the Family Division of the High Court, Somerset House, Strand, London WC2R 1LP. The Agreement is then sealed and a copy sent to each parent.

2.3.2 If the mother does not consent

A father who is not married to the mother of his child can apply to court for a parental responsibility order.

The court's duty is to act in the child's best interest. Generally speaking, a child's interest is best served by the involvement of both natural parents. Indeed that is the philosophy behind the Act unless there are very strong contra-indications such as fear of violence or abuse.

On a father's application to the court for an order for parental responsibility, the court will weigh his commitment to the child and the child's attachment to him. If the court is satisfied, an order in his favour may be made even against a mother's objection.

◆ **Note:** No two cases are the same. It is difficult to predict how the court will weigh a father's application. So in all cases, do seek legal advice.

2.4 Duty to maintain

Every father is obliged by law to maintain his child. This duty is enforceable whether or not the father has a parental responsibility order and whether or not he is involved in any way with his child's life or upbringing.

As we have seen, the law on maintenance for children has undergone radical change. The Child Support Act 1991 came into effect in April 1993. This created a new framework for assessment, collection, and enforcement of payments of child maintenance. A Child Support Agency has been set up staffed by civil servants to assess child maintenance in each case. The assessment is made against an 'absent parent' on behalf of a 'qualifying' child and is worked out according to a statutory formula.

2.5 Proving paternity

If a mother asserts that a certain man is the father of her child and he is therefore liable to maintain her child, this assertion may have to be proved in a court of law. Applications to courts for declarations of paternity were generally heard in 'affiliation proceedings' when a mother applied to court for maintenance for her child and the alleged father resisted the claim. Blood tests could be inconclusive. DNA 'fingerprinting', on the other hand, has made proving the truthfulness or otherwise of an assertion of parentage much more certain.

Today a mother will apply to the Child Support Agency for child support. She will have to give the name of the father except in certain cases where to do so could lead to harm. If the putative father denies parentage, a court can be asked to determine the paternity issue. If a man refuses to have a test, the court can draw inferences against him from his refusal.

The courts will not order a test

- to satisfy a suspicion of adultery; or
- where it would be against the child's best interests.

2.5.1 Retrospective testing?

The courts will order a DNA test to take advantage of genetic fingerprinting even though an earlier blood test proved inconclusive.

You are a married man. A child was born to a woman friend of yours in 1985. She alleged that you were the father of her child and that you were liable to pay maintenance – a claim which you strenuously denied. You took a blood test which proved inconclusive. The mother's claim against you was dismissed. She has now sought to reopen the case and asked the court to order a DNA test. You want to know whether she is entitled to reopen the case.

The answer is 'yes'. There is no rule against retrospective DNA fingerprinting. And, if you refuse to take another test, the court can draw an inference from your refusal.

2.6 Child's passport

Where the parents are unmarried, only the mother's nationality or settled status is relevant with regard to the child's nationality under English law. A child under the age of 16 is entered on to the mother's passport.

3. When parents split up

3.1 Private law

Private law applies when children remain with one or other parent on the breakup of their parents' relationship. Private law is the law between private individuals. Public law in relation to children (see section 4 below) applies when the state intervenes by, for example, taking children into care.

In general the Children Act 1989 stresses the need of *continuing* responsibility of both parents for their child(ren) so as to lessen the impact on the child of the departure of one of the parents. Thus a most significant aspect of the Act is that both parents are still expected to take an active role in bringing up their children despite separation or divorce.

However, the law can only help couples to help themselves. It can only endeavour to assist them in reaching an amicable agreement on the future of their children's wellbeing. Personal issues are not really meant for litigation – particularly where children are involved.

The DIRECTORY at the end of the chapter has an extensive list of organizations which exist to help parents and children in situations of family conflict.

3.1.1 Main features of the Act

(a) The welfare of the child will be the paramount consideration in decisions on the child's future.
(b) Any delay in deciding that future will be considered prejudicial to the child.
(c) The court must pay regard to a principle known as the 'non-intervention principle'. In other words it should only make an order on behalf of a child when it is sure that a court order would be more helpful than no order at all.

3.1.2 Orders available to the court under the Children Act 1989

- *Residence orders:* orders which decide with whom the child should live. Most importantly, a residence order also gives parental responsibility to those who have the child living with them but who are not necessarily the child's parents (e.g. grandparents). This means that parental responsibility can be split amongst several people.
- *Contact orders:* orders to the person with whom the child lives to allow visits from the person named in the order or allow other contact (e.g. by letter or telephone). This would apply most frequently in cases where a father lives away from his child but wishes to maintain contact.
- *Prohibited step orders:* orders which prohibit certain steps being taken in relation to the child without consent of the court (e.g. taking a child abroad on a permanent basis).
- *Specific issue orders:* orders which decide specific questions which have arisen in connection with the child's upbringing (e.g. whether or not to have medical treatment, or to change schools).

◆ **Note:** The court can issue any order in a child's interest – not necessarily the order which was applied for. The orders last until a child turns 16.

3.1.3 Intentions behind the Act

The intentions behind the Act are to encourage

- a non-adversarial approach in deciding on the future of children;
- the love and care of both parents towards their children;
- use of a flexible range of orders so that there should no longer be a question of children being 'won' or 'lost' in court battles;
- both parents sharing responsibility for their children in all crucial matters;
- involvement of other relatives in a child's life.

3.2 Court's checklist

In order to decide whether an order would be justified, the court must consider the following checklist:

(a) the wishes and feelings of the child;
(b) the child's physical and emotional needs;
(c) the likely effect on the child of any change in his or her circumstances;
(d) the child's sex, background, and characteristics which the court considers relevant;
(e) any harm which the child has suffered or is at risk of suffering;
(f) how capable each of his parents or any other person is of meeting the child's needs;
(g) the range of powers available to the court under the Children Act 1989.

3.3 Who can obtain an order

Any person with parental responsibility can apply for an order – i.e. parents or guardians. So can any person with a residence order in their favour (for example, if grandparents have the child living with them under a residence order). An unmarried father can apply for an order even if he does not have parental responsibility.

Children themselves can apply to court for permission for an order to be made in their favour. Their views and feelings must be taken into account in any event. See *Listening to a child's views*, section 1.6 above.

3.4 Who are the orders for? (child of the family)

The orders relate to a 'child of the family' and includes anyone brought up as a family member. This feature is particularly important today where there are so many step-families involving children from previous relationships.

> *When your husband married you, he was a widower and was living with his young son, then aged six. You lived with your husband for four years, during which time you cared for, and looked after his boy. You and your husband have now separated. You quite understand that the son should remain with his father but you would like to continue seeing him even though you have left the family home. However, your husband is hurt and angry and says that he refuses you any contact with the child. Is there anything you can do?*

Contact orders under the Act are made in relation to a 'child of the family'. It includes any child who has been treated by both husband and wife as a child of the family and clearly includes your stepson in your case. You would have to persuade the court that it is in the child's interest to make an order so that you continue to keep in touch with him. (For assistance in these cases, see under DIRECTORY.)

3.5 Family assistance orders

A probation officer or local authority social worker can be appointed by the court to advise, assist, and befriend any parent or guardian of the child, or any other person with whom the child lives, or with whom the child has contact.

A family assistance order can also apply to a child in need of assistance. However, these orders will only be made in exceptional circumstances.

> *Your wife has suddenly left you and your two children and has gone to live abroad with another man. You are in a great deal of distress but want to make all possible endeavours to keep the children at home with you and not to have to put them into care.*

> It would seem that a family assistance order might help you in your circumstances.

These orders are intended as a short term help only. An appointment only lasts for six months.

3.6 The most suitable order

In all cases, the court can make any order which it feels most suits the case before it. In other words, even if you apply to court for a particular order, you may find some other order made on your child's behalf. For example, you might apply to court for a specific issue order that your child should go to a certain school. The court may think it best for the child to issue a prohibited steps order that the child cannot be removed from its present school.

3.7 Conciliation and mediation services

These services are not intended as marriage counselling – the mediators presuppose that there will be a separation but try to make it less painful (see DIRECTORY).

In particular, mediation is advised in order to avoid and/or mitigate parental quarrels over the future of their children.

> *You and your husband have agreed to separate but much bitterness remains and certain key issues, such as the children's future and whether or not to sell your joint home are unresolved. You have seen your own solicitor and your husband has contacted his own solicitor. You feel that a more conciliatory approach, primarily for the children's sake, must be tried. You feel it is too late for marriage guidance because it is help with the separation you most need, not with the marriage which is beyond retrieval. What can you do?*

> There are family mediation services, comprising trained lawyers and volunteers, who work in conjunction with lawyers and the courts. The mediators try to sort out difficulties before the parties turn to litigation.

See also chapter on *Divorce*, section 2.2.

3.8 Which parent?

There are factors which the courts have applied in the past to settle the contentious and painful issue of whether children should live with their mother or father. Although the Act is intended to transform the nature of family proceedings, some of the factors in these cases will, no doubt, apply in the future. The court must consider

- the personality and character of each parent;
- the desirability of a mother caring for young children;
- the need to preserve stability in a child's life and provide continuity of care;
- the need to keep brothers and sisters together.

3.9 No delay

Until October 1991, a divorce could not be made final until the court had considered arrangements for children of the marriage.

Today under the Act, delay is seen as harmful to a child's welfare. The court must only postpone the decree if it needs time for further consideration in the interests of the child.

It will also impose a *timetable* on proceedings so that parents and children have issues decided as speedily as possible. Children's futures are not to be kept hanging in the balance while others wrangle over them.

4. When parents fail

4.1 Public law

Under the heading of 'public law', we will deal with situations in which a local authority intervenes in a child's life.

The public law provisions of the Children Act cover a range of situations – from an everyday case where a mother works and wants to have someone reliable to look after her child in her absence, to an extreme situation where a child is at serious risk of harm and needs care of a very different sort.

It has to be stressed that the 'private law' and 'public law' aspects of the Children Act do not fall into neat categories. Nor are they intended to. The court can take whatever steps it thinks fit in the circumstances of each individual case: for example, in dealing with a dispute over children between private, individual parents, the court may decide that it is in the child's best interests to make a care order in favour of a local authority.

4.1.1 Duties of local authorities

The duties placed on the local authority by the new Children Act 1989 are manifold. Among them are duties to

- register childminders, foster parents, nurseries, and independent schools where there are less than 50 boarders
- take care of children 'in need' in its area (see section 4.2 below)
- protect children in danger
- provide accommodation in children's homes
- take children into care.

In the past, the local authorities have been found to be both

- too officious in taking children away from their parents and putting them into care on mere suspicion of wrongdoing or abuse
- failing in their duty to children who have slipped through the net and have suffered terrible harm and even fatal injury as a result of local authority dereliction of duty.

The Children Act 1989 is intended to assist local authorities to work in conjunction with parents. It is hoped to avoid some of the worst difficulties of the past. It is still early days to assess its effectiveness in this regard but hopes placed on the Act are very high.

4.2 Children in need: orders available

The orders in the Children Act are intended to cover a wide range of situations. They are also intended to give a local authority sufficient flexibility for it to be able to make appropriate and measured responses to the problems it encounters. Orders are directed to 'children in need'. This phrase is given a wide definition i.e. a child is in need if he or she is 'unlikely to achieve or maintain . . . a reasonable standard of health or development'.

It is interesting to note from the definition that not only is a child's physical well-being covered but 'development' relates to a child's emotional and psychological needs as well.

4.2.1 Types of orders

The orders are

- child assessment order
- care order
- supervision order
- education supervision order (see below, section 6.5.3)
- emergency protection order

All these orders, except the education supervision order, are dealt with below (see sections 4.3–4.5). First, however, we must examine some of the tasks imposed on a local authority under the Act:

- it has a general duty to take care of children 'in need'
- it is required by law to work with families of children in need
- it has a specific duty to investigate cases where a child suffers or is likely to suffer significant harm.

4.2.2 General duty

Each local authority has a general duty to safeguard and promote the welfare of children within its area who are in need, and so far as is consistent with that duty, to promote the upbringing of such children by their families.

4.2.3 Need to work with families

As far as possible the Act seeks to avoid the powers which allowed local authorities to take over responsibility from a child's parents and to transfer it to themselves. Its prime concern is to give children in need, as well as their families, the support that they require. Family ties between parents and children are to be fostered, wherever possible, not severed; care provided by a local authority is to be given in partnership with parents – not in opposition to them.

4.2.4 Specific duty to investigate

Where a local authority has reasonable cause to suspect that a child in its area is suffering or is likely to suffer significant harm, it must make enquiries necessary to decide whether to take any action to safeguard the child's welfare.

4.3 Assessment order

This is a new form of order.

- it is not intended to take the place of the old place of safety order
- it is not a care order
- it is not intended to be used in emergencies. (For emergency situations see section 4.6 below, *Children in danger*.)

However, there are cases where a local authority may have reasonable grounds to suspect that a child is at real risk of suffering harm. It may find that those looking after the child do not co-operate when it tries to establish the true position.

An assessment order therefore is intended

- to cover a situation where there is some ground for suspicion that the child could come to harm
- to enable the local authority or the NSPCC to have a medical or psychiatric examination of that child.

The child need not be removed from home for an assessment. Removal can be permitted under the Act if the person who has care of the child fails to produce him or her for assessment. The court must be satisfied that

- there are reasonable grounds for suspecting that the child is suffering significant harm or is at risk of suffering significant harm;
- an assessment is needed of the state of the child's health or development or the way in which he or she is being treated in order to establish whether the child is suffering or is likely to suffer significant harm; and
- it is unlikely that such an assessment will be made in the absence of a court order.

The court must always decide on the basis that

- the child's welfare is paramount
- making an order would be better than not making an order.

The order lasts seven days.

◆ **Note:** the court can issue an emergency protection order (see section 4.6 below) on the evidence before it.

4.4 Care order

Care orders apply to cases where a local authority takes a child into care and assumes parental responsibility for the child. Thus any residence order for the child is terminated. The child is taken from home and placed either in a local authority home or with local authority foster parents.

A care order can only be made by court order. The court must be satisfied

- that the child is suffering or is likely to suffer significant harm (i.e. ill treatment or impairment to health or development) and
- that harm results from lack of reasonable parental care or
- that the child is beyond parental control.

◆ **Note:** the responsibility of the parents of a child in care continues as well so that a local authority cannot

- free a child for adoption or
- appoint a guardian.

The local authority also has parental responsibility for the child under care.

Care orders may also be issued in other circumstances, for example

- in divorce proceedings
- when a child is involved in criminal proceedings.

Care orders can last until a child is 18 but cannot be made for a child over 17.

4.5 Supervision order

This order appoints a supervisor who has the duty to advise, assist and befriend the child. Such an order usually lasts a year. A supervisor can apply to extend the order but its maximum duration is three years; on the other hand, a care order, as we have seen, can last till a child is 18.

4.6 Children in danger

◆ **Note:** a local authority, concerned about a child in a situation of danger or distress, does not have to wait for harm to have actually occurred to the child.

4.6.1 Emergency protection order

A local authority can apply to court for an emergency protection order which replaces the former place of safety order. The order only lasts eight days. Although it can be extended for another 7 days, only one extension may be granted.

Court must be satisfied that

- significant harm has occurred or could happen
- child cannot be seen in circumstances in which significant harm could occur

Court can

- make an order for parental contact
- make an assessment order for a medical or psychiatric examination.

4.6.2 Who can apply to court for any of the above orders?

(a) Assessment, care or supervision orders

Only a local authority or the NSPCC can apply to court for an assessment order, a care order, or a supervision order.

(b) Children in danger – emergency protection orders

Applications for emergency protection orders can be made by

- local authorities
- NSPCC
- any other concerned applicant.

(i) In making application to court for an emergency protection order, a *local authority* has to show that

- it has been making enquiries on the child's behalf
- its enquiries into the child's wellbeing are being frustrated and
- access to the child is required as a matter of urgency.

(ii) The *NSPCC* must show that

- it has been making enquiries which have been frustrated
- access to the child is required as a matter of urgency
- it has reasonable cause to suspect that a child is suffering or is likely to suffer significant harm.

(iii) *Any other applicant* must show that

- he or she has reasonable cause to believe that the child is likely to suffer significant harm if not removed.

4.6.3 Reports by concerned friends or neighbours – confidentiality

Apart from applying for an emergency protection order, a concerned friend or neighbour can approach the court to make a child a ward of court (see *Wardship* below, section 5.4).

If you suspect that a child is being neglected, ill-treated or abused, you can report your suspicions to the local authority or the NSPCC. Confidentiality is ensured.

> *You suspect the family in the next-door flat is abusing their child. You want to report the case to the NSPCC but do not want it known to the parents that you have taken this step. Can you insist that your name will not be divulged in any subsequent proceedings.*

The answer is 'yes'.

4.6.4 Who can apply for release from an order?

- the parents
- the child – provided he or she is of sufficient understanding and maturity
- any other person with parental responsibility
- any person with whom child was living immediately before the making of the order.

(a) When to apply?

An application to discharge an emergency protection order can be made after 72 hours.

4.6.5 Court's considerations

In making any of the above orders, the court is obliged to observe its statutory duties. It must decide that

- an order would be in the child's best interest
- it is better to make an order than to make no order at all
- delay is prejudicial to a child's best interests.

4.6.6 'Looking after' children by local authority: no compulsion

There are many reasons why children are taken into care. The orders dealt with above concern state intervention from outside the family. However, children can be looked after by a local authority on a voluntary basis where it is felt that it would promote the child's welfare. For example, if a parent is ill or otherwise cannot provide the child with proper accommodation or care, a parent can approach the local authority to make application to court for a care order on the child's behalf.

The parents retain responsibility for the child and can remove the child at any time from the accommodation. The local authority is under a duty to

- ascertain the child's wishes
- ascertain the parents' wishes
- ascertain the wishes of any other relevant person.

The child's age and understanding, religion, racial origins and cultural and linguistic background must all be taken into account.

The most important aspect of looking after children in this way is the so-called 'family placement' i.e. foster parenting (see *Other parents* below, section 5).

Your wife recently died. Your teenage daughter was very difficult during her mother's illness, and she has now become uncontrollable. You feel you can no longer cope and that she needs the kind of care which you just cannot give to her. You would like to consider the possibility of fostering.

You can apply to the local authority which will then investigate the entire family situation. Your daughter's views will also be taken into account.

◆ **Note:** it is open to the court to provide for some other form of order, for example, a supervision order which will entail a social worker or probation officer befriending and assisting a child to help over a present crisis (see *Supervision order* above, section 4.5). It can also make a family assistance order (see section 3.5 above).

5. Other parents and carers

5.1 Adoption

Adoption is the total and legal transfer of a child from one set of parents to another set of parents. It is intended to terminate the child's existing legal relationship and to give all parental responsibility to the adopting parents.

Adoption procedures are strictly controlled by legislation and the child's new status is given formal recognition by the court. Even a new birth certificate is entered into the register in place of the child's original birth certificate.

Adopting parents are carefully vetted by an adoption agency or the local authority acting as an adoption agency. Adopting parents are usually

- childless couples or
- step-parents or
- a natural parent, such as the unmarried father of a child.

In 1993, there were 6,757 orders for adoption made in the Principal Registry. Of these, 3,202 were made to step-parents (i.e. 47%).

(At the end of this chapter, there is a DIRECTORY of organizations which give information or advice on adoption issues.)

Where there is a complete severance of all ties between children and natural parents, the child's new family is expected to take their place, as well as the place of other relatives.

You are unmarried and have given full agreement to the adoption of your baby girl aged three months. However, your mother, the child's grandmother, wishes to maintain contact with the child. What is her position?

A natural grandmother would have to make application to the court for a contact order and would have to persuade the court that it would be in the child's best interests for contact to be maintained. The court would also take into account the views and feelings of the adopting parents.

By law local social services authorities and other adoption agencies must

(a) give first consideration to the child;
(b) pay attention to the natural parents' concern for religious upbringing.

5.1.1 Conflicts of interest

The court's role is generally to give formal recognition to the change of status of an adopted child. However, conflicts do arise between a local authority, which has a child in care and wishes to free it for adoption, and the child's natural parent(s). The court thus becomes the final arbiter in disputes where the natural parents – usually an unmarried mother – refuse to agree to an adoption. An adoption agency can submit that the parents are 'unreasonably withholding their consent' and ask the court to override the parents' wishes.

These are some of the most difficult and painful cases which a court has to deal with. The guidelines are that the court must view the case in terms of whether a 'reasonable' parent would see that adoption is in the long-term best interests of the child.

5.1.2 Adoptions from abroad

In this country a couple who wish to adopt a child from another country are advised to go through the proper channels for inter-country adoptions. A draft is already in place for an international convention for co-operation and protection of children for trans-national adoptions.

In this country, the preliminary, official process for an adoption from abroad involves the

- local social services department
- Department of Health
- Home Office and
- British embassy of the country where the child is located.

The procedures are intended to protect the interests of both would-be parents and their prospective adopted child.

5.1.3 Re-establishing contact – child and natural parents

(a) Access to birth records

At the age of 18 adopted children now have access to their original birth records so that they can establish their original parentage.

There are limitations:

- for adoption before 1975, counselling is obligatory
- information against the public interest can be withheld.

See the DIRECTORY for organizations that give counselling and advice on re-establishing contact with your natural parents.

(b) Adoption Contact Register

Relatives of a child who has been adopted can record their details in a register if they wish to resume contact. These details will then be passed on provided that the adopted person – in turn – has indicated that he or she wishes to resume contact.

5.1.4 Changing adoption patterns

Unmarried mothers now receive state support to bring up their babies. The stigma which attached to having children out of wedlock has also largely gone. Termination of unwanted pregnancies is also generally made available. As a result fewer and fewer babies are placed by their mothers for adoption soon after birth. And, as we have seen, about half the annual number of adoptions now take place between children and their step-parents. Increasingly, therefore, adoptions now concern older children, who are placed for adoption by local authorities seeking a home for children in their care.

Thus the concept of a total legal severance of ties between adopted children and their natural parents is no longer always apposite. The law of adoption, therefore, is likely to change, and proposals for reform of the law are already under discussion.

5.1.5 Proposals for reform

Two of the present proposals for reform of the adoption law are that

(a) Adoption should continue as a 'total severance' but with less secrecy, greater openness and flexibility in making adoption orders; or
(b) There should be two types of adoption: a 'total severance' order, or an order for a permanent home in which both sets of parents play a part in the child's life.

In view of the circumstances which prevail in family life today, there are bound to be conflicts on the basis for change. New legislation will have to endeavour to accommodate the wishes of natural parents, adoptive parents, and those of children old enough to know their own minds, as well as the views of local authorities and adoption agencies. The task will not be easy.

5.2 Guardians

Parents who have children under 18 may be anxious about what would happen to them in the event of their death. They can appoint guardians for minor children in their wills. In other words, the guardian takes the place of the deceased parent in the child's life. (This is discussed fully in Chapter 4, *Death – Before and After*, section 9.2.)

5.3 Fostering

A child can be cared for by others under a private arrangement. Notice of such an arrangement must be given to a local authority. Under the Children Act 1989, a private fostering arrangement applies when a child is

- under the age of 16
- living with others (excluding parents, someone with a parental responsibility order, or a relative) for a period of longer than 28 days.

Payment is not a necessary factor.

The Act excludes many situations, for example, where a child is in boarding school. The fact that relatives are excluded too means that common domestic arrangements, for example grandparents looking after a child, do not fall within the Act.

If a private fostering arrangement does apply, the local authority can visit the foster parents and inspect their accommodation. However, the most common fostering arrangements are those in which a local authority takes a child into care and places him or her with foster parents rather than in a local authority home.

5.4 Wardship

5.4.1 What is wardship?

Wardship over children is a power of the court, used in very special circumstances, to transfer to the court all responsibility for a child's life. That child then becomes a 'ward of court'. The child must be a minor, i.e. under 18. No major step can be taken with regard to the child, once he or she has been made a ward of court, without permission of the court.

5.4.2 When is wardship used?

A wardship application is made to court when there is an urgent need to protect a child's interests. It has been used in life-threatening situations, e.g. when doctors wanted to turn off the life-support machine of a dying infant. It has also been used while deciding the question of sterilization of a mentally retarded girl.

However, wardship has been invoked in other circumstances, such as to ensure the proper supervision of property belonging to a child, or to prevent a child from being abducted from home.

The new Children Act is intended to cut down on wardship applications; for example, local authorities will no longer be able to apply to make a child a ward of court in order to take a child into care. Where a local authority does apply to court for wardship, it will have to obtain the court's leave (permission). Leave will only be granted if the local authority can show that

- the other orders available to it under the Act will not achieve the necessary results and
- the child will suffer significant harm if not warded.

In general the courts have stated that wardship will not be granted where an issue can be settled by its powers under the Children Act.

5.4.3 Procedure

Although anyone can apply for wardship of a child, for example a non-relative such as a doctor or social worker, an applicant must have a *proper* interest in the child's welfare. Wardship takes effect immediately even before a judge hears the case. The hearing must then take place within three weeks.

5.5 In need of care from 'carers' — protection for children

As we have seen, the Children Act tries to impose standards on those whose job it is to look after children. However, abuses do take place both within the family and outside it.

The problems are manifold: changing social patterns and attitudes; lack of public resources; conflict between the necessity for state protection of children and the undesirability of obtrusive interference in family life. Where requirements are made too onerous – for foster parents or child-minders, for example – how can local authorities enforce them? Difficulties in legislating and then in implementing the legislation are only too clear.

6. Education

Parent's duty to educate

By law, from the age of five to sixteen all children must receive compulsory full-time education. Moreover, children are legally entitled to receive education which is suitable to their needs and aptitudes. The past decade has seen a mass of legislation in the educational field. The latest in the series, the Education Act 1993, received Royal Assent on 27 July 1993. It is the longest Act on education yet passed; it will be phased in over 12 months. Codification of education law is urgently needed in order to simplify the task of all those who have to implement it in the schools and to interpret it in the courts.

Section 1 of the 1993 Act gives the Minister of Education personal responsibility for overseeing primary, secondary and further education in

England and Wales. The Act sets up a funding authority (the Funding Agency) which will administer funding to the grant-maintained section (see section 6.7.1 below). It gives inspectors power to identify failing schools, i.e. schools which are unlikely to give pupils a proper standard of education. A single curriculum authority (the School Curriculum and Assessment Authority) is created for England. See section 6.3.1 below. (See also DIRECTORY.)

6.1 Schools' changing role

One of the main purposes of the new legislation was to give parents more choice and information over their children's education. It also diminished the role of local education authorities (LEAs).

6.1.1 Parental choice

Parents should be able to make informed choices about the schools in which their children are taught.

6.1.2 Information on offer

The local education authority must produce a booklet of information on schools in its area, including the number of pupils to be admitted in each school and the basis for selection.

Each school must produce its own prospectus. The prospectus must include

- school aims
- subjects offered
- other activities and clubs
- discipline and other measures.

Each board of governors must produce an *annual report* including

- names of governors
- address for contacting school
- information about next parent-governor elections
- details of complaints and appeals procedures
- school budget.

Inspectors' reports must be published of full inspections. Secondary schools must publish a 'league table' of results of all passes at GCSE and A level. Independent schools (i.e. schools outside the state sector) are included in these tables.

6.1.3 Open enrolment

All classes must be filled with the optimum number of pupils. Your child is entitled to a place unless the class is filled to capacity. According to the Parents' Charter parents have the right to a place in the school they want, within their area, unless 'it is full to capacity with pupils who have a stronger claim'.

(a) Enrolment appeals

If there are more applicants than places, the local education authority, or the governors, must apply their own rules on who may be enrolled into the school. If your child is refused a place you can appeal to a committee set up for the purpose.

The composition of the committee and its procedure varies from authority to authority.

The time has come for your eldest child to transfer to secondary school. You have studied the school prospectuses for the local area, as well as the LEA secondary transfer booklet. You have discussed the merits of the different schools with other parents and you have made a number of visits to the various schools on your short list. You now have decided on the school to which you want to send your child. It is some distance from your home. When you make application, you are told that the school enrolment is full. What can you do?

Legally, you have a right of appeal. Your appeal will be heard by an independent committee which your local education authority must set up by law (the details of your LEA will be in the telephone book under the entry for your local authority). If you can persuade the committee of your case and it feels that your reasons are compelling, it can overrule the local education authority or governors.

The procedure differs slightly in each local education authority as the law gives them some autonomy in organizing the appeals procedure. The Council of Tribunals has issued a code of practice, which the committees should follow and which is available for the guidance of LEAs.

The number of appeals is growing – there were about 15,500 appeals by parents not satisfied with a school refusal in 1993. About 30 per cent of appeals are successful. The most successful grounds for appeal are

- the child's brother or sister attends the school
- neighbourhood proximity
- medical or social reasons.

6.2 Schools' structure

6.2.1 School governors

The recent reforms in education have given a great deal of authority to the school governors. The Department of Education and Science is making strenuous efforts to encourage parents and civic-minded people in the community to put themselves forward in the role of governor to give the 'Parents' Charter' a secure base.

For the role of school governors in opted-out schools, see section 6.7.1 below.

6.2.2 Role of head

The role of the headteacher has changed with all the reforms which have been introduced. Heads have to liaise with the governing body, the LEA and the parents, and they can now only exercise their powers over curriculum, staffing, discipline, finance and admission of pupils in conjunction with the governors and in co-operation with them.

The head sets the standards of school behaviour and makes the rules accordingly. He or she alone has power to exclude or expel a pupil (see section 6.4.2 below) but there are rights of appeal thereafter to the governing body.

6.2.3 Role of parents

Parents are represented by their own governors on the school governing body. As we have seen above (see section 6.1.2) they are entitled to certain information by law. They have a right to appeal or complain on many issues (see *Where to turn to for help*, section 6.6 below).

6.3 School syllabus

6.3.1 National curriculum

A national curriculum of core subjects has been laid down. It applies to children aged 5 to 16. The three core subjects are English language, mathematics and science. The seven foundation subjects comprise technology, history, geography, art, music and physical education. A modern language is taught in secondary schools.

All aspects of the curriculum are kept under review by the School Curriculum and Assessment Authority (see DIRECTORY).

At present proposals are being put forward for a national curriculum for religious education (see section 6.3.2 below).

(a) Standard attainment tasks

On the basis of this curriculum children have to perform Standard attainment tasks (SATs).

The school must keep a 'profile of attainment' for each child of how he or she performed in the SATs.

A 'Record of achievement' is compiled for each pupil from the first day of school to the last and covers a broad range of matters and not just test scores.

Senior schools must publish league table results of examination passes.

The introduction of a national curriculum and compulsory school testing in the Education Acts has met with opposition. The plans to launch the first tests for 14-year-olds in English, mathematics and science failed in the summer of 1993. Of about 600,000 pupils only a few thousand sat the tests. The position is being kept under review with regard to future testing.

(b) Access to records

Parents wanting access to school records on their child must approach the head or the board of governors.

6.3.2 Religious education

Every pupil must receive religious education under the Education Act 1988 and take part in a daily act of religious worship. Emphasis is laid on the mainly Christian traditions of this country. At the moment, each LEA draws up its own curriculum within general guidelines laid down by the Department of Education and Science. A national curriculum for religious education is now under consideration. Under the 1993 Act, meetings on the curricula at local level must be held in public and must represent local religions and denominational spread.

Although the religious tradition of this country is mainly Christian, the syllabus must include teaching on the other principal world religions. Children can be withdrawn from assembly on request of the parents on the grounds of conscience. Teachers are also permitted to refuse to teach RE. Pupils who practise other religions can receive their own religious education – apart from the rest of the school – if groups of parents approach the school and alternative teaching can be arranged.

Pupils themselves cannot opt out of RE classes.

> *Your teenage son has asked his form teacher whether he can be excused RE on the ground that he does not believe in the existence of God. The teacher has refused. What is your son's position?*

> It is only the parents who can request the withdrawal of their children from RE classes. Perhaps you could suggest to the teacher that your son's views could be aired in a debate within the context of RE classes.

6.3.3 Sex education

School governors can decide whether the school should give sex education lessons. Pupils are to be encouraged to 'have due regard to moral considerations and the value of family life' in sex education classes.

Parents are entitled to ask for their children to be withdrawn from sex education lessons under the 1993 Act except insofar as the instruction forms part of the national curriculum e.g. in science classes.

> *Your 14-year-old daughter, who goes to the local comprehensive school, receives sex education classes. You would like to have some idea of what she is being taught. You also understand that the school uses an educational video on sex education. You wonder whether you can ask to view the video?*

> You should approach the head and explain the nature of your request and why you are making it. You should receive a sympathetic response. You could also approach the board of governors. Independent complaints committees exist, set up by the local education authorities, to whom you can turn if you are still not happy with the outcome. You can also withdraw your child from the class altogether.

In fact, a survey has shown that one in four schools has failed to draw up a policy document on sex education classes.

Teaching on AIDS and sexually transmitted diseases is not part of the national curriculum.

6.4 School discipline

A statement of school rules should appear in the prospectus.

6.4.1 Corporal punishment

Corporal punishment is not permitted in state schools.

Teachers are not allowed to administer corporal punishment to children who are publicly funded to attend independent schools.

> *Your child has been given a place in an independent school under the Assisted Places scheme. You understand that school discipline is very strict and includes corporal punishment, to which you are opposed. What can you do?*

> By law, teachers in independent schools are not allowed to administer corporal punishment to children who are at independent schools on public funds.

In independent schools, the 1993 Education Act specifies that corporal punishment cannot be given 'by or on the authority of a member of staff', if the punishment is 'inhuman or degrading'. In assessing whether punishment is inhuman and degrading, all the circumstances of the case are to be considered, including

- its reason
- how soon it was given after the event
- its nature and the manner and circumstances in which it is given
- the persons involved and
- its mental and physical effects.

6.4.2 Exclusions and expulsions

Only a headteacher or deputy head has power to exclude a child from a state school.

The head must take reasonable steps to inform the parents without delay of the reasons for the exclusion and how long it is likely to last. Parents are entitled to express their views to the governors or to the local education authority, which can order a reinstatement. The head is obliged to reinstate at their direction.

If a head has decided to exclude for a longer period than five days, the governors and the LEA must be informed. The 1993 Education Act specifies that there cannot be an exclusion for an 'indefinite period' or for one or more periods so that a pupil is excluded for more than 15 days in any term. Children must attend a 'pupil referral unit' for their education.

If a child is expelled, there is an automatic right of appeal to the school governors or the local education authority. Parents can attend the appeal and will be given guidance on how to present their case. However, a pupil under the age of 18 has no right to attend the appeal. If the governors or LEA confirm the expulsion, parents can appeal to a special committee.

According to government research, state schools were expelling too many pupils for insufficiently serious reasons. It was feared that they would then slip out of the school system altogether and form a teenage under-class.

6.5 Other problems

6.5.1 Bullying

The subject of the school bully has received a lot of attention in the media of late. There have been tragic instances of children driven to extremes by the fear of having to face their school 'friends' either in the school playground or on journeys to and from school.

Bullying takes many forms: physical assault, insults, mockery, ostracism, or racial or sexual abuse.

> *Your child has returned home at the end of the school day obviously upset. You notice that his school books have been defaced and that his jacket is torn. He refuses to tell you what has happened but he is a retiring boy and you fear that he may be the victim of school bullies. What can you do?*

The first thing would be to try to get the child to talk to you, but if you are unsuccessful, you may persuade him to talk to another relation or family friend. You should also approach the class teacher in person. You can write to the head, asking that an eye should be kept on the child. Particularly vulnerable times for children who are victims of bullies are when they are not actually under direct supervision, but are moving from class to class or are in the playground. You might suggest to the head that the school governors appoint a member of staff as counsellor whom children can approach.

Much material is now being prepared for class lessons and discussions on the subject of bullying. Do ascertain whether such material is available in your son's particular school.

If your fears about bullying are confirmed, you should make a formal complaint to the board of governors.

In cases of bullying that involve violence or even the threat of violence, an anxious parent can always turn to the police.

In boarding schools, problems of bullying and harassment can be exacerbated because a child is far from home.

There is a helpline available for victims of school bullies. (For further information on the helpline number and organizations to turn to for assistance, see DIRECTORY.)

6.5.2 Truancy

Truancy has become an increasing problem. Many parents are at work and are not in a position to ensure that their child is attending school regularly. As they are obliged by law to ensure that their child is in full-time education, they may find themselves in a situation in which they can be prosecuted and even fined (see section 6.5.3 below).

You are a single parent and work during the day. You were upset to receive a letter from the headmaster stating that your 14-year-old son has been absent from school for some days. You were not aware of the fact that he had been playing truant. You have since heard that the educational welfare officer will be paying you a call at home.

You should try to establish the reason for the truancy – it may be because of bullying or harassment so that your son may be in need of help. You might consult the LEA or the head, about possible transfer to another school.

The educational welfare officer can issue a school attendance order. If your child still does not attend school regularly, in compliance with the order, a local authority can apply to court for an education supervision order (see section 6.5.3 below).

6.5.3 Education supervision order

This is a new order under the Children Act 1989. The ground for such an order is that 'the child . . . is of compulsory school age and is not being properly educated'.

If a child is subject to a school attendance order which is being disobeyed or is registered at school but not attending regularly, it is assumed that he or she is not being properly educated.

The courts must use the Checklist (see section 3.2 above) before issuing an education supervision order and must decide that to issue an order is better than no order at all.

An application to the court must be made by the LEA and both child and parent must be given notice of the application and of the court proceedings. They are entitled to legal aid where appropriate.

If the court is satisfied that your child is not being properly educated, it will appoint a supervisor. It will be the job of the supervisor to befriend and assist the child in his or her difficulties at school.

◆ **Take note:** Parents can be prosecuted and fined for the persistent truancy of their children.

6.6 Where parents can turn for help

Under the 1988 Education Act parents have a specific right of appeal to the governors or the LEA.

◆ **Note:** parents can go beyond the local education authority too.

Section 68 of the Education Act 1944 provides that the Secretary of State can be called upon to intervene where a parent's complaint shows that the LEA or the governors have acted unreasonably. The Secretary of State also has the power to order the governors or the LEA to carry out a duty which they have failed to do.

6.7 Schools outside local authority control

6.7.1 Grant-maintained schools

Until now the focus has been entirely on schools which are within the local authority structure. However, the Education Act 1988 weakened the hold of local authorities over the education system by allowing schools to 'opt out' and become 'grant-maintained', i.e. maintained by central government funding from the Department of Education and Science equal to what the school would have received from the LEA. This process has been given further encouragement by the Education Act 1993. As a result, the system of state education is in the process of very rapid transformation.

In opted-out schools, the board of governors is a formally constituted body which is required to have insurance against accidents, among other matters (see also chapter on *Accidents*).

6.7.2 Voluntary schools

These are schools which function under the local education authority but have a separate existence usually as Church schools.

6.7.3 City Technology Colleges

These are independent schools set up by the Department of Education in conjunction with commercial and industrial sponsors in urban areas. The CTCs are intended to provide a broad curriculum but with a particular emphasis on technology.

6.8 The private sector

In the independent sector, the relationship between parent and school is governed by the contract between them. This covers matters including fees, syllabus, discipline etc.

In a recent case, parents of a child who was expelled from an independent school wanted to use the procedures laid down in the Education Act to appeal against expulsion. The court said that the parents could not resort to the public law in a purely private arrangement with the school.

◆ **Note:** in 1981, the government set up an assisted places scheme to give help with tuition fees at certain independent secondary schools to parents who could not otherwise afford to send their children there. Details are available from the Department of Education and Science (for address to apply for leaflets, see DIRECTORY).

6.9 Home-based education

◆ **Note:** education is compulsory, schoolgoing is not.

You decide you no longer want to send your child aged 10, who is a gifted chess player, to school. You are a former headteacher and a chess player of note and feel that, in the circumstances, your child would be better educated at home. Are you entitled to withdraw him from school?

The Education Act 1944 states that it is the duty of parents of school-age children to ensure that they receive efficient full time education 'either by regular attendance at school or otherwise'. So in fact, while the parents' duty to ensure that their children are being educated is enforceable by law, this education can be 'at school or otherwise'.

Further, the education which every child receives has by law to be efficient, full time, and suitable to his or her needs, age, ability and aptitude.

If you decide to take your child out of school, you would first have to persuade the LEA that you are able to fulfil those criteria with home-based education. There are organizations which give advice and support to parents who wish to educate their children at home. (See DIRECTORY.)

You would be well advised to seek this advice before removing your boy from school.

◆ **Take heed:** Once registered in a school, a pupil's attendance there is compulsory until such time that the LEA agrees to his withdrawal.

7. Children and crime

7.1 Crimes against children

7.1.1 Abduction

With the number of failed marriages and the present general state of flux, the abduction of children by estranged parents is a growing and grave issue. About 200 children a year are abducted within the UK and about the same number are taken abroad. About 90 per cent of abductions are carried out by fathers of whom about one in five is British.

Newspaper and other reports testify to the heartbreak of the parents involved. The traumatic effects on the children involved can only be guessed at. The headlines refer to child abduction as 'tug-of-love' but the end result is human misery.

There are complex legal issues involved particularly in view of the fact that the problem of child abduction often crosses international borders. If you are fearful of a possible abduction, legal advice should be taken as a pre-emptive measure whenever possible.

There are organizations to advise and assist at every stage. The National Council for the Abducted Child (Reunite) is on hand to give advice and has a network of lawyers who have had experience in this field. The Lord Chancellor's Department has a special child abduction unit (see DIRECTORY at the end of this chapter). Two international agreements have been drawn up to facilitate co-operation in the search for missing children.

Where a child is living with someone under a residence order, the child cannot be taken abroad for longer than a month without leave of the court or without the consent of the other parent, a guardian, or any other person who has parental responsibility for that child.

You do not have to wait for the worst to happen before you can act. If you have proper grounds to fear that your child might be abducted, there are immediate steps which you can take.

You are divorced from your American husband who has regular access to your three-year-old son. Both your ex-husband and yourself live in London and he has never indicated in any way to you that he is thinking of taking the child away from you.

However, you learn from mutual friends that he has been making threats to that effect. You wonder if there are any steps that you can take to forestall any such eventuality. The child is registered on your passport.

(1) You must consult a solicitor.
(2) Try to ensure that there is a third party present at all meetings between your child and his father. This could be made a condition of his visits by court order.
(3) You must keep all documents concerning your son (such as birth certificate) so that they cannot be used to enable his father to have his son's name placed on his passport. Also keep a photo of your ex-husband, details of his passport if you have them, and any other information which could assist in tracing him if such a need arose.

Under the Children Act you are allowed to take a child abroad for less than a month without written consent of the other parent.

7.1.2 Sexual offences

It is an offence for a man to have sexual intercourse with a woman he knows to be his daughter, sister or granddaughter. The offence of incest applies also to a half-sister.

Sexual intercourse with a girl under the age of 13 is an offence. It is also an offence to have sexual intercourse with a girl under the age of 16 ('the age of consent'). Her consent is not material.

There is a defence to a charge of unlawful sexual intercourse with a girl aged 13–16 where the man is

- under 24

and he can show that
- he had reasonable cause to believe that the girl was over 16.

The performance of homosexual acts between two men in private is not an offence provided that both are over the age of 18 and both consent. The age of consent for homosexual men was recently reduced from 21 years.

Child sexual abuse is often accompanied by other forms of abuse such as neglect and physical cruelty. (For issues of confidentiality, see section 4.6.3 above.)

7.1.3 Neglect

We have seen that any person who is over the age of 16 and who wilfully neglects or ill treats a child in his or her care commits a criminal offence (see *Duty to Protect*, section 1.4.1 above).

7.2 Crimes committed by children

If a child commits a criminal offence, several rules apply.

7.2.1 Criminal age

Children under 10 cannot be charged with a criminal offence. However, if they have done something wrong which would be a criminal offence in an adult, the social services may institute proceedings. These could involve the child being taken into care in the most serious instances.

A child aged between 10 and 14 who commits an offence must be shown to have a 'criminal mind'. In other words, before a court will prosecute, it must be satisfied that the child could tell the difference between right and wrong.

Until 1993, a boy aged under 14 was deemed incapable of rape. However, the law has now been altered so that a boy aged 10 or over can be found guilty of the offence.

7.2.2 Safeguards

Special rules apply to juveniles aged between 14 and 17. The rules cover the type of court in which they can be charged, called youth courts; procedures governing police questioning and court proceedings; and also safeguards against publicity.

Where a grave crime is involved a child can be remanded in custody. Remittal is to the local authority to provide accommodation which can be secure accommodation if the circumstances warrant it.

On the whole, there is a strenuous endeavour to keep children out of the criminal justice system.

Police can 'caution' young persons rather than involve them further in the criminal justice system. However, a caution can only be imposed when a child admits to a criminal act.

7.2.3 Parental responsibility

Under the Criminal Justice Act 1991, parents can be made responsible for the fines of their children as well as for compensation orders imposed on them. The means of the parents would be taken into account and the fine imposed accordingly.

Under the same Act, a parent can undertake by means of 'recognisances' to take proper care of a child under 16 and exercise proper control over him or her. Recognisances are fixed up to a maximum of £1,000. If a parent refuses consent, a fine of £1,000 can be imposed. Again the means of the parent is taken into account.

A parent can appeal to the Crown Court from an order of a magistrates' court, and to the Court of Appeal from a Crown Court order.

THE STAGES OF GROWING UP

Education

Age 5
You become of compulsory school age.

Age 16
You can leave school. The two school leaving dates are at the end of the spring term and the Friday before the last Monday in May.

Subject to certain exceptions, you are entitled to apply for access to your school records.

Age 18
You alone are entitled to access to your school records.

Age 19
All young people are entitled to full-time education up to the age of 19, either at school or college.

Financial

Age 5
You have to pay child's fare on trains, buses and tubes in London and on buses in most other areas.

Age 7
You can open and draw money from a National Savings Bank account.

Some banks might let you open an ordinary bank account in your own right if they think you fully understand banking transactions.

Age 15
You can open a Post Office Girobank account, but you'll need a guarantor – someone who will be liable for your debts.

Age 16
You have to pay full fare on trains and on buses and tubes in London. You might have to pay full fare in other areas.

You can buy Premium Bonds.

Employment

Age 13
You can get a part-time job but there are restrictions – e.g. you cannot work for more than two hours on a school day or on a Sunday.

Age 16
You can work full-time if you have left school.

You can join most trade unions.

Health

Age 16
You have to pay prescription charges unless you are in full-time education, pregnant, in receipt of income support, on a low income or in certain other circumstances. You have to pay for a sight test and for glasses unless you are in full-time education, you or any other member of your family are in receipt of income support or on a low income or your eyesight is constantly changing. You also have to pay for certain dental treatment if you are not in full-time education.

You can consent to surgical, medical or dental treatment, including the taking of blood samples; and also choose your own doctor. You may not be able to refuse treatment, however. See section 1.4.4(c) above.

Age 18
You have to pay for dental treatment unless you are still in full-time education, or pregnant, or certain other circumstances apply.

Rights and Obligations

Age 5
You can see a U or PG category film at a cinema unaccompanied. In London you probably cannot do this until you are 7. In practice, a cinema manager has complete discretion over admission.

Age 12
You can buy a pet.

Age 14
You can go into a pub but you cannot buy or drink alcohol there.

Age 15
You can see a category 15 film.

Age 16
You can get a National Insurance number.

You can probably leave home without your parents' or guardian's consent.

A girl can consent to sexual intercourse.

You can marry with parental consent. (See chapter on *Setting up Home*, section 1.2.1.)

A boy can join the armed forces with parental consent.

You can apply for your own passport, but one parent must give written consent. You don't need parental consent if you are married or in the armed forces. Below 16, a parent can apply for a separate passport for you.

You can have beer, cider or wine with a meal in the restaurant or other room used for meals in a pub or hotel.

You are legally responsible for a child left in your care and can be held criminally liable if you ill-treat it (see section 1.4.1(a) above).

Age 17
A care order can no longer be made on you, nor can you be received into care.

You can hold a licence to drive most vehicles apart from medium and heavy goods vehicles.

You can buy or hire any firearm or ammunition.

Age 18
You reach the age of maturity – you are an adult in the eyes of the law.

You can vote in local and general elections.

If you are an adopted child, you can look up your birth details (see section 5.1.3 above).

You can serve on a jury.

You have complete contractual capacity so you can own land, buy a house or flat, apply for a mortgage, sue and be sued in your own right. You can act as an executor or administrator of a deceased person's estate.

You can open a bank account or a Post Office account without your parents' signature. You can apply for a passport without your parents consent.

You can make a will. If you're in the armed forces or a marine or seaman you can make a will under the age of 18.

You can buy and drink alcohol in a bar.

You can join the armed forces without parental consent.

You can bring an action for personal injury which occurred within 3 years of your 18th birthday (see chapter on *Accidents*).

You can see a category 18 film. You can buy a video given a certificate for viewing by adults only. Certificates will state a video is suitable for viewing by children of a specified age.

A man may consent to a 'homosexual act' in private if he and his partner both consent.

Age 21
You can become an MP or local councillor.

FAMILY LAW DIRECTORY
Children

Action for Sick Children (National Association for the Welfare of Children in Hospital)
Argyle House
29–31 Euston Road
London NW1 2SD
Tel. 071 833 2041

The Association of Workers for Children with Emotional and Behavioural Difficulties
Charlton Court
East Sutton
Maidstone
Kent ME17 3DQ
Tel. 0622 843104

Boys' and Girls' Welfare Society
Central Offices
Schools Hill
Cheadle
Cheshire SK8 1JE
Tel. 061 428 5256

The Brandon Centre (formerly London Youth Advisory Centre)
26 Prince of Wales Road
Kentish Town
London NW5 3LG
Tel. 071 267 4792

British Association for the Study and Prevention of Child Abuse and Neglect
10 Priory Street
York YO1 1EZ
Tel. 0904 621133

Child Accident Prevention Trust
4th Floor,
Clerks Court
18–20 Farringdon Lane
London EC1R 3AU
Tel. 071 608 3828

Child Abduction Unit
The Lord Chancellor's Department
81 Chancery Lane
London WC2A 1DD
Tel. 071 911 7127

Childline
2nd Floor
Royal Mail Building
Studd Street
London N1 0QW
Tel. 071 239 1000 (admin)
or Childline Freepost 1111
London N1 0BR
(Freephone) 0800 1111

Child Support Agency
PO Box 55
Brierley Hill
West Midlands DY5 1YL
(Enquiry Line) Tel. 0345 133133

Children Need Grandparents
2 Surrey Way
Laindon West
Basildon
Essex SS15 6PS

The Children Panel
The Law Society
Ipsley Court
Redditch
Worcestershire B98 0TD
Tel. 071 242 1222

Children's Society
Edward Rudolf House
Margery Street
London WC1X 0JL
Tel. 071 837 4299

The Children's Society (Advocacy Unit)
14 Cathedral Road
Cardiff
South Glamorgan CF1 9LJ
Tel. 0222 396974

Daycare Trust
Wesley House
4 Wild Court
London WC2B 5AU
Tel. 071 405 5617

End Physical Punishment of Children
(EPOCH)
77 Holloway Road
London N7 8JZ
Tel. 071 700 0627

Independent Representation for Children in Need (IRCHIN)
23a Hawthorne Drive
Heswall
Wirral
Merseyside L61 6UP
Tel. 051 342 7852

Kidscape (campaign for children's safety)
152 Buckingham Palace Road
London SW1W 9TR
Tel. 071 730 3300

National Childcare Campaign
Wesley House
4 Wild Court
London WC2B 5AU
Tel. 071 405 5617

National Children's Centre
The Brian Jackson Centre
New North Parade
Huddersfield
West Yorkshire HD1 5JP
Tel. 0484 519988

National Children's Home
85 Highbury Park
London N5 1UD
Tel. 071 226 2033

National Society for the Prevention of Cruelty to Children (NSPCC)
67 Saffron Hill
London EC1N 8RS
Tel. 071 242 1626

National Youth Agency
17–23 Albion Street
Leicester LE1 6GD
Tel. 0533 471200

Teen Challenge UK
52 Penygroes Road
Gorslas
Llanelli
Dyfed SA14 7LA
South Wales
Tel. 0269 842718

Trust for the Study of Adolescence
23 New Road
Brighton
East Sussex BN1 1WZ
Tel. 0273 6693311

Voice for the Child in Care
Interchange Studios
Dalby Street
London NW5 3NQ
Tel. 071 267 5940
or

Provost's Lodge
22 Hallamgate Road
Broomhill
Sheffield S10 5BS
Tel. 0742 669555

Voluntary Organisations Liaison Council for Under-Fives (VOLCUF)
77 Holloway Road
London N7 8JZ
Tel. 071 607 9573

The Young Homelessness Group
2nd Floor
10 Livonia Street
London W1V 3PH
Tel. 071 494 0333

Young People's Counselling Service
Tavistock Centre
120 Belsize Lane
London NW3

Youth Access (formerly NAYPCAS)
11 Newarke Street
Leicester LE1 5SS
Tel. 0533 558763

Education

Advisory Centre for Education (ACE)
Unit 1B
Aberdeen Studios
22–24 Highbury Grove
London N5 2EA
Tel. 071 354 8321

Assisted Places Scheme
Department of Education
Mowden Hall
Staindrop Road
Darlington
Co. Durham DL3 9EE
Leaflets available (by surname) from:
Tel. 0325 392156 or 0325 392157 for A–E
Tel. 0325 392107 or 0325 392158 for F–P
Tel. 0325 392159 or 0325 392163 for Q–Z

Boarding School Survivors (BSS)
128a Northview Road
London N8 7LP
Tel. 081 341 4885

Campaign for Real Education
12 Pembroke Square
London W8 6PA
Tel. 071 937 2122

Campaign for State Education (CASE)
158 Durham Road
London SW20 0DG
Tel. 081 944 8206

Careers Research and Advisory Centre
(CRAC)
Sheraton House, Castle Park
Cambridge CB3 0AX
Tel. 0223 460277

Curriculum Council for Wales
Companies House
Crown Way
Cardiff CF4 3UT
Tel. 0222 380798

Department of Education and Science
Sanctuary Buildings
London SW1P 3BT
Tel. 071 925 5000

Education Otherwise
36 Kinross Road
Leamington Spa
Warwickshire CV32 7EF
Tel. 0926 886828

English Schools' Athletics Association
26 Newborough Green
New Malden
Surrey KT3 5HS
Tel. 081 949 1506

Family Education Trust
Wicken Manor
Wicken
Milton Keynes MK19 6BU
Tel. 0908 57234

Independent Schools Careers Organisation
12A Princess Way
Camberley
Surrey GU15 3SP
Tel. 0276 21188

Independent Schools Information Service
56 Buckingham Gate
London SW1E 6AG
Tel. 071 630 8793

National Association of Governors & Managers (NAGM)
Suite 36/38
31 Bennetts Hill
Birmingham B2 5QP
Tel. 021 643 5787

National Commission on Education
Suite 24
10–18 Manor Gardens
London N7 6JY
Tel. 071 272 4411

National Confederation of Parent-Teacher Associations (NCPTA)
2 Ebbsfleet Estate
Stonebridge Road
Gravesend
Kent DA11 9DZ
Tel. 0474 560618

School Curriculum and Assessment Authority (formerly National Curriculum Council)
Newcombe House
45 Notting Hill Gate
London W11 3JB
Tel. 071 229 1234

Schools Need Governors
Department of Education
Room 3E1
Sanctuary Buildings
Great Smith Street
London SW1P 3BT
Tel. 071 925 5000

Welsh Office Education Department
Schools Administration Division 3
Phase 11
Government Buildings
Ty Glas Road
Llanishen
Cardiff CF4 5WE
Tel. 0222 761 456 Ext. 5362

Family

British Agencies for Adoption and Fostering
11 Southwark Street
London SE1 1RQ
Tel. 071 407 8800

Courts Family Division
Principal Registry
Somerset House
Strand
London WC2R 1LP
Tel. 071 936 6000

Family Conciliation Service for Northumberland & Tyneside
MEA House
Ellison Place
Newcastle Upon Tyne NE1 8XS
Tel. 091 261 9212

The Family Law Bar Association
Queen Elizabeth Building
Temple
London EC4Y 9BS
Tel. 071 797 7837

Family Mediators Association
The Old House
Rectory Gardens
Henbury
Bristol BS10 7AQ
Tel. 0272 500140

Family Policy Studies Centre
231 Baker Street
London NW1 6XE
Tel. 071 486 8211

Family Rights Group
The Print House
18 Ashwin Street
London E8 3DL
Tel. 071 923 2628

Family Service Units (offices
nationwide)
207 Old Marylebone Road
London NW1 5QP

Family and Youth Concern
Wicken
Milton Keynes MK19 6BU
Tel. 0908 57234

Gingerbread (Guidance for single
parents and children)
35 Wellington Street
London WC2E 7BN
Tel. 071 240 0953

Grandparents' Federation
Room 3
Moot House
The Stow
Harlow
Essex CM20 3AG

Head of Family Law Division
Lord Chancellor's Department
Southside
105 Victoria Street
London SW1E 6QT
Tel. 071 210 2059

Institute of Family Therapy
Family Mediation Service
43 New Cavendish Street
London W1M 7RG
Tel. 071 935 1651

**The National Family Conciliation
Council**
Shaftesbury Centre
Percy Street
Swindon
Wiltshire SN2 2AZ
Tel. 0793 514055

**National Organisation for the
Counselling of Adoptees and Parents**
(NORCAP)
3 New High Street
Headington
Oxford OX3 7AJ
Tel. 0865 750554

National Stepfamily Association
72 Willesden Lane
London NW6 7TA
Tel. 071 372 0844
Counselling Service 071 372 0846

Post-Adoption Centre
8 Torriano Mews
Torriano Avenue
London NW5 2RZ
Tel. 071 284 0555

**Reunite – National Council for
Abducted Children**
PO Box 4
London WC1X 8XY
Tel. 071 404 8356

**Royal Society for Mentally
Handicapped Children & Adults**
(MENCAP)
123 Golden Lane
London EC1Y 0RT
Tel. 071 454 0454

Solicitors' Family Law Association
PO Box 302
Orpington
Kent BR2 6EZ

Parents

Exploring Parenthood
Latimer Education Centre
194 Freston Road
London W10 6TT
Tel. 081 960 1678

Fair Deals for Dads
PO Box 3640
London E14 5DA

Families Need Fathers
Room 2
East Block
38 Mount Pleasant
London WC1X 0AP
Tel. 071 278 0282

National Council for One Parent Families
255 Kentish Town Road
London NW5 2LX
Tel. 071 267 1361

National Foster Care Association
(NFCA)
Leonard House
5–7 Marshalsea Road
London SE1 1EP
Tel. 071 828 6266

Parentline
Westbury House
57 Hart Road
Thundersley
Essex SS7 3PD
Tel. 0268 757077

Parent to Parent Information on Adoption Services
Lower Boddington
Daventry
Northamptonshire NN11 6YB
Tel. 0327 60295

Parents Against Injustice (PAIN)
3 Riverside Business Park
Stansted
Essex CM24 8PL
Tel. 0279 647171

Parents for Children
41 Southgate Road
London N1 3JP
Tel. 071 359 7530

Parents' Lifeline
73d Stapleton Hall Road
London N4 3QF
Tel. 263 2265 (24 hr 840 7000)

Women's Welfare

Lifeline Pregnancy Counselling & Care
The National Administrator
Cae Bach
4 Pant y Wennol
Bodafon,
Llandudno
Gwynedd LL30 3D
Tel. 0492 543741

Mothers Apart From Their Children
(MATCH)
C/o BM Problems
London WC1N 3XX

National Housewives Association Ltd
(NHA)
30 Tollgate
Bretton
Peterborough PE3 9XA
Tel. 0733 333138

Rape Crisis Centre
PO Box 69
London WC1X 9NJ
Help Line London: 071 837 1600
Help Line Birmingham: 021 233 2122/2455

Rights of Women
52–54 Featherstone Street
London EC1Y 8RT
Tel. 071 251 6571

Women's Aid Federation (domestic violence)
PO Box 391
Bristol BS99 7WS
Tel. London: 071 251 6537
　　　 Manchester: 061 839 8574
　　　 Bristol: 0272 633494
　　　 Cardiff: 0222 390874

Women's Link (formerly London Council for Welfare of Women and Girls)
57 Great Russell Street
London WC1B 3BD
Tel. 071 430 1524

408 Consultation Centre (Family planning and related areas)
408 Ecclesall Road
Sheffield S11 8PJ
Tel. 0742 662341

General

British Association for Counselling
1 Regent Place
Rugby CV21 2PJ
Tel. 0788 578328

Citizens' Advice Bureau
National Association
115–123 Pentonville Road
London N1 9LZ
Tel. 071 833 2181

Child Support Agency
PO Box 55
Brierley Hill
West Midlands DY5 1YL
Tel. 0345 133133 (Enquiry Line)

European Commission on Human Rights
Council of Europe
BP 431 R6
Strasbourg 67006 Cedex
France
Tel. 010 33 88 61 49 61

Foreign & Commonwealth Office
Consular Department
Clive House
Petty France
London SW1H 9HD
Tel. 071 270 1500

General Register Office
(Births, Deaths & Marriages)
St Catherine's House
10 Kingsway
London WC2
Tel. 071 242 0262
or
Smedley Hydro
Trafalgar Road
Birkdale
Southport PR8 2HH
Tel. 0704 69824

International Social Service of the United Kingdom (ISS)
Cranmer House
39 Brixton Road
London SW9 6DD
Tel. 071 735 8941

Just Ask (Advisory and counselling service)
46 Bishopsgate
London EC2
Tel. 071 628 3380

Law Centres Federation (offices nationwide)
Duchess House
18–19 Warren Street
London W1P 5DB
Tel. 071 387 8570

The Law Society
113 Chancery Lane
London WC2A 1PL
Tel. 071 242 1222

Legal Aid Board
29–37 Red Lion Street
London WC1R 4PP
Tel. 071 831 4209

Life Cares (Pregnancy, birth, adoption, DSS benefits, facilities for disabled parents or children)
LIFE House
Newbold Terrace
Leamington Spa
Warwickshire CV32 4EA
Tel. 0926 421587

London Friend (Counselling and support for lesbians and gay men)
86 Caledonian Road
London N1
Tel. 071 837 3337

National Association of Councils for Voluntary Service (NACVS)
3rd Floor, Arundel Court
177 Arundel Street
Sheffield S1 2NU
Tel. 0742 786636

Office of Population Censuses & Surveys (OPCS)
Smedley Hydro
Trafalgar Road
Birkdale
Southport PR8 2HH
Tel. 0704 569824

The Prince's Trust
8 Bedford Row
London WCLR 4BA
Tel. 071 430 0524

The United Kingdom Passport Agency
Clive House
Petty France
London SW1H 9HD
Tel. 071 630 1199

Religious Organizations

Baptist Union
Baptist House
PO Box 44
129 Broadway
Didcot
Oxfordshire OX11 8RT
Tel. 0235 512077

Buddhist Centre
51 Roman Road
London E2
Tel. 081 981 1225

Catholic Marriage Advisory Council
Clitherow House
1 Blythe Mews
Blythe Road
London W14 0NW
Tel. 071 371 1341

Church of England
General Synod Enquiry Centre
Church House
Great Smith Street
London SW1P 3NZ
Tel. 071 222 9011

Court of the Chief Rabbi
Beth Din
Adler House
Tavistock Square
London WC1H 9HP
Tel. 071 387 5772

Evangelical Alliance
186 Kennington Park Road
London SE11 4BT
Tel. 071 582 0228

Free Church Federal Council
27 Tavistock Square
London WC1H 9HH
Tel. 071 387 8413

Hindu Centre
7 Cedars Road
London E15 4NE
Tel. 081 534 8879

Jewish Marriage Council
23 Ravenshurst Avenue
London NW4 4EE
Tel. 081 203 6311

London Central Mosque Trust Limited
Islamic Cultural Centre
146 Park Road
London NW8 7RG
Tel. 071 724 3363

Methodist Church
Central Buildings
Matthew Parker Street
London SW1
Tel. 071 222 8010

Registrar of the Court of Faculties
1 The Sanctuary
London SW1P 3JT

The Samaritans
10 The Grove
Slough SL1 1QP
Tel. 0753 532713

Religious Society of Friends (Quakers)
Friends House
173–177 Euston Road
London NW1 2BJ
Tel. 071 387 3601

Seventh-Day Adventist Church
Stanborough Park
Watford
Hertfordshire WD2 6JP
Tel. 0923 672251

The United Reformed Church
86 Tavistock Place
London WC1H 9RT
Tel. 071 916 2020

United Synagogue (Orthodox)
Woburn House
Tavistock Square
London WC1H 0EZ
Tel. 071 387 4300

Vicar General and Master
1 The Sanctuary
London SW1P 3JT
(for issue of a special licence)

See also:

The British Humanist Association
14 Lamb's Conduit Passage
London WC1R 4RH
Tel. 071 430 0908

The National Secular Society
47 Theobald's Road
London WC1R 4RH
Tel. 071 404 3126

The Salvation Army
101 Queen Victoria Street
London EC4P 3EP
Tel. 071 236 5222

4. DEATH – BEFORE AND AFTER

When someone dies, the partner or close relatives have to deal with a multitude of practical matters as well as coping with their emotions. This chapter sets out what must be done. In the short term, the death must be registered, arrangements must be made for the funeral, and the immediate day-to-day expenses of dependants must be provided for. In the longer term, after these urgent matters have been dealt with, the affairs of the deceased person must be settled. This means that someone must take charge of his or her property, personal possessions, debts, business, and so forth, which the law calls by the portmanteau term 'the deceased's estate'.

In this chapter you will find a guide to the formal procedures which have to be gone through when someone dies, and also a detailed explanation of the duties of whoever takes charge of the deceased person's estate – depending on whether or not a will was made – and how their responsibility for winding up the estate must be discharged. This includes the payment of the debts of the deceased and taking care of the property in the estate during the winding up process. Then, after the debts have been paid, the residue of the estate must be distributed to those entitled to inherit: this in turn depends on whether or not there is a will. If there is not, the law lays down who benefits from the distribution.

If someone is disappointed by the terms of a will, or their expectations of inheriting are defeated, they may be able to challenge the will. Alternatively, they may be able to obtain some maintenance out of the estate if no provision was made for them by the will or by the general rules for distribution in the absence of a will.

We all also have not only to think about the death of others, but to anticipate our own demise sooner or later. For most of us, the overriding concern is for our surviving families. How will they manage financially? Who would look after any young children? Would the elderly be provided for and protected? Not surprisingly perhaps, many people tend to avoid thinking about such potential problems. A will enables you to decide exactly who will take charge and who will benefit after your death. Although general rules do exist to cover situations where there is no will, the general rules may not suit your particular circumstances or preferences. For example, the rules favour a surviving spouse of the deceased, which may not be entirely appropriate if the deceased has young children from a previous marriage, or was in a longterm relationship with someone whom he or she never married. This chapter also tells you what will happen to your property if you do not make a will, and explains the advantages of making a will and the procedure for doing so.

Finally, we also look at problems of how to protect minors and the infirm.

Thus this chapter deals with

- registering the death
- immediate financial problems
- the deceased's affairs
- before death – preparing for the inevitable

- making sure a will is effective
- when a will can be challenged
- when there is no will – intestate succession
- provision for dependants
- protecting people who cannot look after themselves.

1. When you have to deal with a death

1.1 Registering the death

1.1.1 The medical certificate

Where a death was due to natural causes, the doctor who was treating the deceased will provide (without charge) a medical certificate of the cause of death, together with instructions on how to register the death in the sub-district where it took place.

If the deceased was being treated in hospital, the doctor may ask the next-of-kin for permission to conduct a postmortem examination, to investigate exactly how death came about.

The doctor must have seen the patient within the fortnight preceding the death. If there was no doctor attending the deceased, a coroner may issue the certificate.

Your husband suffered a mild heart attack when he was 45 years old. Fifteen years then passed and he appeared absolutely fit and healthy for his age. You find him collapsed at the top of the stairs in your home and, by the time you have called the ambulance, he has died from a massive coronary.

If your GP is not prepared to sign the certificate because he had not seen your husband within the fortnight, your husband's death will be reported to the coroner who, in this case, will certify the death as having been from natural causes.

1.1.2 The death certificate

You must register the death within five days with the Registrar of Births, Marriages and Deaths in the area in which the death took place. The address will be listed in your local telephone directory under Registration of Births, Marriages and Deaths.

- Take along the medical certificate of the cause of death. You will also need to know details about the deceased's full names, date and place of birth and marriage, whether she/he was in receipt of a pension, etc.

The death is recorded in a register of deaths, and a certified copy of the entry is called the *death certificate*. The registrar will give you a Green Form giving permission for burial or cremation to take place (to be given to the funeral director) and a certificate of registration of death for social security purposes. As copies of the death certificate will be needed for the will and for dealing with the deceased's property (in particular for making claims on life insurance), ask for several copies of the certificate at the same time. This also reduces the costs.

1.2 Coroners

A doctor must ask a coroner to investigate any death that has taken place

- due to accident or injury
- due to industrial disease
- due to sudden and unexplained events

- under anaesthetic or while undergoing surgery
- while in custody.

Coroners also investigate cases of apparent suicide. The widow or widower or the next-of-kin must be told of the inquest.

If the process may be lengthy, an interim certificate from the coroner confirming the death will be recognized for National Insurance and social security purposes.

◆ **Note:** All deaths of foreigners who die in this country are reported to the coroner.

A coroner may arrange for a postmortem examination without asking permission from the next-of-kin.

Your sister is killed in an accident while hang-gliding. You feel that the hang-gliding school she attended was not taking all proper safety precautions. You understand that there will be a postmortem as well as an inquest i.e. a public enquiry into the death. You want to be informed of the outcome in both cases.

Relatives are able to have a doctor of their choice present when the postmortem is carried out. For the position of a relative at an inquest, see immediately below.

1.2.1 Inquests

If the coroner establishes that a death is not due to natural causes, an inquest must be held.

Relatives are entitled to be legally represented at the inquest although legal aid is not available for this purpose. Other persons may show that they have an interest in the inquest, for example an employer if the death concerned an accident at work.

1.3 Organ donation

If the deceased wanted his organs or body to be donated for transplant or medical research, the medical certificate of death must first be obtained.

Inform the doctor as soon as possible, since organs deteriorate rapidly (e.g. corneas from the eye must be taken within 12 hours of death).

If the whole body is to be donated, contact the anatomy office of your nearest medical school. For general enquiries, contact HM Inspector of Anatomy at the Department of Health (tel: 071-972 4550). It is a good idea to discuss with your relatives your wishes in advance; see section 4.1 below.

1.3.1 Donor cards

Donor cards are available from doctors' surgeries, hospitals and libraries.

1.3.2 Relatives' consent

Your 19-year-old son died suddenly in a cycle accident. He carried a donor card but you would like to know what your legal position is.

Relatives will be asked to consent. It is unlikely that the medical team would override their wishes even though the deceased expressed willingness to act as a donor. In law, it seems that it is only the deceased's willingness which is required, so if there are no next-of-kin, or they do not object, the transplant will go ahead. See also section 1.3.3 below.

1.3.3 Coroner's consent

If a death has been reported to a coroner, his consent is necessary for removing an organ for donation.

1.4 Death abroad

Your parents retired to Spain some years ago. Your mother, who has just died, had always expressed a wish to be buried in England.

(1) Deaths abroad must be registered in the country where they occurred according to local formalities.

(2) If possible, the death should also be registered with the British consul. This will enable death certificates to be obtained in this country (see DIRECTORY for address of the Overseas Registration Section).

(3) The British consul should give you advice about the procedures for bringing the body home.

(4) You should also obtain an authenticated translation of the foreign documents. The death certificate or equivalent will be needed in order to bring the body through British Customs.

(5) You will also need the death certificate to obtain a certificate of 'No Liability to Register' from the registrar of the district in which your mother's funeral is to take place.

1.5 The funeral

1.5.1 The deceased's wishes

Sometimes the will contains instructions about the funeral or cremation, so check if this is the case.

1.5.2 Arranging the funeral

Funeral directors should provide you with price lists and written estimates. If there is to be a religious service, contact the appropriate minister of religion. The funeral director should advise you on this, and on the formalities for cremation. A religious service is not required by law.

1.5.3 Paying for the funeral

If you arrange the funeral you are responsible for payment. If the deceased left enough assets or cash, you may be able to claim reimbursement out of the estate for reasonable funeral expenses. Some pension schemes provide a lump sum to help with funeral expenses, or the deceased may have been a member of a burial or cremation society.

The deceased's bank account is frozen on death (unless it is a joint account), so if you cannot pay and you cannot find sources of income among the deceased's papers, a claim can be made on the DSS Social Fund (which may subsequently claim recovery from the deceased's estate); alternatively ask at your local council offices about help for the funeral (they too may subsequently claim reimbursement from the deceased's estate).

2. Immediate financial problems

2.1 Help in coping

There are various ways in which dependants may seek help if they are in urgent need. A bank loan may be available if it is only a matter of time before funds are released from the estate; or a pension fund of which the deceased was a member may offer benefits. Social security is available to tide over problems.

> *You are an only son, a student at university. Your father died when you were young and your mother did not remarry. Your mother, who was a successful businesswoman, has died suddenly. You understand that you are the sole heir. Until now you received a monthly sum from her personal bank account, but this account is frozen and you are therefore without funds. Her affairs are being well taken care of by a firm of solicitors who have been appointed as her executors, but they cannot make payments out of the estate immediately. What can be done?*

If the estate is substantial, you should approach the bank together with the solicitors to arrange a loan to tide you over until your mother's estate is sorted out.

2.1.1 Turning to social security

The DSS can alleviate immediate problems and have information available on the help which is provided.

> *You married many years ago and received a weekly housekeeping allowance from your husband. He died after a road accident and you find yourself in financial difficulties. In fact you are in need of immediate income support. Your husband was still working as an employee of an engineering firm when the accident happened. He has left no will. You know that he once took out a life insurance policy and you have found the policy document.*

To alleviate your immediate financial problems, you will have to apply to the DSS. For information about which social security benefits you can claim, ask your social security offices for leaflet FB2. This will advise you about widow's benefits, widow's payment, state-earnings-related pension, family credit, and income support.

You will need a certificate of death in order to claim and the hospital administrator should be able to provide one free of charge from the doctor who attended your husband.

Other immediate relief available from the DSS may be in the form of industrial death benefit (for industrial accidents), retirement pensions and war pensions.

2.1.2 Pensions and insurance

If you find yourself in the circumstances outlined above, you must also check with the employers of your late husband regarding his occupational pension scheme and find out who are the trustees of the pension fund. You will have to approach the trustees to establish whether you are entitled to receive the benefit of his pension. If the deceased was retired and cashed in his funds in a personal pension fund on his retirement, depending on its terms there may be no provision for continuing to pay his widow on his death.

His life or accident insurance policy, if taken out for your benefit as his widow, may provide for payment direct to you. Otherwise money payable from life policies falls into the deceased's estate. This means it will only be paid out when the personal representatives have obtained letters of administration. See sections 3.2 to 3.4 below.

2.1.3 Joint bank accounts

Personal accounts are frozen on death. Joint accounts can be operated provided that both signatories are not required to sign every cheque.

> *You and your live-in partner operated a joint bank account. He has died suddenly and your landlord is pressing for the rent. You know that his business account is frozen but would like to pay the rent from the joint account.*

You can operate the joint account provided it only required a single signature. The money in the account is not then considered part of the estate.

2.1.4 Insurance: cars and household

It is most important to note who is the main policyholder on the car and household insurance in the event of a death.

(a) Car

If the policy is in the deceased's name this means that someone else may not be able to drive his or her car until a new policy document is issued. Where there are no other named drivers, but a car is insured 'for any driver', the insurers regard other drivers as driving the car with the policyholder's consent. Such consent, naturally, ceases on death.

> *You and your late wife owned a family car. She always attended to the insurance on the car. You are concerned that the insurance on the car was in her name as the main policyholder, although you were named as a driver in the policy.*

You may not be able to drive the car until the insurance policy is changed for you to become the main policyholder.

> *You return to your home town to visit your ailing, elderly father. You have been driving his car to visit him in hospital when his condition worsens and he dies.*

The insurance on the car may not cover you to continue to drive it; nor will it protect the car against theft. You must inform the insurers of the death as soon as possible and ask them to hold you covered while fresh insurance is arranged.

(b) Household

▶ **Important:** you must notify insurers immediately. Check whether a household contents policy lapses on death. Leaving a house unoccupied with valuable possessions could be a breach of a household policy in any event.

2.1.5 Housing

See sections 7.4 and 7.5 below.

3. The deceased's affairs

3.1 Who to tell and why

3.1.1 The deceased's papers – finding out if there is a will

In all cases, the first thing to establish in dealing with a deceased's estate is whether or not there is a will.

Your uncle, who had no children of his own, died after a long illness. Your aunt is so upset that she has been unable to deal with her late husband's affairs. She asks you to assist in sorting out his papers. She says that she is sure that he left a will as he made changes to the will while he was in hospital. She says that you will also find an antique pistol locked in the top drawer of his desk, for which he had a firearms certificate.

Go through the personal papers left by the deceased. Check with his bank and his past and present solicitors whether they hold his will. It might also have been deposited for safe custody with the Registry of the Family Division of the High Court. (See section 3.1.6 below on guns.)

3.1.2 NHS equipment

Return any NHS equipment lent to the deceased (such as a wheelchair).

3.1.3 Sending back official documents

Other official documents should be sent back to the issuing office, with a note about the date of death.

(a) The passport

The deceased's passport should be returned to the passport office.

(b) The driving licence

The driving licence should be returned to the DVLC Swansea.

3.1.4 Checking with insurers

See section 2.1.4 above.

3.1.5 Tax office

Inform the deceased's Tax Office about the death as soon as possible.

3.1.6 Guns

It is an offence to keep a gun without a firearms certificate. Your uncle's certificate is no longer valid once he has died, so hand the pistol to a firearms dealer for safekeeping (they have special authority for this) pending the settlement of the estate.

3.1.7 Bank direct debits and standing orders

Check all direct debit mandates and standing orders; these cease on death if paid through a bank account in a deceased's sole name. Bills for basic services such as telephone, gas etc., may have been paid in this way.

3.1.8 Credit cards

Make sure that all credit cards are returned with notice of death to the card companies to avoid fraudulent misuse.

3.2 The personal representatives

These are the official representatives of the deceased who 'wind up the estate'.

In one sense, all the deceased's affairs come to a halt at the moment of death; just to cite a single example, bank accounts in his or her sole name are automatically frozen. In another sense, all the affairs of the deceased's estate survive; for example the debts of the deceased still have to be paid.

So someone has to take charge of an estate and sort out all matters relating to it, i.e.

- to take care of the deceased's property
- to pay outstanding debts and taxes
- to ascertain which persons are entitled to what is left (they are called *beneficiaries*)
- to ensure that the beneficiaries are given their proper share in due course.

This is a position of great responsibility, and also involves a fair amount of work, not all of it straightforward.

'Personal representatives' is a generic term which includes both executors and administrators.

3.2.1 Distinction between executors and administrators

The question of who that 'someone' is whose duty it is to take charge of an estate hinges on whether or not there is a will.

(a) If you leave a will, you can decide whom to appoint as your executors who will take charge of your affairs after your death.
(b) If you do not leave a will, the next-of-kin will have to take charge. They are not called executors but are referred to as *administrators* of the deceased's estate.

There need be only one executor or one administrator. Two executors are usually appointed in a will in the event that one might be unwilling or unable to take on the role. If both take on the role they act together. A will can name up to four executors.

◆ **Take note:** although executors can act on behalf of an estate unofficially from the death of the person who appointed them, administrators cannot act until the grant of letters of administration (see section 3.4 below).

In most cases, the executors are also the beneficiaries of the estate, for example a husband or wife will appoint the surviving spouse and/or their children as their executors and beneficiaries who will then wish to wind up the estate as quickly and as cheaply as possible.

3.2.2 A word of caution

◆ **Take heed:** If you deal with any of the property of a deceased person without any authority to do so, you can be liable to penalties. See section 3.4 below.

3.2.3 Obtaining authority to act – probate

If the deceased leaves a will with named executors, the executors must apply to the Probate Division of the High Court for the grant of probate. This gives them official authority to act on behalf of the estate. If you are named and are prepared to act as executor, the procedures for obtaining a grant of probate are set out in a helpful leaflet (Form PA2) produced by the Lord Chancellor's Department.

If there is no will, the administrators of the estate will be granted 'letters of administration' by the same Probate Division.

Both grant of probate and grant of letters of administration are referred to by a generic term: *grant of representation*.

◆ **Help at hand:** the addresses of the Probate Registries are listed in Form PA2. You will be assigned your own probate interviewing officer to deal with you and handle your application to minimize difficulties. Note, however, that their role ends once you are granted probate, and probate officers do not assist in administering the affairs of the estate.

3.2.4 Inheritance tax

If the net value of the assets left by the deceased is more than £140,000, the personal representatives are personally liable to pay inheritance tax on the estate. They must send an account to the Inland Revenue within three months of first acting as personal representatives, or within 12 months of the death, whichever is the later date.

As with lifetime gifts between spouses (see chapter on *Setting Up Home*, section 4.1.8), if the entire estate goes to the surviving spouse, then no inheritance tax is payable. Bequests to registered charities are also exempt from inheritance tax.

> *You are nominated as executor of your stepmother's large estate. You are not able to afford the likely inheritance tax bill and would like to know what you should do.*

> You may have to borrow money to pay the inheritance tax. However, you can claim reimbursement out of the estate when you have received the grant of representation (see section 3.2.3 above). Forms IHT 200, IHT 201 and IHT 202 are the relevant forms.

The housing market's slump and boom cycle can cause great hardship for the beneficiaries who may be liable for inheritance tax on the property – irrespective of whether or not it can be sold to meet the tax liability.

3.3 Acting as executor

There is no legal compulsion to take on the task of executor if named in someone's will.

> *A very close friend asked you whether you would be prepared to act as his executor at a time when he was terminally ill. He said that it would be a simple matter of dealing with his property and personal effects. You agreed to his request and he has named you as sole executor in his will. Now that he has died, you would like some advice on taking on the task.*

> If you are named as executor in a will you are under no legal compulsion to accept the role, even if before the death you promised your friend you would do so.

3.3.1 Taking on the job

If you start acting as an executor you will be regarded as having accepted, so do not begin dealing with the property of the deceased until you have made up your mind (except for urgent matters such as feeding pets or making emergency repairs).

◆ **Take heed:** if you get it wrong, you could be sued by lots of different people. For your own protection, it is well worth while seeking the advice of a solicitor – the costs of which will come out of the estate.

3.3.2 Remuneration and expenses

It is wiser not to become executor of an estate with few assets and many debts. Even if the estate is not bankrupt, if it is fairly large and complicated it may take a lot of your time, and although you will be able to recoup expenses from the estate you cannot charge for your time and trouble (unless the will so specifies or all the beneficiaries agree). For the position of banks or lawyers acting as executors, see section 4.1.1 below.

Out-of-pocket expenses are always paid out of the estate.

◆ **Note:** if an executor or administrator is to be paid for acting in the winding up of an estate, all the beneficiaries must agree in writing by a formal document. In this case, it requires a *deed under seal*. A mere informal written agreement to pay executors for their time and trouble is not enough.

3.4 Appointing an administrator

Letters of administration

Letters of administration must be obtained where the deceased did not leave a will, or left a will but failed to name his executors. Persons who obtain a grant of letters of administration from the Probate Registry are known as the *administrators*. They then take over the deceased's estate dealing with it in the same way as executors.

> *Your late brother has left a will but has not named any executors in it. You have been approached by his live-in partner, who asks you to act as executor. You are quite ready to accept. However, you are not quite sure of your legal position.*

If there is

- no executor named in the will, or
- no will at all

then a grant of letters of administration will be issued by the Probate Registry to next-of-kin.

This is in a prescribed order of priority (see Form PA2) based on the closeness of family relationship. A brother will be appointed as personal representative after

- surviving spouse (which is not applicable in this case); then
- children; then
- parents.

3.4.1 Children of parents not married to each other

Children of parents who are not married to each other are not discriminated against; they can act as administrators if their parents die without a will and they can inherit in the same way and proportion as children of parents married to each other.

> *You have lived with your partner for many years and have had two children by him. He has now died intestate. You would like the children to act as administrators of the estate but have been told by a friend that, because they were born out of wedlock, they are not entitled to act. Is this so?*

The answer is 'no'. For the purposes of the order of priorities of appointment of administrator, the children are your partner's next-of-kin. The fact that you and he were not married is not relevant to the children's status with regard to acting for his estate.

The order of priorities (above) relates solely to the question of who can act as administrator of an intestate estate. There are different rules for who can *inherit* under an intestacy (see section 7 below).

If the whole estate is worth less than £5,000 then a grant of representation may not be necessary (see Form PA2).

3.5 Dealing with the deceased's property

3.5.1 Property in the UK

Once the grant of representation has been issued, the personal representatives can administer the property of the deceased in England and Wales. If there is property in Scotland or Northern Ireland, separate confirmations or grants of representation need *not* be obtained.

Conversely, if the deceased died in Scotland or Northern Ireland, confirmation or grant of representation should be obtained in the country of death, and these will be recognized in England and Wales.

3.5.2 Functions of personal representatives

The function of the personal representatives is to take control of the deceased's property and land, as well as cash and personal effects.

(a) They must keep records.
(b) They must, of course, keep this property quite separate from their own.
(c) They must take reasonable care of the property.
(d) They can take out insurance for this purpose.

They will have to give a rough valuation of the house or flat which the deceased owned to the probate registry. This figure will subsequently be checked by a valuation officer of the Inland Revenue.

Shares are valued as at the day before the date of death. The figures are easily checked from the Stock Exchange Daily Official List.

3.5.3 Taking legal advice

When you should consult a solicitor

- If the estate involves the transfer of ownership of a house or flat
- if the estate involves rented property and the rights of a secure or protected tenant to remain in occupation are at issue
- if there are substantial assets of the estate abroad
- if there are children under 18
- if the estate appears insolvent
- if the deceased was running a business
- if the estate is very large and it would be complicated to administer
- if there is a problem in tracing some of the beneficiaries who might have a claim on the estate
- if the will might have been tampered with – either by the testator or some other person
- if there are likely to be claims against the estate by dependants for whom the will did not make provision
- if the validity of a will is open to question
- if the deceased was killed in an accident in circumstances where his relatives may make a claim for damages under the Fatal Accidents Act (if, for example, he or she was killed in a car crash or work accident); see also *Accidents* chapter, section 11.5.
- if the deceased owned or rented agricultural property.

◆ **Note:** this list is not exhaustive and is intended for guideline purposes only.

3.5.4 Insuring the estate

See section 2.1.4 above for the insurance position immediately the death occurs.

Insurance is always advisable for personal representatives; and since they can be held personally liable to make up any losses caused to a beneficiary or creditor of the estate, make sure any valuables are lodged securely with a bank.

Your co-executor has absconded with some valuable jewellery which your mother-in-law left in her will to her sister. You have been told that you are now personally responsible for making up the loss. You want to know if this is correct.

The answer is 'yes'. You are legally responsible for the actions of your co-executor.

3.5.5 Keeping accounts

At each stage a careful and accurate record should be kept of what is done, as you can be called upon to account for your administration by persons interested in the estate, or by the court.

3.5.6 The deceased's business

If the deceased ran a business, the personal representatives do not have the power to carry on the business except for the purpose of selling it as a going concern. They should see a solicitor if the deceased was a partner in a business or ran his own business through a limited liability company.

3.5.7 The deceased's creditors

The personal representatives are responsible for paying taxes and satisfying debts due by the deceased, out of the assets in the estate. They may advertise for claims from creditors, allowing at least two months for claims to be lodged before paying out to the beneficiaries. Assets may have to be sold to raise cash in order to settle the debts, but beneficiaries under the will (if there is one) may have an interest in particular assets. The order in which assets should be disposed of is laid down by law.

3.5.8 When the estate is insolvent

If there are insufficient assets to pay debts and taxes, the estate is insolvent, i.e. the estate is bankrupt. It must then be administered in accordance with a particular procedure specified in the Administration of Insolvent Estates of Deceased Persons Order (SI 1986 No. 1999, obtainable from HMSO). For example, after paying the expenses of the funeral and administration, and arrears which the deceased owed on social security and pension fund contributions, tax claims by the Inland Revenue must be paid before debts due to ordinary creditors.

Secured creditors such as mortgagees will rely on their security and sell the mortgaged property to recover payment. If the correct procedure is not observed, the personal representatives may become personally liable to creditors.

The next-of-kin are not liable to pay the deceased's debts, if he or she left insufficient assets to pay them.

3.5.9 Paying the beneficiaries

If there are assets left over after paying expenses, taxes and debts, the personal representatives must distribute them in accordance with the will. If there is no will, or no valid will, or the will disposes of only part of the assets, the law prescribes who is entitled to share in the assets of the deceased (see *Intestacy*, section 7 below).

The personal representatives are not obliged to pay out legacies or distribute the assets of the estate to beneficiaries until one year has elapsed since the death.

4. Before death: preparing for the inevitable

The choice is between leaving a will or dying intestate.

A valid will ensures that we can determine what happens to our property after our death.

If we do not make a will, in other words, if we die *intestate*, the law determines how our property will be distributed, to whom, and in what proportion.

4.1 Whether to make a will

As explained above, without a will, assets and belongings will be distributed on death according to the law of intestacy (dealt with in detail in section 7). The intestacy laws benefit blood relatives in the order of proximity, but cohabitees and close friends get nothing.

Good reasons exist, therefore, for choosing to make a will:

(a) to revoke a previous will;
(b) to appoint guardians or set up trusts for your minor children (although this can also be done less formally – see section 9.2 below);
(c) to nominate executors and trustees;
(d) to make gifts to individuals and charities, and to provide for pets;
(e) to prevent family squabbles about who takes what;
(f) to plan, with professional advice, the distribution of your estate so as to minimize inheritance tax and capital gains tax;
(g) to leave instructions about your funeral or cremation, or to leave your organs for research or transplant. But as the will may not be read till after the funeral, you should also tell your family and proposed executor about your wishes in this regard (see section 1.3 above on the matter of donating organs).

◆ **Note:** When you make a will, it is also advisable to sign an enduring power of attorney (see section 9.1 below).

4.1.1 How to go about making a will

Any solicitor will prepare a will for you. The fees can vary from as little as £50 at a High Street solicitor, up to several hundred pounds, depending on

- the size of the estate,
- the complexity of the will itself, and
- the type of legal practice you consult.

Do ask beforehand about legal charges; most solicitors will give you an approximate figure.

If you do not want to consult a solicitor, there are inexpensive customized will-making services available (for example *The Daily Telegraph* offers such a service).

In addition

- various charities such as Oxfam or Help the Aged offer a will-making service
- ready-made will forms are easily available from legal stationers
- there is no legal reason why you should not simply write out a will yourself (but see section 4.1.2).

◆ **Note** that if you nominate as executor a bank or similar organization, or a solicitor or accountant, the will usually includes a clause that they will charge for their professional services (cf. section 3.3.2 above). Their fees may make very substantial inroads into the amount of the estate available for the beneficiaries. Solicitors' fees for acting as executor can be challenged, if the beneficiaries regard them as excessive. The Law Society is promoting legislation to make such challenges easier, in the interests of reducing disputes between lawyers and the public.

4.1.2 Home-made wills

◆ **Take heed:** it is a risky business to try to make a will without some kind of expert advice. Many home-made wills turn out to be invalid for one reason or another. If they are invalid, then the deceased's wishes can be thwarted and the estate will be distributed according to the intestacy rules.

For example, a pre-printed will form may contain a flaw such as omitting to warn that a beneficiary should not be a witness. Customers who buy such a form may have their wishes defeated by the error whereas employing a solicitor would prevent such a problem.

Reputable will-making services carry indemnity insurance against negligence, as solicitors do. However, not all services have insurance. You will then have no proper safeguard, so do check.

4.1.3 Obtaining legal aid

Provided that you meet the legal aid requirements (see chapter on *The Legal System*), legal aid is available for advice and for the preparation of a will

- for persons who are handicapped mentally or physically, or who have sight or hearing disabilities;
- for the parents or guardians of any of the above, who wish to make provision for them by will;
- for testators over 70 years of age;
- for a single parent wishing to appoint a guardian for a minor child.

You and your wife have a child with Down's syndrome and you worry about her future. You would like expert legal assistance in case an accident befalls either of you and your daughter will be left alone.

In this case, you can apply for legal aid, i.e. get State help towards payment of legal fees in drawing up a will best suited to her needs.

Certain organizations such as MENCAP can provide advice on how to set up a trust for a handicapped person out of an estate.

4.1.4 Informal wishes

If after someone's death a letter or note is found among their effects stating that certain objects should be given to particular persons, this has no legal effect unless it complies with the requirements for making a will. It would be unlawful for the personal representatives to pay regard to it unless all the beneficiaries and creditors agree. (See also section 5.3.1 below.)

4.2 Other ways to dispose of property – gifts in contemplation of death

An individual may wish to make a gift during his or her lifetime, with the intention of ensuring that the recipient will receive the gift after the donor's death. Such a gift is said to be 'made in contemplation of death'.

4.2.1 How to make the gift

The gift must be clearly made in the donor's lifetime.

> *Your mother, who knows she is terminally ill, gives you the key to her jewellery box. She tells you that she wants you to have her jewellery after her death. Three days later she dies.*

You can keep the jewellery and it does not fall into the estate for distribution under your mother's will, if she left one, or on intestacy if she did not.

4.2.2 Gift revocable at any time

A gift made in contemplation of death can be revoked at any time during the lifetime of the donor.

> *Three days after giving you the key to her jewellery box and telling you that she wants you to have her jewellery after her death, your mother quarrels with you. She forces open the jewellery box, and gives her jewels to her sister. Soon afterwards, she dies.*

This is a clear indication that your mother revoked her gift to you of the jewellery. It now belongs to her sister. Again it does not belong to the estate after your mother's death.

4.2.3 Gift must be completed

Any gift must be 'completed' before death.

> *At the same time as your mother gives you the jewellery, she gives your brother a cheque for an equivalent amount. She dies before he has deposited the cheque.*

The money represented by the cheque was not a 'completed' gift. Your brother has no claim for that amount – as distinct from any other claim he may have as a beneficiary.

4.2.4 Buildings and land

◆ **Note:** gifts in contemplation of death can apply to house property as well as to personal possessions.

> *Your friend owns little except his house. He has made no will, but while dying in hospital, he tells you that the house is yours. He gives you the keys to the house and tells you where you will find a box in which he kept the title deeds to the property. He gives you the key to the box as well. After his death, his relatives claim the house under the intestacy rules. You want to know whether the gift is valid.*

In a similar case, the court held that the person who received the keys and the title deeds from her dying friend was entitled to the house despite the relatives' claims.

◆ **Note:** It is possible that a gift 'made in contemplation of death' cannot be made in contemplation of suicide.

4.2.5 Distinguished from ordinary gifts

Gifts made in contemplation of death, which are only intended to take effect on death, are not to be confused with gifts made in a donor's lifetime which are intended to take effect immediately. These gifts are a device to avoid inheritance tax and can be made up to the current nil band threshold. If the donor dies within seven years of the gift, the gift attracts inheritance tax; but if the donor survives for longer than seven years, the gift is inheritance-tax free.

5. Making sure a will is effective

Your will cannot be made effective on your death unless it complies with the formalities prescribed by law.

5.1 Formalities

The *testator* or *testatrix* (the maker of a will) must be aged over 18. The will must be in writing. It need not be in English to be valid, if the testator is more familiar with another language.

The will should be clear and legible, though it does not have to be typed. It should not be written in pencil. (For your convenience, keep a copy of the will, which need not be signed.)

5.1.1 Signatures

The will should be signed by the testator *at the end of the document*. This is most important. A signature at the top of the will could be challenged.

The will must be signed by at least two witnesses. They and the testator must all be in the same room at the same time *throughout* the signing session. This fact should be stated in the will, and the date should be inserted.

> You call in two neighbours to witness your will. They are in the room with you while you sign it but one of them refuses to sign unless she reads the will first. She says that otherwise her signature will not be valid.

The witnesses do not have to read the document. They do not even have to know that the document is a will, as long as they know that they are there to witness your signature.

Below the testator's signature the witnesses should then write their usual signatures, and add their addresses and occupations or descriptions.

5.1.2 Who can be witnesses

The witnesses must not be persons who are benefiting under the will. They also cannot be married to persons benefiting under the will.

> Your two sons are to be your sole heirs under your will. You know that neither of them can witness your signature but your daughter-in-law is visiting you and you want to ask her to act as a witness, together with a neighbour.

A person married to someone benefiting under the will cannot act as a witness.

If the testator is very elderly or infirm, one of the persons acting as witness should be a doctor, who should examine him first to make sure he understands what he is doing. The doctor should be asked to keep a record of the examination.

If the testator is too weak to sign, then even a mark will do provided it is made in the presence of the doctor who is acting as witness.

5.2 Where to keep the will

Deposit the signed will in a safe place, perhaps with your solicitor or your bank. It is also possible to deposit a will at any Registry of the Family Division of the High Court.

It is advisable that you tell your executor and family where you have put the will, so that delay in tracing it is avoided. (They will not be able to see it until after your death.)

5.3 Reviewing the contents of the will regularly

The provisions of your will should be reviewed every five years or as your circumstances change. You must certainly consider making a new will when major family events occur, such as marriage, divorce, the birth of a child, or the death of someone close to you. (For the effect of such events on an existing will, see *Revocation of wills* in section 6.4 below.)

5.3.1 Minor amendments and codicils

For a minor amendment to your will, you can consider making a codicil.

Codicils are used for the purpose of making changes to a will where there is no necessity to rewrite the whole will. Two witnesses must witness the signature to the codicil which must be signed and dated in the same way as a will. The codicil is then attached to the will.

Do state that the rest of the will is unchanged, in the codicil's opening sentence.

> *You named two executors for your will but one of them has since died and you would now like to name someone in her stead. Otherwise your will is unchanged. You call in two friends to witness the signing of the codicil and one of them asks whether it is necessary for you to have the same witnesses to your signature of the codicil as witnessed your original will.*
>
> The answer is 'no'. Provided you have two witnesses to the codicil they need not be the same two people who witnessed your signature to the original will.

A letter or memo setting out the testator's wishes will have no legal force although if the beneficiaries agree to abide by its terms and inform the personal representative to that effect, the courts will give effect to such an agreement. A codicil is the simpler and safer way of making sure minor amendments have full legal force.

5.4 Soldiers' and seamen's wills

In certain emergency situations individuals can make a valid will without complying with any of the above formalities. These are called 'privileged wills' and are as effective as a formal written will after the individual's death. The only persons who can make such wills are soldiers on actual military service or mariners while at sea (even if they are under 18). They can even make their will orally, as long as they intended by the statement to dispose of their property on death.

> *Edward, a bomb disposal expert, is injured while carrying out a security operation in England. He gasps out to his comrade: 'If I don't make it, make sure my girlfriend Anne gets all my stuff'.*
>
> This is a valid privileged will, and remains so even if Edward recovers and leaves the army. It remains valid until he makes a new will or he revokes it.

◆ **Note:** the armed forces normally require recruits to make a formal will when joining up.

6. When a will can be challenged

If certain people are dissatisfied with the outcome – either through having been left out of the will or because the intestacy rules have excluded them – they are able to challenge these arrangements.

◆ **Note:** Challengers are not limited to dependants but can include creditors of the deceased.

Anyone is entitled to obtain a copy of a will on payment of a fee, once probate has been granted. It can be obtained from Somerset House, The Strand, London, WC2, Tel: 071-936 7000.

6.1 Grounds of challenge

A person whose expectations of inheriting from the deceased have been disappointed by the terms of a will may wish to challenge the will's validity or effect. There are various grounds on which such a challenge can be made, some of which are described below.

6.1.1 Revocation

It may be claimed that the will was no longer valid because the testator had changed his mind, i.e. the will had been revoked. (See also sections 6.4.2 and 6.4.3 below.)

6.1.2 Mental incapacity

It may be claimed that the deceased did not know or understand what he or she was doing, or its effect, when making the will. See also section 9 below.

6.1.3 Undue influence or fraud

It may be claimed that the deceased was subject to undue influence or fraud when making the will.

6.1.4 Failure to provide for dependants

It may be claimed that the deceased failed to make reasonable provision for a dependant. See section 8 below.

6.2 Costs of challenge

Where legal proceedings are brought to challenge a will, the executor may insist that the beneficiaries indemnify him against the cost of defending the action, before he accepts office. The court will not necessarily order the costs and expenses of the proceedings to be taken out of the estate.

6.3 Reasons for failure of testator's intentions

Even if a will has left you a legacy, various factors may operate to prevent you from receiving the benefit.

6.3.1 Insolvency

If the estate was insolvent, all the assets are used up in paying creditors.

6.3.2 Terms of the will

A gift will also depend on the terms of the will.

In her will your sister left you 'the diamond brooch given to me by our mother'. It now appears that your sister sold the brooch some years before her death.

You will not be able to receive the diamond brooch and cannot claim anything from the estate *in lieu* of the brooch. If she had simply left you 'a diamond brooch' the executor must buy one out of the assets of the estate, provided they are sufficient.

Your uncle's will states that his collection of porcelain should be sold. He directs his executors to buy you a sports car from the proceeds. The executors inform you that the money raised from the sale of the porcelain falls short of the amount needed to buy even the cheapest sports car.

By the terms of the will, the sale of the porcelain must realise sufficient to buy the car; if it does not, the bequest fails and the proceeds from the sale of the porcelain fall into the balance of the estate – the *residue*.

6.4 A will that has been revoked

A will may be revoked by an act of the testator – e.g. by making a later will or destroying a will. Sometimes the law regards a will as revoked automatically, either in whole or in part.

6.4.1 By marriage

A will is automatically revoked by operation of the law (i.e. without any act on the testator's part) if the person who made the will ('the testator') subsequently gets married.

Your husband made a will leaving his estate to you, whom he also named as executrix. After 25 years of marriage, he divorced you and remarried. He died three months later.

In this case, the whole of his will was revoked by his remarriage, so that the estate will be divided according to intestacy, with his second wife taking the lion's share as surviving spouse.

However, you could make a claim under the family provision legislation. The court will weigh up all the circumstances, taking into account your present needs, and the kind of settlement you received when you were divorced (see section 8 below).

This 'revocation by marriage' applies except where a will states that it is made 'in contemplation of marriage'. For example, a couple who intend to honeymoon abroad decide to make mutual wills before their wedding 'in contemplation of marriage'. In that case, their wills are valid.

◆ **Note:** the birth of a child or grandchild does not revoke an existing will. However, it clearly requires consideration to be given to the making of a new will or codicil.

6.4.2 By a later will or codicil

A will is generally revoked by a later will, usually by express words, such as 'This is my last will and testament and I hereby revoke all former wills.'

However, not all later wills expressly revoke earlier ones. If there are no words of express revocation, the effect of the later will depends on its terms, inconsistency with the earlier will, and the implications which flow from the existing wills.

Your father left two wills, the second will having been made about a year after the first one. The later one does not expressly revoke the earlier will and the terms of both wills are similar except for one specific gift. In his first will he left £1,000 to his housekeeper, whom he has since dismissed; the gift is omitted in the second will. You are the sole executor and beneficiary. You would like some advice.

The gift to your father's former housekeeper would no longer be effective.

If a later will does not expressly revoke an earlier one, it can do so by implication. It depends on the terms and whether the second will contains provisions inconsistent with the first one.

If the two wills are not inconsistent, and there is no express revocation of the earlier will in the later, they will both be effective and have combined effect.

If a couple agreed to make mutual wills leaving their property to each other or their children, then after the death of the first, the survivor's ability to make different arrangements by a new will may be limited. A solicitor should be consulted in these circumstances.

6.4.3 By destruction

Clearly a will is revoked if the testator destroys it. Only actual physical destruction – e.g. burning it, or cutting it up – is a revocation, and then only if it is done intentionally by the testator or, if by someone else, in his presence. Striking out pages, by drawing a line through the words, is insufficient; but cutting out the signatures, or crossing them through so thickly that they cannot be made out, operates as a revocation.

You understand that your cousin telephoned her solicitor and asked him to destroy her will. He properly advised her that she should destroy it herself, and posted it to her. She has since died and you have found her will among her papers, heavily scribbled on and with the word 'Cancelled' written at the top. The will can still be read, although with difficulty, as can the signatures. You would like to know whether the will is valid.

In all cases where the validity of a will is open to challenge, it is advisable to consult a solicitor. However, in a case similar to this one, the court held that where the will and its signatures could still be read, it was valid.

6.4.4 By divorce

If the testator gets divorced after the date of the will, the will is partially revoked; the will remains valid but any appointments of the former spouse as executor, and bequests to him or her, are deleted. Separation without divorce has no effect on the will.

Your mother made a will naming your father as co-executor with her brother. She left your father two-thirds of her estate, with the other third going to you. Thereafter she divorced your father. She has recently died and you would like to know the present position.

As a result of the divorce, your father, as your mother's ex-husband, has to be left out of account in dealing with her estate – both as legatee of the two-thirds of her estate and as co-executor. As a result you will receive one-third of the estate under the will, and the other two thirds will devolve as on intestacy (see section 7 below), with her brother acting as the sole executor.

If your father cannot support himself, he could apply for family provision (see section 8 below).

6.5 Mental incapacity

For wills to be valid, testators must have known and understood what they were about at the time of making the will. If they subsequently become senile or mentally ill this does not revoke an earlier will.

A valid will can be spiteful or eccentric, unexpected or capricious – this fact alone does not cast doubt on the testator's mental capacity. All that is required is that testators have the capacity to understand the nature of a will, the extent of their property and the claims on their bounty of their relatives and friends.

If the will was made when the testator was very elderly or was known to have suffered from mental illness, a doctor may have been asked to witness the will, and if so may have kept a record of the testator's state of mind at the time.

A situation analogous to lack of capacity arises where there is a suspicion that the testator did not understand or approve the will he signed. If this can be proved, the will is invalid.

> *Nina, a wealthy, infirm and frail widow of 91, lived in a nursing home run by Mr and Mrs Smith. A letter signed by Nina was sent to solicitors she had never consulted previously, asking them to draw up a will leaving her estate to Mrs Smith. They sent the will to her which she signed. The solicitors did not see Nina personally, and during visits to Nina by her relatives Mr or Mrs Smith were always present. After Nina's death her relatives challenge the validity of the will.*

> Given the highly suspicious circumstances the court is unlikely to find that Nina knew and approved the contents of the will when signing it.

6.6 Undue influence and fraud

Where the testator was *persuaded* to make a will in particular terms – such as leaving large sums to a religious sect – this will not invalidate the will unless the testator was subjected to excessive pressure or coercion. The mere fact the beneficiary was in some position of authority or influence over the testator (as doctor, priest or solicitor, for instance) raises no presumption that excessive pressure was used.

> *James, after a marriage of many years to Celia, separates from her and starts a relationship with Beth. Beth, with whom James is obsessed, persuades him to make a will leaving his substantial property to her to the exclusion of his wife and children.*

> On James's death the will is valid. (However, Celia and the children can claim family provision out of the estate – see section 8 below.)

7. Where there is no will: intestate succession

Only about one in three of the population bothers to make a will at all. Many others may intend to do so but just do not get round to it. In the event, whether they wish it or not, they are relying on the rules of distribution of their estates under the intestacy laws. These laws, generally speaking, are designed to follow a deceased's own wishes; in other words, the law assumes that people who leave no wills would wish their estate to benefit their closest relatives.

However, since the intestacy rules were drawn up there have been noteworthy changes in home ownership patterns: about 70% of houses are now owner-occupied today, compared with only about 30% forty years ago. This fact, taken together with the marked increase in the numbers of people who have pensions and life insurance, as well as owning property, means that the intestacy rules, intended to act as a safety net, can instead sometimes work in an arbitrary and unfair way.

7.1 Who inherits?

Intestate succession proceeds in accordance with the diagram overleaf.

7.2 Who is a 'spouse' of the deceased?

As we can see from the diagram, the surviving spouse is given the first £125,000 of an estate where there are children (and £200,000 where there are no children). Therefore the definition of a 'spouse' is critical for the purposes of division.

▶ **Remember:** Under the laws of intestate succession property left by a deceased person is distributed according to set general rules. As a result they can have unintended results.

> *You parted from your wife and contact between you and her just about ceased once your only son was grown up. You were never formally divorced, however. Your son now tells you that she has died intestate. He says that by law you are entitled to all her personal possessions, as well as a share in her estate up to £125,000. Thereafter you have a 50 per cent share in the life interest in the remainder, with your son having the other share. He feels that this is most unfair in view of the fact that he has been living with his mother all the time, while you, in fact, had deserted them to live with another woman for the past 15 years.*

Under the intestacy rules, the estate will be divided as stated by your son. If you and your wife had divorced, on the other hand, you would not have received anything from her estate.

In the present case your son could apply under the laws for family provision (see below) but he would have to show that he was dependent on his mother at the time when she died.

7.3 Who is a child of the deceased?

Under the intestacy rules, the children who qualify are

- legitimate and illegitimate children
- adopted children

but *not* stepchildren.

> *When you were six years old your mother married for the second time. Your stepfather was a very wealthy man who has recently died. His will failed because it did not comply with the legal formalities of making a will. A friend tells you that you are entitled to a share of an estate as a 'child of the family'. You wonder if this is correct.*

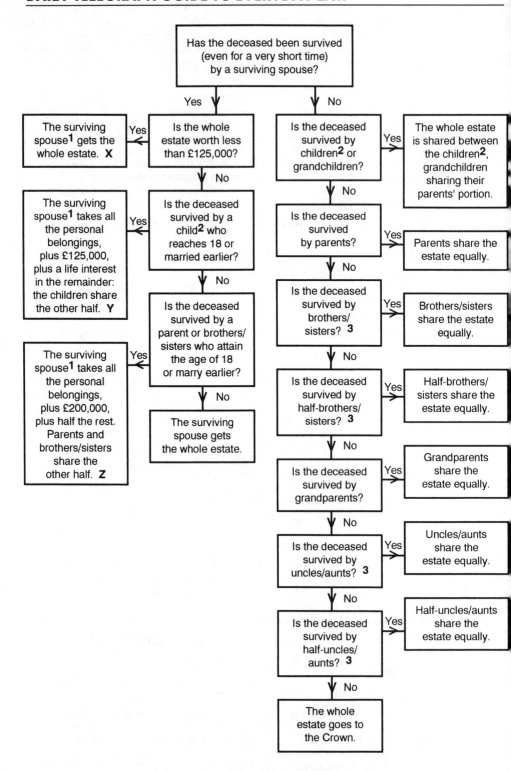

Has the deceased been survived (even for a very short time) by a surviving spouse?

Yes → Is the whole estate worth less than £125,000?
- **Yes** → The surviving spouse[1] gets the whole estate. **X**
- **No** → Is the deceased survived by a child[2] who reaches 18 or married earlier?
  - **Yes** → The surviving spouse[1] takes all the personal belongings, plus £125,000, plus a life interest in the remainder: the children share the other half. **Y**
  - **No** → Is the deceased survived by a parent or brothers/sisters who attain the age of 18 or marry earlier?
    - **Yes** → The surviving spouse[1] takes all the personal belongings, plus £200,000, plus half the rest. Parents and brothers/sisters share the other half. **Z**
    - **No** → The surviving spouse gets the whole estate.

No → Is the deceased survived by children[2] or grandchildren?
- **Yes** → The whole estate is shared between the children[2], grandchildren sharing their parents' portion.
- **No** → Is the deceased survived by parents?
  - **Yes** → Parents share the estate equally.
  - **No** → Is the deceased survived by brothers/sisters? **3**
    - **Yes** → Brothers/sisters share the estate equally.
    - **No** → Is the deceased survived by half-brothers/sisters? **3**
      - **Yes** → Half-brothers/sisters share the estate equally.
      - **No** → Is the deceased survived by grandparents?
        - **Yes** → Grandparents share the estate equally.
        - **No** → Is the deceased survived by uncles/aunts? **3**
          - **Yes** → Uncles/aunts share the estate equally.
          - **No** → Is the deceased survived by half-uncles/aunts? **3**
            - **Yes** → Half-uncles/aunts share the estate equally.
            - **No** → The whole estate goes to the Crown.

Notes to the diagram for intestate succession

(1) 'Spouse' means a person to whom the deceased was married at the date of death, even if separated or estranged. A cohabitee, however long the relationship, has no right to inherit on intestacy. So for the purposes of the rules of intestacy, 'spouse' includes a separated or estranged spouse but not a divorced spouse.

(2) 'Child' includes an adopted child and an illegitimate child, but not a stepchild or the child of a cohabitee and another person.

(3) The children of any one of these will inherit in their place.

> *John, who dies without leaving a will, is survived by two nieces, the children of his predeceased sister Diana, and by his uncle Harry. The entire estate will be shared between the nieces, who take the place of Diana and thus exclude the category to which Harry belongs.*

(4) Boxes X, Y and Z: see section 7.4.2 below.

The answer is 'no' – you are not entitled to share in your stepfather's estate. However, if you can show that your stepfather was maintaining you at the time of his death and that you were dependent on that maintenance, you could apply under the law which makes family provision for dependants (see section 8).

7.4 Property issues

In all matters concerning property, do seek legal advice.

7.4.1 The matrimonial home

The outline below only lists the general rules which apply to inheriting property on an intestacy. There are solicitors who will give an interview at a fixed fee (or without charge) and their names are listed in the Solicitors' Regional Directory (available from a Citizens' Advice Bureau or the public library).

7.4.2 Owner-occupied property

Under the law of intestacy the surviving spouse of the deceased (most often the widow) is not necessarily entitled to the matrimonial home unless it was jointly owned.

- If the house was jointly owned then the survivor normally acquires it automatically in addition to his or her share of the estate as detailed above.
- If the house is mortgaged, and it passes to the surviving spouse under a joint ownership, mortgage repayments must be kept up to avoid repossession. Many people take out insurance (either life insurance or endowment policies) to pay off the mortgage on the matrimonial home. Do check all policy documents.
- If the house was in the name of the deceased alone, and its value is less than the statutory entitlement (see boxes marked X, Y and Z on the diagram opposite), the survivor can insist that it goes towards that entitlement.
- If the house was in the name of the deceased alone, and it is worth more than the statutory entitlement, the survivor can only claim it as his or her share if he or she has other assets out of which the excess can be paid.

You are recently widowed and would like to continue to live in the family home which was in your husband's sole name. You have no children. Your husband died without leaving a will and the house has been valued at £300,000.

You are only entitled to £200,000 out of the estate and your in-laws would be entitled to the balance. Therefore if you wish to keep the house, you would have to find the £100,000 to pay them the excess.

7.4.3 Rented property

▶ **Remember:** never negotiate with a landlord without first getting legal advice.

If the first-dying spouse was named as the tenant under the lease, check the wording to see whether the death automatically brings the lease to an end.

If the landlord knows of the tenant's death, but continues to accept rent from the surviving spouse, he may be accepting the survivor as the tenant in place of the deceased.

◆ **Note:** where there are two persons who can succeed to the tenancy – for example, a surviving spouse and another member of the tenant's family – then the spouse takes preference.

These rules do not apply where the spouse or member of the family is a successor already (see also chapter on *Landlords and their Tenants*).

7.5 Cohabitees

7.5.1 Position on intestacy

◆ **Take heed:** A cohabitee has *no* entitlement on intestacy, but may be entitled as a dependant (but see under *Provision for dependants*, section 8 below).

7.5.2 Occupation of property

With regard to house ownership, the position for cohabitees is much less favourable than for a surviving husband or wife. If the home was not jointly owned, but was in the name of the first-dying, the cohabitee cannot claim any share in it unless (s)he made a substantial contribution to its acquisition or improvement.

For the position where property is rented, see chapter on *Landlords and their Tenants*.

8. Provision for dependants

Provision is available to a limited group of people – whether or not the deceased left a will.

◆ **Note carefully:** the law limits those who can challenge the division or sharing out of an estate on the ground of dependency to a narrow class of people.

(See section 6 above for details of other grounds for challenging a will, for example, that it is invalid.) On the question of dependency, the class of people who can challenge a will is confined to those who might have expected something from an estate through their relationship with the deceased, but who have been left in need.

It is the *relationship* with the deceased, plus dependency on him or her, that gives a legal opportunity to make such a challenge.

8.1 Who can apply

In 1975 the Inheritance (Provision for Family and Dependants) Act was passed to ensure that a limited class of dependants of a deceased person – those with a legitimate expectation of receiving something on his death – could be provided for out of a deceased's estate.

8.1.1 Relationship with deceased plus dependency

The Act applies both

- where the rules on intestacy (see above) fail to provide for such a dependant, and
- where the deceased made a will which did not make any adequate provision for his dependants.

In either case an application can be made to the court.

8.1.2 Time limits

◆ **Note:** the application must be made within six months from the date of grant of representation to the personal representatives.

8.2 Gifts during the deceased's lifetime

The deceased may have given away assets during his lifetime precisely in an attempt to defeat the legitimate expectations of his family. Persons who received such gifts from the deceased less than six years before his death may have to return their value to the estate to meet claims under the Act.

8.3 Reasonable maintenance

When considering these applications, the court is not trying to decide what would have been a fair apportionment of the estate, nor whether it was unreasonable or unjust of the deceased not to have left something to one of the applicants. Instead, the court will consider objectively what is reasonable maintenance for the applicant, taking into account the size of the estate and the needs of the applicant.

8.4 The surviving spouse

Only the surviving spouse of the deceased may be entitled to more than reasonable maintenance. Other applicants – if successful – will get simply what is reasonable for their maintenance. This is a much more restrictive test.

Your estranged husband has left you nothing in his will even though he was a wealthy man. You have been advised to claim under the family provision scheme. You wonder how the courts assess the position of a widow in these circumstances.

The claim of the spouse is for such financial provision *as it would be reasonable for her to receive in all the circumstances* irrespective of what is required for her maintenance. If the estate is large she will be awarded substantially more than she needs to maintain herself – and is unlikely to get less than she would have received on divorce. If the marriage was a fairly long one she will probably get at least half the estate.

Apart from a surviving spouse, the following persons can apply to court under the Act: an ex-spouse, a child, a person who was supported by the deceased.

8.5 The ex-spouse

As the financial claims are likely to have been settled on divorce, it is only in very exceptional cases that an ex-spouse will get anything extra under the 1975 Act.

> *At the time of your divorce from your husband, you were running a very successful estate agency business. You opted for a 'clean break' settlement with him as your maintenance was met out of your own earnings. Since then, however, your business has had to be wound up. Your ex-husband has now died leaving his estate to his second wife and their children. You would like to make a claim on the estate.*

This is a situation where the court may well take the view that notwithstanding the divorce, your circumstances have altered in such a way as to entitle you to a share of the estate.

8.6 Children

A 'child of the deceased' includes an illegitimate child or a child adopted by the deceased.

'Reasonable provision' here will depend on the circumstances; a minor or young person may get the costs of completing education or training, if the deceased was paying for this during his lifetime, whereas an adult child who is able to earn, or is being adequately supported by a spouse, is unlikely to succeed in an application – even if help would be welcome (and even if the deceased failed to fulfil his financial responsibilities when the child was a minor).

If there are special circumstances even an able-bodied adult child may succeed, e.g. if (s)he gave up work to care for the deceased during illness, or ran the deceased's business unpaid.

A person treated by the deceased as his/her child, such as a stepchild, who was being supported by the deceased, is treated in the same way as a child by blood.

8.7 Persons who were supported by the deceased

Dependants of the deceased may include cohabitees, elderly relatives etc. In fact, any person who was receiving a degree of regular maintenance from the deceased, whether or not a relative and whether or not living in the deceased's household, could be eligible.

The most common situation here is where two people – e.g. friends, sisters, cohabitees – share a home and expenses, and the owner of the home dies without making provision for the survivor.

For the deceased to have provided rent-free accommodation is in itself a significant contribution towards maintenance, especially in the case of an OAP.

> *You lived together with your partner in his house. You took care of the house, and when your partner became disabled and frail, you nursed him devotedly for several years. His will gave the house to his children from an earlier marriage, with no provision for you. You have made a claim for maintenance out of the estate. Your partner's children argue that by your loving care you were in effect 'paying' for board and lodging received, i.e. that you were not a dependant but a contributor to the household.*

In a similar case, the court held that loving care and attention were not 'payment' for the claimant's board and lodging; and the surviving partner was therefore entitled to reasonable maintenance out of the estate.

◆ **Note:** 'maintenance' out of an estate could include a share in the home.

9. Protecting people who cannot look after themselves

The financial affairs of someone who has become incapable through age or illness can cause great anxiety to the relations. They may see bills being left unpaid or valuable assets being disposed of for a fraction of their value.

If the sick or elderly relative agrees, and if it is a matter of increasing forgetfulness, using a form from the bank to add another signatory to their bank account may solve the problem and means bills can be paid.

If the relative can be persuaded to give a power of attorney to someone to handle their affairs while, for example, they are ill or in hospital, problems can be dealt with by the appointed agent. Unfortunately, however, an ordinary power of attorney becomes ineffective if the donor loses mental capacity. The law has provided for this by introducing 'enduring power of attorney' (see section 9.1 below).

If, as is often the case, the relative's increasing incapacity is accompanied by suspicion and paranoia, it may be difficult to persuade them to sign over any powers of authorization to those who wish to protect them. In such a case it may be necessary to apply to the Court of Protection to act as their statutory guardian (see DIRECTORY). An enduring power of attorney, if obtained in advance when mental capacity is still present, avoids these problems.

Living wills

An adult of full mental capacity may direct that particular medical procedures, including life-saving ones, should not be used on him at a time in the future, a so-called 'living will'.

Such documents are currently being made available by certain organizations, including the Voluntary Euthanasia Society and the Terence Higgins Trust. A patient's refusal to give consent to treatment may be effective, even if it was expressed at an earlier time, before he became unable to express that refusal. Such a document will have legal force, although there may be difficulties about proving that the document still represents the patient's wishes in the circumstances which have arisen. The document cannot, however, legally authorize active steps to terminate life.

English law is unclear about the validity of the prior appointment of a proxy decision-maker with power to refuse consent to treatment on a patient's behalf. An enduring power of attorney (see below) can only authorize dealing with the patient's property and other affairs, not his health.

Most US states accept and regulate advance directives of this kind, as do some jurisdictions in Australia and Canada. Problems have arisen about defining the 'trigger event' activating such an authorization, and about ensuring that it can be revoked if the patient changes his mind.

9.1 Enduring powers of attorney

Provision has been made in law for an enduring power of attorney which becomes operable on incapacity.

Your elderly father has for many years collected military medals, and his collection is now valuable. He also owns his own home. You are concerned that he is losing concentration and is becoming forgetful. You often have to deal with letters threatening to cut off his electricity for unpaid bills.

If your father will sign a form authorizing his bank to accept your signature on his cheques, you will be able to pay his bills without troubling him (see section 9 above).

In order to ensure that at least he does not sign away rights to his property or enter into other deals, you should arrange for your father to sign an enduring power of attorney to protect him from his vulnerability. This power of attorney is on a prescribed form which incorporates an explanation of its effect (see section 9.1.1 immediately below).

If your father sells his medals or makes other deals when he has become actually incapable of understanding a transaction, the deals will be invalid if those who dealt with him knew of his incapacity. The fairness of any contract will also be a significant factor. However, whether the transactions could be set aside by the courts would naturally depend on whether the dealers could be traced.

9.1.1 Procedures for an enduring power of attorney

The enduring power of attorney need not be drawn up by a solicitor but it is sensible to take legal advice.

(a) It must be signed by the donor on a prescribed form (obtainable from law stationers) which incorporates an explanation of its effect to the signatory.
(b) The signature of the person receiving the power of attorney is also required.
(c) Each signature must be witnessed – not necessarily by the same witness.
(d) When it is needed, the document must be registered in the Court of Protection.
(e) Next of kin must be informed prior to registration, since they could be affected by the use of the document.

◆ **Note:** the document becomes effective only when the incapacity actually materializes and the registration procedures have been complied with. It remains effective until the donor's death, unless he revokes it when he has regained the ability to deal with his own affairs. It is advisable to sign an enduring power of attorney when you make a will.

9.1.2 Court Receiver

If someone has become so mentally impaired that he or she is not in a position to sign an enduring power of attorney, a receiver can be appointed by the Court of Protection to administer his or her property (see chapter on *The Legal System*, section 11, for further details.

9.2 Appointing a guardian

If you have minor children, the appointment of a guardian should always be considered. You should then decide whether the guardian is to be appointed to act as such

- jointly with the surviving parent, or
- only after the death of both parents.

9.2.1 Who can appoint a guardian

The *mother* of a child can appoint another person to be guardian to the child after her death. If she was married to the child's father at the time of the birth, the guardian will act jointly with the father after her death – unless she specifies that the guardian should only act after the father's death.

The *father* of a child has the right to appoint a person to be guardian to the child only if

(a) he was married to the child's mother at the time of the child's birth; or
(b) he was given 'parental responsibility' for the child by a court order; or
(c) he entered into a 'parental responsibility agreement' with the child's mother in statutory form (see chapter on *Children*).

Unless the father specifies that the guardian's appointment is to take effect only after the death of both parents, the guardian appointed by the father will act jointly with the mother.

9.2.2 Appointment by will

If you are making a will, the appointment of a guardian should be made in the will, with the formalities prescribed for all wills as set out above (section 5.1). If you then change your mind and want to appoint someone else, you could do it by codicil.

> *You are a single man. You and your former girlfriend have a little boy. She made a will nominating you as guardian of the child in the event of her death. You parted and she married another man. You now learn that she has died and her mother is caring for your son. You tell the grandmother that you are the child's legal guardian but she disputes this. What is your position?*
>
> (1) Your girlfriend's will, including the nomination of you as guardian, is automatically revoked on her marriage (see section 6.4 above).
> (2) However, if you had entered into a parental responsibility agreement in the legal form, you would have become guardian of your son on her death. The agreement (unlike the will) is not revoked by her marriage. A parental responsibility agreement can only be revoked by a court of law.
> (3) Her husband, who is your little boy's stepfather, does *not* become a guardian on her death unless his wife had appointed him to this capacity.

As to legal aid, see section 4.1.3 above.

9.2.3 Informal appointment

If you do not wish to make a will, perhaps because you are satisfied with the statutory scheme for intestacy, or because you have insufficient assets to be worth the bother and expense, it is also possible to make an informal appointment of a guardian.

The only formalities required are that

(a) the appointment must be in writing
(b) it must be signed
(c) it must be dated.

There is no *legal* requirement for witnesses, but it may be a sensible precaution to have at least one witness to your signature, who, after seeing you sign, should write his usual signature below yours with his address and occupation.

The informal appointment can be revoked by

- a later will; or
- the destruction of the written appointment by the person making it; or
- a new informal appointment of a guardian by the mother or father.

9.3 Statutory wills for the mentally impaired

A person who lacks the understanding to make a valid will may still possess some property. The court can be asked under the Mental Health Act to make a will for the patient, in such terms as the patient might be expected to have intended if of sound mind.

DIRECTORY
Death – Before and After

Age Concern England (National Council on Ageing)
Astral House
1268 London Road
London SW16 4ER
Tel. 081 679 8000

The British Humanist Association
14 Lamb's Conduit Passage
London WC1R 4RH
Tel. 071 430 0908

Centre for Policy on Ageing (CPA)
25–31 Ironmonger Row
London EC1V 3QP
Tel. 071 253 1787

The Compassionate Friends
53 North Street
Bristol BS3 1EN
(Helpline) 0272 539639
(Admin)   0272 665202

Court of Protection
Stewart House
24 Kingsway
London WC2B 6JX
Tel. 071 269 7300

The Cremation Society of Great Britain
Brecon House
Albion Place
Maidstone
Kent ME14 5DZ
Tel. 0622 688292

Cruse – Bereavement Care
126 Sheen Road
Richmond
Surrey TW9 1UR
Tel. 081 940 4818

General Register Office
(England & Wales)
St Catherine's House
10 Kingsway
London WC2B 6JP
Tel. 071 242 0262

The Foundation for the Study of Infant Deaths
35 Belgrave Square
London SW1X 8QB
Tel. 071 235 0965
Cot Death Helpline 071 235 1721

Home Office
50 Queen Anne's Gate
London SW1H 9AT
Tel. 071 210 3000

National Association of Widows
54–57 Allison Street
Digbeth
Birmingham B5 5TH
Tel. 021 633 4663

National Association of Funeral Directors
618 Warwick Road
West Midlands B91 1AA
Tel. 021 711 1343

National Association of Memorial Masons
Crown Buildings
High Street
Aylesbury
Buckinghamshire HP20 1SL
Tel. 0296 434750

The National Secular Society
47 Theobald's Road
London WC1R 4RH
Tel. 071 404 3126

Overseas Registration Section
General Register Office
Trafalgar Road
Birkdale
Southport PR8 2HH
Tel. 051 471 4801

Terence Higgins Trust
52 Grays Inn Road
London WC1X 8LT
Tel. 071 831 0330

Voluntary Euthanasia Society
13 Prince of Wales Terrace
London W8 5PG
Tel. 071 937 7770

See also *Religious Organizations* on pages 96–97.

129

5. LANDLORDS AND THEIR TENANTS

Some of the most basic terms of English property law, such as 'freehold' and 'leasehold', go back to feudal times. Land, and the buildings on it, last longer than we ourselves do. Hence the need for formality in dealing with or 'conveying' property. Clearly, owning, dealing in, or renting property is quite different from owning, dealing in, or renting our other possessions. Moreover, buying a flat or house is usually the most expensive transaction we ever undertake and paying rent or a mortgage is usually the most expensive item in any budget.

However, despite the fact that property law dates back for centuries, it is not immune to change. It reflects the pressures of the times as does any other body of law. A recent example of such a change is the steady liberation of rented accommodation from the laws which were intended to give security to tenants. The driving force behind this legislation is a clear policy decision to encourage the private rental sector of the property market.

Other examples of policy decisions which have determined the present course of property law can easily be found: for instance, the 'Right to buy' legislation which allows tenants in the public sector to buy their own homes. This has much altered the position of local authorities as landlords.

The latest example is the law which gives long leaseholders the right to buy their freeholds. The law has only just come on to the statute book and we have – as yet – no certainty as to how it will work out in practice.

On the whole, these laws have been passed piecemeal to reflect very different political and ideological approaches to property-holding. At the same time, all the legislation has been superimposed on the system of landholding developed under the common law with its ancient roots.

Today, therefore, all common law property principles must be read as subject to overriding Acts of Parliament. For example, under common law, a tenant must leave the premises when a lease expires. So much of statute law, however, lays down requirements which a landlord must meet before he may recover his property from the tenant.

As a result of these and other factors, property law should be regarded as a job for experts. In this chapter, we focus on the landlord and tenant aspects of property law on the understanding that generally, when buying or selling property, persons seek help from their solicitor, chartered surveyor or licensed conveyancer.

Even in the field of landlord and tenant relationships, however, it cannot be over-emphasized that you are entering a minefield of legal complexity. If you are uncertain of your rights – whether as landlord or as tenant – you must seek informed advice.

In this chapter we look at

- some fundamental aspects of the landlord and tenant relationship
- covenants between landlord and tenant
- renting in the private sector

- public sector accommodation
- protection from harassment and eviction
- the resident landlord
- assignment and subletting
- death of a tenant
- buying a long leasehold
- managing agents and service charges
- buying the freehold
- extending your lease.

1. Some fundamental aspects of the landlord and tenant relationship

1.1 Similarity in diversity

There are all kinds of lease. They may cover business premises which might comprise several city blocks; council houses in the public sector; flats bought on long leases; private rented accommodation which could consist of no more than a bedsitter; vast agricultural estates or small-holdings.

However, all forms of lease have several factors in common which distinguish them from owning your own home. These factors also distinguish *leases* from *licences* which are generally a mere permission to use premises in a particular way or for a particular time.

1.2 Outlines of the relationship

(a) A lease always entails at least two parties: a landlord and a tenant. A landlord grants to the tenant the exclusive use of property on certain conditions and for a certain time. There can, of course, be joint tenants and joint landlords; or subtenants.

(b) A lease is thus bound by time limits: this can be for a week, a month, a year or a fixed period of years. The longer the period, say 999 years, the more the lease resembles absolute ownership. However, the obligations under the lease (called *covenants*, see section 4 below) – of both landlord and tenant – still have to be observed. Indeed, long leaseholds have been an effective way of ensuring that property is kept up. For example, we shall see that a restrictive covenant can only be negative (see chapter on *Neighbours*, section 7.1). You cannot have a restrictive covenant to paint the outside of your property. A landlord can, however, insist on such a term in your lease.

(c) An essential aspect of a lease is the need for exclusive possession. This is dealt with more fully (see section 1.5.2 below). In return for being granted possession for a fixed term or a periodic term, i.e. on a weekly, monthly or yearly basis, the tenant must pay rent to the landlord. Again the amount is infinitely variable, from a token amount for ground rent, say a peppercorn or £100 per annum on a long leasehold flat, to hundreds of pounds per week for furnished residential accommodation. Rent can also be in the form of services in exchange for accommodation.

(d) Both landlord and tenant are bound by a complex network of duties and obligations, called covenants, which are found in all leases. Some of these covenants may be implied by law (i.e. the law 'writes' the covenants into the lease, even if the parties fail to do so themselves; see section 2 below on *Covenants*).

(e) When a lease expires, the property which comprises the lease must go back or 'revert' to the landlord (a landlord is sometimes called a 'reversioner' for this reason).

131

(f) However, as we all know, the position of a tenant is very often protected by legislation so that instead of the property reverting to the landlord, the tenant of rented accommodation may be able to stay on. This is known as 'security of tenure' (see below, section 3.2).

(g) If a tenant on a long lease (i.e. for over 21 years) wishes to leave, he is usually entitled under the terms of the lease to sell the remainder of his lease. Under general circumstances, a landlord cannot reasonably refuse permission for the sale. For example, having bought a flat ten years ago on a 75-year lease, you could sell the 'remainder of the term', i.e. the 65 years of the lease which is still left to run. This sale for the remainder of the term of the lease is called an 'assignment' (see below, section 7). The person to whom the tenant sells will step into his or her shoes and be bound by the covenants of the lease. In the same way, a landlord can sell his reversion. The new landlord is then also bound to the tenant under the covenants of the lease. In other words, persons can change – whether as landlord or as tenant – but the lease continues. (In exceptional cases, there may be essentially personal covenants between landlord and tenant. These would not bind future landlords and tenants.)

(h) Freehold and leasehold property both comprise what is known as an 'estate in land'. This means that they are both forms of land ownership defined in terms of their duration. They are, in fact, the only forms of landholding available in law. Both, therefore, require written formalities in creating these estates and in dealing with them.

1.3 Distinction between leasehold and freehold property

Having outlined the common factors of a lease, it is easy to highlight the contrast with freehold property – also in outline.

- freehold property does not involve two parties; the property belongs to the owner, therefore there is no reversion
- it does not have time limits on its ownership
- rent is not payable.

1.4 Where the lines are blurred

1.4.1 Limitations on ownership

Nothing in property law is simple: while one can state in bald outline the clear distinction between outright ownership of one's own home and renting one's home or buying it on a long lease, there are nonetheless limitations on owning one's own home too. New legislation – to some extent – may lead to an erosion of the clear distinctions between the two forms of property holding with their roots in antiquity, namely freehold and leasehold.

(a) Absolute ownership is not what it seems; there are all sorts of limitations on the property; for example, it can be compulsorily acquired under the planning laws.

(b) The leasehold reform acts allow conversion to freehold status on certain conditions; in particular, under the Leasehold Reform Housing and Urban Development Act 1993 which came into force on 1 November 1993, long leaseholders may be able to acquire the freehold to their properties on certain conditions and in certain circumstances (see section 11 below).

(c) Even with freeholds, there may still be rights against the property in the form of easements or restrictive covenants (see chapter on *Neighbours*).

1.5 Distinction between lease and licence

Instead of leasing property, you may wish to use it – or only be allowed to use it – in a limited way. In other words, you will not be granted a lease by your landlord but only a licence.

A licence, like a lease, can entail the payment of rent and be limited in time. So how does a lease differ from a licence?

Among other differences, a licence does not usually give exclusive possession of property (see section 3.2.2 below).

1.5.1 The need for a clear distinction

The distinction between a lease and a licence is of critical importance. If you have a lease, you will generally have some form of protection – in particular, you may be able to stay on in the premises when your lease expires. Licensees never have this protection; they have to leave once their licence is revoked although the landlord must still get a court order for eviction. They are thus still protected against harassment and being unlawfully turned out of the premises (see section 5). In order to get round the protection which the law gives to tenants on a lease, where the landlord has to prove certain grounds before getting a court order (see section 3 below), landlords have resorted to the ruse of calling a lease 'a mere licence'. With the shift in legislation towards greater incentive for landlords and less security for their tenants, no doubt this ruse will be less used. Nonetheless, the distinction between a lease and a licence remains crucial.

1.5.2 Exclusive possession

A tenant has exclusive possession of the premises which are leased to him or her. A licensee generally does not.

> You are a single person occupying the double room of a flat in which there are two other single bedrooms. The 'landlord' made it clear when letting you into possession that if he can find a couple to take over the double bedroom, you will have to move into one of the single bedrooms. He now states that you are occupying the double bedroom under licence only. You wonder what your position is.

You are a mere licensee as you would not be able to assert a right to a double bedroom. The position might have been different if you occupied it with your boyfriend (see section 3.2.2 below).

1.5.3 Does it matter what your landlord calls your agreement?

The courts will look at the substance of the agreement and not at a label which the parties give to their agreement. There have been many attempts by landlords to get round the security-of-tenure provisions of the Rent Acts by calling their agreements with their tenants 'licences'. However, this has singularly failed to wash with the courts. Unfortunately, however, the lines between lease and licence can get blurred.

1.5.4 Other forms of licence

Other forms of licence exist even when an occupier of the premises may have exclusive possession. For example, in the public sector, local authorities may licence housing associations to allow persons into short term property (usually property earmarked for redevelopment) in exchange for rent. As the housing association is only a licensee, the temporary occupiers are also only licensees.

Accommodation may be provided rent free in return for the tenant providing services e.g. as caretaker. This can constitute a tenancy but very often it is a mere licence.

2. Covenants

◆ **Note:** Even if certain covenants are not written into the lease (although they usually will be), the landlord and the tenant are still obliged to perform them. They are covenants which the law will *imply* as duties in the landlord and tenant relationship. These covenants are considered to be so crucial that the lease would not be effective without them.

No other covenants are implied by law other than those listed below.

In general, express covenants (those written into the lease) still take precedence over implied ones – but not invariably (see section 2.1.4 below).

2.1 The landlord's implied covenants

2.1.1 Covenant for quiet enjoyment

This covenant generally applies to interruption of the physical use of the premises. The interruption must be substantial.

> *You have taken out a lease on one of the four flats in a converted house. Your flat is periodically flooded from the flat above. It transpires that the landlord has converted the flats so badly that the drains are totally inadequate for their purpose. The insurers tell you that you will have to leave your flat for several months for proper work on the drains to be put in hand.*

In such a situation, quite apart from the question of nuisance (see chapter on *Neighbours*), the courts would be entitled to hold that the landlord is in breach of his covenant for quiet enjoyment.

However, breach of a covenant for quiet enjoyment does not apply to mere temporary inconvenience.

> *You have taken out a lease on one of the four flats in a converted house. You have explained to the landlord that you are buying the flat because of its peaceful situation. The landlord lives on the premises and decides to convert two of the flats into a large family-sized flat for himself. There is noise and interruption which you find difficult for your working and living conditions. You wonder if he is in breach of his covenant for quiet enjoyment of your own property.*

The answer is probably 'no' – although in all such issues, it is a matter of fact and degree.

2.1.2 Covenant not to detract from the value of the lease

This covenant, spelled out in legal terms, is the covenant of the landlord 'not to derogate from his grant'. In effect, it means that a landlord cannot grant you a lease and then take action which in effect detracts from what he has already granted to you under your lease.

> *You have a flat with a terrace and an outside staircase leading to a communal garden. Your landlord intends to build a conservatory which would entail removing the staircase. You wonder what the position is.*

Your landlord may be in breach of his covenant by detracting from the value of the lease which he has granted to you. However, you would have to look at the terms of your lease very carefully to see what the landlord's rights might be.

2.1.3 Fitness of premises

In short term lettings, there is an implied covenant that the premises should be fit for habitation.

◆ **Note:** This covenant is overlaid with statutory law which imposes on the landlord an obligation to keep premises in repair. See also second paragraph of section 2.1.4 immediately below.

When buying a long leasehold, a lease will usually contain express terms on the landlord's duties to maintain the premises. The outlay is usually recovered from the long leaseholders under the lease in the form of service charges (see below, section 9).

2.1.4 When an implied covenant conflicts with a lease's express covenant

If there is a contradiction between a covenant implied by law and the express terms of your lease, then the express terms generally prevail. For instance, a landlord may wish to build a tarred roadway past your block of flats to serve his neighbouring block: if your lease allows him to reserve a right of way, then he will be allowed to do so – in other words, he can 'derogate from his grant' because the lease allows him to do so.

◆ **Note:** A landlord cannot contract out of certain repairing covenants, imposed by law. Where he is under a statutory duty to keep premises in repair, he will not be able to write a term into the lease which will allow him to evade his legal obligations.

A landlord cannot regain possession of residential accommodation without a court order unless the tenant leaves willingly.

2.2 The tenant's implied covenants

2.2.1 To pay the rent

There is usually an express clause in the lease concerning payment of rent. In any event, such a clause would be implied into a lease. If a tenant fails to pay rent, the landlord is usually entitled to seek possession of the premises.

◆ **Note:** we usually associate payment of rent with payment of money. However, premises can be let in exchange for services – for example, you could be the tenant of a cottage in the grounds of a club or a house in return for acting as caretaker.

2.2.2 To pay certain charges

(a) Long leases

In long leases (i.e. more than 21 years) a tenant may be obliged to pay service charges. This again is generally an express covenant found in most leases (see section 10 below).

(b) Short term lettings

If a short-term letting does not so expressly provide, it would generally be an implied term that the tenant should pay for ordinary outgoings such as electricity or gas bills.

It is axiomatic that the more specific a lease is with regard to such matters, the less scope there is for disagreement. For example, it is generally agreed that, in furnished lettings, the tenants should pay the council tax. That is still no reason, however, why the lease should not specify that the tenant is obliged to make this payment.

2.2.3 Not to 'commit waste'

As we have seen, a fundamental doctrine of landlord and tenant law is that the property 'reverts' to the freeholder when the lease expires. The tenant, therefore, is under a duty, implied by law, not to take any action which would diminish the value of the premises on their reversion to the landlord. For example, you may rent a cottage with wooded grounds on a long lease. You would be liable, as tenant, if you cut down the trees or demolished a wing of the cottage. Again, like so many matters in law, it is a matter of fact and degree. The actions described above are positive actions which are clearly harmful to the landlord's interests. But what if a tenant is merely neglectful or forgetful?

You go away for a Christmas break and omit to empty the water tanks. There is a sudden freeze, and you return to find the premises flooded after a thaw. Your landlord says that you are liable for the damage. You wonder what your position is.

The court will consider the terms of your lease and the type of your tenancy (for example, whether you are a weekly tenant or in the house for a longer term) as well as for how long you left the premises empty. The terms of the landlord's insurance policy will also be relevant. In one case, it was held that a two-day break during a very cold spell was not sufficient to make the tenant liable for ensuing damage.

2.2.4 To allow the landlord to enter the premises

It is reasonable that if a landlord is responsible for maintaining the premises and keeping them in repair, he should be allowed to view them to establish whether repairs are necessary. He should give the tenant reasonable notice of his intention to view the premises. However, in the case of an emergency, for example a power failure, the landlord should be allowed to enter without notice.

2.3 Other covenants usually found in leases – express terms

This section deals with some covenants which are often – but not always – expressly written into a lease. In any event, they will not be implied into a lease by law.

2.3.1 Covenants concerning use

Some leases will contain clauses which forbid the tenant to use the premises in a certain way. For example, a lease in a residential block of flats will usually have a covenant against using the flat for business purposes. This covenant is enforceable against anyone to whom the tenant may sell the flat, and is known as a covenant which touches and concerns the land.

2.3.2 Covenants controlling assignment

This is dealt with in section 7 below. In general terms, a landlord often insists that his permission should be sought and obtained before a tenant can let someone act as tenant in his or her stead.

2.3.3 Insurance

Leases generally provide that the landlord will insure the premises. In long leaseholds (i.e. over 21 years), the insurance premiums are usually recoverable from the tenants on a proportionate basis.

2.3.4 Terminating a tenancy

Leases usually contain clauses which allow a landlord to regain the premises in certain circumstances, for example, if a tenant fails to pay rent or uses the premises in breach of the user covenant. In legal terms, the lease is 'forfeited' and the landlord can 're-enter' – subject always to the laws which protect tenants against eviction (see below, section 5).

3. Renting in the private sector

This section applies to property which is let on a

- weekly
- fortnightly
- monthly or
- yearly basis

or for leases of less than 21 years.
(For leases of 21 years and over, see *Long leaseholds*, section 9 below.)

For many years now, the government has been anxious to promote private-sector lettings. It was felt that the main obstacle to developing the private rental market was the fact that landlords were reluctant to let their properties because of

- the difficulties in ensuring that tenants vacated their premises when their leases expired; and
- the difficulties in ensuring a market rent for their properties.

In other words, laws which had been passed to give protection to tenants militated against the private rental market.

Thus, in order to encourage landlords to let privately, new legislation was passed to enable landlords to recover their premises more easily.

Most importantly in this connection, a new form of rental was established – known as 'assured shorthold' – which gives tenants a very minimum of security. (This is dealt with below, see section 3.6.)

It remains to be seen whether these changes in the law will stimulate private sector lettings to the extent that is hoped.

◆ **Note of warning:** In general the law on private-sector lettings is a very complex area. It is difficult not only for the unwary but even for those who think they know their business! The courts resound to litigation between landlords and tenants locked in bitter dispute over their rights.

3.1 The Housing Act 1988

In 1988 a new Housing Act was passed which was intended to ease the landlords' position. This Act now determines private-sector lettings of residential accommodation after January 15 1989. Thus all new lettings, entered into after that date, are now governed by the Housing Act 1988.

These provisions co-exist with earlier legislation, in particular the Rent Act 1977, which had quite different policy goals: its concern was to protect the position of the tenant. However, this chapter focuses primarily on the current legislation as it applies to private-sector lettings after January 15 1989.

Under the Housing Act 1988, there are two types of tenancy:

- Assured tenancy
- Assured shorthold tenancy.

◆ **Note:** new rules have been introduced to streamline possession proceedings for these two types of tenancy. Under the new procedure, district judges will be able to grant a possession order without a court hearing, if the tenant is unlikely to have a defence (see section 3.7 below).

3.2 Some general principles

In order for there to be security of tenure of rented accommodation, certain basis rules must be applicable.

For protection, there must be a letting of a dwelling house as a separate dwelling;

- it must be let under a lease and not on a licence
- the tenant must be an individual, i.e. company lets are not protected
- the dwelling house must be occupied as the tenant's only or principal home
- it must not be a tenancy specifically excluded from protection by the Acts (holiday lettings, for example, are specifically excluded from protection).

All of these points will be dealt with below.

3.2.1 It must be a dwelling house let as a separate dwelling

The term 'dwelling house' has been given the widest interpretation. It must be a fixed abode where a tenant can sleep, cook and eat. These are considered the basic activities for which we use our living space. Thus 'dwelling house' covers, for example, a permanently moored boat.

3.2.2 What does 'let as a separate dwelling' mean?

The requirement that the accommodation is let as a separate dwelling means that each tenant must have exclusive possession of his or her living area.

To be a tenant, you must have exclusive possession of the premises which are let to you. It does not mean you have to rent a whole flat or a whole house. You can have exclusive possession of a single room, such as a bedsitter.

> *You have rented a room in a flat with your boyfriend. You have both signed an agreement with the landlord. You have a double room and there is one other single bedroom which is occupied by another tenant. You share the kitchen and bathroom with the other tenant and you all use the communal lounge.*

You and your boyfriend have exclusive possession of the double bedroom.

(a) Difficulties which can arise in practice

Problems frequently arise in regard to exclusive possession. As we have seen, a tenant can have exclusive use of a bedroom but the other areas of the house such as the kitchen or bathroom will be shared. (For the position where there is a resident landlord, see section 6 below.) There may be other arrangements with the landlord – for example, that he can require a tenant to move out of one room and into another. We are back to a problem we have encountered before, *viz.* is the letting a lease or a licence? (See above, section 1.5.2.) Hence the importance of ensuring that the agreement reflects the true position between landlord and tenant.

(b) Company lets

Company lets are excluded from the provisions of the Rent Acts, hence the regularity with which advertisements appear in newspapers stating that 'company lets only' will be accepted. The company rents the accommodation and its employee who lives there is a mere licensee.

3.2.3 Occupied as the only home or as a principal home

A tenant who has moved out of the dwelling house cannot claim protection of the Rent Acts. He or she is no longer occupying it as their principal home. However, protection is not withheld if an absence is short relative to the time which the tenant has lived in the premises. Again it becomes a matter of fact and degree.

> *You are a tenant of a flat in which you have lived for a number of years. Your employers send you abroad for three months. During this time, you do not sublet the flat and you continue to pay rent.*

You have not jeopardized your position with regard to protection vis-à-vis your landlord.

However, the flat must be your only, or your principal, home. A person cannot have two main homes. If you work in London during the week and live in a rented flat, returning to your country cottage at weekends, you will have to persuade the court that the rented flat represents your principal home.

3.2.4 Position on divorce

As part of a property settlement on divorce, a court can usually assign a lease or tenancy from one spouse to the other.

3.3 Encouraging private lettings under the Act

There were two particular aspects of the earlier landlord and tenant legislation which the 1988 Act addressed. The one concerned rent and the other concerned the type of tenancy (see section 3.6 below). The Act created two new types of tenancy, assured tenancy and assured shorthold tenancy; it also allowed a landlord to claim a market rent.

3.3.1 Rent

'Regulated' rents still apply to tenancies which came into existence before the 1988 Act. They were governed by the 'fair rent' procedure.

(a) The 'fair rent' procedure

Under earlier legislation, rent was registered as a 'fair rent' in a register maintained by the local authority. It was determined by various factors, such as location and type of accommodation. However, it was not a market rent and was not fixed according to whether or not there was a shortage of properties in the area. If either landlord or tenant regarded the level of rent as not 'fair', there was an appeal to the Rent Assessment Committee of the area. Its decision was final. Moreover, an application for an increase or decrease could be made only after two years from the last registration.

The 'fair rent' procedure was seen as a deterrent to private-sector lettings.

(b) The present procedure

Under the 1988 Act, with regard to an assured tenancy, a landlord can serve a notice, on a prescribed form, giving notice of a new rent. This notice can be served when the lease expires. Alternatively the lease itself can have included a term for a regular rent increase.

If the tenant refers the rent to a rent assessment committee, the committee must consider the rent the letting would get in an open market.

◆ **Note:** the tenant can only take the rent issue to the rent assessment committee when the lease expires.

Under an assured shorthold tenancy, a tenant's rent can also be increased and the tenant can take the matter to a rent assessment committee. The committee will only consider the rent if it is 'significantly higher' than the landlord ought to receive – in other words, if it is excessive.

3.4 Tenancies: regaining possession

As we have seen, there are two main types of tenancy under the 1988 Housing Act:

- an assured tenancy
- an assured shorthold tenancy.

The question of regaining possession of the premises depends on which type of tenancy exists.

3.4.1 An assured tenancy

(a) The notice

A landlord can only get possession if he obtains a court order. Under the Act, in general, a court cannot make a possession order unless the landlord has served a proper notice on the tenant as specified by the Act.

(b) Meeting the grounds for possession

The landlord can only obtain a court order for possession of a dwelling house under an assured tenancy, if he can prove one of 16 grounds specified in the Act. On grounds 1–8, the court must order possession. On grounds 8–16, on the other hand, the court must be satisfied that not only has the ground been proved but that it is *reasonable* to grant possession. In other words, on one of those grounds, the court *may* order possession.

3.5 The grounds

There are 16 grounds for obtaining possession.

Grounds 1–8: the court *must* order possession if the landlord proves one of them. There is no need to show 'reasonableness'.

3.5.1 Mandatory grounds

Ground 1:

- The landlord lived in the premises at some time as his principal home; or s/he desires to use it in this way at some future date.
- he or she gave notice to the tenant in writing at the beginning of the tenancy of an intention to return at some stage;
- and that landlord now wishes to return.

The landlord may be able to use this ground even if s/he wants to sell the house, provided it was previously used as his or her only or principal home.

Ground 1 also applies if someone acquires the property as an inheritance or as a gift from a landlord who already had a right to rely on this ground. It does not apply, however, to someone buying the property after the tenancy has already begun.

◆ **Note:** It can apply to the spouse of the landlord.

You and your wife let your only home when you were relocated by your firm. You inform the tenant in writing that it is your principal home and that you intend to return to live in it. Your wife is very unhappy with the relocation and wants to return home to live there with the children. You want to know what is your position.

On these facts, it would seem that the court would give you possession on ground 1.

Ground 2: A mortgagee of the property wishes to obtain possession in order to exercise its power of sale with vacant possession. Again, notice of the fact that the property was mortgaged should be given by the landlord to the tenant at the beginning of the tenancy.

◆ **Note:** If you buy a property on a mortgage and then let it to a tenant, you may be in breach of your mortgage agreement. You must get permission from your building society or bank before you let it out to others.

Ground 3: The house is usually used for holiday lettings. A landlord can let a property to the tenant who does not want it for a holiday for a fixed term of not exceeding eight months provided that

- the tenant was informed that it would be required for letting for four months (usually the summer period) after the eight-month period and
- the house had been let as a holiday home in the year before the tenancy began.

Ground 4: The premises belong to an educational institution which normally lets them to students, and which wants the premises back again for this purpose.

Ground 5: The premises are normally used by a minister of religion and they are required again for this purpose.

Ground 6: The landlord intends to demolish the whole or a substantial part of the dwelling and the works cannot be carried out with the tenant in occupation.

Ground 7: The person residing in the premises after the death of the tenant is not entitled to succeed to the tenancy (see below: *Death of a tenant*, section 8 and see also chapter on *Death – Before and After*).

Ground 8: There are arrears of rent which exceed

- 13 weeks if rent is payable weekly or fortnightly
- three months if rent is payable monthly
- three months if rent is payable quarterly
- three months if rent is payable yearly.

3.5.2 Discretionary grounds

In these cases the court may order possession on one of these grounds if it thinks it *reasonable* to do so:

Ground 9: Suitable alternative accommodation is available for the tenant if an order for possession is granted.

Ground 10: Some rent is in arrears but not for the length of time set out in ground 8 (above).

Ground 11: There is persistent delay in paying rent which is lawfully due.

Ground 12: There is a breach of the tenant's obligation.

Ground 13: There is deterioration of the property through the tenant's waste or neglect.

♦ **Note:** this ground applies not only to the premises occupied by the tenant but also to the common parts. It also applies if someone living with the tenant is responsible for the deterioration.

Ground 14: The tenant, or anyone residing with the tenant, has been a source of nuisance or annoyance to neighbouring occupiers.

Ground 15: The tenant, or anyone living with the tenant, damages the landlord's furniture.

Ground 16: The tenant was an employee of the landlord and the employment has come to an end.

3.6 Assured shorthold tenancy

This form of tenancy provides the tenant with virtually no protection. However, a landlord still has to apply to court for an order if a tenant does not leave willingly.

A landlord must be granted a court order if a tenant stays on after expiry of the tenancy provided that the conditions for an assured shorthold tenancy have been met. There is no need to prove any of the 16 grounds above.

3.6.1 The main elements

- the tenancy is a fixed term for at least six months;
- the landlord cannot bring the tenancy to an end before the six months expire;
- the tenant has received proper notice at the beginning of the tenancy, and this notice
  - (a) is in prescribed form
  - (b) is served at the beginning of the tenancy
  - (c) is served by the landlord on the tenant
  - (d) states that it is an assured shorthold tenancy.

3.6.2 Continuing the tenancy – no need for new notice

If the same landlord and tenant wish to continue on the same terms with reference to the same premises, there is no need to serve another notice. The assured shorthold tenancy continues.

3.6.3 Tenancies excluded from the Act

Certain tenancies are excluded from the provisions of the Act.

Several grounds are set out in the Housing Act 1988, of which the principal one concerns 'resident landlords' (see below, section 6).

Other grounds include

- holiday letting of the property
- the giving of services, rather than rent, in return for the accommodation. For example, you may occupy a flat rent-free in a block of flats in return for your services as a porter.

For protection of tenants, see also below, *Protection from harassment and eviction*, section 5).

3.7 Accelerated possession procedure

New rules came into force on November 1 1993 which deal with possession proceedings for assured and assured shorthold tenancies. The rules are intended to streamline possession proceedings in certain cases. They enable a judge to make a possession order on written application without necessarily requiring the parties to attend in court for a hearing.

◆ **Note:** the rules apply only to tenancies under the Housing Act 1988.

3.7.1 Assured tenancies

If a landlord wishes to recover possession of a dwelling house on grounds of

- landlord occupation
- former holiday occupation
- former student letting

or

- occupation by a minister of religion

and provided the tenant has been given proper notice, the landlord can file all the relevant information with the court together with his application for possession. The information required is stipulated in the rules and must be on a prescribed form. The landlord must also serve a copy on the tenant.

A tenant has 14 days in which to make a reply.

If there is no reply, the landlord may make a written request for a possession order.

If there is a reply the judge can

- make an order after considering the reply, or
- fix a day for a hearing.

3.7.2 Assured shorthold tenancies

The rules apply where a landlord intends to recover possession when the tenancy has come to an end.

◆ **Note:** The accelerated procedure can only be used to recover possession; it cannot be used if there is another action by the landlord against the tenant as well, for example for non-payment of rent.

4. Public sector accommodation

The local authorities' position as landlords has undergone dramatic changes in the past decade. Their powers in relation to planning and compulsory acquisition have remained largely the same; their duties to provide homes for the homeless and the needy have grown as the requirements of our changing society have to be met. However, the actual housing stock has been diminished through the 'right to buy' legislation and the current limitations on local government finance.

4.1 How housing is allocated

Each council allocates its rental property to persons who make application for a council house according to a set of criteria. Priority is given, for example, to an applicant who has spent a long time on the waiting list; to single-parent families; and to personal factors such as health or disability, etc. The position of priority for single mothers is currently being reviewed.

4.2 Security of tenure – exclusions

In general council tenants are secure tenants. There are certain exclusions however. Among them are:

(a) Licensees: short term lets where the land or properties are to be re-developed. Often this land is licensed to housing associations which, in turn, allow persons to occupy the property in the short-term. The agreement between council and housing association specifies that it is a licence only. As the housing association as 'landlord' only has a licence, so in turn is any one living in the property a licensee only.

(b) Employees: residential accommodation can be let as part of a contract of employment, e.g. to members of the police or fire services. The criterion is whether the accommodation is necessary for an employee to be able to carry out his duties properly. Tricky questions sometimes do arise concerning whether or not the accommodation was really needed for employment purposes. For example, the headmaster of a school may live as a tenant in a property owned by the local authority on or near school grounds. He may resist possession proceedings on the ground that he is a secure tenant; alternatively he might wish to exercise his right to buy the premises (see below, section 5.5).

(c) Certain others on short term lets, such as homeless persons or job seekers.

4.3 Tenant's rights

Under the Housing Acts, most tenants have security of tenure. This means the right to remain in the premises for the tenant's lifetime and also allows for succession after the death of a tenant (see below, section 7).

However, the Council can gain possession of premises from a secure tenant in certain circumstances and on certain grounds; moreover,

- the Council can only gain possession of its premises by court order
- the Council must persuade the court that it is a reasonable order for the court to make.

4.3.1 Among the grounds for possession are:

- rent arrears or some other breach of tenancy (for example, a council might prohibit the keeping of pets; a persistent breach of this condition, by keeping a dog in your flat, might result in a possession order)
- causing a nuisance or annoyance to other occupiers
- allowing the premises you occupy, or the common parts, to fall into a state of disrepair
- obtaining the tenancy by means of a false statement
- exchanging the tenancy and taking a premium on the exchange
- misconduct, where the tenant occupies the premises in connection with employment
- the premises were given to the tenant as a temporary measure while repairs were carried out to his or her usual dwelling house.

4.3.2 Suitable alternative accommodation

In the following cases, an order for possession is *mandatory* (i.e. the court must order possession) if one of the following grounds is established. However, the Council must show that it can offer suitable alternative accommodation once the order comes into effect. The grounds are that:

- the premises are overcrowded
- the landlord has to demolish or reconstruct the premises and cannot do so without gaining possession of them
- the whole estate is to be disposed of and vacant possession must first be obtained

- the tenant occupies the accommodation from a charity – such as a charitable housing trust – and the tenant no longer meets the purposes of the charity. For example, a charity might have been set up for tenants with mobility problems but you are now able to get about.

4.3.3 Some other categories for possession

There are certain cases where, in order to get possession, the Council must prove that

- it is reasonable to evict and
- suitable alternative accommodation is available.

In other words the court has a *discretionary* power; compare section 4.3.2 (above) where the court must order possession in the circumstances. In these cases

- the tenant was formerly an employee of the Council and the premises are needed for a new employee
- the premises were adapted for a person with a disability and let to a disabled person who no longer lives there.

Your husband was handicapped and was housed by the Council in accommodation adapted to meet his disability. He has since died and you have succeeded him to the tenancy (see below, section 8, Death of a tenant*). You have now been told that the Council requires the premises for someone else with a disability but can offer you accommodation elsewhere.*

Provided the accommodation is suitable, the Council has good grounds for possession in your case.

- In the case where one tenant succeeds to a tenancy, the premises may be too large for the present single occupant and the Council wishes to move him or her to smaller premises. For example, you and your late husband occupied a two-bedroomed council flat. You have succeeded to the tenancy. The Council may decide that a one-bedroomed flat now suffices for your purposes. See section 8.2 below, *Death of a tenant.*

4.3.4 'Suitable' alternative accommodation

The court will take into account all sorts of factors with regard to the accommodation such as present facilities, locality, and proximity to amenities. It will also take into account the needs of the tenant relating to age, employment etc.

4.4 Right to buy

Council tenants have a statutory right to buy their own houses. This far-reaching change of policy was introduced by the Housing Act 1980. It has since been amended and added to and, until recently, the current provisions were found in the Housing Act of 1985. However, there was another change in 1993. The right to buy has been given a further legislative boost by the Leasehold Reform, Housing and Urban Development Act 1993. This latest Act has introduced a 'rent to mortgages' scheme to assist even those on very low incomes to buy their own homes.

4.4.1 The basic rules

The basic rules covering the right to buy concern

- who qualifies

- how the price is calculated
- how the purchase will be financed.

(a) Qualifying tenants

The tenant must have been in occupation for two years.

(b) Price calculation

The price payable is the market price for the property less a discount which is calculated on the basis of how long the tenant has stayed in the house.

(c) Financing the purchase

Councils have been under a statutory duty to supply a mortgage to finance purchases under the Right to Buy legislation. Now this duty has been repealed. A 'rents to mortgages' scheme has been introduced in its stead – to assist in particular those tenants on low incomes. Very briefly, this allows a tenant to buy the property on a mortgage whereby the loan is calculated so that the outgoings are no more than the rent would have been had the tenancy continued.

5 Protection from harassment and eviction

There are two forms of protection against harassment and eviction:

- criminal prosecution
- civil action for damages.

5.1 Harassment

Harassment is any action likely to interfere with the peace or comfort of the residential occupier or any member of his or her family. It also covers withdrawal of services reasonably needed for residential occupation. In short, it is any action deliberately intended to make an occupier

- give up the property or
- feel too intimidated to exercise his or her legal rights.

Examples of harassment include

- changing the locks
- uttering threats and using other forms of intimidation
- disrupting basic services
- accumulating rubbish on the premises
- removing light bulbs in common parts.

◆ **Note:** victims of harassment can include licensees who do not have protection of Rent Acts. The statutory provisions apply to 'all lawful residential occupiers'.

Usually criminal prosecutions for harassment and/or eviction are brought by the local authority.

5.1.1 Civil actions for damages

The courts can award significant sums to tenants who have been unlawfully put out of their dwellings.

Damages can be obtained by tenants or by mere licensees if they prove unlawful eviction. Damages for their goods can also be claimed.

Awards can be very high to deter unscrupulous landlords. In one case a tenant who was forced out of her bedsitter was awarded £31,000 in compensation. Her landlord had woken her at 2 a.m. to ask for rent, played loud music, come into the bathroom when she was using it, and changed the locks when she fled the place. While she was out of the premises he then smashed her belongings.

5.1.2 Injunctions

A tenant can apply to court for an order (an *injunction*) to stop the unlawful action. If the landlord breaches the injunction, he is then liable for contempt of court.

5.1.3 The landlord's defences

The landlord has certain grounds on which to make a case that his action either was lawful or, in the case of reinstatement, is no longer unlawful.

(a) Reinstatement

If a landlord is being prosecuted for unlawful eviction or sued for civil damages, he can offer to reinstate the tenant so that the action against him will be dropped. However, merely handing a tenant a key to the front door is insufficient. There must be a genuine reinstatement to the premises together with the tenant's possessions. It is no use inviting a tenant to go back to a room which has been totally wrecked. Of course, it can be difficult to enforce such orders.

(b) Genuine belief that the tenant has left

A landlord might be able to persuade the court of his genuine belief that a tenant has left.

> *Your tenant has been several weeks in arrears with her rent. All attempts to contact her are to no avail. Other tenants tell you that her post is accumulating outside her corridor. You decide to change the lock to the flat and put her goods into storage. The tenant returns after a three-month trip abroad and threatens to sue for unlawful eviction.*

A court will take heed of your defence to her claim and assess its genuiness in the light of the circumstances of the case.

5.2 The need for a court order to evict

If premises are let as a dwelling and the tenancy comes to an end but the person occupying it continues living there, the owner can only recover possession by commencing court proceedings.

Court proceedings can begin only after a valid notice to quit has been given to the tenant and the period of the notice has expired. For the accelerated proceedings in assured and assured shorthold tenancies, see section 3.7 above.

5.2.1 Valid notice

A notice is valid if it is both

- in writing and
- given at least four weeks before the date on which it is to take effect.

5.2.2 Excluded licences or tenancies

There is no need for a court order where

- the occupier shares accommodation with a resident landlord or with a member of the landlord's family. They must live in the same premises. If your landlord only uses a room in your flat occasionally, you *share* the accommodation but he does not *live* there.
- it is a holiday let
- no rent is being paid.

However, even in these cases, although a court order is not required, reasonable notice is required and, most importantly, no harassment can be used to get the occupier out of the premises.

6. A resident landlord

A letting of a property cannot be on an 'assured tenancy' basis if the landlord is 'resident'. What is a *resident landlord* for the purposes of the 1988 Act?

6.1 Some general rules

(a) The property rented by you must be part of the same premises in which the landlord lives. Thus it could be a single flat in which you both live. Where the flat is part of a purpose-built block, your landlord can be resident if, for example, he has a long lease on a three-bedroomed flat. You rent one of the bedrooms and your landlord and his son occupy the other two rooms. It is perfectly clear that he is a 'resident' landlord for the purposes of the Act. Do take note, however: if you live in a flat in a purpose-built block of flats and your landlord lives in *another* flat in the same block, he is *not* a resident landlord.

(b) The landlord must be an individual (not a company).

(c) The landlord must have resided in the same building since the commencement of the tenancy.

(d) He must use the premises as his home.

(e) He must be in continuous residence. (This does not mean he has to stay there every night.)

> *You rent a flat in central London with two bedrooms – one of which the landlord reserves for himself. He has two homes, one of which is in the country about 100 miles away. He uses the London accommodation two nights per week. He wants you to quit the premises when your lease expires on the grounds that he is a resident landlord. You dispute this.*

> In all such cases, it is a matter of fact and degree. There is nothing to stop a landlord having two homes if he has reason to be in London on those particular nights of the week. He also does not have to be in residence every night of the week. If he reserved one room as an office, however, which was only occasionally used, you could assert that he is not a resident landlord.

6.1.1 If a 'resident landlord' sells the property

The new landlord can continue 'residence' provided

(a) he moves in within 28 days; or

(b) he notifies the tenant in writing of his intention to move in within 28 days and

(c) he moves in within six months.

6.1.2 If a resident landlord dies

A successor has two years in which to move in.

◆ **Note:** The issue of whether or not there is a 'resident' landlord also applies when tenants seek to buy their freehold (see below, section 11).

7. Assignment and sub-letting

7.1 What is an assignment?

A tenant may be allowed to 'assign' the whole of the remainder of his lease in the tenancy. For example, you rent a property on a three-year lease, and you spend a year living there. Your firm then wants to send you abroad for a year and you therefore wish to dispose of your lease for the remaining two-year period. You must establish whether you have a right to assign the property i.e. whether you can let another tenant take over in your stead.

7.1.1 Absolute prohibition

A lease may have an absolute prohibition against assignment by the tenant.

7.1.2 Qualified prohibition

More generally, a lease has a qualified prohibition against assignment, i.e. a tenant can assign with consent. The landlord's consent is not to be unreasonably withheld. Under the Landlord and Tenant Act of 1989, a landlord has to

- answer within a reasonable time
- give reasons why he withholds his consent
- give his reasons in writing.

You wish to assign the remainder of your two-year lease to a friend of yours. Your landlord has to consent to the assignment. She refuses her consent in writing within a couple of weeks on the grounds that your friend has failed to supply adequate references for credit-worthiness.

All a tenant's covenants have to be performed by a new tenant on an assignment. Therefore it is reasonable for a landlord to enquire whether the person you are proposing in your stead will be able to pay the rent.

7.1.3 Unreasonable withholding of consent

What happens if a landlord refuses consent to assign and the tenant thinks the refusal is being unreasonably withheld?

A tenant can apply to court for

(i) a declaration that the landlord's consent is being unreasonably withheld;
(ii) damages.

7.1.4 No prohibition against assignment

The lease may have no prohibition at all against assignment and, in such a case, a tenant is free to assign.

7.2 Enforcing covenants against others

A landlord, as we have seen, expects a tenant, on an assignment, to perform all the covenants in the lease which 'touch and concern' the land. These are the covenants which are intrinsic to a lease, for example, to pay rent, to pay service charges, to use the premises in accordance with the lease, and not to commit waste.

7.3 Sublettings

7.3.1 What is a subletting?

A subletting takes place if a tenant lets his property for less than the remainder of his term. For example, if you have a three-year lease and you go abroad for a year, and let your property for the year that you are away, that will be a subletting. The terms of the lease will generally contain a covenant which specifies whether or not there can be a subletting. If the lease does allow a sublet, it may be on terms; for example, the landlord's consent.

A subletting also applies to a let of part of your premises. For example, you rent a two-bedroomed flat and you only occupy one of those rooms. You decide to rent out the other room. Before doing so, you must check the terms of your lease; many residential leases contain an absolute prohibition against subletting part of the premises.

♦ **Note of warning:** If you assign your lease, you will lose assured tenancy protection. You will not be able to claim that the premises are your principal home once you cease to occupy it. The same warning must be borne in mind for a sublet – where it will be a matter of fact and degree. For instance, if you sublet the whole premises while you go on holiday or for a stint of work elsewhere, you may keep the protection. If you cease to occupy the premises, you will probably lose it. However, you will not lose your status if you sublet part only of the premises – provided your lease allows you to do so.

♦ **Note:** it is advisable to check with your insurers. Even if your landlord insures the building and the subtenant insures his or her possessions, you will want to insure your own possessions too – such as carpets, curtains, kitchen equipment etc.

8. Death of a tenant

8.1 Private sector

8.1.1 An assured tenant under the 1988 Act

(a) Periodic tenancy

If a tenant who rents property on a 'periodic' basis (i.e. from week to week, month to month or for some other period which is not fixed in advance – see *Fixed-term tenancy* below) then dies, leaving a spouse or cohabitee who lived with the tenant as husband or wife and who was resident at the time of the tenant's death, then the landlord has no grounds for possession. The survivor can continue to live in the premises.

♦ **Note:** there is one important proviso to the above right of succession. The tenant cannot himself or herself have been a successor. In other words, if you succeed to a tenancy as the widow or widower of a tenant, and then remarry, your second spouse cannot succeed to a periodic tenancy.

(b) Fixed-term tenancy

If a tenant dies who has a fixed-term tenancy (i.e. a tenancy for a period which has been fixed in advance, for example, for 15 years), and this has not expired, the balance of the tenancy will pass to a beneficiary either under a will or on an intestacy. The landlord cannot recover in these circumstances.

8.1.2 Different rules apply to tenancies under the Rent Act 1977

If the original tenant dies leaving a spouse or cohabitee in the house, that survivor will become a statutory tenant and can remain in occupation. If the original tenant dies and there is no surviving partner, another member of the tenant's family is entitled to an assured tenancy governed by the 1988 Act.

If the successor dies, a second successor can take over if

- he or she was a member of the family of both the original tenant and the first successor; and
- he or she lived with the first successor for at least two years prior to the first successor's death.

8.2 Public sector

If a tenant is a *secure* tenant in public sector accommodation, as most tenants generally are (see section 4 above), then family members can inherit on the death of a tenant.

8.2.1 Spouse (including cohabitee)

A wife or husband of the tenant (including a cohabitee) can inherit provided it was his or her main home.

8.2.2 Other members of the family

Another member of the family of the deceased tenant may succeed to the tenancy provided he or she had lived with the tenant for 12 months before the tenant died. There is no need to prove that they lived in only one property during those 12 months; for example, two brothers may occupy a council flat, and then arrange to exchange the flat for another one; shortly after they move the tenant dies. The brother can succeed him provided that their total residence together was for 12 months or more in council property.

A person cannot inherit from a council tenant where that tenant was already a successor.

9. Buying a long leasehold

For the purposes of landlord and tenant law a long leasehold is one that extends for 21 years or more.

As we have seen, a lease is a formal document which sets out the duties, rights, and obligations of both landlord and tenant.

9.1 Need for care

Great care must always be taken in purchasing a long leasehold. In fact, the complexities are such that, although in some ways you are buying something 'less' than a freehold, you are also buying something 'more' than a freehold in other ways. You are bound to a landlord by terms, obligations and duties specified in your lease. These can be onerous.

You are committed to paying service charges which may increase with great rapidity. Your decisions are no longer your own – not only with regard to the fact that you now have a landlord. You also have to take into account the wishes and needs of all the other long leaseholders. For example, a decision can be taken by the other tenants that the whole block needs repainting. This will cost something in the region of £100,000. You might prefer to spend your share of that sum in renewing the carpets in your own flat. You may find yourself short of money and not wish to spend anything at all – nonetheless, you will be bound to pay your contribution.

9.2 Maintenance and management

When buying a long leasehold, a lease will usually contain express terms on the landlord's duties to maintain the premises. The outlay is usually recovered from the long leaseholders under the lease (see section 10, *Managing agents and service charges* below).

This is one of the areas in landlord and tenant law which generates much heat. Lessees have suffered on three counts:

- Their landlords have neglected their premises.
- Their landlords have charged exorbitant amounts for necessary works.
- The managing agents do not fulfil their tasks.
- The landlords have carried out unnecessary works.

9.2.1 Neglect of premises

Blocks of flats were sometimes allowed to fall into disrepair. A landlord might have appointed managing agents who did not perform their duties properly. What were tenants to do? Under the Landlord and Tenant Act 1987, the courts are allowed to appoint a manager to carry out repairs and to collect the money to do so.

9.2.2 Service charges – control

Service charges are amounts payable for 'services, repairs, maintenance or insurance or the landlord's costs of management'.

With regard to those charges

(a) the landlord is not supposed to make a profit;
(b) they must be reasonably incurred; lessees can refuse to pay excessive amounts;
(c) when building work in excess of £50 per flat or £1,000 per block is to be carried out, two estimates must be obtained. A residents' association must be shown the estimates;
(d) service charges cannot be recovered after 18 months unless there has been proper notice;
(e) a residents' association is entitled to request copies of the estimates and of management accounts. (For a fuller discussion, see below, section 10.)

9.2.3 Repossessions

Particular care needs to be taken when acquiring repossessed property on long leasehold. Has the landlord gone bankrupt? Who is acting in his stead? Against whom can you enforce the maintenance covenants? How can you establish the level of service charges? Who is paying the insurance?

Do seek professional advice on all these counts, exercising your own discretion, too, on whether the answers you receive satisfy you enough to go ahead with the purchase. The attraction of repossessed property is that it is often so cheap – one doesn't want unexpected and unexplained expense afterwards.

10. Managing agents and service charges

As we have seen, a problem of the leasehold system is that landlords do not always carry out their duties.

▶ **Remember:** many landlords, of course, see that the premises are well managed. Their tenants receive an annual bill for service charges which are kept to a reasonable level. Their managing agents, if there are such appointed, carry out their duties efficiently.

However, difficulties do arise in practice, as we all know. Legislation has endeavoured, in piecemeal fashion, to deal with these problems.

One of the difficulties is that service charges and managing agents' fees can be out of line with apparent requirements. In other words, long leaseholders feel that they are being taken advantage of. Another difficulty is that managing agents are appointed by the landlord but paid for by the tenants; this could entail conflicts of interest.

10.1 Appointment of managing agent

Under the Landlord and Tenant Act 1987, a tenants' association may serve a notice on the landlord asking to be consulted on the appointment of a managing agent. The landlord has to reply to such a notice by giving

(a) the name of the person he intends appointing;
(b) a list of the duties which the landlord intends the managing agent to fulfil on his behalf;
(c) an opportunity for the association to make their comments on the appointment.

10.1.1 Employment of managing agent

A residents' association is entitled to serve a notice on a landlord concerning a managing agent who is already being employed for their premises. The landlord has to reply stating the obligations which the agent is carrying out on his behalf; and giving a reasonable period for the association to comment on the manner in which the agent has been discharging those obligations and whether it is desirable that he should continue to do so.

10.1.2 Code of conduct for managing agents

The Leasehold Reform Housing and Urban Development Act 1993 gives the Secretary of State authority to approve a code of conduct to promote 'desirable practices' in the management of residential property. Among other matters, the code should provide for

(a) resolving disputes between landlord and tenant;
(b) ensuring competitive tendering for works in connection with the property;
(c) administering money paid for service charges.

The standards which will be set by the code are also relevant to determining whether management is 'efficient and effective' if a management audit is carried out (see below, section 10.2).

10.1.3 Failing to comply with the code

However, if a manager fails to comply with the code, this will not, of itself, make him or her liable for any proceedings. Such failure can be used in evidence, however,

- if proceedings arise and
- the failure is relevant to the question in dispute.

10.2 Management audit

The Act also makes provision for a management audit. If two-thirds of the qualifying tenants agree, they can appoint a surveyor or accountant to carry out an audit to determine whether

- there is efficient and effective management and
- their service charges are 'being applied in an efficient and effective manner'.

10.2.1 'Qualifying' tenants

Tenants can qualify for the purposes of appointing an auditor if they

- have a long lease and
- pay service charges.

10.2.2 Costs

The tenants will have to pay for the costs of the audit. Furthermore, if the landlord incurs costs in making copies of documents etc. available to the auditor, the landlord is 'not precluded' (as the Act primly puts it) from recouping these costs from the service charges.

10.2.3 Service charges – need to inform

The management audit provisions follow on earlier legislation which provide for the need to inform tenants of their service charges. Under the Landlord and Tenant Acts 1985 and 1987, tenants are entitled to

- be informed of how the figure for the service charge is reached
- inspect accounts and receipts
- be consulted concerning major works which cost over £1,000 or £50 per flat multiplied by the number of flats – whichever is the greater
- be shown at least two estimates of the works
- be certain that their service charges are held in trust.

11. Buying the freehold

New legislation enables tenants to buy their freehold. Under earlier legislation (in particular, the Leasehold Reform Act 1967) only tenants of houses on long leaseholds at low rateable values could buy their freehold. Now, it is possible for tenants of flats – as well as of houses – to buy the freehold. Owners of houses of high rateable value are also enabled to purchase their freeholds. This is known as enfranchisement.

11.1 Long leaseholds – flat dwellers

Under the Leasehold Reform Housing and Urban Development Act 1993, which came into force in November 1993, long leaseholders who qualify will be able to acquire the freehold to their properties on certain conditions. This is a group action. However, individual leaseholders who qualify will be able to renew their leases for a further 90 years (see below, section 12) – if they choose not to go in for enfranchisement.

There are certain features of the Act that are worth noting at the outset:

(a) It alters the relationship between landlord and tenant to a significant degree.
(b) The legislation is very complex and few of its provisions have yet been tested in the courts.
(c) For tenants who wish to buy the freehold, professional advice is essential:

- valuation advice must be obtained from surveyors or incorporated valuers
- legal advice must be sought on the mechanics of the purchase.

◆ **Note of warning:** there are as yet no experts in the field of enfranchisement – the Act is a wholly new field of legislation to both landlords and their tenants, as well as to their professional advisers.

11.2 General observations

Under the 1993 Act, leaseholders will have two basic rights subject to conditions: to club together to buy the freehold or to extend their individual leases.

Thus the Act has not done away with the leasehold system. Indeed the long leasehold form of property-holding might be strengthened by the Act, not weakened by it, as tenants who qualify now have the right to renew their leases for 90 years (see section 12 below).

◆ **Note of warning:** The Act is extremely complicated and there are already disagreements between experts as to the meaning and interpretation of certain of its terms.

The Department of Environment has issued a guide to the Act in the form of a booklet (see DIRECTORY: telephone number 071 276 3398). The booklet states that the DoE cannot give advice on individual cases but can answer general enquiries.

An independent advice agency – the Leasehold Enfranchisement Advisory Service – has been set up to give general basic information and initial advice on the workings of the new Act. It does not undertake individual casework. The agency is funded by the private sector and the DoE and publishes advisory material, as well as running seminars (see DIRECTORY).

11.3 Buying the freehold

For enfranchisement, both the tenant and the building must qualify. In other words, certain conditions have to be fulfilled before landlord and tenant can begin to enter into negotiations under the terms of the Act.

11.3.1 The qualifications

- At least two-thirds of the flats must be long leaseholds (more than 21 years at the time that the leases were granted)
- At least 90 per cent of the floor space of a block must be residential
- There must be low rent
- Fifty per cent of the leaseholders must have used the flat as their main residence for a year
- Two thirds of the residents must agree to make the purchase
- If a block is converted or has fewer than four flats there must be no resident landlord on the premises.

Long leasehold
As we have seen, a long leasehold is one that was granted for more than 21 years. However, that does not mean that the lease presently has to have 21 years or more to run.

In 1983, you bought a flat in a house converted into four flats. It was then on a 27-year lease and you acquired it very cheaply as it was regarded as a 'wasting asset'. The lease now only has 17 years to run. You want to know whether you qualify for enfranchisement.

The answer is 'yes' – provided that the other criteria are met, for example, that you bought the flat at a low rental and the other tenants wish to enfranchise too.

Moreover, the long lease does not have to have been first granted to you.

You acquired your flat from a man who was not the landlord. The freeholder had sold him 125-year leases of ten flats in the block to redevelop. He sold the flat to you on a 99-year lease. You want to know whether you are the qualifying tenant or whether this is the person who sold you the flat.

The answer is that you are the qualifying tenant – provided that the other stipulations are met.

Moreover the long lease does not have to have been granted to you alone.

You and your husband jointly own a flat in a block of flats. You want to know which one of you is the qualifying tenant.

The answer is that you together constitute the qualifying tenant.

11.3.2 The 'low' rent

You would be advised to seek professional advice to answer the question of whether or not your flat qualifies as a lease granted at a low rent.

11.3.3 Company-owned flats

There is nothing in the Act which defines a 'tenant' for the purpose of qualifying for enfranchisement. However

- a company cannot satisfy the residence test (see below)
- if either a tenant or a company owns two or more flats in the same building, then none of those flats can qualify for the purposes of calculating either the two-thirds or the residence test.

11.3.4 The residence qualification

At least fifty per cent of the tenants must have lived in their flats as their main home for

- the last year

or

- periods which total three years in the last ten.

You own a flat in London where you lived for two years from 1983 to 1985. You were then relocated to Birmingham for four years, i.e. until 1989. You then returned to London for a year before moving to Brussels on another assignment.

You have met the criteria for residence of having spent three years in the last ten in the flat as your main home.

11.3.5 Does the building qualify?

For a building to meet the enfranchisement qualifications

- there must be more than two flats in the building
- ninety per cent of the floor space is residential (this is intended to exclude buildings which are largely commercial with only some living accommodation)
- there are two-thirds or more qualifying tenants in your building.

Certain buildings are excluded altogether – for example a building on land held by the National Trust, or one with a resident landlord.

11.3.6 The valuation

Valuation is based upon the following:

Open market value of the building which is for enfranchisement: the value of the interests which the landlord holds in the property assuming that the tenants are not in the market to buy.

'*Marriage value*': extra value brought about by the fusion of the freehold and leasehold interests; these are considered to be worth more if they are to be owned by the same person.

Compensation: where your purchase would lower the value of your landlord's other property. For example, your landlord has converted two semi-detached houses into flats. He lives in one of the flats in House A. He might feel justified in asking compensation for a lowering in value of House A as a result of the tenants' purchase of House B.

11.3.7 If you fail to agree on a valuation

The valuation can be determined by a leasehold valuation tribunal.

11.3.8 The nominee purchaser

The tenants must appoint a nominee to act on their behalf to conduct the purchase.

11.3.9 Costs

The tenants will have to pay

- costs of their own professional advisers
- the landlord's reasonable costs including the costs of the landlord's professional advisers
- costs of setting up a company to run the block (if the residents form a company to act as the nominee purchaser (see section 11.3.8 above).

11.4 Buying the freehold outside the confines of the Act

The Act may encourage tenants and landlords to reach agreement on the purchase of the freehold without entering into its statutory complexities.

Once a landlord knows that the tenants' bargaining power has been increased by the Act and that they may be in a position to insist upon a sale, he may decide that it is in his best interests to proceed directly with the negotiations outside the confines of the Act. By the same token, tenants too may find it simpler to negotiate directly while knowing that they can have recourse to their rights under the Act if they need to.

12. Extending your lease

The 1993 Act allows tenants to enfranchise as we have seen above. However, it also gives tenants an additional right to extend their leases by 90 years. In fact, it is this right which may be more used by tenants who own flats on long leases. It is an individual right, not a group action. Immediately, the expenses are less and the complications are fewer. Moreover, tenants will be able to extend their leases for a further 90 years so that most tenants will own what in effect will be a perpetually renewable lease. Far from destroying the concept of leasehold property, therefore, the Act in certain ways has strengthened it. At the same time, the Act has done away with the anxiety of owning a lease which is a 'wasting asset' (i.e. as the years go by, the lease's term, and with it its value, diminishes).

12.1 To qualify for extension

You must have

- a lease for more than 21 years
- a lease at a low rent (for establishing a 'low rent' see advice in *Enfranchisement* above, section 11).

You must satisfy a residence requirement:

- you must have lived in the flat as your main or only home for three years or
- you must have lived there for a total of three years in the preceding ten.

12.2 Owning more than one flat

Unlike leasehold enfranchisement, you can own more than one flat in the block and can apply for an extension to all the flats which you own (in enfranchisement, if you own more than one flat, none qualifies for the purpose, see above, section 11).

12.3 Assessing the value of extending the lease on your flat

You should call in a professional valuer to give you a valuation of an extended lease on your flat. As you will have to give your landlord detailed information on your flat (see below, section 12.4.2), this information will have to include the price which you would be prepared to pay for the 90-year extension. You must also give your landlord or his agent access to the flat to make their own valuation.

12.4 Failure to agree on flat's value

If you and your landlord cannot agree on the price, you can apply to a leasehold valuation tribunal to set the price for you.

12.4.1 The basic procedure

You must serve a notice on your landlord. This is known as a section 42 notice.

12.4.2 The section 42 notice

The section 42 notice must contain certain basic information including the following:

- details of the flat
- details of the lease and why it qualifies for the 'low rent' provision
- residence details
- the price which you are prepared to pay
- the date by which you expect your landlord's response – it must be within two months after your notice.

12.4.3 The landlord's counter-notice

The landlord can accept some – but need not accept all (or any) of this information.

- he can put forward his own terms for negotiation
- he can deny that the tenant qualifies under the Act
- he can refuse to extend if he can show that he intends redeveloping the premises.

12.4.4 Failure to agree

If there is a failure to agree on price, we have seen that the matter can be referred to a leasehold valuation tribunal. If there is a refusal to accept the tenant's qualifications, however, a different tribunal will decide the outcome. This matter has to be referred to a county court.

12.5 Direct negotiations

As with enfranchisement, both landlord and tenant may decide that they can reach a better, and possibly more amicable, agreement outside the terms of the Act. They can therefore leave it to one side altogether and enter into direct negotiations to extend the term of the lease.

DIRECTORY
Landlords and their tenants

Architects and Surveyors Institute
St Mary House
15 St Mary Street
Chippenham
Wilts SN15 3JN
Tel. 0249 444505

British Property Federation
35 Catherine Place
London SW1E 6DY
Tel. 071 828 0111

Building Societies Association
3 Saville Row
London W1X 1AF
Tel. 071 437 0655

College of Estate Management
Whiteknights Park
Reading RG6 2AW
Tel. 0734 861101

Corporation of Estate Agents
PO Box 151
Gloucester GL19 3RY
Tel. 0452 840726

**Incorporated Association of Architects
and Surveyors**
Jubilee House
Billing Brook Road
Weston Favell
Northampton NN3 4NW
Tel. 0604 404121

**Incorporated Society of Valuers and
Auctioneers**
3 Cadogan Gate
London SW1X 0AS
Tel. 071 235 2283

Institute of Rent Officers
Musgrave House
Musgrave Row
Exeter EX4 3TW
Tel. 0392 72321

Lands Tribunal
48–49 Chancery Lane
London WC2A 1JR
Tel. 071 936 7200

**Leasehold Enfranchisement Advisory
Service** (LEAS)
6/8 Maddox Street
London W1R 9PN
Tel. 071 493 3116

**National Federation of Housing
Associations**
175 Gray's Inn Road
London WC1X 8UP
Tel. 071 278 6571

**National Federation of Housing
Cooperatives**
88 Old Street
London EC1V 9AX
Tel. 071 608 2494

National Association of Estate Agents
Arbon House
21 Jury Street
Warwick CV34 4EN
Tel. 0926 496800

National Tenants' Organisation
Voluntary Action Centre
51 Grove Road
Hounslow
Middlesex TW3 3PR
Tel. 081 690 8920

**Royal Institution of Chartered
Surveyors**
12 Great George Street
London SW1P 3AD
Tel. 071 222 7000

Small Landlords Association
28 Rosedene Avenue
London SW16 2JH
Tel. 081 769 5060

6. GOODS AND SERVICES

In a modern industrialized society, we are constantly acquiring, producing or selling products or services, weaving a web about us of legal rights and obligations. Each time you hop on a bus, buy a pint of milk or leave your suit at the cleaners, you are entering into contractual relationships which have legally enforceable consequences.

The law used to stand back as far as possible from contracts of all kinds, taking the view that it was up to each individual to negotiate terms and conditions in order to protect his or her position. In a mass age, this was increasingly seen as unfair, if not unworkable. The result is that today the law regulates the content of most types of contract, which have particular legal results whether the parties know of this or not at the time. At the same time, the need to prevent individuals being taken advantage of by those with greater muscle, or from being cheated by the dishonest, has created an ever-strengthening legal shield to protect the consumer from dangerous products, from being misled by false claims, from being taken advantage of financially, and so forth.

Even where this protective legislation exists, it is still up to individuals actively to protect themselves by taking precautions, reading the small print, shopping around where possible. This chapter is designed to help you to take such precautions; but, of course, also to tell you about your remedies if things go wrong. In most cases, tradesmen and retailers are honest and doing their best; if things go wrong, they will often respond to a complaint, in order to keep a customer happy, without the letter of the law having to be invoked.

Unfortunately, of course, things do not always run smoothly. When this is the case, complain first, clearly and promptly. If this is unsuccessful, in the last resort you can sue the supplier; if you use the small claims procedure this will not be very expensive, but it is often less trouble and quicker to complain to the trading standards department of your local authority. Sometimes, you may be able to seek recourse through the trade association, if there is one, which if it cannot mediate the dispute may run an arbitration scheme. With some disputes, e.g. with a building society or insurance company, there may be an Ombudsman who will investigate your complaint.

Suing will always be a last resort – but obtaining legal advice should not be. This can be obtained from a solicitor, a citizen's advice centre or law centre. You may be able to get government assistance for legal fees (legal aid), if your financial situation is within the limits laid down for this. Ask a solicitor who does legal aid work for a fixed fee interview or the Green Form Scheme, if you are worried about the expense (see also chapter on *The Legal System*).

In this chapter we look at some of the ways of acquiring goods or commissioning services which arise most frequently in our lives:

- purchase and sale of goods – foodstuffs, clothing, cars etc.
- other ways of acquiring goods, e.g. hire-purchase, lease or contracts for services, from plumbers to aromatherapists or estate agents

- dangerous products
- dealing with financial institutions – your bank and your insurance company
- credit and debt
- contracts for pleasure – eating or drinking out, going on holiday in this country or abroad, buying timeshares.

1. A matter of contract

Whenever you enter into an arrangement to obtain goods or services you are entering into a contract.

No writing may exist, indeed words may not even be exchanged, as when you get on a bus and tender the correct fare. But it is a contract which you have entered into nevertheless and if something goes wrong – such as an accident – your rights and obligations can be legally enforced.

What distinguishes a contract from other situations with legal consequences is that in a contract there are mutual reciprocal rights and obligations. Both parties give something and receive something.

1.1 Written contracts

If there is a written contract, it will define your legal position whether you read it or not. Terms and conditions, a ticket or receipt can be part of the contract and define your position under it, even if you have not signed it. Only if someone is unable to read or understand a document, and is misled about its nature, may he or she be able to escape the consequences of signing.

1.1.1 Signing a contract

If you are asked to sign something, read it first or ask to take it away to study. Once it bears your signature you will be bound by its terms whether or not you knew of them. Never sign a blank or partially completed form.

Contracts for large items such as computer systems or cars often contain an 'entire contract' clause which states that the documents contain the entire agreement between the parties. If you agree to this clause you will lose your right to complain of any misrepresentation that was made to you *before* you signed.

> *You buy a car that has only done about 10,000 miles. Before you buy it, you point out to the salesman that one bumper is badly dented. He says that it will be no problem to replace it when you bring the car in for its first service. When you do bring the car in, the salesman has left the firm and the person in his place says that you accepted the car with all its defects. You have signed an agreement with an 'entire contract' clause.*

In this case, you have no redress. However, even if you had not signed such a contract, it may be difficult to enforce an oral representation of this sort, so always make a note of what is said and ask the salesperson to sign it too.

1.2 Unwritten contracts

There is no legal requirement that contracts should be in writing; contracts are equally enforceable in law whether written or oral. Most of our day-to-day contracts are oral – as when you buy goods in a shop. In fact, it is not even necessary that words should be exchanged at all, as when you buy a ticket from an automatic vending machine at a car park or Underground station. Contracts can also be partly oral and partly in writing.

1.2.1 Being bound by terms

Few of us read printed clauses on the back of a ticket, or a reference to terms and conditions in a timetable or insurance policy (often available in a separate document). However, these terms still bind us in the event of a mishap.

Sometimes there are no written terms and the absence of writing may mean difficulties in proof. In certain contracts, terms can be implied by law, i.e. 'written' into the contract (see section 2.1 below).

1.3 Who has rights under contract

◆ **Note:** only persons who are actually parties to the contract can rely on its terms even as modified by the law. If you buy a food processor which does not work, you have contractual rights against the shop. If you give the item to your niece as a wedding present, she has no rights at all under the contract because she was not one of the parties to the sale.

If her gift food processor doesn't work, she can either ask you to enforce the shop's obligation under the contract, or find out whether the shop will ignore the legal position and deal direct with her in the interests of goodwill. If however, the food processor is actually dangerous, she can complain to the shop under the Consumer Protection Act – whether or not she was a party to the contract. She can also complain to her local trading standards officer. If she is injured by the dangerous defect she could sue the manufacturer for damages (see also section 6).

1.4 Non-contractual arrangements

Not all transactions are contractual, of course.

> *A friend asks you to drive him to the airport to catch a flight to New York. You oversleep and turn up late so that he misses his plane.*

Because you were doing him a favour and not receiving payment, there are no legal consequences, although he could have sued a taxi firm in similar circumstances.

A minor does not incur contractual obligations except in limited circumstances. For the purposes of the law of contract, a minor is anyone aged under 18.

> *A 17-year-old neighbour, a trainee hairdresser, offers to do your hair for a fee, with disastrous results.*

You can't sue her for breach of contract, although you might have been able to sue an adult in the same circumstances. Probably you could sue for negligence (see *Accidents* chapter), if you could prove negligence on her part. On the other hand, you may have voluntarily assumed the risk by going to her in the first instance.

2. Consumer protection

In theory, there is 'freedom of contract' in English law. This means that, generally speaking, people can put any terms they like into their contracts which the other side is then free either to accept or to reject.

In reality, of course, consumers are often faced with a choice of accepting fixed terms which a business may offer, or going without. You cannot usually negotiate all the terms of your car insurance, but are offered a printed policy, take it or leave it; and if you leave it you will probably find other companies' policies are very similar.

The law has intervened to correct the balance in favour of consumers in certain ways.

First, where it considers conduct sufficiently grave, it has made wrongful trading a crime. So it imposes *criminal* penalties if a trader attempts to mislead potential customers. The system of prosecuting businesses for false trade descriptions (see section 2.2 below) is an example. Other examples would be traders who serve short weights or measures, or dealers trying to pass themselves off as private sellers.

It is the responsibility of Trading Standards Officers, who are employees of local councils, to enforce these laws and prosecute traders committing offences. All breaches of trading standards should be reported to them (see your telephone book for your local trading standards office – sometimes called the Consumer Protection Department – of your local authority). Should you have to report an offence against the food safety provisions, you should contact your local authority Environmental Health Officer.

Second, the law writes certain terms into contracts for the sale of goods – whether or not the parties to the contract have included them. In other words, the law intervenes directly in the contractual process. See section 2.1 below.

2.1 Implied terms

The law defines the content of the parties' respective rights and obligations, by providing that all contracts of a particular type automatically *include* certain terms – such as that all goods sold should be fit for their purpose and of merchantable quality (see section 3.1.1 below). Or, in a sale of goods contract, the law will always imply a term that the goods which are sold will match a sample provided by the seller.

It also decrees that certain terms are automatically *excluded* from all contracts ('excluded terms') – for example, under the Unfair Contract Terms Act, a business is not allowed, by law, to exclude its liability for causing death or personal injury.

These implied terms are generally not enforced by criminal sanctions. However, a consumer can bring a legal action in the civil courts for damages where a trader has breached a term – for instance, where a shopkeeper has sold a faulty product.

English law has reacted in a piecemeal way to consumer problems so that the law on the subject is intricate.

2.2 Criminal sanctions

In the interests of protecting consumers against unfair trading practices, there are many regulations in effect prescribing codes of conduct for business. Breaches give rise to criminal liability rather than to compensation claims, but the possibility of being reported to trading standards officers may lead a trader to mend his ways and offer an informal settlement (see further, section 6.4 below).

2.3 European law

EC law has already had an impact on consumer law in this country, most noticeably in imposing uniform liability for dangerous goods in the interests of consumer safety (see *Dangerous products*, section 6 below).

3. Sale of goods

The first principle is that whenever and wherever one buys goods, there is a contract with the seller. This is so whether one signs a long complicated document or signs nothing. There is a contract even when the transaction is conducted without words – as when you choose goods off a shelf and pay for them at a supermarket till.

Under a contract of sale both buyer and seller have defined rights and obligations.

3.1 Obligations of seller

The seller's obligations are more complex than the buyer's, because the law implies (see section 2.1 above) certain terms in every contract of sale.

3.1.1 Merchantable quality and fitness for purpose

Every seller is responsible for the quality of the goods which he or she sells. In the words of the law, goods must be of 'merchantable quality'. The goods must also be fit for their normal purpose.

Of course, these two conditions can overlap: for example, a hair dryer with a faulty thermostat which overheats is not of merchantable quality and is not fit for its purpose. Sometimes, however, these two conditions can be distinguished: if you ask a dealer for a word processor with some computer functions and he sells you a dedicated WP with no computing power, the WP is merchantable but is not fit for your purposes.

On the other hand, inadequate instructions can make a product unmerchantable, e.g. a lawn weedkiller with instructions which do not make it clear that it will scorch the grass if applied in hot weather.

Even if a purchase is in good working order, it will not be of merchantable quality if it is bought new but its appearance is impaired, e.g. it is dented or scratched, *unless* it is sold as 'shopsoiled' or 'imperfect'.

From January 1995, under a new Act, goods will no longer have to be of 'merchantable quality' but will have to meet a condition of 'satisfactory quality'. This means that a reasonable person would regard the goods as satisfactory, taking into account appearance and finish, safety, durability and the absence of minor defects, as well as fitness for the usual purpose for which the goods are being bought.

Although a buyer of a secondhand car cannot complain that it is not of merchantable quality just because it needs certain repairs, it is a criminal offence to sell a car in an unroadworthy condition.

> You bought a car which had done only 5,000 miles from a dealer, and you had to replace a hub cap. You are now very upset to discover that the brakes are defective.

> With regard to the brakes, the dealer is in breach of his contractual duty to provide you with a car of 'merchantable quality'. He has also committed a criminal offence. However, with regard to a replacement hub cap, it is not unreasonable for the purchaser to have to make some replacements in a secondhand car – even a 'nearly new' one. See also the chapter on *Motoring*.

A shop cannot get out of its legal obligations by putting an exemption clause in the contract. Equally, displaying notices such as 'No refunds or returns' will not exempt a shop if it sells unmerchantable goods.

You bought an electric toaster at a sale at a reduced price. Sale goods were advertised as being on a 'no returns' basis. The toaster simply does not work and you ask the shop to take it back.

The fact that the goods were bought for a reduced price or during a sale is irrelevant. You are entitled to your money back, or a working replacement if you would prefer it.

If you tell the seller you are buying goods for a specific purpose, they must be fit for that purpose. Thus a computer shop is in breach of this obligation if it sells you software which is incompatible with your hardware when you had asked for advice, or which cannot produce spreadsheets if this is what you said you needed.

◆ **Note:** Goods must be fit for their purpose *provided* that they are subjected to normal use.

You buy a kitchen knife, which has a laser-edge guaranteed for five years. You use it as a screwdriver and the point breaks off.

It is doubtful whether using a kitchen knife as a screwdriver would be classed as normal use.

Goods are considered fit for their purpose if most consumers would be satisfied with the product. If you have a particular problem which you have not made clear at the time of purchase, you cannot claim that a product is not fit for its purpose when you find it unsatisfactory.

You suffer from an allergy to a particular chemical used in fabric conditioners. You use some conditioner in your washing machine and get dermatitis as a result.

If you failed to establish the ingredients at the time when you bought the conditioner, and if most consumers would not suffer from the same problem, you probably would not be able to ask the shop to take the package back or to refund you.

3.1.2 Goods must meet description

There is another obligation on the seller: The goods must also be *as described*.

You buy a scarf from your local boutique after having been told by the sales assistant that it is cashmere. Afterwards, you see the same scarf on display in a big department store as 'angora and wool mix'.

You are entitled to take the scarf back and ask for a refund. You would also be entitled to complain to your local trading officer of your local authority for breach of trading standards.

Goods are too often misdescribed; for example, a label on a packet may describe its contents as 'pure' fruit juice whereas they are actually water in which fruit pulp has been soaked.

Food manufacturers have been prosecuted under the Trade Descriptions Act for describing a product as 'tender chopped chicken breasts' and 'pure ground beef burgers' when they were composed of re-formed meat and soya.

There are cases that go the other way, of course. In one case, a seller of T-shirts bearing the logo of well-known companies such as Levi, Adidas and Reebok, was prosecuted. He was acquitted of applying a false trade description because the goods were sold beside a notice saying 'brand copies'. He also gave an oral explanation to buyers that the branded items would cost £12–£15. His T-shirts, although costing £1.99, were of reasonable quality and would wash well. As the public would not have been misled, he had committed no offence.

3.1.3 Seller must give title to goods

There is an implied term that the seller has the right to sell the goods. If you buy golf clubs at a car-boot sale, which subsequently turn out to be stolen and which are reclaimed by their owner, you are entitled to a full refund of the price from the seller – if you can trace him! (See also *Stolen Goods*, below, section 4.6.)

3.1.4 Seller must deliver in time

If you are not taking the goods with you at the time you buy, because they are to be delivered later, the seller is under a duty to deliver within a reasonable time. Otherwise he will be in breach of contract. If you want the goods by a particular date make sure you specify this at the time – preferably in writing. The seller is not entitled to deliver by instalments – unless that was agreed – if you buy a dining room suite he is in breach of contract if he delivers the table and then makes you wait several weeks for the chairs.

3.2 Obligations of the buyer

A buyer is obliged to pay the agreed price and to take the goods. So once you have agreed to buy, you cannot change your mind because you've spent more than you should have or seen something you like better in another shop. Even if you only paid a deposit and then try to get out of the contract, the seller would still be entitled to keep the deposit and possibly to claim the balance of the price as well.

If you are selling goods such as a car, it is risky to let the buyer take it away before paying you. You may have no remedy if he gives a false address and his cheque then bounces. Insist on receiving payment first, in cash, by bank draft, or a *printed* (not handwritten) building society cheque. A guide to selling or buying a used car is available from the Office of Fair Trading Publications Department, Field House, 15–25 Bream's Building, London EC4A 1PR – Tel. 071-269 8890. See also chapter on *Motoring*.

3.2.1 What if the price changes after the contract?

You order a three-piece suite from a furniture shop, to be covered in the fabric you choose from a catalogue in the shop. You are told the price is £1,500 and that delivery will take six to eight weeks. You pay the £1,500, but after a month the shop informs you that the factory has put its prices up and asks for an extra £200.

Unless you were told at the time of contracting that the price could be varied, you can insist that the shop bears the excess, or you can cancel the contract and claim compensation e.g. for the extra inconvenience you will suffer in not having the suite if you have to place a new order elsewhere.

◆ **Note:** Shops are entitled to charge more if you do not pay cash (e.g. by negotiating credit). However, shops must give clear notification of the fact by notices displayed at the entrance and at each till or checkout point (see below, section 7.3.1).

3.2.2 Paying in advance by credit card

If you have paid in advance but the goods are not received you would be protected if you paid by credit card – and could claim a refund from the credit card company. This only applies if the price was between £100 and £30,000; otherwise, if the seller goes bust after you have paid in advance, you may have only a claim in the liquidation. For example, a customer pays £600 by cheque for a pine bed; the shop then closes down. She cannot get a refund or the bed because the liquidator, who has to wind up the business, has to sell it to share the proceeds out among all the creditors, of which the unhappy customer is only one. It would not matter if the customer paid by cheque or in cash. However, paying by credit card protects you against such an event. If not paying by credit card take the goods with you or have them delivered as soon as possible – the same day if you can.

3.3 Buyer's remedies

Quite often when you complain to a shopkeeper about faulty merchandise, he or she may tell you to write to the manufacturer. However, remember that your contract is with the shopkeeper. It is for the shop to enforce its own rights against its supplier or manufacturer.

3.3.1 Getting a refund

If the goods are totally unusable or unsatisfactory from the start, a customer is entitled to a full refund.

You bought a clockwork train set for your grandchild's birthday. When the present was opened, it was immediately apparent that one carriage only had three wheels, and that the engine could not be wound up because the key did not fit. When you complain to the shopkeeper she tells you to write to the manufacturer.

Do not let the shopkeeper try and shelter behind the manufacturer. Your contract is with the shopkeeper, and not the manufacturer. You are entitled to pursue any claim against the shop itself. You are not obliged to accept a credit note for the broken toy nor are you obliged to accept a replacement, although this may be the most convenient course.

If you do take a replacement, in its turn the new model train set must satisfy all the requirements as to quality explained above.

3.3.2 Rejecting the goods

In certain circumstances, you may be said to have 'accepted' faulty goods. This will apply in particular if you do not act quickly in returning your purchase, or if you let the shop repair it.

You bought a new car. Three weeks after taking delivery, when the car had only done 142 miles, the engine seized up on the M1. In your view the car is clearly defective and not of merchantable quality, and you want to return it. The garage proprietor refuses to take it back and says that it can be repaired.

In a similar case, the court held that the buyer could not get his money back, because by keeping it for three weeks he had 'accepted' it under the contract. He was only entitled to have it repaired at the supplier's expense, plus compensation for getting stuck on the motorway.

When you take defective goods back to the shop and agree to let them repair them, you are also accepting the goods under the contract. You will lose your right to claim a refund if the repairs don't cure the problems.

If you do reject the goods and tell the seller so immediately (confirm this in writing), you are not bound to return them – it is the seller's responsibility to repossess. Often, though, customers are quite willing to return portable goods to the shops from which they were bought. In any event, do not use them while you are waiting for them to be collected or are intending to return them.

3.3.3 Manufacturer's guarantee

If there is a guarantee from the factory, it may give you additional rights against the manufacturer, but these will not necessarily be worth pursuing e.g. if you have to pay the costs of packaging the goods and returning them. Unless the goods are actually dangerous, you may have difficulty in legally enforcing the terms of a guarantee, if the manufacturer's response is unsatisfactory.

▶ **Remember:** The existence of such a guarantee in no way reduces the scope of your rights against the shop with whom you actually dealt.

3.3.4 Buyer needs to act promptly

If you do have any complaint, you must act quickly or you may be taken to have accepted the goods (see section 3.3.2 above). In that case you will have lost the right to a refund, although you may still be entitled to a rebate on the price and compensation for loss.

4. Other ways of acquiring goods

4.1 Mail order

You have the same rights as any buyer when you order goods by post, but it may be harder to enforce those rights. Keep a copy of all relevant data – the ad, the journal and the date on which it appeared, all correspondence, and the counterfoil of your cheque or postal order as proof of payment. It is always safer not to pay money in advance if possible.

4.2 Hire purchase and hire

It is important that you check precisely who the seller is. When you buy goods on HP or under a conditional sale agreement, the supplier of the goods is not, technically, the seller; the finance company is, and it is primarily against them that your rights will have to be enforced. You may also have rights against the dealer if you relied on assurances by his staff about the quality of the goods. In practice the finance company and the supplier may have arranged that the latter will deal with your complaints, but in law your rights are against the finance company.

When you hire goods (e.g. a digger to excavate a garden pond) or buy them on HP, you have similar rights in respect of the goods hired as a buyer has, as far as quality is concerned. The goods must be as described and fit for their purpose (see section 3.1 above). If you hire a TV set you do not lose your right to reject the set and end the contract, even if you let the hire company have a go at repairing it (as a buyer this would prevent you cancelling the contract of sale, see section 3.3.2 above).

4.3 Part exchange

You have the same rights as any buyer paying in full in money when the deal includes a trade-in, e.g. when your old cooker or car is taken in part exchange.

4.4 Auction sales

Land and many types of goods are bought at auctions, and on the whole the law is the same for all, from the valuable fine art auction houses to sales of livestock in the country.

4.4.1 Making the contract

Once the bid has been accepted by the auctioneer and his hammer falls, a contract is formed. The seller of the 'lot' is legally obliged to give it to the successful bidder, who is legally obliged to pay the price to the auctioneer. Even in the case of land no formal written contract is necessary but there must be a written memorandum of the sale after the auction.

4.4.2 Misdescriptions

A potential buyer should always take the opportunity to inspect the property or the 'lot' in which he is interested, before the auction takes place. In the case of buildings, have a survey carried out and make mortgage arrangements *before* the auction. You are nevertheless entitled to expect an accurate description of property or goods in the auctioneer's catalogue. The conditions of sale usually exclude liability for terms implied by law into other sales, but they cannot unreasonably exclude liability for misdescriptions. The position is the same even if the misdescription is an oral statement by the auctioneer during the sale. If the goods were misdescribed, the buyer should act promptly to reject the goods and claim back the price. The lapse of even a few days may mean you have accepted them, and although you can claim compensation you are then stuck with the contract.

4.4.3 Reserve price

The conditions of sale should also make it clear whether the seller has fixed a minimum price, and whether the seller can bid against potential purchasers as a way of encouraging higher offers.

4.4.4 The buyer and the auctioneer

The auctioneer is the agent of the seller, and receives a commission on the sale. The price must be paid to the auctioneer (who can sue for it), but apart from this the contract is made between the seller of the goods and the successful bidder, and it is between them that any disputes about the property should be settled in the civil courts. But the auctioneer can be liable for selling goods which the seller had no right to dispose of, so if you bid for an antique table which turns out to have been stolen and it is subsequently reclaimed by its true owner, you can get damages from the auctioneer.

4.4.5 Criminal offences

Criminal legislation outlaws dealers' bidding rings (where dealers agree not to bid against each other, thus keeping bids low) but this is very difficult to prove. It is also an offence for anyone to conduct a mock auction.

4.5 Private sellers

Unlike commercial traders, a private seller can exclude liability for defects in quality, but is still required to ensure that goods satisfy their description. If your neighbour sells you a 'leather suitcase' you can complain if it isn't leather, but not if the lock is defective. (Note that traders who pretend to be private sellers are committing a criminal offence.)

4.6 Stolen goods

A particular danger with private sellers is that the goods may not be theirs to sell. If the car you bought privately turns out to be stolen and is reclaimed by the true owner, you can claim the full price from the seller, if you can find him.

4.6.1 Cars under HP agreements

In the case of cars – not other goods – which are wrongly sold by someone who had possession under an HP agreement, an innocent purchaser will not have to hand the car back to the HP seller, if unaware of this fact. See chapter on *Motoring*.

4.6.2 Stolen goods in open market

In 1993 two valuable paintings were stolen from Lincoln's Inn. A purchaser bought them for £145 at Bermondsey Market; he took them to Sotheby's who valued them at £65,000. The purchaser acquired ownership of the paintings because of an old rule, which provided that if goods were bought in good faith at a public, legally constituted market, the purchaser acquired good title and the original owner could not claim back the goods. The rule has been much criticized as protecting the disposal of stolen goods.

On November 3 1994, Parliament acted to abolish it. This will mean that wherever the goods are bought, the original owner will be able to reclaim them from the purchaser. However, until the Act comes into force, sales made in open market will still be governed by the old rule.

5. Services

In the ordinary course of life you enter into many contracts for services throughout the day – when you leave your suit at the drycleaners, take a cab, visit the hairdresser, hire an electrician or a music teacher, or leave your car at the garage to be serviced. In all such cases you are entering into a contract governed by the Supply of Goods and Services Act, even if the transaction is entirely oral and nothing is signed.

5.1 Obligations of supplier

Under the Act, certain terms are implied into a contract for services, in the same way that, as we have seen, certain terms are implied into a contract of sale for goods. See sections 2.1 and 3 above.

5.1.1 Reasonable competence

Where a contract has been entered into, the provider of the services is under a duty to carry out the services with reasonable care and skill. His or her lack of formal qualifications or experience is no excuse. However, a specialist must show a higher standard than a non-specialist.

> *You call in your builder/odd-job man to give you a hand with painting the kitchen walls. A kitchen tap springs a leak and he offers to repair it with disastrous results. Your kitchen is flooded.*

In similar circumstances, you could certainly have sued a firm of plumbers called in to repair the leak. However your rights against a decorator, who did not hold himself out as a specialist, are probably minimal.

You visit the hairdresser and ask her to apply a colouring tint to your hair. The hairdresser carelessly allows it to drip so that it stains your dress.

You can claim for cleaning, or if this is not possible, replacement (second-hand value) of the dress.

◆ **Note:** the legal requirements of reasonable care and skill only apply when the provider of the services is acting under a contract.

If your aunt offers out of affection for you to make up curtains from new fabric which you have purchased, you cannot sue her if the curtains are a failure. If you agreed to pay her for her services, however, you could claim compensation (if you are hard-hearted!) even though she is not in business as a curtain-maker.

If your hairdresser ruins your hairstyle, so that on your wedding day you look like a hedgehog, you can claim compensation. But you would have no claim just because you do not like the style or colour as long as it was competently done.

5.1.2 Reasonable charges

If a price for the services is not agreed at the time of entering into the contract, the customer is under a duty to pay no more than a reasonable charge. It is always sensible to ask for a fixed price in advance, especially for emergency or out-of-hours services. If you are asked to pay an exorbitant price you can make payment under protest and then reclaim the excess. What is a reasonable charge depends on the circumstances.

Sometimes you will be asked to pay part of the charge in advance – as a decorator, for example, may need to lay out money buying lining paper and paint before he can start the job. Only pay enough to cover the cost of the materials. If you pay in full in advance you have no bargaining counter left if things do not go according to plan.

5.1.3 Reasonable time for providing services

The provider of services is also under a duty to carry out the services within a reasonable time. A simple or routine job will naturally take less time than a specialized or complicated one; but it is wise to agree the date by which you expect the job to be done.

After a heavy storm, you ask a roofing firm to replace some loose tiles on your roof. After stripping off the loose tiles they cover the hole in the roof with polythene sheeting and then, despite repeated telephone calls, do not reappear to complete the job for ten days. During this time there are heavy rainfalls and rain gets in under the polythene. The walls below are stained and furniture and carpets damaged.

You are entitled to compensation for the damage. You should also call in another firm to complete the repairs so as to prevent further damage.

You will also be entitled to compensation if the provider of the service fails to turn up at all; for example if a wedding photographer failed to attend the wedding.

5.2 Excluding liability

You may be asked to sign a form which contains a clause limiting or excluding a firm's liability, or there may be a notice on their premises to the same effect, e.g. 'Cars Parked at Owner's Risk' in a parking garage; or in a drycleaners', 'No liability is accepted for belts, buckles or trimmings'. Such clauses are valid if they are fair and reasonable in the circumstances.

> *You take an entire film of photographs at your daughter's graduation. The photographic shop accepts the film on the basis that their liability is limited to the cost of a replacement film. They lose the film.*

You are entitled to say the exclusion clause is unreasonable and therefore ineffective. If however they had made it clear when accepting the film that when a higher charge is paid they accept full responsibility, the exemption on the normal charge contract would be reasonable as you would then have had a choice.

If the firm or its employees are grossly negligent it is unlikely an exemption clause will enable them to avoid liability.

> *You take a two-piece suit to the cleaners for the removal of a stain. The manager points out that they cannot guarantee that the stain will be completely removed, which you accept. There is also a notice in the shop stating 'While all care will be taken we cannot be held liable for loss or damage'. When you return to collect the suit you find that they have lost the jacket.*

The shop probably has a responsibility to pay for a replacement suit, despite the oral disclaimer and the notice.

Any notice or term in a contract which exempts or limits liability for death or personal injury resulting from negligence is totally ineffective in law.

> *You take your young son to a local fairground and give him a ride on a helterskelter. Due to its negligent maintenance or operation you are both flung out of the seats and are injured.*

Despite any exempting notices you can both sue for full compensation (see *Accidents* chapter).

5.2.1 Consumer protection

◆ **Note:** Many suppliers of services belong to trade associations which issue codes of practice. These lay down certain standards to which their members are expected to adhere. On the one hand, the extent to which an individual member abides by these standards is a voluntary matter and a dissatisfied customer would certainly not be able to enforce them by law. On the other hand, customers do have some recourse to a trade association where a member has provided a below-standard service. Certain trade associations also provide arbitration and complaint procedures.

It is a criminal offence to make in the course of trade or business, false statements about the nature or provision of services, such as if an unqualified masseur claims to be a fully trained physiotherapist. Inform the local trading standards officer, who may prosecute.

5.3 Supply of goods plus services

In many situations, a contract requires the provider of services to supply goods as well as do work, for example a central heating engineer may also supply the boiler which he is to instal.

In these situations the law implies certain requirements into the contract (unless expressly excluded by agreement between the client and supplier). The main requirement is that the materials or goods supplied will be fit for their purpose and of reasonable quality. In the case of building services to a house, a builder may be responsible even to *subsequent* owners for faulty workmanship or materials.

If the goods supplied are unsuitable or defective, you should act as soon as possible to make it clear that you are rejecting them and that you expect them to be replaced or repaired as appropriate.

In providing goods or material it is no defence for the provider of services to say that reasonable care and skill were used in selecting the goods (unless there is a reasonable exemption clause in the contract).

5.4 Sub-contractors

Sometimes your arrangement for services does not necessarily contemplate the supplier doing all the work himself. For example, a small jobbing builder doing a house conversion will subcontract out part of the work to plasterers, electricians, etc. Similarly most opticians do not make spectacle lenses personally but order them to be made by specialist firms. If the work is badly done or not in accordance with what you specified, the builder or optician cannot shelter behind the subcontractor with whom you never dealt. As far as you are concerned you dealt only with the builder or optician. Whether he does the work himself or through someone else is beside the point. He is liable to you whether or not he can claim reimbursement from the subcontractor.

5.5 Customer's duty to pay

The customer must pay the fee he agreed to pay, within a reasonable time. If no fee was agreed, he is obliged to pay a reasonable charge (see section 5.12 above). Providers of services, such as hoteliers or repairers, are usually entitled to keep any of your property in their possession until their charges are met. Even solicitors and accountants will have a right to keep your papers and can refuse to return them until paid.

If you pay in advance it is safest to do so by credit card. Then if the services are not provided (because, for example, the firm goes bust) you can still recover the money from the credit card company (provided the payment is between £100 and £30,000).

If you do not return within a reasonable time the firm may need to dispose of the goods to recoup their losses. Frequently there will be a notice to this effect on the premises, e.g. in shoe repairers' or electrical goods shops. If there is no such notice, the goods can only be sold if the contractor takes reasonable steps to trace the tardy customer to tell him of the impending sale in writing, giving enough time for the customer to turn up, pay the fee and collect his property. As to payment by credit card, see section 3.2.2 above.

The courts have held that a clause in the contract that you must pay the full price in spite of any set-off, is invalid because it is unreasonable. So if you feel you have a claim that the services are not satisfactory, you could deduct the shortfall from the due price.

5.6 Professional services

You only have a legitimate complaint about professional services on the basis of the quality of their services, not on the basis of the results. Doctors do not guarantee a cure, nor do solicitors guarantee a successful outcome to litigation. As long as they have acted with the degree of care and skill reasonably to be expected from their profession you cannot complain. On the other hand, there are cases of professional negligence where you have a good claim for compensation.

> *You buy a property to which access can only be obtained via a narrow lane. The solicitor acting for you in the purchase fails to discover that the lane actually forms part of the property of a neighbouring landowner, who begins to build on it, effectively blocking access.*

The solicitor is responsible for your damages.

An architect who designed a house extension failed to warn the client that the extension would block the neighbour's right to light. When the extension was built the client had to pay compensation to the neighbours but could sue his architect for reimbursement as the litigation was foreseeable. See also chapter on *Neighbours*.

Solicitors, doctors and other professionals will be insured against liability. Make a complaint as soon as possible after the event. If you get no satisfactory response you can complain to the supervising professional body (see DIRECTORY, and also see *Accidents* chapter, section 9).

In the case of surveyors, case law has established that they can in some circumstances be held liable to pay compensation not only to their own clients but also to some third parties.

> *You buy a house without instructing your own surveyor, but relying on a valuation report carried out by the surveyors instructed by the building society giving the mortgage (for which you have been charged by the building society). You subsequently discover that the surveyor negligently failed to notice that when the chimney breasts had been removed the chimneys remained inadequately supported, with consequent damage to the roof.*

You may be able to recover damages from the surveyor in negligence although you had no contract with him.

5.7 Estate agents

The vast majority of people selling or renting property use an estate agent although you can do so privately or through a property shop. If you do decide to use an estate agent, you will be entering into a contract for his or her services. As with any other contract for services, the estate agent must show reasonable care and skill in carrying out the duties contracted for.

> *Smith, who owns a house, asks estate agents to find him a company tenant for the house while he is working abroad. They put in as tenant Jones, who claims to be a senior employee of a cricket club, but who is in fact only a part-time barman at the club.*

If the estate agents had checked with the club they would have discovered the true position, but they failed to make such checks. When Jones falls into arrears with the rent, Smith can sue the estate agent for compensation.

5.7.1 Regulation by law

Although they deal with the largest and most important transaction in people's lives – the purchase and sale of property – estate agents are not required to have undergone any professional training, nor do they require a licence. Many do in fact have a surveyor's or auctioneer's qualification.

However, estate agents are subject to increasing regulation by law. The Director General of Fair Trading can act to prohibit an individual from continuing to act as an estate agent if the legal requirements are not observed. In particular, these require estate agents (a) to keep any of the customer's money which they receive in a separate deposit account, and to keep it insured; (b) to inform a potential customer (seller) of their itemized charges before any commitment is entered into, and (c) to disclose to both potential buyers and sellers whether they have any financial interest in the property. An individual can also be declared unfit to be an estate agent if he fails to inform the seller in writing about all offers from potential purchasers (e.g. because they did not agree to accept mortgage or insurance services from him), or if he misrepresents offers received.

5.7.2 Regulation by Association

The National Association of Estate Agents is open to persons practising as estate agents. It lays down rules of conduct and has a guarantee bonding scheme to protect clients' deposits. It also offers correspondence courses which lead to certificates at senior and junior levels (see DIRECTORY). There is also an Ombudsman for corporate estate agents (see DIRECTORY).

5.7.3 Commission

(a) *Effective cause*

If property is put up for sale through an estate agency, the agents are entitled to commission (usually 1–2% of the price) from the seller if they are the effective cause of the property being sold.

> *Brown, a prospective purchaser, is introduced to Green, the seller, by an estate agent, ABC, but Green rejects his offer as insufficient. Brown then receives details of the same property from another estate agent, DEF, and due to the efforts of DEF his subsequent offer is accepted by Green.*

Depending on Green's agreement with ABC, it would seem that only DEF is entitled to commission from Green, as DEF was the effective cause of the sale.

The estate agent must act with due care and skill, which includes telling the seller if another purchaser materializes who offers a higher price. If he or she fails to do so, no commission is payable.

The terms on which the estate agent will be appointed must be communicated to potential sellers in writing before they commit themselves to a particular firm. Scrutinize the terms carefully, and make sure that you do NOT agree to pay the estate agent commission

(a) if the property is sold through the efforts of another agent;
(b) if the property is sold entirely through your own independent initiative;
(c) if the sale falls through for whatever reason.

Avoid agreeing to pay commission merely on the 'introduction' of 'a ready, willing and able purchaser'. If possible, you should only agree to pay commission if the estate agent introduces a purchaser who completes the deal.

It is advisable to check also whether the agent's expenses, e.g. for advertising the property, are included in the commission, or whether they are payable in addition. Note that VAT will be payable on the commission. If the agent gets a discount from a newspaper for advertising he must pass this on to you. Estate agents must also tell you what services they will offer to potential purchasers of the property, and whether they have any financial interest in it.

(b) *Sole agency*

If you have given a 'sole agency', put a time limit on it so that if the property is not sold within, say, six or eight weeks, you can go to another firm. Before the time limit expires do not deal with another estate agent, or you could end up being liable to pay commission to both.

> *Ellen enters into a sole selling agreement for the sale of her bungalow with estate agents JKL. Without any involvement on their part she then sells the bungalow to her cousin Jack. Does she need to pay commission to the agency?*

> Because she gave JKL a sole agency, Ellen must pay JKL commission on the price she received from Jack.

The estate agent is obliged to explain (in terms laid down by Parliament) precisely what is meant by the phrases 'sole selling rights', 'sole agency', and 'ready, willing and able purchaser'.

5.7.4 Sign boards

You are entitled, as part of the contract with the estate agents, to stipulate that no 'For Sale' or 'Sold' boards should be erected on the property, although you could only get nominal damages if the agent puts up a board. If more than one board is put up, however, an estate agent may be committing a criminal offence.

5.7.5 Misdescriptions

The estate agent is the agent of the seller, and it is the seller who is responsible to the buyer if the estate agent has misdescribed the property.

Ask to see a draft of any advertisements before he publishes them or circulates details about your property. If you subsequently become aware of errors in those details, you must tell your conveyancer and ask him to inform the purchaser before the transaction is completed. The 1991 Property Misdescriptions Act extends criminal liability for misdescriptions to builders and property developers as well as to estate agents. It applies to both commercial and residential property. A private seller incurs no criminal liability under the Act for misdescriptions, although like all sellers he can of course be held liable for misdescription in the civil courts.

> *A firm of auctioneers and estate agents described a property in the auction particulars as 'a wine bar by day, cocktail lounge by night', with accompanying photograph. Graham successfully bids for the property, which he is buying as an investment, but then discovers that the local justices have revoked the liquor licence for the wine bar and the cocktail lounge.*

> Graham can withdraw from the contract with the seller and claim damages from him, as the particulars given had wrongly induced him to believe the wine bar was a going concern bringing in a regular rent. The seller may be able to claim a contribution from the estate agents if they were in breach of their contract with him; and they will also be criminally liable under the Property Misdescriptions Act.

5.7.6 Buying or renting through an estate agent

It is a criminal offence for an estate agent to apply a false description to goods or services he offers.

An estate agent is the agent of the seller, not of the buyer (he is paid by the seller). Agents usually disclaim liability for misdescriptions, so if you are a purchaser you should take steps to check all the particulars yourself; ideally, get your own survey done.

If you pay a deposit to the estate agent, to show that your offer to buy is serious, the estate agent is under a legal duty to keep it in a separate 'client account'. You will not normally get interest on it even if the transaction is prolonged, so keep the sum as small as possible. You can try and specify when making the payment that it is paid on condition that you will be entitled to interest.

Payment of such a deposit does not mean the sale is legally binding; until the contract is signed on both sides the seller can still accept a higher offer or withdraw the property from sale, and equally the buyer can change his mind and back out. You can enter into a 'lock-out' agreement with the seller, however. This means that the seller agrees not to enter into any other negotiations for a limited period. Because the estate agent is acting in the seller's interests, he must tell him of higher offers made by other potential purchasers. It is only when property is bought at auction that the sale is binding without a written contract, simply on the fall of the auctioneer's hammer.

If the seller has authorized the estate agent to receive the deposit on his behalf, the seller will be obliged to refund the deposit to the buyer if the estate agent becomes insolvent or misappropriates the money.

6. Dangerous products

When we shop, we anticipate with pleasure using the goods which we purchase. We seldom think that the goods we are buying may cause us grief! But misfortunes do occur, even with the best-run of shops and the most careful of customers. This is not necessarily because of a defect in the product, it may be due to faulty design.

If damage or injury does result, it is not only the person who contracted to acquire it who may suffer. Anyone who is hurt or whose property is damaged may be able to claim compensation from the manufacturer or supplier. Liability does not depend on the existence of a contractual relationship.

We could get sick or hurt when we buy something because

(a) it is inherently dangerous (e.g. contaminated food, or fireworks);
(b) it is wrongly used (e.g. a drug which is safe in a limited dosage but dangerous if an overdose is taken);
(c) it is badly marketed (e.g. it is misleadingly labelled, is supplied with inadequate instructions, or is in an unsafe container).

From these examples, we can see that sometimes blame for the accident can be laid at the door of the shop or manufacturer. Of course, sometimes our own lack of care can be blamed – for example, if we hurt ourselves on a new pair of scissors.

6.1 Having to prove negligence

Where a manufacturer or retailer could have foreseen that there was a chance that a consumer might get hurt, then those responsible for the article, its condition or its supply will be classified as negligent. If this can be proved, they will be liable to compensate the victims of the accident under common law. The product must have been used for its *intended* purpose and not for some other purpose – for example, using in a kitchen drain cleaner which is only meant to be used out of doors would disqualify the user from compensation.

A manufacturer of an article will also be liable for faulty components, even if these were manufactured by someone else, or for faulty packaging if it is this which caused the damage (e.g. an ill-fitting stopper on a container of dangerous chemicals).

Where the product is safe if used correctly, a manufacturer or supplier is responsible for providing adequate instructions or appropriate warnings.

> *You purchase hair dye and apply it to your hair in accordance with the printed instructions. It gives you dermatitis.*

> The manufacturers of the hair dye are liable in negligence for failing to include a warning that before use the product should first be tested on a small area of skin.

However, a victim of such an accident has to overcome the real difficulty of proving that it was the hair dye which was the cause of the dermatitis.

6.2 Difficulties in proving negligence

What has to be proved is that danger should have been known and guarded against. Difficulties in proving negligence have led to changes in the law in the interests of consumer safety, imposing liability without proof of fault – see section 6.3 below.

6.2.1 Who can be found liable?

It is not only manufacturers who can be held liable for negligence. Decided cases have fixed liability on negligent assemblers, distributors, installers, repairers and builders. Accordingly, a garage mechanic is liable to those injured if an accident results from his negligent repair of a car's brakes, and those who instal a lift negligently are responsible for a resulting accident to a passenger in the lift. In all such cases liability is based on fault and this will have to be proved, although in some cases it is obvious. It is no defence for the manufacturer to prove that the product was as safe as those of its competitors, because the common practice of the industry may itself be unsafe or negligent.

The courts have said that a manufacturer who discovers a danger in a product is negligent if he fails to recall the product from buyers, by appropriate action. We have all seen advertisements in the newspapers where manufacturers call for the return of certain products – even cars.

6.2.2 No liability for misuse

As we have seen, a manufacturer or supplier is not liable, of course, if an accident resulted from the product being wrongly used. If a doctor negligently prescribes an excessive dose of an otherwise safe drug, the manufacturers of the drug are not at fault. Similarly, while a hammer has the inherent potential to crush a thumb, it is not defective merely because it has done so. Misuse will reduce or even prevent damages for compensation.

In order to claim for negligence, then, fault must be established. A retailer or other seller is not negligent just because he or she sold the product.

6.2.3 Position of the seller

Against the seller, the remedies lie in the law of contract. A customer can sue the seller for breach of the obligation implied by law that goods shall be (a) of merchantable quality, (b) reasonably fit for their purpose and (c) in compliance with their description (see section 3 above). It is not necessary that there should have been a written contract – a verbal sale over the counter will also be treated as containing these terms. The seller's liability under these implied obligations does not depend on his being at fault, and he cannot escape these obligations by putting up notices that no responsibility is accepted for the goods' condition, safety, etc. But because this liability arises out of contract, it can be relied on by the buyer, and no-one else.

> You buy an electric lawnmower from B Ltd. Your son-in-law borrows the mower and receives an electric shock due to an electrical fault while it is being used, causing burns.

> He has no claim against B Ltd in contract, as he was not the purchaser of the article.

B Ltd may however, be liable in *negligence*, if they should have known the mower was defective; or under the Consumer Protection Act (see section 6.3 immediately below).

6.3 The Consumer Protection Act

Since March 1988, the limitations of both proof of negligence or proof of a contract have been largely made irrelevant by an Act of Parliament embodying a consumer protection Directive from the European Community.

The EC has also proposed that similar 'no fault liability' should be imposed on the suppliers of services. The proposal means that an injured person would be relieved of the burden of having to prove negligence on the part of the person who provided the service.

6.3.1 Who is liable under the Act?

Under this legislation, strict liability without proof of fault has been imposed on

- the manufacturer of a product (including the manufacturer of a component part);
- firms which market goods under their own label (whether or not they are the manufacturer), and
- the firm or person who first imported the goods into the European Community.

6.3.2 When is a product defective?

The Act gives consumers a right to claim compensation for injury or loss caused by defective products. It applies to products which must be found to be defective in the sense that their safety is not such as persons generally are entitled to expect.

Liability arises where the defect causes death, disease or other personal injury, or property damage exceeding £275 in value.

♦ **Note:** The Act does *not* apply to building construction and does not cover unprocessed food such as fruit, meat or fish. However, processed food ranks as a product.

The Act does not apply where the goods are simply shoddy or malfunctioning, such as an iron which fails to heat up, or where the only damage is done to the product itself, for example where the iron's temperature control fails so that the heating element in the iron melts. If the fault in the iron causes a fire which damages the kitchen, however, the consumer can rely on the Act. The dangerous defect can be in the packaging or in the instructions for use which accompany the product.

An injured consumer must establish that the injury was caused by a defect in the product. It was this hurdle that prevented compensation for children who alleged that they suffered brain damage as a result of receiving the pertussis (whooping cough) vaccine.

If it can be proved that the product had a safety defect, and that it caused the damage, it is not necessary to prove negligence or other faults in the design, product or quality control procedures.

However, it seems that manufacturers will not be liable for a latent danger which could not have been known at the time they supplied the product. It is not clear how much research they should have done before they can escape liability under this heading.

6.3.3 Exclusion clauses

The manufacturers, suppliers or own-branders whom the Act makes responsible to compensate consumers cannot escape from their liabilities by exclusion clauses in any notice or contract, or in any 'guarantee' given to the consumer. In fact, the legal effect of such a guarantee is not entirely clear in law.

Even if the guarantee does create a contract, it does not necessarily cover all the manufacturer's possible liability, for example it may guarantee free replacement parts but not free labour or refund of postage. If the damage caused by the defect is substantial, the victim is probably on more reliable ground if he insists on his rights under the Consumer Protection Act rather than confining himself to the 'guarantee'.

6.3.4 Liability of retailer

It will be noticed that the Consumer Protection Act does not impose a primary liability on the retailer who sold or hired out the defective product. The Act does oblige him to inform a consumer of the name of the manufacturer or importer, and he can be held liable himself if he does not.

Any claim under the Act must be made within three years from the time that the claimant knew of the damage or injury, the defect in the product and the identity of the producer, subject to a cut-off point of ten years from the date of the product's first being put into circulation. Where the consumer's own lack of care contributed to his loss or to his injuries, his damages will be reduced to reflect this.

6.4 Criminal liability

It should be noted that the law also imposes criminal penalties on those who manufacture or supply unsafe products, or whose products do not comply with the safety standards laid down by various sets of regulations. It is of great assistance to a claimant if a criminal prosecution is brought, because the court can award compensation when convicting and this is likely to be much speedier than bringing a civil case. It will also be of help in establishing the claim if civil compensation has to be sought.

Note that if a victim is injured by defective equipment at work, he can recover damages from his employer (who can in turn hold the manufacturer of the goods responsible) – see section 6.5 below on defective equipment at work. If an accident is due to defective products installed in a building, such as faulty electrical plugs, the builder is liable just as he is if the work is done negligently.

♦ **Note:** When purchasing, always remember to pay heed to the safety marks on products (for example, the *kitemark*). This means that the product has passed the British standards safety tests.

6.5 Defective equipment at work

An employee who is injured by equipment provided by his employer can claim damages from the employer under the Employers Liability (Defective Equipment) Act 1969. This right does not depend on the employer being at fault in choosing equipment or his knowledge of the defect.

The employer will be able to claim reimbursement from the manufacturer of the equipment.

7. Financial institutions

In almost all cases when you are contracting with financial institutions, you will be using their standard forms. Although you can shop around, there will not be major differences between the terms institutions use – which puts consumers in a disadvantageous 'take it or leave it' situation. If the standard terms do not suit, negotiate if you can.

7.1 You and your bank

When you open a bank account, you enter into a contract with the bank. Under this contract, the bank undertakes to honour cheques up to the amount deposited into an account or up to an agreed overdraft limit. A 'cash card' is an entitlement to draw cash from automatic vending machines also up to an agreed limit.

It is a simple fact that if we draw out more money than we are entitled to, and an account is overdrawn, we are in debt to the bank. Banks can charge compound interest on the debt. The bank can 'dishonour' (i.e. refuse to pay) your cheque if there are insufficient funds to meet it, or if the overdraft limit has been exceeded. A bank can also refuse to honour a cheque for any one of the following reasons:

- the cheque is incorrectly written, e.g. the words and figures differ, or it is undated
- the bank is notified of the death of the account-holder (which freezes the bank account until an executor takes control of it – see chapter on *Death – Before and After*)
- the cheque is 'stale', i.e. more than six months old, although technically a cheque is valid for six years.

♦ **Note:** To give someone a cheque knowing it will bounce because of insufficient funds is a criminal offence under the Theft Act.

7.1.1 Stopping a cheque

You have a right to stop any cheque by instructing your bank not to pay. You can phone your bank and explain that as a matter of urgency it should take your verbal instructions and that you will send in written confirmation later. Banks charge for putting a stop on a cheque.

You gave a plumber who did some emergency repairs a cheque for £45. You want to stop the cheque as you now discover he failed to fix the leak.

If he asked for your banker's card to guarantee the cheque for the amount, you will not be able to stop it.

You gave your brother-in-law a cheque, which he cashed immediately, just before the bank's closing time. You told your bank to stop the cheque first thing next morning.

As the cheque had already been paid out, the bank is entitled to debit your account with the amount of the cheque.

◆ **Note:** even if you have stopped a cheque you may still be liable on the underlying transaction. For example, you may owe the unpaid price for goods you have bought. So if you give a cheque in payment for a word processor you bought from a shop, but overnight realized that you could have bought it more cheaply from another dealer, you will still owe the shop the amount of the price, even though the bank will follow your instructions to stop the cheque.

If you lift a stop on a cheque but the bank in error fails to pay it, the bank is in breach of contract.

7.1.2 Crossed cheques

A person to whom a cheque is made out (the payee) can exchange the cheque for cash at the issuing bank. Crossing the cheque means it can only be paid through a bank account, which provides some safeguard against its falling into anyone else's hands. The best way to ensure that only the payee gets the money is to add the word 'only' after the payee's name, cross the cheque, and write the words 'not negotiable, a/c payee only' in the crossing. This is often printed on the cheque by the bank.

7.1.3 Lost or stolen cheques

If a cheque is lost or stolen, the bank should be informed immediately so that the account-holder is not responsible for cheques written out by anyone else. If the bank then happens to pay out on such a cheque it cannot debit the account. It also cannot debit your account if it pays out on altered or forged cheques, provided you did not draw the cheque in such a way as to facilitate forgery, e.g. by leaving large spaces between words when writing the amount.

Banks are liable to meet cheques presented by retailers even with forged signatures, where they have been supported by a cheque guarantee card.

The banks are presently trying out various methods to try to obviate fraud by giving customers 'smart' cheque cards.

7.1.4 Credit cards, cash cards and cheque guarantee cards

Cards should only be issued to customers who request them, or to replace or renew those previously issued. If you do not wish to use those functions on a card operated by a personal identification number (PIN) you can request that no such number be issued to you. If you have a PIN make sure you do not write it on the card or keep a note of it with the card, or you may have to bear the losses if the card is misused by some unauthorized person. Under the Consumer Credit Act you, the customer, are liable only up to £50, provided you were given details of a telephone number and an address to contact to report the loss or theft of a card. (If you were not given such contact details you are not liable at all.)

7.1.5 Bank's errors

Where the bank by mistake credits your account with more money than you have paid in (e.g. by confusing your account with that of another customer with the same name) you can refuse to pay the money back if you did not know of the mistake. You are not obliged to check your bank statements to see if they have overcredited you.

What if the bank dishonours a cheque which it should have paid? This can cause great embarrassment and inconvenience, because, for example, a creditor may insist on being paid in cash in future. Technically, it could be libel on the bank's part. In practice few of us are likely to take our bankers to court over a refusal to honour a cheque which should have been paid out.

A letter of explanation from the bank to the aggrieved creditor would probably help to smooth things over. An apology from the bank would be helpful too.

If you feel that your bank's wrongful refusal to honour a cheque may lead to a run on your credit, do take legal advice.

See also *Bank charges*, section 7.1.9 below.

7.1.6 Confidentiality

The bank is under a duty to keep confidential any information about your account.

> *You have an overdraft. An employee of your bank tries to telephone you at your place of work, and in the course of conversation with your boss, the bank clerk mentions that you have not paid instalments due to the bank, and that you may be betting on the horses. As a result of this conversation, you lose your job.*

> The bank is liable to you in damages for breach of its contractual duty of confidentiality.

There are certain exceptional circumstances where a bank may be obliged by law to disclose details of the account to the police or the Serious Frauds Office, for the purposes of their investigations into certain criminal offences such as major frauds, tax offences, insider dealing, proceeds of drug trafficking, or terrorist links. The bank is under no obligation to inform you about any such investigation.

The bank should not disclose information about you or your account, even to other companies in the same banking group, except with consent, but there is evidence that some banks may not always observe this – as the receipt of marketing material about other financial services shows.

7.1.7 The Banking Ombudsman

If you are unhappy about the way the bank is handling your account, and get no satisfaction from the manager of the branch or from the head office, you can complain to the Banking Ombudsman (see DIRECTORY).

He can award compensation of up to £100,000 (but cannot act where the aggrieved account-holder is a limited company). The bank will be bound by the Ombudsman's decision, but a customer who remains dissatisfied still has the option of taking legal action against his or her bank.

7.1.8 Traveller's cheques

Usually there are terms in the purchase conditions which exempt the bank issuing the traveller's cheques from liability to give a refund unless the purchaser has properly safeguarded the cheques. Where there is such a condition, purchasers can only obtain a refund for stolen or lost cheques if this occurred without their carelessness – which they would have to prove. Some institutions' traveller's cheques may not contain such a condition, in which case the purchaser's claim to a refund may be valid even if he or she was seriously at fault.

Some terms go further – for example, traveller's cheques can be issued with the condition that a refund will not be due if the purchaser gives the cheques to another person or company to keep. If you cautiously deposit your unused traveller's cheques in the hotel safe you would be in breach of such a condition!

Not all banks operate a bring-back service to redeem unused traveller's cheques. It makes financial sense to buy from a bank which does.

7.1.9 Bank charges

The Code of Banking Practice states that banks will notify customers of any changes in the terms and conditions, with reasonable notice of variations before such variations are applied.

It is up to each bank to take commercial decisions on the rates they charge or pay, as long as customers are given proper notice of this and changes are not made without due warning. You cannot complain to the Ombudsman if you were notified of the charges or rates; your only sanction is to move the account to another institution.

The Banking Code of Practice which e.g. requires banks to publicize their charges, also limits loss to £50 if a cash withdrawal card is used by someone else without the customer's negligence. However, some banks have rejected the Code as a basis for doing business.

Always check your bank statements. There are a growing number of complaints about errors, such as that banks mistakenly charge a higher rate of interest on overdrafts than agreed; they may debit payments twice due to computer error; may not show credits; or may delay direct debits.

7.2 You and your insurance company

An insurance policy is a contract between a policyholder and an insurance company under which, in return for a stipulated fee (a 'premium'), the company will pay a sum of money on the occurrence of a specified event, such as death, fire, burglary etc. Certain insurance policies are compulsory – for example, third party cover for car owners.

◆ **Take note:** Insurance contracts have several special features which do not occur in other types of contract.

7.2.1 What you can insure

You can only take out valid insurance to cover an eventuality where you stand to lose financially, technically called your 'insurable interest'. For example you cannot insure property unless you stand to lose if it is damaged or destroyed.

You run a successful desktop publishing business from a suite of offices which you rent. You have now formed your business into a limited liability company. However, you continue to insure the premises and assets of the business in your own personal name.

The insurance policy will be void as you no longer have an insurable interest in the premises and assets. You must take out a new policy and name the company as the policyholder.

Life insurance: the law assumes you have an insurable interest in your own life and that of your spouse, but you cannot insure the lives of others you care for – a favourite pop star, say, or even your own child. However, if your children are giving you financial support which will cease on their death, you will have an insurable interest in their lives, and can take out such insurance on their lives.

7.2.2 Telling the company everything

Generally, persons entering into contracts with others have no obligation to volunteer information about themselves or the subject matter of the contract to those others, although of course they must not actually misrepresent the facts. But insurance contracts are different. Every insurance contract carries with it the duty to make disclosure of all relevant facts. This means that not only must you give accurate and truthful answers to all questions in the proposal form, but you must in addition *volunteer* information which could be relevant. If you do not, the insurance company can treat the policy as void. In fact, if the proposal form states, as they usually do, that the answers form the basis of the contract, *all* information – even if not particularly relevant to the risk insured against – must be correct and honestly given.

When filling in a proposal form to insure your car, you inadvertently give an incorrect address for where the car will be garaged, and also fail to volunteer information about a previous minor motor accident in which you have been involved.

The insurance company can avoid liability on the grounds of either the inaccuracy or the non-disclosure.

▶ **Very important:** If the insurance contract is renewable, for example annually, each renewal is treated as making a fresh contract and the duty to disclose arises again – so if the facts have changed make sure you tell the company.

A broker or agent may fill in the proposal form for you. If they do, you should read it carefully – never sign it without checking it first. Even though they get their commission from the company and not from you, as far as filling in the form is concerned they are your agents and if information is not correctly recorded you lose your insurance cover. If, however, they fail to obtain the cover you requested or if on renewal a new exclusion clause is put into the policy without your knowledge, you could sue the broker for professional negligence.

7.2.3 Sticking to the letter of the contract

The Unfair Contract Terms Act, which prevents businesses from putting terms in their contracts that limit their liability, does not apply to insurance contracts.

Insurance policies always contain terms about what the policyholder must or must not do, and if these are not strictly abided by the insurance company can refuse to pay out. For instance, a home contents' policy may require you to instal and use a properly functioning burglar alarm.

P's car was stolen from outside his house. He admitted that due to a fault in the ignition barrel he had for two years left the key in the ignition and taken no steps to have the car repaired.

His insurance company was entitled to refuse to pay out on the policy because he had not taken reasonable precautions, as the policy required, to prevent loss.

A firm manufacturing jewellery takes out insurance to cover its jewellery being transported by salesmen around the country. The policy states that the jewellery must not be left unattended. One of the salesmen parks his car in a layby, locking the suitcase containing the jewellery in it, and goes behind some bushes to answer a call of nature. During the time the car is out of his sight a thief breaks into it and steals the suitcase.

The insurance company may not compensate the firm, as the salesman did not adhere to the terms of the policy.

In certain cases, the courts have said that the insurers should pay out where money or jewellery has been stolen from a parked car. However, it is always better to stick to the terms of your policy and err on the side of being too careful, rather than relying on the insurers' goodwill in paying out to you in the event of a mishap.

7.2.4 Being under-insured

Am I under-insured with regard to my home contents' policy?

Review the amount you have insured for, periodically, to take account of new acquisitions, increases in value, etc. If you overvalue the insured property this may invalidate the policy, but if you undervalue it you may not get even the amount at which you valued it.

You take out £5,000 fire insurance for property worth £10,000.

When half of it is destroyed by fire, you will get only £2,500.

You can limit your cover by insuring for a specific amount. In turn, the insurance company will limit its liability by imposing an 'excess', so that claims below a certain level will not be paid out.

If your holiday insurance specifies an excess of £200, and your pocket is picked and £200 or less is taken, the loss will be treated as not covered by the insurance.

Some policies also exclude items exceeding a particular amount in value, so particularly valuable items have to be separately insured.

If you have to get a valuation of lost or stolen goods to make the claim, include the cost of obtaining the valuation in your total claim on the policy.

7.2.5 Excluded risks

Policies generally contain a list of 'excepted perils' namely, the risks which are not covered by the policy; for example, damage caused by 'war, riot or civil commotion'. The terms of the policy can also cut down the scope of protection in ways you may not expect, for example home contents policies may exclude cash, cheques and documents, which may have to be insured separately. The Insurance Ombudsman has ruled that all exclusions must be set out fairly and must satisfy the test of reasonableness. You should ask about particular items and risks you want covered – it may be necessary to shop around to obtain cover. You may have a claim against your broker if he or she did not obtain cover which you specified was needed. Homeowners may find that their household contents' insurance excludes plants, garden ornaments and pets. Note that you will not be covered for loss or damage occurring before the start of the insurance period.

7.2.6 No-claims bonus

Insurers limit their liability by trying to reduce the number of claims made, by giving policyholders an inducement not to claim – in the form of a discount or no-claims bonus. If the amount of the claim is less than that of the no-claims bonus, it will not be worth claiming, but it is probably sensible – in the light of your duty of disclosure – to tell the insurers of the loss anyway, making it clear that this is for information only.

7.2.7 Police notification

In the event of theft, always inform the police promptly, as your insurers will insist on a report from the police as a precondition of paying out.

7.2.8 Time limits

Policies usually fix time limits for the notification of a claim, as a condition of the company's liability. It is always prudent to inform the insurers as soon as possible that a claim is to be made, even if you do not yet have full details of the value of the loss.

7.2.9 Insurance losses

The insurance industry has had to pay out a record amount through claims for a series of unprecedented natural disasters in recent years. There have also been large, recession-related claims such as mortgage indemnity cover, as well as massive payouts on losses from theft.

In addition, insurers feel that they have become the victims of all sorts of fraudulent claims or scams from members of the public, such as when someone holidays abroad, spends all his money, and then, on returning to England, claims for a 'theft' of traveller's cheques which never took place. It is not surprising, therefore, that insurers would want to sift through claims very carefully in order to trap those that may not be above board. However, if you have had your money stolen on holiday and your claim is genuine, you may be upset and resent any delay on your insurer's part. Remember, though, that the cost of fraud will be recouped by the insurers in increased premiums, so reduction of fraud is in your own interest.

◆ **Note:** For certain claims, your insurance company may employ the services of a loss adjuster to assess the potential loss. The loss adjuster's report may then be used by your insurers as the basis on which to pay out your claim.

7.2.10 Uncooperative insurers

If you have a dispute with your insurers, persist in your claim by, if necessary, going up through managers and directors to the very top. If you still can't get satisfaction, within six months you can complain to the Insurance Ombudsman (see DIRECTORY). He has the power to award compensation of up to £100,000 against an insurance company, and getting his award does not prevent you taking subsequent legal action if still unhappy.

Alternatively, you can have your claim arbitrated through the Personal Insurance Arbitration Scheme (PIAS), run by the Chartered Institute of Arbitrators (see DIRECTORY).

◆ **Note** that both these schemes are voluntary, so that not all insurance companies participate in them.

7.3 You and your debts

The law is concerned to oversee the business of lending money. It tries to ensure – within the limits of usual business practice – that the innocent are not taken advantage of and that persons who lend money are properly licensed (see *Consumer protection*, section 7.3.5 below).

7.3.1 Getting different types of credit

It is usually cheaper to buy for cash than on credit, as the price will have added on to it the amount of interest and additional charges. Some forms of credit will be cheaper than others, so just as you would do for anything else, it is sensible to shop around to find the best source. Sometimes goods are advertised at 0 per cent interest, but then there may be some other hidden cost – for example, loss of a discount on a new car. In recessionary times, of course, when consumers hold back from spending in the High Street, ever-increasingly attractive offers are put out by shops and other businesses to tempt reluctant customers. Interest-free credit does not mean that regular repayments do not still have to be made. Credit card borrowing may be more expensive than borrowing elsewhere, if you do not repay the credit card bill in full each month.

▶ **Remember:** As always, take time to consider before you sign anything.

7.3.2 Standard credit agreements

There are various forms of standard credit agreements but the main forms of credit for retail sales are

- hire purchase agreements
- conditional sale agreements
- credit sale agreements

(a) Hire purchase agreements

A standard HP agreement reflects a situation where a customer wants to buy goods from a shop on credit. He or she makes the purchase and the shop then sells the goods to the finance house which, in law, becomes the seller. The finance house makes finance available to the customer who has to repay it in instalments. The customer 'hires' the goods, which do not actually become his property until the last instalment is paid. Technically, he has the option to become the owner at this point. In some cases, the dealer or retailer may himself provide the finance in which case he is both seller and lender, but this is not as common as finance house agreements.

(b) Conditional sale agreements

In a conditional sale, which is more unusual than HP, a customer 'buys' the goods on instalment from the finance house. Again, the goods belong to the finance house and not to the customer until the last instalment is paid. Unlike an HP agreement, the customer is under a legal obligation to buy the goods at the end of the instalment period.

(c) Credit sale agreements

In a credit sale agreement, the customer also buys goods which he or she pays for by instalments. However, the goods actually belong to the customer from the outset of the contract – unlike a conditional sale agreement.

7.3.3 Legal controls on lenders and other creditors

All these agreements are governed by statute. The law lays down who can finance them; how they are to be financed; what documentation should be used; and how the customer should be protected.

Persons who offer finance must be licensed to do so by the Office of Fair Trading. It keeps a register which is open to members of the public who can inspect the register for a fee.

It is important that you check precisely who the seller is. When you buy goods on HP or under a conditional sale agreement, the supplier of the goods is not the retailer, as we have seen. It is the finance company which in law 'sells' the goods and it is primarily against them that consumer rights will have to be enforced. There may also be rights against the dealer if you relied on assurances by his staff about the quality of the goods. In practice the finance company and the supplier may have arranged that the latter will deal with complaints, but in law rights are against the finance company.

By law all advertisements for and offers of loans and credit must specify the APR. This stands for Annual Percentage Rate, and is meant to enable you to compare overall the cost of borrowing from different outlets. In practice, the APR has come in for criticism as being deliberately confusing to the customer.

7.3.4 Giving security

If you can give security you may get a cheaper loan. However, be on guard against lenders who want you to put up your home as security; by law, their advertisements must make it clear that this is the security they require. If you cannot keep up the instalments you may end up with no roof over your head.

Also be wary of acting as guarantor for someone else's debt – if they default you will have to pay the creditor. Always check the details of the debtor's agreement with the creditor before you sign any guarantee to make sure you could afford to pay if you have to.

So it is wise to get independent legal advice before you sign a transaction

- where its purpose is to benefit someone else (i.e. where you are acting as guarantor for someone else's loan) or
- where you may lose your home.

It is also illegal for anyone to ask for your social security benefit books as security for a loan. You must report any such request from a creditor to the local Trading Standards Officer.

7.3.5 Consumer protection

The safest procedure when asking for a loan or credit is to ask for a written quotation and take it home to study. If you sign an agreement in business premises you will be bound by it, whereas if you sign at home you may have a 'cooling-off' period during which you are entitled to cancel the agreement if you have second thoughts. If you look at the agreement you will see whether it contains, as the law requires, a clear notification to you about your right to cancel. *Never* sign an agreement in blank or without all the details being filled in. If you agreed to the loan or credit arrangement over the telephone, even from your home, you will not have the right to cancel.

Always fill in an application for credit yourself or check it carefully before signing it. If the details are inaccurate, you may be committing a criminal offence.

If you exercise your right to cancel, you will be entitled to the return of any deposit paid and goods given in part exchange. At the same time you will have to return the money borrowed or the goods you received.

Once you have signed the agreement you must be sent another copy through the post. keep it in a safe place, together with a record of each payment you make and any correspondence you have with the lender. If these get mislaid, on payment of 50p to the creditor you are entitled to receive a copy of the agreement and a statement of instalments paid and balance owing.

7.3.6 Credit cards

If you have used a credit card such as Access or Visa (as distinct from a charge card or debit card, e.g. American Express or Diner's Club) to buy goods or services worth more than £100, you can hold the credit card company liable, together with the defaulting trader, if you do not get what you paid for. This does not apply to hire purchase transactions (and see also *Tour operators* below 9.2.4).

7.3.7 Defaulting on a debt

If you buy goods on hire purchase and then find you cannot keep up the payments, do not be tempted to sell the goods to raise funds. You have no right to dispose of them until all the instalments have been paid, and you may be committing a criminal offence if you do. Further, if you offer to return the goods to the seller, be warned that your liability to keep up instalments does not automatically terminate – ask them to agree to this in writing when you relinquish the goods.

> *You bought an expensive hatchback car on HP at a time when you were earning considerable sums as a broker in the City. You have since been made redundant and cannot afford the payments on the car. You have seen an advertisement in a local paper from what seems to be a reputable firm offering to take over your car and to make the payments on your behalf.*

> Do not be tempted. You may find that although you part with your car and log book, so losing your vehicle for good, the payments may not be made on your behalf so that you are still liable to the finance house for a car you no longer have. It would be better by far to approach the finance house and ask for advice on how best to get out of your present plight (see *Ending the Agreement*, below, section 7.3.10).

Failure to pay means that the goods can be repossessed, but a court order is necessary to enter your home without your permission. If you have paid more than one-third of the instalments, there cannot be a repossession at all without a court order. If a creditor takes you to court and gets a judgement against you, which you pay off, that may not be the end of the matter. You may end up on a register of debtors which will seriously affect your chances of getting credit again. You can be deleted from the register of debtors, provided you obtain a certificate of satisfaction from the County Court (cost £1). County Court judgements are passed to the Registry Trust, which are consulted by credit rating agencies and mortgage institutions, so it makes sense to have your name removed – which can be done if you paid the debt within 28 days of the judgement. If you pay after 50 days your name will remain on the register for six years although the debt is recorded as satisfied. (The Registry Trust Limited can be contacted at 173–175 Cleveland Street, London W1P 5PE.)

Do not pay anyone to 'repair' your credit rating. The Office of Fair Trading has a free booklet *No Credit* which explains how to correct information held by credit reference agencies (see below).

7.3.8 Credit reference agencies

If you find yourself unable to obtain credit from a particular firm, it may be because your name appears on a credit reference agency's records, e.g. because a judgment for debt has been obtained against you. If you think this may be the case, and the amount involved is under £15,000, you are entitled on request to be told the name of the agency used, so that you can ask them for a copy of the record affecting you. The credit reference agency is obliged to send you a copy of the record for a fee (at present £1). If the records are inaccurate you can have them amended. The Office of Fair Trading booklet *No Credit* sets out the procedures which you must take. It is important to note carefully the time limits which the booklet lays down for these procedures.

Information about organizations which hold personal information about individuals on computer file can be obtained free from the Data Protection Registrar, Wycliffe House, Water Lane, Wilmslow, Cheshire SK9 5AF; Tel. 0625 535 777. Guidelines about the holding of personal information on computer systems were published in September 1993 by the Department of Trade and Industry.

7.3.9 Extortionate interest

If you think you are paying interest at extortionate rates, you may be able to have the agreement set aside by the courts. Take legal advice before you stop payments, however, as it is extremely rare for this to be allowed. The courts will not regard a high rate as extortionate if the creditor has run an extra risk in giving you the credit.

7.3.10 Ending the agreement

If after embarking on a hire-purchase agreement you wish to terminate it, you can pay off all the instalments ahead of time. If you want to do this, write to the creditor and ask him about the rebate to which you are entitled because of the early payment. On the other hand, if you want to terminate the agreement and give back the goods, you will have to pay up to half the price for the privilege of doing so. If you default on the instalments and the hire-purchase company wish to enforce the agreement, they must send you a default notice. If you cannot pay off the arrears when you get this, take legal advice immediately – you may be able to ask the court for a 'time order' giving you extra breathing space.

If you get into difficulty with debt, write and tell the creditor about the problem. Most creditors would prefer not to go to court and would rather make arrangements for the repayments if feasible. Where you owe money to more than one creditor, inform all of them about your difficulties rather than skimping on one creditor's repayments in order to satisfy another's.

Dickensian debtors' prisons are a thing of the past, and it is a criminal offence for a creditor to harass a debtor. If you do get sued, get legal advice from a solicitor or consumer adviser. Always try to put before the court realistic proposals about the amounts you can afford to repay regularly.

8. Eating and drinking out

8.1 Pubs

For many years, pub hours were strictly controlled. The licensing laws regulating pub hours were introduced during the First World War and it is only recently that these regulations have been relaxed. Pubs can now remain open throughout the day. However, publicans still often maintain a routine for their opening hours, particularly on Sunday afternoons, and it is advisable to check. Licensed restaurants are allowed to serve alcohol in certain circumstances, for example, with 'substantial food'.

8.1.1 Who can be served?

Until now the law has endeavoured to keep children out of pubs. It is a very familiar and very English scene to see, on summer days, parents bringing out lemonade and packets of crisps to their bored children waiting about in pub doorways and parking grounds. Proposals are now being put forward to allow children more readily into pubs.

Regulations governing the offences of serving alcohol to minors fall heavily on the publicans themselves. They are forbidden to sell alcohol to anyone under 18 – whether they know their age or not. In fact, even serving a drink to an adult who intends it to be consumed by a minor is a criminal offence. Children over 14 are allowed into a bar as long as they do not drink, but under 14s may not enter a bar at all unless to use a facility such as a toilet. 16- to 18-year-olds are allowed to have beer or cider with a meal in a pub – provided that it is not taken at the bar but in an area usually set aside for the provision of meals.

A publican must also refuse to serve someone who is already drunk – of whatever age. Moreover, he or she is under a legal duty to tell a drunk or violent person to leave the premises. Such a person commits an offence if he does not then depart.

8.1.2 Publican's duty

On the other hand, it is clear that a publican will be committing an offence if a refusal to serve someone is based on that person's race, sex or ethnic origins.

8.1.3 Credit

It is illegal for a landlord to sell drinks on credit. However, it is perfectly legal to pay by credit card for a meal at a pub provided the drinks are paid for separately.

8.1.4 Weights and Measures Act

If you order a drink in a pub, you can expect it in a specified quantity which has been laid down by the Weights and Measures Act. It is a criminal offence if short measures are served, e.g. if beer is served with an excessive head of froth. Equally, it is a criminal offence if a publican draws too much and serves over the measure although there are likely to be few complaints about this to the local trading standards officer!

8.1.5 Displaying prices

Prices of drinks and foods must be displayed on notices which are visible where they are served.

8.2 Restaurants

Certain problems crop up again and again with restaurants. What should be a pleasant evening out can be marred by off-hand service, poor food, over-expensive menus, and imbroglios over lost property. Not all these problems can be solved by legal redress – often one simply decides to grin and bear it – but it is as well to know what are one's rights in law.

8.2.1 Food description

The food served must be fit for its purpose, comply with its description and be of a quality reasonably to be expected in an establishment of its kind. If you are dissatisfied with the food on tasting or inspecting it, complain at once.

▶ **Beware:** if you take more than a few mouthfuls you will be regarded as having 'accepted' the food and will have to pay for it.

If the food is not as described (e.g. a 'mixed seafood platter' which contains only one kind of fish), tell the local trading standards officer.

However dissatisfied you are, do not just walk out without paying! You could be committing an offence under the Theft Act. At the very least, give your name and address to the manager before you leave.

8.2.2 Food Safety Act

The Food Safety Act 1990 makes it a criminal offence to sell food which is injurious to health, or is not of the nature, substance or quality demanded, or does not comply with the food safety requirements. If you are served food which makes you ill, report the restaurant to the local environmental health officer.

> *You book several tables at a restaurant to celebrate your silver wedding with a dinner among 30 friends. Everyone at the party gets food poisoning after the meal.*
>
> The restaurant will be liable to pay damages to everyone who suffered to compensate them for the illness, and will be liable to criminal penalties under the 1990 Act (which could result in them being closed down temporarily if not permanently).

Note that doctors are under a statutory duty to inform the authorities about any patient suffering from food poisoning.

8.2.3 Displaying prices

A restaurant menu with VAT-inclusive prices must be displayed at the entrance, or in the case of a self-service cafeteria at the point where the food is selected.

8.2.4 Service charges

If the service is unreasonably bad you are entitled to refuse to pay a service charge. There is no requirement by law that you have to tip – unlike, for example, the legal requirement that menus must state prices inclusive of VAT. So even though a menu may state '10 per cent added for service', you can withhold it if the circumstances warrant it.

8.2.5 No-shows

▶ **Do remember:** when you make an advance reservation at a restaurant, you are entering into a contract. If you fail to turn up and the restaurant cannot fill the table with other guests in your place, you could be held liable to pay damages.

Conversely, if after you booked you turn up at the restaurant to find no table has been kept for you, you could claim compensation from them, for, say, the costs of the wasted journey.

8.2.6 Belongings

If a careless waiter spills soup on your suit, compensation (for example, the cost of cleaning) is due from the restaurant, because they are responsible for the negligence of their staff.

> *You are sitting at a table in a restaurant. As you lift your glass of red wine, another customer pushes past your table jogging your arm, so that the wine spills on your dress.*

The proprietor is not responsible for the cleaning or replacement of the dress (unless you could prove that the placing of the tables was such as to make such an accident reasonably foreseeable).

On the same principle, if your coat is stolen from coathooks placed in the restaurant for the convenience of customers, the restaurateur is not responsible. However, if you hand your coat over to a waiter who then disappears with it and the coat is stolen, the restaurant would be responsible for its loss.

> *As you enter a restaurant, a waiter approaches you and gestures towards the cloakroom where there is an attendant. After pausing for a moment, you decide to hand over your briefcase together with your coat. When you return, the briefcase is missing. The manager points to a sign above the attendant's desk which says that property is left at the customer's own risk.*

It would seem that the disclaimer would be effective if the sign is sufficiently prominent for you to have noticed it when you handed over your belongings.

A disclaimer would not be effective, however, if the attendant had been negligent – if, for example, during a slack moment she had wandered over to chat to the barman.

Different considerations would apply where you are told to leave your belongings at a cloakroom and you have no choice in the matter. For example, for security reasons one cannot take umbrellas or briefcases into an art gallery. It would seem that under these circumstances, the management takes complete responsibility for them and owners are not leaving the goods at their own risk.

9. Going away on holiday

9.1 Hotels

Given the nature of the trade, it is not surprising to learn that an hotelier is under a legal duty to take all comers if there are rooms available.

A distinction is drawn between hotels on the one hand, and boarding houses, residential hotels and bed-and-breakfast establishments on the other hand, which are not expected by law to take in all would-be guests.

It is of course an offence to refuse to serve someone solely on account of race, sex, or ethnic origins – whatever the nature of the establishment.

9.1.1 Displaying charges

An hotel must display its charges and specify which meals – if any – are included in the price. This information must be clearly available at reception – it is insufficient to put a notice on the back of a bedroom door.

9.1.2 Cancellations

As with booking a restaurant table, a contract is made with an hotel on booking a room. In the event of a failure to take up a booking, the hotel is entitled to charge a reasonable amount for lost profits if it cannot relet the room.

> *You have booked an hotel room and given your credit card number to the receptionist to make sure of your reservation. You cannot keep the booking and you telephone the hotel to cancel it. You are dismayed to see that you have been charged the full amount for you and your wife on your credit card statement which you receive a month later.*

> If you book a room in an hotel but cancel your stay, you are still liable to pay something towards the hotel. However, you are not liable in law for the full cost of the room, as the hotel has saved on providing food, laundry, etc. Hotels are supposed to charge a reasonable amount only on lost profits but of course, these can form a considerable proportion of the amount charged for an overnight stay.

If you can persuade your credit card company that the hotel charges are exorbitant, it may take action on your behalf.

If you had paid a deposit instead of giving your credit card number, the hotelier would be entitled to keep it – again within a reasonable amount.

In recessionary times, hoteliers and restaurateurs are not always able to fill rooms and tables which have been booked. Their proprietors are therefore much more likely to take a tough stance against 'no-shows' than at other times.

9.1.3 Overbookings

Conversely, if you book a room but when you arrive find the hotel is full, the hotelier is liable to you for any extra costs involved in staying somewhere else (which could include your travel costs to the alternative place).

9.1.4 Specific requests

If particular requirements, such as a sea view, are specified at the time of booking, an hotel is in breach of contract if the room does not meet the specification.

> *You have a mobility problem and find stairs difficult. You ask for a ground floor room when you book at an hotel in the Lake District. When you get there you find that the hotel's only ground floor room is occupied by another guest and you have to climb a flight of stairs to get to your room.*

> In such a case, you are entitled to a deduction, and even to cancel.

9.1.5 Guests' property

Once you are a guest in an hotel, it is responsible for the safety of your property (though not for your car or items left in it unless the hotel's employees are negligent). You can claim compensation for the loss or theft of your belongings on hotel premises.

In most cases, the hotel will have limited its liability, as it is entitled to do, by putting up a notice in the reception area or in the entrance, making clear that it will only be liable for up to £50 per item or £100 per guest. The figures for compensation for loss were laid down in the 1950s and are clearly quite out of date.

A notice limiting liability must be in the front of the hotel and a notice which is only put up in a bedroom has no legal effect.

The hotel is then only liable to pay more than these statutory amounts if its employees are grossly negligent or if the property is deposited for safe custody with the management.

> You book into an hotel for a weekend. There is no notice in the reception area, but after you have signed the register and are shown to your room, you see a notice limiting the hotel's liability prominently displayed in the room. Your jewellery case is stolen from the room while you are out.

> The hotel must pay you the full value of the jewellery as the notice in the bedroom is insufficient in law to limit its liability.

(For the liability of the hotel for accidental injuries, see *Accidents* chapter, section 4.5.4. For package holidays, see *Tour operators* below, section 9.2.)

9.2 Tour operators

So many things can go wrong with a holiday – from the bankruptcy of a travel organizer to an hotel being unsuitable or overbooked – that it is essential to take out travel insurance to cover against as many eventualities as possible. Make sure in particular that the policy

(a) gives cover for cancelling at short notice;
(b) gives adequate cover for medical expenses abroad (skiers and tourists to the United States be warned!);
(c) covers the full replacement value of possessions which might get lost or stolen.

A package holiday is just what its name would imply. It is an all-inclusive deal which covers travel and hotel. Package holidays are booked by coach, train or plane, and are arranged for travel both in Britain and abroad. A package holiday is also one of the few items you buy where you cannot know the final cost when you enter into the contract, i.e. at the time of booking.

By law, the travel organizer must – *before you book* – give you information about visa and health requirements, and details about the security of any money you pay over, e.g. as a deposit. The protection of deposits is not necessarily guaranteed, however.

9.2.1 Surcharges

Surcharges to cover variations in transport costs, taxes and exchange rates are commonly payable under the booking conditions – if they are not expressly mentioned you cannot be invoiced for them. After you have booked it is only in limited circumstances, which must be clearly set out in the brochure, that the organizer can change the price of the holiday. No one can be asked to pay a surcharge within 30 days of the commencement of the holiday. If the price of the holiday has been increased significantly you may be entitled to cancel the holiday without penalty and claim reimbursement. If the travel agent or tour operator is affiliated to ABTA (the Association of British Travel Agents), the ABTA Code protects against alterations being made less than two weeks before the start of the holiday.

9.2.2 Compliance with brochures

▶ **Don't forget:** the brochure's glossy pictures and enticing descriptions form part of your contract with the tour operator. This applies to all package holidays, whether you book for an hotel or choose self-catering accommodation through a tour operator.

Of course, booking conditions also form part of the contract but the tour operators cannot rely on these conditions unless they have been properly communicated to you. The question is what recourse a holidaymaker has where there are clauses which limit or exclude liability – if, for example, a promised swimming pool is unexpectedly closed.

9.2.3 Whose fault is it anyway?

If the accommodation and facilities fall short of your expectations, the tour operator might claim to be relieved of any liability by the inclusion of clauses in the booking conditions limiting or excluding its liability. Under the Unfair Contract Terms Acts such clauses are invalid unless they are reasonable, and cannot in any event exclude liability for negligence resulting in death or personal injury.

The trouble, legally speaking, with package holidays is that when something goes wrong with transport or accommodation, tour operators have often claimed that they cannot be held responsible for the running of airlines and hotels over which they have no control.

EC regulations require airlines which have overbooked passengers to pay compensation of up to £210. Passengers also have the option of being re-routed or taking a refund. Under an EC Directive on package travel, the organizers can now be held responsible for the failure of others such as airlines or hotels to carry out the obligations paid for by the customer – unless the failure was unforeseeable or unavoidable. This will not apply to all packages however – individually tailored holidays and fly-drive arrangements, for instance, will be excluded from the Directive's scope.

▶ **Take heart:** no exemption clause in the booking conditions will protect the tour operator if it fails to provide what was substantially the holiday you bought, even if there is a term allowing the substitution of hotels or resort.

> *You book a holiday in a 3-star hotel. When you arrive you are told the main building is full and you are offered a dirty room in a dilapidated annexe infested with beetles.*

> You are not obliged to accept this substandard accommodation, and the tour operator is responsible for finding you an appropriate alternative and for paying compensation.

Equally, you are not obliged to accept a room in a large hotel in a noisy city resort, when you were buying a holiday described in the brochure as a small family hotel in a quiet resort village.

If the brochure describes the hotel as having such facilities as an English-speaking management, a paddling pool for toddlers, a beauty salon, a discotheque, or house-party atmosphere, then when any of these are absent or inadequate you can claim substantial compensation from the tour operator.

> *Mr Jackson paid £1,200 and bought his family of four a holiday in Sri Lanka at a hotel described in the brochure as luxurious with many specified facilities. The hotel turned out to be dirty and badly run, and most of the promised facilities did not exist or were unusable; halfway through the holiday they were moved to a better but only partly-built hotel.*
>
> He sued the tour operator and was awarded £1,100 (including damages for the disappointment of the whole family).

♦ **Note** that you do not have to accept an alternative if one is offered, although you may prefer to do this rather than lose the holiday altogether. In any event, complain to the local representative immediately, and keep a written record of your complaints and their response. Take photographs if appropriate (of, for example, locked fire escapes, unhygienic eating areas, dangerously low balconies) and try and get the names and addresses of other holiday-makers who can support your allegations if they are contested.

9.2.4 Paying by credit card

If you pay by credit card for a holiday costing more than £100, the credit card company can also be held liable. This may not apply if you paid the travel agent and not the tour operator direct.

If you have paid by credit card direct to an airline, which has gone out of business, you can expect a refund from your credit card company. If you had paid a travel agent by credit card for the same air ticket, you would not be refunded. Credit card companies argue that the contract is not between the cardholder and the credit card company, the contract is with the travel agent, who should reimburse the customer.

9.2.5 Complaints

If the tour operator does not accept your legitimate complaint, and it is a member of ABTA, try the Personal Insurers Arbitration Scheme (PIAS) run by the Chartered Institute of Arbitrators (see DIRECTORY).

You can also complain to your local trading standards officer about misdescriptions in the brochure. If he or she successfully prosecutes the tour operator the court may make a compensation order in your favour. This will not be for as much as you might get through litigation, but it costs you nothing.

9.2.6 When the tour company goes bust

If a holiday firm goes under and it is a member of ABTA, holidaymakers who have paid in advance can expect to receive their money back. Moreover, they will not be stranded away from home if they are already on holiday when their firm collapses. Under the EC Directive, all tour organizers must now provide security against their going insolvent, so the problem of stranded holidaymakers should, it is hoped, be a thing of the past.

9.3 Activity holidays

Despite well-reported accidents such as the death of four teenagers on a canoeing course in Dorset in 1993, there is no national code of safety laid down for the organizers of such courses or holidays. The governing body of some sports, e.g. rock climbing, does lay down strong guidelines but not all activities have a ruling body.

Before going on such a course or allowing your children to do so, make enquiries about the instructors' qualifications, the safety standards and the insurance cover of the organizers, and obtain full insurance cover yourself.

9.4 Timeshares

A large number of people every year buy timeshares, and the high-pressure (and often dubious) selling methods of the companies involved led to the passing of the Timeshare Act 1992.

9.4.1 Details of the Timeshare Act

This will require a timeshare company which offers you a contract to inform you in writing that

(a) You have the right to change your mind and withdraw from the contract.
(b) You must receive a blank cancellation form.
(c) You will be entitled to the return of your deposit.
(d) You have 14 days from the date of the contract to exercise this right, so do not give in to pressure to confirm the agreement sooner.
(e) If you do cancel, you can cancel any financing arrangements.
(f) You must then repay the whole of any credit given to you within one month but you will not have to pay interest.
(g) If you received no notification of your right to cancel, you can cancel the agreement at any time.

Failure on the companies' part to comply with the provisions of this Act will be an offence.

9.4.2 Limitations of Act

▶ **Beware:** The provisions of this Act only apply to timeshare agreements entered into under British law, or where one of the parties signs the agreement on British soil; but in these circumstances it does apply even if the accommodation is abroad.

If you buy a timeshare abroad, you are bound by the laws of the country in which you have bought.

> *While in Spain, you buy a timeshare there, but regret your decision when you return to the UK three days later.*

> Unfortunately for you, Spain has no legislation in force at the moment to allow you a cooling-off period although such a law is currently under way.

The text of a draft European Directive was agreed in September 1994 which, when it comes into force, will give buyers a cooling-off period of 10 days. No advance payments may be made within that period and buyers can withdraw without giving reasons. France, Greece and Portugal have also enacted specific legislation to deal with timeshare purchases.

Misdescription applies to timeshare properties as much as to any other contract for sale.

> *You bought a timeshare property from a firm in England. The property, in Tenerife, was described as a 'luxury development' with sensational views. When you arrive, you find that the*

building is on a bare hillside overlooking a building site and the builders' ablution block.

You should report the matter to your local trading standards department for a criminal prosecution for making false statements, as well as suing the firm itself for damages. A successful prosecution always assists in a civil case for damages.

In a similar case, the disappointed customer was awarded by the court one-third of the price he had paid plus £1,050 for the distress and disappointment of a ruined holiday.

DIRECTORY
Goods and services

Advertising Standards Authority
Brook House
2–16 Torrington Place
London WC1E 7HN
Tel. 071 580 5555

Air Transport Users' committee (AUC)
2nd Floor
Kingsway House
103 Kingsway
London WC2B 6QX
Tel. 071 242 3882

Association of British Insurers (ABI)
51 Gresham Street
London EC2V 7HQ
Tel. 071 600 3333

Association of British Travel Agents
(ABTA)
55–57 Newman Street
London W1P 4AH
Tel. 071 637 2444

BBC Television Consumer Programmes:
Watchdog (BBC1)
BBC Television
White City
201 Wood Lane
London W12 7TS
Tel. 081 743 5555

The Travel Show (BBC1)
BBC Manchester
New Broadcasting House
Manchester M60 1SJ
Tel. 061 200 2000

BBC Radio Consumer Programmes:
Face The Press (Radio 4)
Does He Take Sugar? (Radio 4)
You and Yours (Radio 4)
In Touch (Radio 4)
Jimmy Young Programme (Radio 4)
Broadcasting House
Portland Place
London W1A 1AA
Tel. 071 580 4468

Punters
BBC Radio 4
Bristol BS8 2LR
Tel. 0272 742186

Banking Ombudsman Bureau
The Office of the Banking Ombudsman
Citadel House
5–11 Fetter Lane
London EC4A 1BR
Tel. 071 405 9944

British Bankers' Association
10 Lombard Street
London EC3V 9EL
Tel. 071 623 4001

British Insurance & Investment Brokers'
Association (BIIBA)
BIIBA House
14 Bevis Marks
London EC3A 7NT
Tel. 071 623 9043

British Holiday and Home Parks
Association Ltd.
Chichester House
31 Park Road
Gloucester GL1 1LH
Tel. 0452 526911

British Standards Institution
Information Services
Linford Wood
Milton Keynes MK14 6LE
Tel. 0908 226888

CCN Credit Systems Limited
Consumer Affairs Department
PO Box 40
Nottingham NG7 2SS
Tel. 0602 868172

The Chartered Institute of Arbitrators
24 Angel Gate
City Road
London EC1V 2RS
Tel. 071 837 4483

Commission for Local Administration in England
21 Queen Anne's Gate
London SW1H 9BU
Tel. 071 222 5622

Commission for Local Administration in Wales
Derwen House
Court Road
Bridgend
Mid Glamorgan CF31 1BN
Tel. 0656 661325

Consumers' Association
2 Marylebone Road
London NW1 4DF
Tel. 071 486 5544

Consumer Credit Association (UK) (CCA)
Queens House
Queens Road
Chester CH1 3BQ
Tel. 0244 312044

Consumer Credit Trade Association
Tennyson House
159–163 Great Portland Street
London W1N 5FD
Tel. 071 636 7564

The Consumer Policy Committee
BSI
2 Park Street
London W1A 2BS
Tel. 071 629 9000

Consumers in the European Community Group
24 Tufton Street
London SW1P 3RB
Tel. 071 222 2662

Department of Trade & Industry
Consumer Affairs Room 404
10–18 Victoria Street
London SW1H 0NN
Tel. 071 215 3316

Direct Marketing Association
Haymarket House
1 Oxendon Street
London SW1Y 4EE
Tel. 071 321 2525

Direct Selling Association
29 Floral Street
London WC2E 9DP
Tel. 071 497 1234

Federation of Independent Advice Centres (offices nationwide)
13 Stockwell Road
London SW9 9AV
Tel. 071 274 1839

Federation of Small Businesses
140 Lower Marsh
Westminster Bridge
London SE1 7AE
Tel. 071 928 9272

Finance & Leasing Association (FLA)
18 Upper Grosvenor Street
London W1X 9PB
Tel. 071 491 2783

Food and Drink Federation
6 Catherine Street
London WC2B 5JJ
Tel. 071 836 2460

General Medical Council
44 Hallam Street
London W1N 6AE
Tel. 071 580 7642

Health Services Commissioner (Ombudsman) for England, Scotland, Wales
Church House
Great Smith Street
London SW1P 3BW
Tel. 071 276 2035

Incorporated Society of Valuers and Auctioneers (ISVA)
3 Cadogan Gate
London SW1X 0AS
Tel. 071 235 2282

Independent Television Commission
33 Foley Street
London W1P 7LB
Tel. 071 255 3000

Institute of Trading Standards Administration (ITSA)
4/5 Hadleigh Business Centre
351 London Road
Hadleigh
Essex SS7 2BT
Tel. 0702 559922

Insurance Ombudsman Bureau
City Gate 1
135 Park Street
London SE1 9EA
Tel. 071 928 4488

Law Centres Federation (offices nationwide)
Duchess House
18–19 Warren Street
London W1P 5DB
Tel. 071 387 8570

Local Authorities Coordinating Body on Food & Trading Standards (LACOTS)
PO Box 6
Robert Street
Croydon CR9 1LG
Tel. 071 688 1996

London Regional Passenger Committee
Golden Cross House
8 Duncannon Street
London WC2N 4JF
Tel. 071 839 1898

Mailing Preference Service
FREEPOST 22
London W1E 7EZ
(to get off mail order listings)

Ministry of Agriculture, Fisheries and Food
Whitehall Place (West Block)
London SW1A 2HH
Tel. 071 270 3000

National Association of Estate Agents
Arbon House
21 Jury Street
Warwick CV34 4EH
Tel. 0926 496800

National Consumer Council
20 Grosvenor Gardens
London SW1W 0DH
Tel. 071 730 3469

National Consumer Credit Federation
98–100 Holme Lane
Sheffield S6 4JW
Tel. 0742 348101

National Federation of Credit Unions
5th Floor,
Provincial House
Bradford BD1 1NP
Tel. 0274 753507

The Office of the Building Societies Ombudsman
Grosvenor Gardens House
35–37 Grosvenor Gardens
London SW1X 7AW
Tel. 071 931 0044

Office of the Data Protection Registrar
Wycliffe House
Water Lane
Wilmslow
Cheshire SK9 5AF
Tel. 0625 535777

Office of Fair Trading
Field House
15–25 Breams Buildings
London EC4 1PR
Tel. 071 242 2858

The Office of the Ombudsman for Corporate Estate Agents
Beckett House
4 Bridge Street
Salisbury
Wiltshire
SP1 1LX
Tel. 0722 333306

Office of the Parliamentary Commissioner for Administration
Church House
Great Smith Street
London SW1P 3BW
Tel. 071 276 3000

OFTEL
Export House
50 Ludgate Hill
London EC4M 7JJ
Tel. 071 822 1600

Personal Insurance Arbitration Service
Chartered Institute of Arbitrators
International Arbitration Centre
24 Angel Gate
City Road
London EC1V 2RS
Tel. 071 837 4483

Registry Trust Limited
173–175 Cleveland Street
London W1P 5PE

Retail Motor Industry Federation
201 Great Portland Street
London W1N 6AB
Tel. 071 580 9122

Royal Institution of Chartered Surveyors
12 Great George Street
London SW1P 3AD

Solicitors Complaints Bureau
Portland House
Stag Place
London SW1E 5BL
Tel. 071 834 2288

7. WORKING FOR A LIVING

The laws which govern relations between employers and employees clearly reflect the social, political and economic attitudes of our times. Since 1978, eight major Acts of Parliament on employment law have been passed. Among the many matters which this enormous mass of legislation deals with, trade union law, in particular, is addressed.

The impact of European law on our domestic labour relations law also cannot be over-emphasized. Indeed, some of our recent Acts of Parliament have been passed as a direct consequence of the UK's need to conform to its EC Treaty obligations.

However, Acts of Parliament are only a means to engender good industrial relations. For example, we can only legislate up to a point for the fair treatment of women or minorities. It is what happens in shops, offices and factories, throughout the country, which truly determines these and other issues.

Then again, the effectiveness of much industrial relations law depends on the industrial health of our economy. It stands to reason that if jobs are scarce, employees are not in a strong position to assert their rights. By the same token, employers in recessionary times may find that economic exigencies can and do force them into making difficult decisions to keep their businesses afloat – for example, making staff redundant.

In order to deal with the ever-growing volume of industrial relations law, industrial tribunals were set up in the 1970s. They were intended to settle industrial relations disputes effectively, speedily, and cheaply. They were also intended to be more informal than the ordinary courts, allowing unrepresented employees to bring their own actions.

At the moment, industrial tribunals have a very heavy workload. This entails longer waits for hearings. The hearings themselves are becoming more technical under the pressure of difficult legislation. The delays, complications of procedure, and structure of industrial law would soon become totally unacceptable, the court stated in a recent case. It called for a prompt and thorough review of the whole field.

About 4,500 cases are heard per year by the tribunals. Of these more than half concern unfair dismissal. Another 35,000 cases per annum are withdrawn or a settlement is reached before a hearing.

In this chapter we look at

- formalities on entering employment
- an employer's duties
- an employee's duties
- continuous service
- gender issues
- race discrimination
- dismissal
- redundancy
- trade union activities.

1. On entering employment

It is clearly in the interests of both employer and employee to understand – at the outset of their relationship – the terms and conditions of employment.

1.1 Written terms

Employees are entitled by law to have their terms of employment set down in a 'statement'.

1.1.1 Mandatory terms

The mandatory terms must state

(a) the parties to the contract of employment
(b) the date of commencement
(c) continuity of service, i.e. whether employment with a previous employer is to count as part of the employee's continuous service and the date on which such continuous period started (see also section 4 below).

1.1.2 Other written terms

In addition, they should also state

(a) rate and frequency of pay
(b) hours of work
(c) holiday entitlement and holiday pay
(d) sick pay
(e) pension rights
(f) notice
(g) job title
(h) disciplinary procedures.

At present, these terms need not be specified in one document. For example, an employee can be directed to a collective agreement or a works book to establish the terms of an item concerning disciplinary procedures (however, see section 1.2.2 below).

1.1.3 Time limits

The legislation sets down the time in which

- a statement must be served
- a statement's terms can be altered.

(a) Statement of terms within 13 weeks

The statement of terms and conditions must be furnished to employees within 13 weeks of starting work (also see section 1.2.3 below).

(b) Changing the terms

Employees must be notified of any change in the terms within 4 weeks.

1.1.4 Failure to provide a statement

If an employee is not supplied with a statement, he or she can go to an industrial tribunal which can determine what particulars should have been provided.

1.2 Statements – changes to requirements

Under the Trade Union Reform and Employment Law Act 1993 (TURELA), in addition to the above terms, an employee is entitled to

- Job description as an alternative to a job title
- Date on which a fixed term contract is due to end
- Place of work
- Details of collective agreements
- Details of work abroad if for more than a month.

1.2.1 Form of written statement

There must be a principal statement setting out items concerning names; date; terms of pay and hours of work; holidays; job title or description, and place of work. Other details can however follow in instalments.

1.2.2 References to other documents under TURELA

Particulars will have to be spelt out in the document given to the employee. There cannot be a reference to a collective agreement as the law presently stands.

(a) Notifying changes

Changes must be given to an employee within four weeks at the latest.

1.2.3 Time limits

The terms must be given to every employee who works eight or more hours a week, within two months of starting work.

2. An employer's duties

There are certain general duties which an employer owes to all employees. These need not be written into the contract but are implied by law. They include the following:

- The obligation to pay an employee for work done
- The way in which an employee is treated
- The obligation to take reasonable care for employees' health and safety (see chapter on *Accidents*, section 7).
- The obligation to provide equal treatment for men and women in an 'equality clause' (see section 5.1.1(a) below).

2.1 Implied duty to pay

An employer is clearly obliged to pay an employee for work done. The amount must be specified in an itemized pay statement which must be provided to an employee by law.

2.2 Implied duty to provide work?

There is no obligation on an employer to provide work for an employee so long as he or she is still being paid. However, a contract of employment can make provision for

- lay-off
- short time working.

2.2.1 Lay-off

This can arise when an employee's pay depends on being provided with work and he or she is not entitled to be paid under the contract when no work is provided.

The question then arises of whether a lay-off is a temporary suspension from work or a dismissal with a prospect of re-engagement. If it lasts for more than four consecutive weeks, or more than six weeks in any thirteen weeks, an employee can give notice that he or she intends to claim redundancy.

2.2.2 Short-time working

This can arise when the amount of work required of an employee is reduced. However, short-time working only applies if less than half the normal week's wages is being earned. An employee can claim redundancy if four consecutive weeks of short-time working have elapsed or short-time working has been applied for six out of thirteen weeks.

2.2.3 Contractual rights are paramount

To sum up, the contract itself must allow for lay-offs or short-term working before an employer can resort to them.

You work for an advertising agency but business has fallen off badly in the recession. You go to your office every day but find yourself doing crossword puzzles for most of the day. Your employer says that he will be withholding some of your salary pending an upturn in business. He says that he is entitled to lay off staff or to insist on short-time working in view of the exigencies of his situation. You wonder what your position is.

Even if no work is provided, your employer is under a general duty to pay you once you are willing and able to work. He has no automatic right to lay off staff or put them on short-time working and must have a contractual right to do so either by an express or implied term in the contract of employment. However, in recessionary times, staff will often accommodate their employers rather than see them go under!

2.2.4 No work

If an employer becomes insolvent the employment contract comes to an end. Employees should be entitled to wages owing to them and to redundancy pay (see section 8 on *Redundancy* below). If administrators carry on the business in order to realize its assets, they 'adopt' the contracts of employment. Employees' wages then take priority over the administrator's expenses.

2.3 Implied duty to treat employees properly

An employer is expected to treat his staff properly. This duty is implied in every contract of employment. The cases speak of a relationship of trust, confidence and respect. For example, an employer has failed to treat his or her employees properly when

- in a big business with many employees, s/he has refused to allow an employee to leave the premises to deal with an emergency at home
- s/he has refused to give one employee an increase in salary awarded to all other members of staff.

Your boss has been humiliating you in front of your work colleagues. You feel quite persecuted and wish to resign. There is nothing in your contract of employment which specifies that you are to be treated with respect.

The law will imply such a term in your contract on your behalf. Employers are not allowed to behave in an arbitrary or malicious manner towards employees.

2.4 Duty to ensure health and safety

An employer is under a duty in law to provide

- competent staff
- a safe system of working
- proper safe equipment and plant.

Details are discussed in the chapter on *Accidents* (see section 7).

2.5 Providing references – is it a duty?

An employer is not under a duty to provide a reference for employees.

You have always worked conscientiously. You now wish to apply for a job with another company. You have asked several times for a reference but your employer has not written one out for you.

There is nothing you can do to insist upon being given a reference.

2.5.1 Reference must not be malicious

However, if an employer does provide a reference, he or she is then under a duty to ensure that the reference is not malicious. If it is malicious then the ordinary laws of defamation will apply.

An employee, whom you disliked, has left you and has applied for another post. You are asked to supply a reference.

As we have seen, an employer is not obliged to supply a reference. However, if you do write one, you are under an obligation to ensure that your personal dislike does not lead you into writing a reference which is actuated by malice.

2.5.2 Is an employer under a duty of care for inaccuracies?

If a statement in a reference is inaccurate because of a negligent mistake, then an employer is liable to his former employee if he fails to get a job because of the negligent misstatement.

Thus an employer owes an employee a duty to make sure that the reference contains only accurate statements.

3. Employee's duties

Employees have a general duty to

- carry out their tasks and
- conduct themselves in such a way as to serve their employer's interests.

They are also under a duty to keep secret their employers' confidential information (see section 3.3 below).

3.1 Obeying orders

All lawful and reasonable orders should be carried out with reasonable skill and care.

3.1.1 Illegal orders

An employee is not under a duty to obey a plainly illegal order – such as falsifying the accounts or driving a vehicle with faulty brakes.

3.1.2 Unreasonable orders

An employee is under a duty to obey reasonable orders. What is an unreasonable order? This is much harder to ascertain than establishing an illegal order. What is reasonable to one person may appear quite unreasonable to another. Problems frequently arise with questions of overtime or of moving to another place of work at an employer's request.

It is plainly a matter of fact and degree.

3.2 Part performance

If an employee refuses to carry out contractual duties, an employer can withhold payment as long as it had been made clear that a partial performance would be unacceptable.

> *You have informed your employer that you are no longer prepared to work on Saturday mornings although your contract specifies that you have to work one Saturday morning in four. You come to work on Mondays to Fridays as usual. Your month's pay in its entirety has been withheld.*

Your position will depend on whether you knew in advance that a refusal to work on Saturday mornings would be regarded as a non-performance of your contractual duties.

3.3 Confidentiality

3.3.1 Present employees

Employees are under a general duty not to disclose confidential information relating to their employers' affairs which they might obtain in the course of their work. (For the definition of 'confidential information' see section 3.3.3 below.)

They are also under a duty not to assist a competitor of their employer. This is the employees' side of the duty to ensure that the relationship between employees and employers is one of trust.

3.3.2 Ex-employees

The question is what happens when an employee leaves his or her employer? How much of the employer's confidentiality should s/he still observe?

The answer is that confidential information is not to be disclosed but that employees can use general information they have acquired during their employment.

3.3.3 Confidential information

Whether a particular piece of information comes within this duty of confidence depends on the following factors.

(a) Nature of job

Certain jobs where confidential information is dealt with on a regular basis would indicate a high obligation of confidentiality. This might even be written into the employment contract.

(b) Nature of information

Not all information obtained in the course of employment is of equal weight. Distinctions must and can be drawn between trade secrets and other information.

(i) Trade secret

The information must be a trade secret or material so highly confidential that it requires the same protection as a trade secret. How is a trade secret determined?

(ii) Employer's attitude

If the employer stresses the confidential nature of the information it might show that s/he regards it as a trade secret.

(iii) Whether separable

If a particular piece of information cannot be separated from a package of information, which is generally not confidential, it might throw doubt on its designation as a trade secret.

3.3.4 Patent or invention

Any patent or invention an employee has made – provided it was in the course of normal duties and s/he has a special obligation to an employer because of those duties – belongs to the employer. However, an employee may still be entitled to be compensated for any 'outstanding benefit' an employer receives as a result of the patent.

3.3.5 Preventing wrongful use of information

An ex-employee is *not* at liberty to use information regarded as confidential to set up a rival business or to help a competitor. An ex-employer can ask the court for an injunction to prevent such misuse. If the court thinks an employer has made out a case, an injunction can be granted whether there is an express covenant not to disclose confidential information or a covenant which the court implies.

(a) Express covenants

In general, express restrictive covenants are there to protect confidential information which an ex-employee has acquired – for example, from an employer's mailing lists. To protect their business, employers also often insist in their contracts of employment that their employees sign a covenant not to compete with them if they leave – 'restrictive covenants' (or 'covenants in restraint of trade' as they are also called); see below, section 3.4.

(b) Implied covenants

Even if an employee has not entered into an express covenant with an employer s/he may be restrained from using confidential information acquired during the course of employment. This is because every contract of employment contains an implied term not to use or disclose such information.

However, in such a case, an ex-employee is entitled to approach customers, suppliers or contacts of a former employer although s/he must not make any list or memorize the names of customers etc. before s/he leaves. That would be in breach of the implied duty of fidelity during the subsistence of the contract of employment.

3.4 Restrictive covenants

The law realizes that employers want to protect their business against competition. At the same time, there is a strong perception that ex-employees are entitled to make a living as best they can. Their chances of doing so should not be unfairly curtailed by their relationship with an ex-employer.

So a restrictive covenant will only be enforceable if it can be shown that it is *reasonable* and is *in the public interest*.

Restrictions are more likely to be regarded as unenforceable if their terms are very wide.

3.4.1 The restriction must be reasonable

As a general rule, the parties themselves are regarded as the best judges of what is reasonable between them. Two key factors in assessing reasonableness are time and distance.

(a) Time

A contract term for a year would be regarded as reasonable whereas a seven-year restraint would be regarded as unreasonable – depending on the type of contract.

> *You were a director of a mail order firm in charge of preparing a catalogue. You left and went to work for a rival. Your former employers have applied to the court for an injunction to prevent you working for their competitors on the ground that you signed an agreement that you would not join any rival firm for 12 months.*

In this case, the restriction could be regarded as reasonable for a person of your seniority.

(b) Distance

> *You are a solicitor and have a contract with your firm, which is in the City, not to practise within a 10 mile radius of the City of London for five years if you leave. You are now offered a job with another firm of solicitors situated in the West End of London.*

It is likely that the court would consider the density of the population as a factor in deciding whether the restraint is reasonable. A ten-mile radius restriction might be a more reasonable term in a contract between solicitors in a small country town than in one between London solicitors.

3.4.2 The restriction must be in the public interest

In deciding what is in the public interest, the courts will always favour the right of someone to find work. They will protect an employer's legitimate interest – but only insofar as that is necessary and specific.

3.4.3 The restriction must be enforced in ordinary courts of law

The rights and duties of an employer and employee in relation to restrictive covenants are only enforceable by bringing proceedings in the ordinary courts. They do not involve industrial tribunal hearings.

4. Continuous service

4.1 Rights dependent on continuous service

As we have seen, many of an employee's rights depend on the need to show that he or she has worked for the appropriate period. This is known as continuous service. Generally, the stipulated periods are

- two years' full time (for more than sixteen hours per week) or
- five years' part-time (for between eight and sixteen hours per week).

(See Department of Employment Booklet 11: *Rules governing continuous employment*).

(a) Two years' continuous service (full-time)

Employees must show that they have worked for their employers for two years continuously at the effective date of dismissal (where they work for at least 16 hours per week).

(b) Five years' continuous service (part-time)

Under the employment legislation, a part-time worker, who works between eight and 16 hours per week, has to work for five years' continuous service to qualify for unfair dismissal and redundancy protection. The House of Lords has ruled that, as most part-time workers are women, the requirement for five years' continuous service for those working between eight and 16 hours per week to qualify for unfair dismissal and redundancy – conflicts with the right of men and women to receive equal pay for equal work. Only two years' continuous service should be required to qualify – as with full-time workers. Those working less than 8 hours per week are unaffected by this ruling.

(c) When continuity begins and ends

Continuous service starts on the day the employee begins work. Any week in which an employee works for 16 hours or more will be included in the calculation of continuous employment. Periods such as overtime are not included in the computation.

Where an employee has worked under multiple contracts with the same employer, he or she may not be entitled to aggregate the hours of work where the contracts are separate and distinct.

There is a cessation of work when the employer has no work available for the employee to do. Whether or not the absence is temporary is a question of fact to be determined by an industrial tribunal. (See also above, *Employer's duty to pay*, section 2.1.)

(d) Must be with one employer

An employment must usually be with one employer only, in order to be treated as continuous.

However there are exceptions where

(a) a trade, business or undertaking is transferred
(b) an employer dies
(c) there is a change of partners, personal representatives or trustees
(d) an employee works for an associated employer.

There must be a transfer of a business as a going concern and the new business must be the same as the old.

Two employers are treated as associated if one is a company of which the other directly or indirectly has control, or if both are companies of which a third person has control.

(e) Interruptions

If the continuity is broken, an employee has to start all over again in accumulating the legally required period of continuous service.

(f) Interruptions which do not count

Continuous service is not interrupted if

(a) There is a break in service for no more than 26 weeks because of sickness or injury; it still counts as normal employment.

(b) An employee is loaned to another employer for a period of time.

(c) Absence from work is due wholly or partly to pregnancy and the other conditions of maternity leave apply. A woman must return to work when her maternity leave comes to an end (see *Gender issues* below, section 5).

(d) Absence from work for the whole or part of a week is due to a 'temporary cessation' of work.

(e) An employee takes part in a strike. The period during which s/he stops work will not be counted as a break in his or her continuity of employment. Its effect is to postpone the date on which the employee started work by the number of days on which s/he was on strike.

(f) Interruptions are relatively short in relation to the period worked.

5. Gender issues

5.1 Equal pay

The cases show that the law is particularly dynamic in the sphere of discrimination on grounds of sex or race. The law has to address difficult and touchy issues, as well as having to adapt to changing social modes and work patterns. European law has a continuing impact in the sphere of sex discrimination provisions. Again and again our national law has been obliged to alter in order to accommodate European judgments and directives.

5.1.1 A right by law

In 1970, the Equal Pay Act was passed in order to lay down the principle of equality between the sexes in employees' terms and conditions. Under the Act, a woman can claim equal pay with a man if she is employed in 'like work' or 'equivalent work' or where her work is of 'equal value' to that of a man in terms of the demands made on her.

◆ **Take note:** a man is just as entitled to receive equal pay under these provisions as is a woman. However, in discussion, we will refer to women – who are usually found to be most in need of the protection afforded by the terms of the Equal Pay Act – rather than to men.

(a) Equality clause

Every contract of employment includes an equality clause either express or implied. If a term in a woman's contract is, or becomes, less favourable than a term in a man's contract, that term will be modified to make it as favourable as the corresponding term in the man's contract.

The only time when an equality clause will not operate is where an employer can prove that the variation is genuinely due to a material factor other than that of sex (see *Material factors*, section 5.1.1(e) below).

(b) Same employment

A man is in the *same employment* as a woman if he is employed by the same or an associated employer at the same establishment or at establishments in Great Britain which include that one. There must be common terms and conditions of employment either generally or for employees of the relevant class.

(c) Like work

A woman is to be regarded as engaged in *like work* with a man if her work and his are of the same or broadly similar nature and the differences, if any, between the things they do are not of practical importance in relation to the terms and conditions of employment.

(d) Equivalent work

A woman is employed on work *equivalent* to that of a man if their work has been given an equal value in terms of the demands made on the employee under various headings.

This requires the carrying out of a job evaluation scheme (JES). Jobs are evaluated in terms of the demands made on a worker under headings such as skill, effort and decision-making. Once a JES has been carried out and the woman's job is found to be of equal value with that of a man, the woman may claim equal pay.

(e) Material factors

An employer may defeat a woman's claim for equal pay if it can be shown that the pay differential is due to some objectively justifiable reason other than sex ('material factors').

To show that discrimination is objectively justified, an employer must show that s/he is

- taking measures which correspond to a real need of the business
- that the measures are appropriate in the circumstances
- and that they are necessary to meet the need.

For example, a health authority decided to attract qualified and experienced persons from the private sector to get a particular service started by offering them a higher salary. A woman who qualified and came directly into the service wanted to be paid at the higher rate. It was held that there had been a material factor, namely the need to attract private-sector personnel, to justify the higher pay rate. That had nothing to do with sex.

If it is shown that there is a significant imbalance between the wages of a man and a woman, the burden is on the employer to justify that imbalance.

For a defence of material factor to succeed, an employer must show that any difference is material and it must be material between the man's and the woman's case.

For example, a male canteen worker was paid more than a woman for doing like work. The employers claimed that special arrangements had been made in the man's case because of the difficulties in recruiting night shift workers and that was not a difference related to sex. The court held that the employers had not shown that there was a material difference between the man's case and that of the woman to which the difference was genuinely due. The man was being paid at a higher rate in order to secure his services and that was not a material factor between the case of the man and that of the woman.

Factors such as additional obligations and amount of responsibility attached to the job, experience and length of service, and the job's location may all be regarded as material factors.

(f) Impact of European law

Article 119 of the EC Treaty provides that member states should ensure and maintain the application of the principle that men and women should receive equal pay for equal work. The Equal Pay Directive (75/117) and Equal Treatment Directive (76/207) deal with the general implementation of the equal pay and equal treatment principles. Those provisions are now being relied on by employees in this country who feel that UK law is not providing the same comprehensive rights as are available in EC law.

A recent example is the House of Lords ruling that part-time workers (i.e. those working between 8 and 16 hours weekly) should be accorded the same rights to claim compensation for redundancy and unfair dismissal as those in full-time work. As most part-time workers are women, the House of Lords stated, they are being discriminated against if they would have to work for five years continuously as under the present law.

5.2 Sex Discrimination Act

This Act was passed in 1975. It makes it unlawful to discriminate against men and women on the grounds of their sex. It must be stressed that the Act is applicable to both sexes. In fact the Equal Opportunities Commission (see DIRECTORY and chapter on *The Legal System*) has found that 40 per cent of complaints to it about sex discrimination in recruitment are from men.

5.2.1 Direct discrimination

Direct discrimination occurs when, on the basis of sex, a man or a woman receives less favourable treatment than their female or male counterpart.

A well-intentioned motive is not a defence.

You and a colleague are the only two men in an otherwise all-female team. Your male colleague leaves his employment and you are withdrawn from the team and placed in another department. Your employers state that the reason for your withdrawal is that, in the past, a sole male found it difficult to work in an all-female team.

This is an instance of direct discrimination, the good intentions of your employers notwithstanding.

However, instances of direct discrimination – for good or bad motives – are usually hard to prove. For that reason, the Sex Discrimination Act includes the concept of indirect discrimination.

5.2.2 Indirect discrimination

Indirect discrimination occurs when an employer imposes a term or condition which is such that the proportion of persons of one sex who can comply is considerably smaller than that of the other sex and

- the term cannot be justified irrespective of the sex of the person to whom it is applied
- and it is to that person's detriment that he or she cannot comply with it.

As we will see below, a term or condition may be justified where there is a genuine occupational qualification (see section 5.2.4 below).

5.2.3 Other discriminatory acts

The Act also stipulates that there must be no discrimination in

- the arrangements made for the purpose of deciding who to employ
- terms on which employment is offered

- refusing or deliberately omitting to offer employment because of a person's sex
- the way access to promotion, training etc. is offered
- dismissing a person or subjecting him or her to detrimental treatment.

As we can see the terms are very wide.

5.2.4 Genuine occupational qualification

There is no discrimination if it is specified that it should be a man or a woman who is employed in a job where their sex is a genuine occupational qualification. The following are some examples of where this would be the case:

- where physical characteristics are needed for authenticity (e.g. a male actor is employed to play a male role)
- where decency or privacy might otherwise be infringed (e.g. the attendant in a women's changing room is female)
- the post involves a single-sex institution (e.g. the matron in a girls' boarding school is female).

If you are an employer wishing to employ someone in your own home, you are entitled to specify the sex of that person. However, there cannot be an official policy determining that sex – e.g. that an *au pair* should always be female.

5.3 Maternity rights

There are many detailed and complex rules on the subject of the rights of pregnant employees. It is important that employers should spell them out to their employees and explain them as fully as possible. It is unfortunate for both employers and employees that this particularly sensitive area of employment law should be as complicated as it is. New rules will be coming into operation in November 1994 which are superimposed on the old regime – no doubt adding to the difficulties in interpreting the law (see section 5.4 on *Projected changes* below).

Employees should seek advice from their trade union representatives or from other organizations (see DIRECTORY).

There are certain basic statutory rights.

5.3.1 The right not to be unfairly dismissed on grounds of pregnancy

The dismissal of a woman because she is pregnant or for any reason connected with pregnancy ('inadmissible reasons') is automatically unfair under the Sex Discrimination Act. Remedy is via an industrial tribunal.

◆ **Take note:** the dismissal will not be automatically unfair if her pregnancy makes it impossible for a woman to do the job properly and there is no suitable alternative work she can do.

In this case, the ordinary redundancy rules apply (see section 8 below).

5.3.2 General rights

The Employment Protection Act gives pregnant employees other rights, in addition to protection against unfair dismissal. These rights are

(1) The right to time off work for ante-natal care (this can include relaxation classes)
(2) The right to maternity leave

(3) The right to return to work after maternity leave

(4) The right to statutory maternity pay.

5.3.3 Ante-natal care

An employee is entitled to be paid the appropriate hourly rate for any periods of absence to receive ante-natal care.

There is no minimum qualifying period of employment before this right is acquired.

> *Your secretary, who has been working for you for under a year, says that she is pregnant and will need to see a doctor during working hours. You ask whether she has already made an appointment and whether she can re-arrange her working hours so that she can see a doctor in her own time.*

Your secretary is under no duty to rearrange her working hours or to make up lost time. Her right is to time off during working hours.

The fact that she has not worked for you for a qualifying period does not affect her minimum right to time off work to receive appropriate ante-natal care. It will affect her entitlement to the level of maternity pay, which she will receive, and to maternity leave, however (see immediately below).

The appointment to receive ante-natal care must have been made on the advice of a doctor, midwife or health visitor and you are entitled to see her doctor's certificate and appointment card after her first visit.

5.3.4 Maternity leave

Employers must not allow a woman to return to work within two weeks of having her baby. If they do, they can be fined up to £500.

There is now a two-tier system for women whose babies were born on or after October 16 1994. All pregnant women irrespective of length of service or hours worked have a right to a basic 14-week maternity leave period. All women with more than two years' service also have the right to return to work within 29 weeks of the birth as follows:

A pregnant woman has the right to return to work provided

- she has worked for the same employers
  (a) for two years full time or
  (b) for five years part time
- she works at least until the end of the 12th week before the expected confinement date
- she gives proper notice of
  (a) when she is taking leave and
  (b) when she will return to work
- the firm can take her back (see also section 5.3.5 below).

If, after the start of the sixth week before the expected week of the birth, the employee is absent because of pregnancy or childbirth, maternity leave will start automatically on that date.

Leave can commence at any time within 11 weeks of the confinement date and can last for up to 29 weeks. For rules concerning returning to work afterwards, see below.

(a) Leave – need to give notice

Proper notice is crucial.

A woman must notify her employer that she is going to be absent from work wholly or partly because of her pregnancy or confinement.

Notice must be given at least 21 days before the planned absence. Notice must be in writing. If notice has not been given 21 days beforehand, it should be given as soon as is reasonably possible.

(b) 'Notified date of return'

A woman must give notice in writing to the employer of her intention to return to work at least 21 days before the day on which she intends to return. This is a strict requirement with *no* exceptions. It is very important to give such notice as all the other rights to which she is entitled follow on from it.

◆ **Note** that by giving notice a woman is *not obliged* to return to work. She is merely keeping her options open.

(c) Postponement of return to work

Return to work may be postponed by

- the employer or
- the employee

An employer may postpone a woman's return to work provided that s/he notifies the woman when she can return within a four-week period of notification and gives reasons for the postponement.

An employee may postpone her return for up to four weeks provided that she furnishes a doctor's certificate to the effect that she is not able to return to work.

(d) Returning to the same work

Provided all the proper conditions are met, a woman can return to

- the job in which she was employed under her original contract of employment and
- on terms and conditions which are not less favourable than those which would have been applicable to her if she had not been absent because of her pregnancy.

(e) Failure to return to work

If a woman fails to return to work after the end of her maternity leave – without proper notice of her intention to postpone her return – she will lose her statutory rights.

5.3.5 Where an employer cannot offer the old job back

(a) Redundancy situation

Where a redundancy situation arises while the woman is on maternity leave, it may not be possible for her to return to her old job. However, if there is a suitable vacancy, the employer must offer her alternative employment and the terms of her new employment must not be substantially less favourable than her old contract. The job must also be suitable and appropriate for her to do.

Where there is no suitable vacancy, the woman will be entitled to claim a redundancy payment.

When deciding which of several employees to make redundant, an employee must disregard the inconvenience arising from the fact that one is pregnant and will be taking maternity leave. If the employer does not do so and makes absence on maternity leave the factor determining the pregnant woman's dismissal, then it will be unfair.

(b) Small firms

If the number of employees working for the employer before the start of the woman's maternity leave was five or less, the employer's refusal to allow her to return may not amount to a dismissal if it was not reasonably practicable for her to return or for the employer to offer her suitable alternative employment.

5.3.6 Statutory maternity pay (SMP)

(a) Obligation to pay SMP

An employer is obliged to pay SMP for 18 weeks.

◆ **Take note:** this obligation applies whether or not an employee intends to return to work provided that continuity-of-service requirements are met.

(b) Two rates of pay

There are two rates of SMP:

(a) 6 weeks payable at the higher rate (90% of average earnings); and
(b) 12 weeks at the lower rate (currently £52.50 – the amount changes annually in April).

(c) Computing earnings

Earnings include bonuses, overtime, statutory sick pay, and arrears. However, redundancy payments, reimbursement of business expenses, benefits in kind and pension payments are excluded.

(d) Other allowances

To be entitled to the higher rate SMP, a woman must have been continuously employed for two years and have worked 16 hours or more per week. If she has worked part-time, i.e. between eight and 16 hours per week, she will need to have been continuously employed for five years. However, see changes to the legislation, section 5.4 below.

To be entitled to the lower rate SMP a woman must have 26 weeks' continuous employment. There is no minimum working hours' requirement but her average weekly earnings must be at or above the lower earnings limit (LEL) of £56 from April 1993);

The actual maternity pay period is flexible and need not be restricted to the 11th week before the anticipated confinement date.

> *You are in your sixth month of pregnancy, in fulltime employment, and would like to work up until the sixth week before the baby is due. You are concerned as to whether you will jeopardize your rights to SMP.*

You can choose to work up until the sixth week before the expected week of confinement and still retain your right to the full 18 weeks' SMP.

(See also *Employers' Guide to Statutory Maternity Pay* (NI257); *Statutory Maternity Pay: An Employer's Training Brief*; and Table of Dates (SMP55), published by the Department of Society Security.

> *You have only been in your present position as legal researcher for two months when you discover that you are pregnant. You know that you do not qualify for SMP as you lack sufficient continuity of service, but would like to know what other benefits you may receive.*

Any woman, who is not eligible for SMP at the higher or lower rate, may be entitled to claim maternity allowance direct from the DSS. Entitlement depends on the employee's NIC record rather than continuity of employment with one particular employer.

▶ **Do remember:** SMP is subject to PAYE income tax.

(e) Appeal against refusal to pay

If an employer refuses to pay a woman SMP, she is entitled to ask an adjudication officer of the DSS for a formal decision. Both the employer and the employee must send written submissions to the adjudication officer stating their positions although they need not attend in person.

5.4 Changes to present legislation

The current legislation is in conformity with an EC Directive on pregnant women at work for women whose babies were due on or after 16 October 1994. A 'maternity leave period' will be granted to all employees irrespective of length of service or hours worked. It will last for 14 weeks. Six months' employment is required to qualify for statutory maternity pay at the higher rate.

New provisions on dismissal state that a woman will automatically be deemed to be unfairly dismissed if the principal reason for dismissal is that she is pregnant or for any other reason connected with pregnancy (e.g. morning sickness).

She is also entitled to written reasons for dismissal, if she is dismissed at any time during pregnancy or maternity leave. There is no minimum service requirement and she should not have to request the reasons – they should be given as a matter of course.

5.5 Compensation for discrimination

The European Court ruled in August 1993 that the purpose behind the sex discrimination provisions was to guarantee real protection for employees and to act as a real deterrent to discrimination by employers. Therefore it was unlawful for a State to set a fixed amount so as to limit the compensation which a victim of sex discrimination could receive from the national courts. Every case depended on its particular circumstances. A fixed award of damages might not be an accurate reflection of the actual loss suffered.

6. Race discrimination

It is unlawful to discriminate against a person on grounds of colour, race, nationality and ethnic or national origins (see the Race Relations Act 1976).

The Commission for Racial Equality keeps the 1976 Race Discrimination Act under review and may advise, assist or give legal help to individuals (see DIRECTORY). It also issues a Code of Practice in order to assist employers to establish procedures and records for monitoring the ethnic composition of their workforce.

6.1 Defining ethnic origins

The term 'ethnic origins' embraces more groups than the term 'race'. In law a person's ethnic origins are determined by his ethnic group. An ethnic group is a distinct community on account of its

- long shared history
- cultural traditions, including family and social customs.

These two characteristics are regarded as essential.

In addition, the following characteristics are considered relevant:

- common geographical origins or common ancestry
- common language and literature
- common religion
- being a minority group or
- being part of a minority or an oppressed majority (for example, a conquered people) within a larger community.

6.1.1 Selecting for employment

An employer must not discriminate against a person as regards

- making arrangements for job offers
- terms on which jobs are offered
- recruitment or selection for employment.

6.1.2 Prospects in employment

Once a person is employed he or she must not be discriminated against on grounds of race

- in the terms of employment
- in opportunities for training and promotion etc.
- with regard to other benefits
- as reason for dismissal.

6.2 Direct discrimination

There is direct discrimination where one person treats another less favourably on grounds of race, colour, nationality or ethnic origins.

Segregation constitutes less favourable treatment but voluntary con-segregation (living as a separate community) is lawful.

The motive for discrimination is irrelevant. A worthy motive may still be unlawful discrimination. For example, an employer might refuse to take on a Jewish applicant simply in order to shield him from antisemitic remarks from other members of staff. The employer would nevertheless still be guilty of racial discrimination.

6.2.1 Difficulties in proving direct discrimination

Generally speaking, it is not easy to prove that an employer has discriminated against an employee on the grounds of race. So if the facts of the case indicate discrimination and no other reasonable explanation is forthcoming, then the court may assume that discrimination occurred.

6.3 Indirect discrimination

There is indirect discrimination where an employer

(a) applies a requirement or condition to a job
(b) the proportion of persons from one racial group who can comply with it is smaller than the proportion of persons from other racial groups
(c) the requirement or condition is not justified irrespective of the racial group of the person to whom it is applied; and
(d) it is to the person's detriment that he or she is unable to comply with the requirement or condition.

6.3.1 When a condition does not amount to indirect discrimination

(a) An employer may be able to justify a condition which would otherwise amount to indirect discrimination, provided it is not imposed for discriminatory reasons.

For example, a food company imposed a rule prohibiting the employment of persons with beards or long hair. A Sikh applied for a job and when he was turned down, he claimed indirect discrimination on grounds of race. The Court of Appeal dismissed his claim.

The court held that although the requirement did indirectly discriminate against Sikhs, it could be justified on grounds of health and hygiene.

(b) An employer may be able to justify a condition where it is just one of a number of factors which are taken into account in assessing a candidate's suitability for a job. In other words, it is not a condition with which an employee *must* comply.

For example, an inner London borough advertised for a head of its legal department. One of the criteria was experience in the borough. A candidate felt that it was indirect discrimination because the number of persons from his racial group who could comply with that condition was smaller than from other racial groups. However the Court of Appeal found that the condition was not a 'must' – it was just one of a number of factors for drawing up a shortlist.

6.4 Reverse discrimination

Discrimination in favour of an ethnic minority can also breach the provisions of the Act.

> *A local authority advertised for a manager in its housing department but insisted upon someone from the ethnic minorities in order to deal with housing problems in a racially mixed area. You are not from an ethnic minority but feel that your qualifications entitle you to apply for the job.*

If your application is turned down out of hand because you do not qualify on the grounds of race, you can make a legitimate claim of discrimination to a tribunal.

◆ **Note:** in certain welfare tasks (as opposed to managerial jobs), requirements as to race do not constitute discrimination (see section 6.10 below).

6.5 Victimization

A person is victimized if he is treated less favourably because he has

- brought proceedings claiming discrimination on grounds of race
- given evidence or provided information in connection with such proceedings

or

- made allegations of an unlawful act of discrimination.

However a person is not victimized if he is less favourably treated because his allegations were untrue and not made in good faith.

6.6 Putting pressure on employees to discriminate

It is unlawful to engage in discriminatory practices, to publish discriminatory advertisements, to give instructions to other persons to discriminate or to put pressure on a person to discriminate.

You are offered a job in a pub but the landlord tells you to take as long as possible before you serve a black or Asian customer. You do not intend to carry out his instructions. You also would like to report it to someone in authority.

An unlawful act of discrimination such as this should be brought to the attention of the Commission for Racial Equality (see DIRECTORY).

6.7 Individual's remedies

A person who feels that he or she has been discriminated against may complain directly to an industrial tribunal. If the tribunal finds the complaint is well-founded, it can make a declaration of rights, award compensation or recommend that the employer should take steps to remove the effects of the discrimination.

6.8 Proving your case

It is notoriously hard to prove that a particular act has been motivated by race discrimination. Even an employer who decides not to employ someone from an ethnic minority may not admit to himself or herself – let alone to others – the real reason for refusal. Even a professed desire to employ someone 'who will fit in' can disguise discriminatory intent.

You have been thwarted in gaining promotion in your firm. You suspect it is because you are from an ethnic minority. It is of course very difficult to prove your case and you want a tribunal to draw the inference that you are the victim of racial discrimination. You would also like information from your employers concerning the ethnic composition of their workforce in order to show that they generally operate discriminatory practices.

The courts are well aware of the difficulties of proving racial discrimination in the workplace. Usually an employee can only point to certain facts which are consistent with having been treated less favourably on the grounds of race. It is then up to the employer to furnish a convincing alternative explanation – for example, that there were other good reasons for taking that particular action. If no good explanation is put forward, then a tribunal could well infer discrimination.

The courts will order an employer to provide information on the ethnic composition of the workforce in a race discrimination case, provided it is reasonable to impose such an order.

For example, if the data already exists, then it is not asking too much from an employer to provide it. However, where the information is not available and it would take great expense and trouble to assemble it, then an order is unlikely to be made.

6.9 Exceptions to the rule – where there is no discrimination

(a) Discrimination on grounds of birth, nationality, descent or residence is permitted in the civil service.
(b) Employment in private households is not covered by the Race Relations Act.
(c) If particular occupational qualifications are required, discrimination is permitted. Thus an employer may discriminate against a person on grounds of race in very particular circumstances – where race is a 'genuine

occupational qualification' for the post (see section 6.10 immediately below).

6.10 In what circumstances might belonging to a particular racial group be a 'genuine occupational qualification'?

(a) Where an employee will be required to participate in a dramatic performance or other entertainment and someone from a particular racial group is needed for purposes of authenticity.

(b) Where an employee will have to act as an artist's or photographic model and authenticity is needed.

(c) Where an employee will be working in a place where food or drink is served to members of the public in a particular setting and a person of a particular racial group is needed for purposes of authenticity (for example a Thai waitress in a Thai restaurant).

(d) Where an employee will be providing welfare services to a particular racial group, which could most effectively be provided by a member of that group.

The question of what are welfare services has been considered by the courts. The term is given a wide interpretation. However it will not apply, for example, where the services – even in a welfare department – are of an administrative nature which could be performed by someone from any racial group.

7. Dismissal

There are two types of dismissal: wrongful dismissal and unfair dismissal.

The common law allows an employee to bring a claim for *wrongful dismissal* in the ordinary courts. At common law an employer could end an employee's contract of employment by giving proper notice or payment in lieu. A failure to give proper notice was treated as a breach of contract and an employee could sue for damages for wrongful dismissal.

This right still exists.

Statute law allows an employee to bring a claim for *unfair dismissal* in an industrial tribunal.

Changes have been introduced so that industrial tribunals are now able to hear both types of dismissal cases (see section 7.1.3 below).

If you are in any doubt as to what action best suits your particular situation, you must seek legal advice.

7.1 Wrongful dismissal

So in certain circumstances, a claim for wrongful dismissal may still be more to an employee's advantage than pursuing a claim for unfair dismissal under statute. Also, a claim for wrongful dismissal may be the only avenue open to an employee – for example, when s/he has not worked the continuous period necessary to qualify for his or her statutory rights.

7.1.1 Conditions of wrongful dismissal outlined

(a) An action for wrongful dismissal only arises where there has been a breach of contract.

(b) There is no maximum award in damages for wrongful dismissal.

(c) A claim for wrongful dismissal does not involve a continuous service requirement (see section 7.2.3 below).

(d) The court will not normally order that an employee be reinstated in an action for wrongful dismissal.

(e) There is no age barrier to a claim for wrongful dismissal, whereas under statute, an employee past the normal retiring age cannot claim for unfair dismissal.

(f) A claim for damages may be brought within six years from the date of the alleged breach of contract, whereas under statute an employee must generally bring an action within three months.

(g) There is no ceiling on damages in a wrongful dismissal case. A highly paid employee with a long notice provision may be entitled to sue for considerable sums of money. In one case an employee entitled to 30 months' notice was awarded over £70,000 damages.

7.1.2 Criticism of present two-tier system

The fact that there are two types of dismissal claims, heard in two different sets of courts, has evoked criticism. It has been suggested that these claims should all be heard in industrial tribunals.

7.1.3 Streamlining of procedures

Under the Trade Union Reform and Employment Law Act 1993 (TURELA), section 39, regulations were introduced to widen the tribunals' jurisdiction to hear claims for employers' breach of contract. Jurisdiction was extended from July 1994 to cover claims for damages for breach of contract and sums due under contracts of employment, e.g. notice pay. Thus employees who wish to bring an unfair dismissal claim (see section immediately below) and a breach of contract claim can bring them both together instead of in two actions. An employer can also counter-claim (i.e. put in a claim of his own against an employee). Damages are limited to £25,000.

7.2 Unfair dismissal

The provisions relating to unfair dismissal are now contained in the Employment Protection (Consolidation) Act 1978.

(a) There may be a case of unfair dismissal even where there has been no breach of contract.

(b) The maximum award of compensation for unfair dismissal is normally £11,000 (from 1 June 1994) plus a basic award.

(c) Employees generally require two years' continuous service before they can bring a claim for unfair dismissal.

(d) An industrial tribunal may order reinstatement or reengagement of an employee.

(e) An employee who is over normal retiring age is not entitled to bring a claim for unfair dismissal.

(f) There is a time limit of three months for bringing a claim for unfair dismissal.

7.2.1 Tribunal workload on unfair dismissal claims

Over fifty per cent of all cases brought before industrial tribunals concern unfair dismissal.

The law endeavours to strike a balance between the needs of the workforce to be protected against arbitrary and unfair dismissal and the needs of management to run their businesses efficiently.

7.2.2 Employee's rights against unfair dismissal

By law, an employee has the right not to be unfairly dismissed by his or her employer.

The above statement is subject to certain reservations.

(a) While a dismissal in certain instances may appear to be unfair, an employer can put forward reasons to show why the dismissal was fair in the particular circumstances of the case (see section 7.3 below).

(b) In general an employee must have worked for a qualifying period (see continuous service, section 7.2.3 below). However in certain instances, there is no need for a qualifying period (see section 7.2.3(a) below).

(c) In certain capacities employees have no protection – for example, members of the armed forces or the police.

7.2.3 Continuous service

To bring a claim for unfair dismissal, an employee must show that he or she has worked for the appropriate period. This is known as continuous service (see section 4 above).

(a) Where there is unfair dismissal and no requirement of continuous employment

If a dismissal is based on

- sex discrimination
- race discrimination
- trade union activities or membership
- non-membership of a trade union

there is *no* requirement of continuous employment before a claim can be made. The minimum number of hours per week, however, do apply.

(See Department of Employment, Booklet 11: *Rules governing continuous employment*.)

(b) Lockouts

When an employer closes the place of employment or refuses to continue employing staff, then there is a lock-out.

An industrial tribunal can only determine whether there has been an unfair dismissal if (i) other employees were not dismissed; and (ii) if they were dismissed, they were re-engaged within three months. This is the 'no picking and choosing' rule.

(c) Strikes

An industrial tribunal has no jurisdiction to determine whether a dismissal was unfair where, at the time of the dismissal, the employer was conducting a lock-out or the employee was taking part in a strike or other industrial action.

However the employer has no right to pick and choose who he dismisses in such circumstances. He must dismiss all those who are on strike at the time of the dismissal and must not re-engage them for three months. If the employer dismisses or re-engages only some, those persons who were not re-engaged, or were dismissed, may bring a claim of unfair dismissal before an industrial tribunal.

Employees who, at the time of dismissal, are taking part in unofficial action are excluded from the right to bring a claim of unfair dismissal.

7.3 When an employer claims a dismissal was fair

An employer may defend a claim of unfair dismissal by establishing a potentially fair reason for the dismissal. Among these reasons are

(a) the capability or qualifications of the employee; poor performance; or ill health

(b) the conduct of the employee

(c) redundancy (see *Redundancy*, section 8 below)

(d) illegality (it would be potentially fair for an employer to dismiss an employee if he would be breaking the law if he continued to work; e.g. it would be fair to dismiss a driver who had lost his licence)

(e) some other substantial reason (see ACAS advisory booklet: *Discipline at Work*); this may include such things as unacceptable absence levels, criminal convictions, etc.

Even if an employer has dismissed an employee fairly, the employee is still entitled to a period of notice.

7.4 Dismissal which is automatically unfair

There are some dismissals which are automatically unfair. Unfair circumstances of dismissal include

(1) where an employee is a member of a trade union

(2) where an employee is involved in union activities

(3) where an employee refuses to join a trade union

(4) closed shop dismissals

(5) where an employee is pregnant and the principal reason for dismissal is her pregnancy

(6) where an employee has been selected unfairly for redundancy

(7) where there has been a transfer of the employer's undertaking

(8) where the dismissal is on grounds of sex

(9) where the dismissal is on grounds of race.

7.5 Reasons to be in writing

An employee may request a written statement of the reasons for dismissal (fair or unfair). To be entitled to such a statement, an employee must have completed six months' continuous employment with an employer at the effective date of dismissal (two years if s/he commenced employment on or after 26 February 1990).

The statement should be provided within 14 days of requesting it. An employer cannot unreasonably refuse to provide a statement.

7.6 Time limit for claims

A claim for unfair dismissal must be presented within three months from the effective date of termination.

7.7 Summary dismissal

In certain exceptional circumstances, an employee can be dismissed without notice. The dismissal takes effect immediately. The courts require 'gross misconduct'.

Summary dismissal has been justified

- where an employee has acted dishonestly
- where an employee has gained unauthorized access to computer records
- where an employee has knowingly breached an express contractual term (e.g. where a coach firm expressly forbids drinking on or off duty and one of its long-distance drivers reports for work over the limit).

8. Redundancy

Employees are entitled to payment of compensation if made redundant. This means that employment has been terminated because an employer

- ceases altogether to carry on business
- ceases to carry on business in the same place
- ceases to need some employees.

8.1 When redundancy occurs

Redundancy occurs

- if an employer ceases or intends to cease carrying on the business for the purposes of which the employee was employed;
- if an employer ceased or intends to cease carrying on the business in the place where the employee was employed; or
- the needs of the business for an employee to carry out work of a particular kind, or to do so in the place where he worked, have ceased, or diminished, or were expected to do so.

8.2 When an employee can claim

To claim a redundancy payment an employee

- must be aged between 18 and 65
- must have been employed for at least two years continuously (see section 4 above for computing 'continuous service') and
- must work for 16 hours or more each week.

8.2.1 When part-time workers can claim

If a person works for between 8 and 16 hours per week s/he must have worked for five years continuously. A person who works for fewer than 8 hours a week is not allowed to claim a redundancy payment.

◆ **Note:** the House of Lords has held that only a two-year qualifying period should apply for part-time workers employed for between 8 and 16 hours per week.

8.2.2 Presumption

There is a presumption that an employee who is dismissed has been dismissed for redundancy and is entitled to a redundancy payment.

8.3 Employer's defence to claim – reasonable alternative

An employer can prove that an offer of suitable alternative employment was made and the employee refused it unreasonably.

8.3.1 When an employee's refusal of alternative employment is justified

Employees can refuse alternative employment if it is unsuitable. An unsuitable offer entails

- a significant loss of pay, including the opportunity to earn over-time and bonuses; or
- radical changes in hours of work.

You have been a long-serving headmaster. Your county council has now proposed to offer you a job as a supply teacher as an alternative to redundancy. You have refused and claim redundancy payment.

Your refusal would probably be considered reasonable as the council has made an unsuitable offer of alternative employment.

8.4 Redundancy procedure: fair dismissal procedures

An employer must follow certain steps in order to carry out a fair dismissal on grounds of redundancy. There must be

(a) Consultation with trade union representatives within 30 or 90 days as appropriate, on the steps to be taken (e.g. selection criteria, alternatives to dismissal etc.). The 90 day period applies where 100 or more employees are to be dismissed in any one establishment. The 30 day period applies where ten or more employees are to be dismissed.
(b) Consultation with non-union staff individually or collectively.
(c) Determination of the number of redundancies necessary.
(d) A call for volunteers.
(e) Consideration of the possibility of re-deployment within the organization or an associated company, with the possibility of retraining.
(f) Selection of employees to be dismissed made according to agreed procedure or custom and practice.
(g) Notification of dismissal to those concerned as soon as possible.
(h) Reasonable paid time off during working hours to seek alternative employment.
(i) Notification to Department of Employment of impending redundancies within 30 or 90 day period as appropriate.
(j) Issue of notices of dismissal.
(k) Calculation of redundancy payments and issue of statement of calculations to each employee to be dismissed.

8.4.1 Importance of correct procedures

Prior consultation and warnings of impending redundancies are most important.

An employer will not normally be considered as acting reasonably unless he warns and consults any employees affected, or their representatives; adopts a fair basis on which to select for redundancy and takes such steps as are reasonable to avoid or minimize redundancy by redeployment within his own organization.

9. Trade union activities

9.1 Time off for trade union duties

Any employee who is a union official has the right to have paid time off during working hours to carry out certain union duties and to train for those duties.

9.1.1 What are trade union duties?

For the rule to apply, the duties must concern the following matters:

- terms and conditions of employment or working conditions
- engagement, termination or suspension of employment
- allocation of work
- disciplinary matters
- trade union membership
- provision of facilities for trade union officials
- negotiation or consultation machinery.

These duties are likely to be defined in a clearcut way.

You are a teacher and a member of a teachers' union. You object strongly to a bill currently before Parliament which is intended to introduce a new curriculum. You wish to lobby Parliament during the debate. That would entail leaving school during working hours. You argue that you are entitled to the time off with pay as it involves a question of working conditions and allocation of work.

It is unlikely that a tribunal will decide that lobbying Parliament falls within 'trade union duties'. It is more likely to be seen as generalized political activity.

9.1.2 What is trade union training?

For an employee to qualify for time off for training certain conditions are also laid down:

- it must be relevant to his particular trade union duties and
- it must be approved by either the TUC or the official's own union

9.2 Dismissal connected to unions

9.2.1 When dismissals are automatically unfair

An employee will be automatically regarded as having been unfairly dismissed if the principal reason for his dismissal is that

(a) he was a member of an independent trade union or
(b) he had taken part in the activities of an independent trade union at an 'appropriate' time (i.e. either outside working hours or within working hours when it has been agreed that he is permitted to take part in such activities), or
(c) he was not, and refused to become, a member of any trade union or of one particular trade union, or
(d) his dismissal was a closed shop (union membership agreement) dismissal.

Employees who are dismissed on any of those grounds do not need the requisite qualifying service before they can bring a claim for unfair dismissal.

9.3 Redundancy: need to consult unions

An employer who intends to make employees redundant must consult with the trade union of which his employees are members, if any. Consultation must take place at the earliest opportunity.

9.3.1 Information must be in writing

Certain information must be disclosed in writing to the union for the purposes of consultation (see also section 9.3.5 below):

(a) the reason for the redundancies
(b) the number and categories of employees to be affected
(c) the total number of employees in the categories to be affected
(d) the selection criteria to be applied
(e) the method of carrying out the redundancies to be used, having regard to any agreed procedures.

9.3.2 Consideration of union views

The employer must consider any representations made by the union and state his reasons for rejecting them. An employer need only comply with those requirements in so far as it is reasonably practicable.

9.3.3 Special circumstances

If there are special circumstances which make it not reasonably practicable for an employer to comply with the statutory provisions, he must take all steps which are reasonably practicable.

Examples of special circumstances:

(a) Insolvency will only be regarded as a special circumstance if it results from some unusual or unexpected event.

(b) The failure to renew trade with an important customer may be a special circumstance.

(c) The sudden withdrawal of credit facilities may be a special circumstance.

9.3.4 Failure to comply with statutory requirements

If an employer fails to comply with the statutory requirements of consultation and consideration of representations, the union may appeal to an industrial tribunal for a declaration that the employer has not complied with the statutory requirements and for a protective award.

(a) Consultation

Employers should consult at the earliest opportunity. Where between 10 and 99 employees are to be made redundant, consultations must take place at least 30 days before the first dismissal takes effect. If 100 or more employees are to be made redundant, 90 days for consultation must be allowed before the first dismissal takes effect.

(b) Protective awards

The award is remuneration for a protected period for the employees who have been dismissed.

That period is

- 90 days where 100 or more employees are affected
- 30 days where ten or more employees are affected
- 28 days where less than ten employees are affected.

If the employer does not comply with the protective award order the employee himself can apply to the tribunal for an order.

9.3.5 Fine for failure to provide information

The Department of Employment issues Form HR1 for notification. A copy of this must go to a trade union recognized by the employer. It is an offence not to provide the requisite information, involving a potential fine of up to £5000 on a summary conviction.

DIRECTORY
Working for a living

Advisory, Conciliation & Arbitration Service (ACAS)
27 Wilton Street
London SW1X 7AZ
Tel. 071 210 3000

Central Office of Industrial Tribunals
93 Ebury Bridge Road
London SW1W 8RE
Tel. 071 730 6105

Certification Officer for Trade Unions and Employers' Associations
27 Wilton Street
London SW1X 7AZ
Tel. 071 210 3734

Commission for Racial Equality
Elliot House
10/12 Allington Street
London SW1 5EH
Tel. 071 828 7022

Commissioner for the Rights of Trade Union Members
First Floor
Bank Chambers
2a Rylands Street
Warrington
Cheshire WA1 1EN
Tel. 0925 415771

Commissioner for Protection against Unlawful Industrial Action
Second Floor
Bank Chambers
2a Rylands Street
Warrington
Cheshire WA1 1EN
Tel. 0925 414128

Department of Employment
Caxton House
Tothill Street
London SW1H 9NF
Tel. 071 273 3000

Department of Social Security
Millbank Tower
21–24 Millbank
London SW1P 4QU
Tel. 071 210 5983

Employment Appeal Tribunal
Audit House
Victoria Embankment
London EC4T 0DS
Tel. 071 273 1041

Employment Department Redundancy Payment Offices:

Statutory Redundancy Payment Helpline: 0800 848489

Aytoun Street
Manchester M60 2HS
Tel. 061 236 4433

2 Duchess Place
Hagley Road
Birmingham B16 8NS
Tel. 021 456 1144

Arena House
North End Road
Wembley
London HA9 0NF
Tel. 081 900 1966

The Employment Service Disability Services Branch
Courtwood House
c/o Mayfield Court
56 West Street
Sheffield S1 4EP
Tel. 0742 739190

Equal Opportunities Commission
Overseas House
Quay Street
Manchester M3 3HN
Tel. 061 833 9244

Health and Safety Executive
Public Enquiry Point, Information Centre
Broad Land
Sheffield S3 7HQ
Tel. 0742 892345
(has regional office network)

Industrial Relations Services
18–20 Highbury Place
London N5 1QP

London Hazards Centre
308 Gray's Inn Road
London WC1X 8DS

Manpower Services Commission
Moorfoot
Sheffield S1 4PQ

Maternity Alliance
15 Britannia Street
London WC1X 9JN
Tel. 071 837 1265

National Association of Careers and Guidance Teachers
Portland House
4 Bridge Street
Usk
Gwent NP5 1BG
Tel. 0291 672985

Office of the Parliamentary Commissioner for Administration
Church House
Great Smith Street
London SW1P 3BW
Tel. 071 276 3000

Public Concern at Work
Lincoln's Inn House
42 Kingsway
London WC2B 6EN
Tel. 071 404 6609

Trades Union Congress (TUC)
Congress House
Great Russell Street
London WC1B 3LS
Tel. 071 636 4030

Training Agency
236 Grays Inn Road
London WC1X 8HL
Tel. 071 278 0363

Wages Inspectorate
Employment Department
Clifton House
83–117 Euston Road
London NW1 2RA
Tel. 071 387 2511

8. NEIGHBOURS

Most people live amicably enough with their neighbours, helping and supporting each other in a myriad different ways. In such cases, we do not think in terms of legal relationships. The questions of how the law governs our immediate environment or how it endeavours to resolve disputes between neighbours simply do not arise.

In many of the issues that can and do arise between neighbours, however, the law tries to strike a balance. On the one hand, householders should be free to use their property and to behave as they like with the minimum interference from others. On the other hand, we have to use our property and behave in such a way that we do not interfere with the way our neighbours choose to enjoy *their* home environment. So the law strives to apply the maxim of 'give and take' – in the hope (sometimes a vain hope) of reducing the scope for quarrels between neighbours.

To those not involved, quarrels between neighbours may seem trivial indeed. Why should one litigate over a few inches of brick wall? What purpose can such litigation possibly serve? Can a few inches of wall, land or overhanging shrub ever justify the costs and the heartache? But we should never underestimate the anger and bitterness of those involved in such disputes.

There are organizations which endeavour to take this particular aspect of social relations outside the sphere of the law courts altogether. Their view is that a court case is not the best way to solve problems between people who have to live in close proximity to each other for years. Mediation on a voluntary and friendly basis may be the best solution by far (see the DIRECTORY, at the end of this chapter).

Arguments between neighbours have led to more than bad feelings and ensuing litigation: in one case, a feud over the volume of sound from the stereo in a neighbouring flat caused an arson attack and the deaths of two people. In another, a barbecue party led to a quarrel between neighbours which also resulted in a death.

In this chapter, we look at

- the 'neighbour' principle
- problems with peace and quiet
- problems with boundaries and fences
- problems with nuisance
- problems with smoke and fumes
- problems with gardens
- problems with rights and properties.

1. The neighbour principle

1.1 We have many neighbours in law

The line of the song runs 'Next door is just a footstep away.' However, the law takes a much wider view of the people we can and must call our 'neighbours'.

1.1.1 Defining 'duty of care'

In the legal sense, our 'neighbour' is any person whom we should reasonably have in mind if we were to act so carelessly as to cause him or her harm.

1.1.2 Reasonableness

Who are these people we should have in mind? Among other elements, the law defines the duty of care we owe to them on the basis of 'reasonableness'.

Of course, stating the principle on paper is easy; implementing it in practice is more difficult. Fine lines have sometimes to be drawn. Actual situations, as we all know, are infinitely variable.

> *In order to deter birds from eating the ripening cherries in your garden, you fire blanks into the air. Your garden is close to a road. A passing motorist is so frightened by the sound of the shots that he loses control of his vehicle and careers into a passing cyclist. What is your responsibility for the accident?*

In law, both the car driver and the cyclist would be considered your 'neighbours'. You should have realized that the sudden sound of gunshot near a well-used road might cause a panic reaction.

However, if you live in a very isolated spot and choose to frighten birds from your garden with blank shots (as you regularly have done in the past), you would probably not be responsible if a cyclist a couple of miles away fell off his bicycle from fright. He is not your 'neighbour' in the legal sense. It would not be 'reasonable' to expect you to have considered the possible harm to him in these circumstances.

Thus the emphasis is on the word 'reasonableness'. You don't owe a duty to take care of someone else's welfare if their presence is so remote that you couldn't be expected to be conscious of their wellbeing. In other words, you don't owe a duty of care to everyone in the world; you owe a duty to take care only to those who are reasonably likely to be affected by your careless actions.

In general, of course, the very people who do become involved in neighbourhood disputes are those who live close at hand. They are 'neighbours' in the most accepted sense of the word. But it is important to know that the legal definition of a 'neighbour' can take us well beyond those who live in our immediate vicinity.

2. Problems with peace and quiet

2.1 Noise as form of pollution

Of all the complaints which neighbours make against each other, the commonest concern noise. It can come from loud music, crying children, barking dogs, or DIY equipment; in summer, when one should most enjoy being out of doors, neighbourhood noise can become even more disturbing – whether it be the sound of lawnmowers and hedgetrimmers or of music through open windows.

Noise, quite rightly, is considered in law to be a form of pollution under the law of nuisance (see section 4, as well as section 2.3.2 below).

(a) Modern society

Changing social and domestic patterns have also added to the problem: large houses which were built for one family are often subdivided into several flats with inadequate sound insulation; unemployment often means that the elderly and the relatively young find themselves sharing the same space during the day; the young may be inconsiderate and play music loudly; the elderly may be deaf and they too may turn the volume up.

Finally, hi-tech also works against those who like peace and quiet; stereo equipment is getting more and more sophisticated – as well as portable – so an escape from unwanted sound becomes increasingly difficult.

Motor traffic and aircraft pose problems of their own. Their volume grows all the time with its concomitant effects on the environment. However, the laws governing noise from traffic and overflying aircraft are largely outside the scope of this chapter.

2.2 Interpersonal attempts to combat noise

In all disputes with neighbours, resort to the law should be your last course of action. There are many other routes to explore first.

> *You have put up with the fact that your neighbours lock their dog in their house when they are out so that it howls. You have put up with the fact that they play their radio loudly when they are home. But lately, they have been giving all-night parties with what sounds like professional disco equipment. What do you do?*

The answer involves several factors. To take the social aspects first:

It is always best to try to settle problems amicably, particularly with people you may have to co-exist with for years to come. But in view of the fact that you have already put up with a reasonable amount of disturbance, from their radio and dog, you are entitled to feel that the noise from disco parties is unreasonable. 'Reasonableness' is the key aspect of the case.

2.2.1 Talking to your neighbours

The first thing is to approach your neighbours and speak to them about the noise: try to establish whether there was a run of recent celebrations that has now come to an end. If not, ask them whether they would agree to break up their social gatherings at a reasonable hour so that others may sleep.

2.2.2 Contacting other neighbours

If, despite your request, they refuse to be more considerate, speak to your other neighbours to find out whether (a) they are affected by the noise and (b) whether a concerted approach with them may help.

2.2.3 Keeping written records

It would be advisable at this stage to put your complaints in writing to your noisy neighbours – very politely – and keep copies of your letters as well as any reply. Also keep a log of the noise, of all kinds, that you suffer from. Take note of when the parties begin and when they end. (See section 2.3.2 below.)

2.2.4 Contacting the landlords

In a block of flats, approach the Residents' Association if there is one, the managing agents, or the landlords. The noisy neighbours are probably in breach of the terms of their lease.

Where there is a speculative conversion of a house into a couple of flats, you may find out that the 'landlord' is a shell company and that there is little help to be had from that quarter.

In public sector housing, contact the Housing Officer.

2.2.5 Seeking mediation

Try to establish whether there is a mediation service in your area that could act as go-between between yourself and your neighbours (see DIRECTORY).

2.3 Legal attempts to combat noise

If all else fails, you have to consider your legal position.

2.3.1 The police

You could telephone the police and no doubt they get many such calls in the middle of the night. But the police are only likely to intervene if there is, or is likely to be, a criminal offence.

There are, however, alternative remedies that the law supplies.

2.3.2 Local authorities

You can complain to the Environmental Health Department of your local authority. Someone will come round to investigate – usually in office hours – so that is why if you are complaining of all-night parties you will need evidence to back up your complaint.

◆ **Note:** some local authorities do run call-out squads who do operate at night, so check the position in each case.

Local authorities are getting so many complaints of noise, some 70,000 per year, that they have great difficulty in dealing with them all on their available resources. In order to streamline procedures, certain local authorities have devised standard forms for the complainant to fill in so that the authorities can make their own assessment of the seriousness of the complaint. They may then get an officer to make a follow-up visit. It is the intermittent nature of noise – as well as the fact that it often takes place at night – which makes this aspect of the environmental health officer's job so difficult.

But if he or she is satisfied that the complaint is genuine, the EHO might write an informal letter to the noisy neighbour. In the majority of cases, that might suffice. However, if the problem persists, the local authority can serve a notice under section 80 of the Environmental Protection Act 1990 that the noise levels are to be reduced or curtailed. Your neighbour ignores the notice at his peril. If he fails to observe it, the authority can prosecute.

▶ **Remember:** by contacting the local authority, you might prevent the dispute ever reaching the courts. If nevertheless it has to be litigated the local authority does so on your behalf. In a recent case, the EHO – to the delight of the neighbours – even seized some offending stereo equipment.

2.3.3 Going to magistrates

You can yourself go to a magistrates' court under section 82 of the Environmental Protection Act 1990. Before you do so you have to give your neighbour formal written notice of your intention of taking out proceedings – and that may even be sufficient to stop the noise. Otherwise you will have to make an appointment with the court and produce your evidence to them.

The court will need to be satisfied that you have genuine cause for complaint, so you must specify time, date, duration of the noise, the nature of the noise and why you think it is a genuine nuisance. (For the definition of nuisance, see section 4 below.) In effect, you are launching a private prosecution. If satisfied by the presentation of your grievance, the court will issue a summons against your neighbour.

2.3.4 Going to county court

Going to the county court is another route you could follow. You could begin a civil action in a county court for an injunction to stop the noise. (An injunction is a remedy which the law provides – in this case, telling the other party to refrain from acting in a particular way.)

You could also sue for damages. However, you would have to establish that you have suffered damage to your health or depreciation in the value of your property. On the whole, going to court is the most risky and costly approach.

The outcome of litigation is always uncertain. In one case, the plaintiff (the person who brings the action) complained of noise from his neighbour's chickens. The judge granted an injunction against the neighbour (the defendant) which forbade her to allow her cockerel to crow between midnight and 7 am.

In a case with quite different implications, the neighbours had complained to their local authority about a trumpeter who practised next door. The musician won his appeal, which he brought with the support of the Musician's Union, against a notice which the local council had imposed on him forbidding him to practise.

2.4 Checklist

Do's

- Do examine your own feelings to see that you are not being hypersensitive and that your reactions are reasonable.

- Do satisfy yourself that an attempt to solve the problem by legal action would be worth the increase in neighbourly ill will.

- Do check with other people in the street as to their feelings.

- Do keep careful records.

- Do get statements and/or co-operation from other neighbours when making your complaint.

Dont's

- Don't put up with the noise until you reach bursting point. You also weaken your case if you do not take some measured steps to indicate your displeasure.

- However, do not assume that going to law will bring speedy relief – it is generally slow and expensive. There is also no guarantee of success.

- Don't ignore the various kinds of conciliation procedure.

- Don't, on the other hand, be too faint-hearted in pursuing your rights.

In all cases, it is advisable to seek help before resorting to legal action. In the chapter on the *Legal System* there is information about solicitors, as well as other sources of legal advice, who may be in a position to help you.

2.5 Building standards

The discussion above concerns problems faced by one particular person who has to deal with a noisy neighbour. However, all the neighbours – for example – in a block of flats or in a terrace – may share the common problem of inadequate sound insulation in the building.

The Department of Environment issues guidelines concerning requirements on sound proofing and also density requirements for party walls, stairs etc. However, these requirements are not mandatory.

The Building Research Establishment tests sound proofing to establish whether the level of noise penetration is reasonable.

2.6 Other sources of noise

2.6.1 Noise in the streets

A recurring problem is noise from faulty alarms, both car alarms and house alarms, which can ring and ring while the owners are away. In one case, a car alarm went off every night for several months, apparently set off by the wind! A maddened householder eventually tried to get into the car and was arrested for criminal damage. He was not charged but was bound over to keep the peace (see *The Independent* June 28 1991).

2.6.2 Statutory powers to deal with street noise

In order to combat these problems, a Noise and Statutory Nuisance Act was passed in 1993. It came into effect in January 1994. It extends the scope of the Environmental Protection Act 1990 so that street noise is also classified as a statutory nuisance (see below, section 4.3).

(a) What is included

The Noise and Statutory Nuisance Act 1993 covers nuisance from vehicles, machinery or equipment in the street. It deals in particular with car alarms and burglar alarms (see sections 2.6.2(c) and (d) below).

'Street' not only covers a highway or road, but extends to a footway, square or court open to the public 'for the time being'. It would therefore cover a situation where a car with a faulty alarm is parked in a residential square – the parking being limited to residents only.

'Equipment' includes musical equipment – so that it would appear to cover the faulty, or even the persistent, bell of an ice cream van. Whether or not it could apply to busking remains to be seen.

(b) What is excluded

The Act does not apply to traffic noise, political demonstrations or noise made by 'any naval, military or air force'.

(c) Car alarms

(This is also dealt with in the Chapter on *Motoring*, see section 2.2.)

The person 'responsible' for a car with a faulty alarm is

- the person whose name is registered as owner with the DVLC
or
- any other person who 'for the time being' is the driver of the vehicle.

An environmental health officer (EHO) can serve an abatement notice on that person to remedy the fault. If the vehicle is unattended the EHO can put a notice on the vehicle and if, after an hour, nothing further has been done or the person responsible has not been found, the EHO can

- immobilize the alarm

or

- remove the vehicle.

The EHO can open and enter the car provided there is 'no more damage than is necessary'. It must also be secured against theft 'as effectually' as when it was found!

(d) House alarms

Householders have to inform their local authorities of alarms which they instal. The alarm must meet prescribed requirements and the police must be notified of the names, addresses and telephone numbers of current keyholders.

If any alarm operates for more than an hour after it has been activated so as to annoy people nearby, an officer of the local authority can turn off the alarm by entering the premises provided he has authority to do so. He can obtain a warrant from a justice of peace to enter the premises – if need be by force – provided stringent stipulations are met. No more damage is to be caused than is necessary, the alarm should be re-set if reasonably practicable, and he must leave the premises – also so far as is reasonably practicable – as effectually secured against trespassers as when entered.

The owner can be called upon to reimburse the local authority for expenses incurred.

2.6.3 Noise from children

There is not much a neighbour can do if there are rowdy children in the house next door, the street, or the block. Speaking to their parents may only antagonize them, and the parents themselves may be powerless to stop the noise. In any event, parents cannot be held answerable for their children's bad behaviour unless they themselves can be shown to be at fault.

If children are playing truant, or appear to be playing truant, they should be reported to the education officer of your local authority. Similarly, if there is anxiety that a child's persistent crying could be the result of cruelty or neglect, the matter should be reported to the social services office of your local authority or to the NSPCC (this matter is dealt with more fully in the chapter on *Children*).

2.7 Changes proposed for the future

(1) There has been a White Paper on setting up noise neighbourhood watch schemes to combat neighbourhood noise, modelled on neighbourhood watch schemes for crime prevention.
(2) A private member's bill is aimed at transferring noise control to the police.

3. Problems with boundaries and fences
3.1 Establishing boundaries

There is no rule of law that requires you to mark the boundary of your property or to enclose it with a fence. If there are stipulations about these matters, they will be as a result of

- an agreement with your neighbour or
- an obligation in your conveyance or lease.

But even if there are no such legal rules or no particular stipulation in your conveyance, it is always advisable to reach agreement with your neighbour about the boundaries between your properties.

3.1.1 Note of warning

The courts resound to quarrels between neighbours over the position of the fine line which divides their properties. Litigation reaches the highest courts over a matter of inches.

These cases can lead to the recovery of a disputed piece of land or the demolition of an offending fence for the winning party, who may also win damages. In fighting a hopeless cause, however, the other side can end up much worse off than before – indeed their entire property may have to be sold in order to pay a huge bill for costs on both sides – in addition to the damages which they may have to pay. Even those on the winning side can find themselves out of pocket in a law suit (see chapter on the *Legal System*).

What is striking – and disheartening – is how fiercely both sides feel and how absolutely convinced they are that the other side is in the wrong.

The battle is over the boundary, the battlefield is the court. The judge endeavours to resolve the issue on legal grounds. Nonetheless it is often a profound clash of personality which is the significant factor in the litigants' presence in court at all.

3.1.2 Prevention is always better than cure

If you are buying a property, always try to establish in advance where the boundaries to the property lie. Ascertain the rights of way and parking rights, if any.

It is much better to sort out all these matters in advance than to try to assert your rights once you move in.

Be particularly wary of buying a property where the plan does not tally with what you actually see on the ground (see immediately below). If in doubt, contact the Boundary Skills Panel of the Royal Institution of Chartered Surveyors (see DIRECTORY).

3.1.3 When there is a plan

In general, in any conveyance there *should* be a plan, annexed to the title deeds, which is supposed to show where the boundaries to a property lie. But a plan can be misleading, inaccurate or out-of-date. If you have not established the boundaries before you moved in, or you are unexpectedly under challenge from a neighbour, what do you do then?

3.1.4 The objective test

In general, the court takes an objective view of a factual situation. It asks itself the question 'What would a reasonable person think that he or she was buying at the time and in the circumstances of the case?'

> *You bought a bungalow which was built by the seller on part of his land. The seller still lives in the house next door. At the time of the purchase, you explained to him that you were thinking of building an extra room because you and your wife were expecting another child. The plan which the seller attached to the title deeds was not up to date. As far as you were concerned you assumed you were buying an extra ten feet of land next to the garage on which you intended to build. The seller now says that that strip of land belongs to him. What can you do?*

The court will look, in such a case, not just at the plan in isolation but at all the surrounding circumstances, the negotiations leading up to the sale, and at the other documentation, such as the solicitors' enquiries.

Then the court will ask itself the question: 'What would the reasonable person think he or she was buying?' The answer to that question may not necessarily be the answer that you would wish to hear – the court may decide that you simply acted on the assumption that the land would be yours but failed to ascertain your position properly.

3.1.5 When there is no plan

We have looked at the situation in which a plan can be misleading. There are also situations where there is no plan attached to the title deeds.

Where there is no plan of your property at all, certain legal presumptions come in to play, i.e. the law makes certain generalizations about boundaries.

(a) Ditches

If there is a man-made ditch at the 'end' of your garden which is not marked on any map or plan, then the law assumes that the boundary runs up to the near side of the ditch.

(b) Hedges

If there is a hedge at the 'end' of your garden, your boundary will incorporate as much of the hedge as you trim; if you trim the whole of the hedge, then you may be able to claim that it is all yours. Otherwise the boundary is assumed to be the middle of the hedge.

(c) Hedge and ditch

If there is a ditch and then a hedge, you are presumed to own the land as far as the near edge of the ditch. It would not be neighbourly practice, in the eyes of the law, to dig a ditch on someone else's land. If there is a hedge and then a ditch, you are presumed to own the land up to the further edge of the ditch. It is assumed that the ditch digger has thrown the soil onto his own land when digging the ditch, and has then planted the hedge on the bank of soil.

(d) Right of way

Where there is a right of way, a boundary is assumed to run in the middle of the right of way. In the same way, a boundary is said to run in the middle of a natural stream or river.

◆ **Note:** these presumptions (or generalizations) are not binding rules. They can be displaced if you have other cogent evidence to the contrary. But they do serve a useful purpose in specifying certain guidelines in determining this kind of dispute.

3.2 Fences

Even where there is no demarcation dispute over a boundary to a property, a frequent source of ill-feeling between neighbours arises from the fence between them. Who owns the fence? Who should keep it in repair? Must it be kept in repair?

The answers to these questions ought to be amicably sorted out with goodwill on both sides. Too often, however, angry litigants ask the courts to supply the answers; this means there has to be a winner and a loser – with regard both to the issue at stake and to the costs which litigation inevitably entails.

3.2.1 General rules regarding ownership

Again there are certain presumptions regarding fences. Do be warned that these presumptions can be displaced by other evidence.

(a) Plan with 'T' marks

The general rule is that where the title deeds have a plan, the usual practice is for there to be a 'T' mark on one side of the fence. If the 'T' mark falls on your side of the fence, then you are the owner.

(b) No 'T' marks or no plan at all

If there is no 'T' mark, or no plan to the deeds, then there is a general presumption that you own the fence if the supporting posts are on your land.

(c) Party fences

You can decide to have a party fence with both sides owning the fence and both sides contributing to its cost of repair.

3.2.2 Mending fences

In general, if a fence belongs to your neighbour and it falls into disrepair, s/he is not under an obligation to repair it unless there is some obligation which has been written into the conveyance (in new housing estates, for example, there are often obligations of this kind imposed). You can only insist on repair if it is more than an eyesore and presents an actual danger to you on your side of the property. In that case, you could approach the environmental health officer of your local authority to complain of a private nuisance (see *Nuisance* below, section 4).

If you need to repair the fence at your own expense because it constitutes a danger, you might have to ask your neighbour's permission to go on to his land. Otherwise you would have to apply to court for leave to go on to his land (see *Access to neighbouring land*, section 8.1 below).

◆ **Note:** All rules regarding fences, boundaries and party walls are in general terms, so do not assume that you are in the right in a dispute with your neighbour!

3.3 Party walls

In theory, the neighbour on each side of a party wall owns half the wall (whether the division is made vertically or horizontally).

Moreover, where two buildings have been standing for 20 years or more, each neighbour acquires a right, called on *easement*, against the neighbour on the other side for the right of support to their property. (See *Rights of support*, section 7.2.5 below.)

Rights, as well as ownership, generally entail duties too, and party walls are no exception.

3.3.1 General duty to take care

It is reasonable for the law to impose a duty to take care on the owner of a party wall, so that whether he uses it, removes it, builds on it, or repairs it, he must minimize the possibility of damage to neighbouring property.

▶ **So remember:** proper skill and care must be used in any work or repair which could expose a party wall to risk of damage.

Similar rules apply to contiguous roofs and to floors in flats which form the ceiling of the flat below.

(a) Nuisance

Allowing a party wall to fall into disrepair can cause a nuisance. An adjoining owner could then sue for damages. For example, if your neighbour allows dry rot on her side of the wall to spread to your side, she would be liable for damages if she knew that it could happen but failed to take any steps to deal with the dry rot and to halt its spread.

(b) Liability of owners for third party contractors

Your home is one of a Victorian terrace of houses. Your roof has been leaking and you decide that it would be best to replace the tiles. You engage a builder, who has been highly recommended to you, and the job seems well done. You are now approached by your immediate neighbour who says that the wall and ceiling of an attic room in his house are showing signs of damp. You endeavour to locate the builder as you understand that, as an independent contractor, he is liable for any damage. You discover that he has gone out of business. Your neighbour commences litigation for the cost of the repairs to his house. He says that it is no concern of his that your builder was at fault and is no longer available. What is your position?

Where there is damage to an adjoining building as a result of work to a party wall, roof, or basement, the owner may have to bear the responsibility if the builder disappears.

3.3.2 Rules within London

As far as London is concerned, there is specific legislation which deals with party walls.

(a) You do not own half a party wall and you do not have to wait 20 years to acquire a right of support. In effect, each side of a party wall owns the wall in common with his neighbour on the other side.

(b) Each side therefore has the right to carry out work on his or her side of the wall. However, this right is subject to protection for the owner on the other side.

You live in a two-storey terraced house in inner London. Your next-door neighbours have decided to convert their ground floor into an open-plan living area. They have begun work which involves redistribution of the loading on the party wall. This has only just come to your attention and you are told by a friend, who is a surveyor, that there is a strong risk of possible damage to your own home. What can you do?

You must inform the local authority immediately and ask for a Stop notice. Your neighbour is under a legal obligation to you under the London Building Acts to give you two months' notice before he does any work which could affect a party wall.

4. Problems with nuisance

There are three categories of 'nuisance' in law:

- private nuisance
- public nuisance
- statutory nuisance.

4.1 Private nuisance

A private nuisance has been defined as something that occurs on someone else's property which detrimentally affects your property or your enjoyment of your own property.

> *Your next-door neighbour is a DIY enthusiast. Lately he has decided to sand down all the floors of his house and the noise and vibrations from the sanding equipment interfere with your TV reception. Does this qualify as 'nuisance'?*

The answer would depend on the degree of the noise, the hours at which the sanding takes place, the time that it might take him to finish his floors, and the extent to which your television reception is impaired. If the sanding goes on at reasonable hours and he only intends to use the sanding equipment for a one-off job which should finish in a matter of weeks, you are unlikely to be able to complain of nuisance.

> *Meanwhile, however, he has installed equipment in his garage to pursue his hobby of gemstone polishing. There is no prospect of the interference to your TV reception coming to an end.*

You could complain that your neighbour was using his property in such a way as detrimentally to affect the peaceful enjoyment of your own amenities.

Equally, something which occurs on your property can be a source of nuisance to your neighbours and interfere with the enjoyment to which they also are entitled. For example, your son is a car enthusiast. He spends hours in the back garden stripping down cars and souping up their engines. Your neighbour complains of the noise of revving engines and the smell of chemicals from bodywork repairs.

Of course, it is always a matter of degree but, again, there is no doubt that these activities can constitute nuisance.

4.1.1 Scope of private nuisance

The examples given so far all concern nuisance emanating from neighbouring properties. There is a query whether someone can cause nuisance (in the legal sense) from or on your own property, such as if your ex-partner tries to deprive you of the use of your telephone by interfering with your telephone line.

4.1.2 The need for some continuity

In general nuisance denotes some notion of continuity – particularly in establishing nuisance against a neighbour. However, a one-off event could also be a nuisance; for example, a sudden and unexpected inflow of chemicals from neighbouring land that pollutes your stream.

4.1.3 The need for a measured response

A problem with nuisance is that you do not want to over-react and to antagonize your neighbours. On the other hand, the longer the delay, the more difficult it becomes to prove a case of nuisance. In other words, some form of measured response should be made promptly.

4.2 Public nuisance

A public nuisance is something that, as the name suggests, detrimentally affects a large group of people and not only an individual. It often concerns obstructions on the highway.

◆ **Note:** neighbours can band together in residents' committees to act as a pressure group against certain kinds of nuisance. For example, they try to prevent heavy traffic using certain roads by lobbying for the installation of 'sleeping policemen'.

4.3 Statutory nuisance

Certain kinds of nuisance are covered by legislation. In particular the Environmental Protection Act 1990 has laid down various matters, associated with property, that qualify as statutory nuisances. As the name of the Act would suggest, the law is primarily concerned with those who use (or neglect) their property in such a way as to cause a potential health hazard. The Act refers to the state of premises, the state of an animal kept on premises, smoke, fumes, dust, and any 'accumulation or deposit' of substances that could be prejudicial to health or could cause a nuisance.

It is the well-being of the population as a whole that the Act is concerned to protect. However, you can use its provisions for the protection of your own wellbeing by notifying apparent breaches to your local authority which has a duty, under the Act, to ensure that the Act's provisions are observed.

The local authority has to inspect its area from time to time and to detect any statutory nuisances;

- if a complaint is made, it has to take such steps as are reasonably practicable to investigate the complaint;
- if it is satisfied that a statutory nuisance exists, or is likely to occur or recur, it must serve an abatement notice (i.e. a notice on the person causing the nuisance to take steps to end it);
- it may take proceedings; it may abate the nuisance and 'do whatever may be necessary' to execute the notice.

The house next door was sold to a buyer who has been living abroad. Twelve months have elapsed and he still has not taken up occupation. During the year, his garden has grown ever more unkempt and has become an eyesore. Animal feedstuff has apparently been left in the garden shed. When you last looked out of your window and glanced towards the next door house, you were appalled to see a large rat scurry towards the back fence. What can you do about it?

You must complain to your local authority environmental health officer (the details can be looked up in your telephone book). Under the Act it is up to the environmental health officer (EHO) to take action on your behalf. If the premises next door are in themselves a hazard to health, by, for example, containing something that gives off a noxious smell, quite apart from the presence of vermin, they could certainly consitute a nuisance under the Act.

4.4 Combatting nuisance

In general, the council is under a duty to investigate your complaint. The EHO will try to get the owner of the premises to take action to remove or abate the nuisance. But in a case such as this, where the owner might not be traced, the council itself can take steps under the Act to remove the feedstuff and makes the premises vermin-free.

4.4.1 Neighbourhood groups

As we have seen above, neighbours often band together to combat a nuisance which affects them all. Neighbourhood groups have been proposed to deal with noisy neighbours – along the lines of crimewatch schemes.

5. Problems with smoke and fumes

There are many forms of pollution which can affect our immediate environment: dust, noise, chemical or noxious fumes, pollutants in water, blocked drains. One of the commonest that leads to disputes between neighbours is smoke. Smoke can come from a bonfire in someone else's garden or from a barbecue party next door. Again it becomes a question of degree. When does one person's pleasure become a pain to others?

5.1 Reasonable use

In general, the law looks to property owners to make reasonable use of their premises. If a person wishes to complain about how a neighbour uses his premises, he or she must show unreasonable use, that is, must show some sort of harm such as damage to health or to enjoyment of property. In other words it must constitute a legally defined wrong. It must be a nuisance, a trespass of some sort, or a hazard. These are quite high thresholds to cross.

Furthermore, we must take our neighbourhoods into account. If we buy a house in a semi-industrial area, we may have to put up with a greater degree of pollution in the form of noise or chemicals than we would in a residential area. If we buy our house in a semi-rural area, we may not be able to complain about noise from a nearby farmyard. If we buy a flat in a high street, we may have to put up with the smells from take-away food shops.

5.1.1 Smoke

As we have seen, smoke, fumes or dust can be a nuisance under the Environmental Protection Act 1990. The question – as always – is what point must be reached in order to transform an everyday nuisance into a 'nuisance' in law.

> Your neighbour is a most enthusiastic gardener so she has lots of garden clippings to burn. You find that quite often the smoke from her bonfires spoils what would otherwise be a couple of pleasant hours in your own garden. It soils your washing if there is any on the line. Even more problematic and unpleasant, however, is the fact that her children sometimes throw household rubbish on to the fire and the dense fumes from this burning rubbish irritate your chest. What should you do?

The first thing is to establish whether you really have grounds to complain of a nuisance. Keep a diary and take a note of how often the bonfires next door affect you, how long they usually burn for, whether a fire is lit irrespective of the time of day or the weather (for example, on a windy day the effects from smoke will be worse), what sort of rubbish is being burnt and causing dense smoke. Then speak to your neighbour to try to establish some sort of amicable arrangement. For example, perhaps she will agree to light bonfires only on the days when you are out. You might persuade her that her children should not amuse themselves at the fire – for their own good as much as for yours.

If all this is to no avail, and you feel a cause for complaint to the local authority is justified under the Environmental Protection Act 1990, you can call in the environmental health officer. The local authority will then decide whether or not to take action under the Act. It can issue a notice to the person to put an end to the nuisance (an abatement notice) if

(a) it is satisfied that a nuisance exists and
(b) the nuisance is likely to recur.

5.1.2 Barbecues

Alas, barbecues have become a very frequent source of dispute since so many more people today own them – coupled with the fact that there has been a series of hot summers.

A barbecue party can lead to a combination of factors which can annoy one's next door neighbours; there is the smoke, the smell, and probably noise too. There are not even walls to absorb some of the sound from an outdoors party!

In one tragic case, a neighbour in an upstairs flat doused the barbecue in the patio of the people living downstairs by throwing two buckets of water on to the flames from his upstairs balcony. A quarrel ensued in which a person died.

5.1.3 Insecticides and pesticides

The use of insecticides or pesticides can be a statutory nuisance under the Environmental Protection Act 1990 if their use is prejudicial to health or a nuisance. Their use can also cause damage under the common law rule of negligence.

> *Your neighbour knows that you keep bees. Nonetheless she goes ahead and uses insecticide on her rose bushes and the breeze wafts the substance on to your land. As a result, your bees are killed. What can you do?*

As in all instances, one wants to try the 'softly-softly' approach with neighbours – you should ask that it should not happen again in the future and perhaps ask for compensation for the loss of your bees. However, if your neighbour refuses to co-operate, you might have a case to sue for damages – possibly in the small claims court (see Chapter 12, section 5.1). You could also ask a county court for an injunction to stop her using harmful substances.

6. Problems with gardens

6.1 Intrusions from next door

Trespass and/or nuisance are the most common aspects in which the law is invoked in connection with gardens and neighbours' disputes.

Trespass, as we all know, usually involves people or animals (see chapter on *Accidents*, section 4.3.2 and chapter on *Countryside*, section 3.1.1(f)). It may come as a surprise therefore to discover that trespass can also be committed by plants or trees. These can either overgrow your property or – more insidiously – grow beneath it.

6.1.1 Overhanging plants and trees

The general rule is that you are entitled to your own 'space' – in, under, and, to some extent, above your own property. So branches from neighbouring trees or shrubs which overhang your garden are intrusions into your space, therefore they can be regarded as trespass and a nuisance.

> *Your neighbour has a very fine apple tree. Several branches, laden with fruit, overhang your garden where you have planted a delicate clematis against the fence. You have asked him several times to do something about the branches but he has taken no action. What can you do?*

You are entitled to lop off those branches which actually intrude over your side of the fence. You must take great care that only those branches, and no others, are pruned. You are supposed to return the branches to your neighbour and are certainly not entitled to any of the apples!

However, to take unilateral action against a neighbour's tree, even if you are entitled to do so in the strict legal sense, may not be the best policy when you have to live next door to him. It might be better to ask his permission to prune beforehand, or even to consider simply planting a hardier shrub against your fence.

♦ **Note:** under the Access to Neighbouring Land Act 1992, you can apply to court for an access order to deal with trees or shrubs on someone else's property. (See section 8.1 below.)

6.1.2 Roots growing underground

Trespass and nuisance can be caused by roots that grow underground and into and under neighbouring property just as much as by branches that overhang property from next door.

> *Your neighbour has written to you stating that the roots of one of your birch trees is in danger of causing settlement to her house. She is threatening you with an injunction to restrain you from continuing to permit the intrusion. Can she ask the courts for such a drastic remedy?*

The answer is 'yes'. Where roots cause material damage to adjacent property, the householder can sue for damages and ask for an injunction. The two remedies can be sought at the same time and are not mutually exclusive.

See also *Access to neighbouring land*, section 8 below.

6.1.3 If your neighbour fails to take action

If there is a shrub, climber or tree in your garden which poses a danger to a neighbouring property, your neighbour is not under a *legal* duty to take action.

> *You have planted a Virginia creeper against your back wall. You notice that it is now beginning to extend to your neighbours' tiled roof. You point this out to them and ask them to ensure that the tendrils do not damage their tiles. They do nothing about it. Thereafter, in the winter they complain to you about a leak from their roof.*

It is your responsibility to have ensured that no damage was done to their roof from your climber. Moreover, you are liable for the cost of repair, although the court may reduce the compensation you will have to pay, if your neighbour fails to mitigate the damage.

6.1.4 Interference with sunlight

With regard to gardens, you are not entitled to ask your neighbour to cut or prune branches of trees to ensure that you have uninterrupted sunlight. You are only entitled to reasonable airspace above your own property – you cannot impose airspace on neighbouring property.

You also cannot insist that your neighbour prunes his hedge to a certain height even if it is a party hedge. You are only entitled to prune your half to the height that you prefer – unless a maximum height has been stipulated in the conveyance. (See section 7.2.2 below with regard to the 'Right to Light' for your premises.)

6.2 Dangerous trees

Your local authority is under a statutory duty to ensure that trees do not pose a danger to other persons or to their property.

Any person who thinks that a tree is in a dangerous condition (whether in a public place such as a street or on private property such as a neighbouring garden) has the right to notify the local authority. The authority is then compelled, by law, to take action by tracing the owner of the land and giving notice of a 21-day period in which he or she must ensure that the tree is made safe. If there is no action and the owner does not appeal against the notice, the local authority can take the necessary action to make the tree safe.

(See also *Access to neighbouring land*, section 8 below.)

6.3 Protecting trees

It is a welcome feature of our law that trees are given special statutory protection.

> *You have recently sold your large Victorian house to a couple who intend to turn it into a residential home for the elderly. There are some very fine and unusual trees in the garden which you feel add much to the amenity of the area. If the couple build on to the house, as they intend to do, the trees may be felled. What can you do?*

If you think that there are trees which should be protected, you can write to your local planning authority under the Town and Country Planning Act 1990. If you offer convincing reasons, the planning authority will order its own inquiry and then may impose a tree preservation order on the trees to protect them from harm.

7. Problems with rights and properties

7.1 Restrictive covenants

In order to protect the amenities of an area, particularly a residential neighbourhood, property owners have frequently resorted to imposing restrictions on the way that neighbouring property owners may use their land.

There is a real problem, however. Property changes hands all the time; you may agree with someone that land, or the buildings on it, should only be used in a certain way (for example, that the land should not be built on, or the house should never be converted into flats). But can that agreement be enforced if the property is sold to someone else?

In order to enforce such agreements, property owners impose restrictive covenants on the property. These covenants are then registered and will pass with each conveyance. Restrictive covenants are usually imposed when a property is being developed or sold.

> *You have a house with large grounds. There is an old boiler house at the bottom of the garden. You obtain planning permission from the local council to allow a 'back garden' development to convert the boiler house into a studio flat. You intend to sell the flat once it is built. However, you would like to restrict the use that any potential buyer might wish to make of the studio. For example, you might want it to be for residential purposes only or you might want to make sure that a would-be purchaser does not build any extension on to the studio. What can you do to ensure these conditions?*

In the deed of sale you stipulate that these conditions of sale are restrictive covenants which your solicitor must then register as land charges. These are registered in the Charges Register as an interest affecting the property.

7.1.1 Rules on restrictive covenants

(a) Two properties are necessary

Restrictive covenants always need two properties: the *dominant* property for the benefit of which the covenant is made in the first place; and the *servient* property, i.e. the property on which the covenant is imposed. In the example above, the dominant property is the main house because the main house has the benefit of the ban on any further building. The studio is the servient property which has the detriment of a restrictive covenant against building imposed on it.

(b) Must be negative covenants

Restrictive covenants are negative in nature. You cannot use a restrictive covenant to insist that the purchaser of your studio paint the outside of the building at regular intervals.

You cannot even disguise a positive obligation under a negative cloak – for example, to stipulate that 'the purchaser shall not let the studio go unpainted'. Its effect, even though expressed negatively, is to impose a positive obligation to paint the studio.

(c) Enforcing covenants which 'run' with the land

Even if you sell your house, the new owner should be able to enforce the restrictive covenant provided it 'touches and concerns the land' or 'runs' with the land – as the lawyers say. This means that not all restrictive covenants can be enforced against new ownership. It only applies to covenants that directly affect the land itself – for example a covenant not to build.

Thus the owner of the studio could not wait for the sale of the main house and then carry out plans to build an extension. The covenant becomes attached to the properties, irrespective of who owns them. In such a case the restrictive covenant will continue to 'run with the land' unless other steps are taken to remove it (see below).

(d) Indemnity covenants

In order to make certain that a covenant will be respected, sellers sometimes insist that an indemnity covenant be entered into by the purchaser.

Under an indemnity covenant, the buyer agrees to indemnify the seller if any of the restrictive covenants in the title deeds are broken. Subsequent purchasers generally then enter into the same indemnity covenant so that the original purchaser is protected against any breaches by them. Indemnity covenants have the effect of a guarantee. The chain of indemnities protects the original buyer who could otherwise be sued by the seller long after he has left the property.

(e) Removing covenants

Application to a Lands Tribunal
Application can be made to a Lands Tribunal to have a restrictive covenant removed.

> You have bought a Victorian house in the high street of a busy market town. The house has a restrictive covenant on it that it must be used for residential purposes only. However, you would like to convert the ground floor into an office suite for your own use and use the upper storeys for a maisonette in which you would live. All the rest of the street now comprises offices and shops and the restrictive covenant appears wholly out of date.

You would seem to have a good case in seeking the discharge of the restrictive covenant as an unreasonable restriction on the use of your property. Always take proper advice on these issues first, though. You would also have to check on the 'change of use' provisions of the planning legislation. (See section 7.3.)

(f) By agreement

Another way of getting round a restrictive covenant is to persuade the other owner(s) of the property who benefit from it to forgo their rights. In this case, you may have to pay them compensation.

(g) Leasehold property

One of the features of leasehold property is that positive obligations can be imposed on tenants under the terms of their lease. The circumscribed nature of restrictive covenants does not apply in a lease – for example, tenants can be required to paint the outside of the building every five years (see chapter on *Landlords and their Tenants*). For that reason, too, certain residential estates, concerned about upkeep, will sell houses on their estate on long leasehold, such as 999 year leases.

7.2 Easements

7.2.1 Rules on easements

Restrictive covenants must be negative as we have seen above. There are, however, certain positive rights which properties can and do acquire against neighbouring properties. Such rights are called *easements*. Common examples of easements are rights to light, and rights of way over someone else's land.

(a) Easement entails two properties

Like a restrictive covenant, an easement also involves two properties: a dominant one and a servient one. The dominant property has the benefit of the easement while the servient property has the burden, i.e. the easement, imposed on it.

If we take the example above of the studio flat built in someone else's grounds, we can now see that the roles can be reversed from those in the situation under the restrictive covenant against building. For example, if the owner of the main house agrees that the buyers of the studio can use his main driveway for parking their car, the studio will benefit from the right of way and so it becomes the 'dominant' property, while the main house and grounds, on which the right of way has been imposed, will now be the 'servient' property.

(b) An easement can be positive

Unlike a restrictive covenant, which must always be negative, (e.g. an agreement not to build), easements can be positive in nature. Thus an easement can impose on land a positive duty, such as the duty to permit someone else to lay services over or under your land, to walk across it, or to support an adjoining building.

(c) An agreement 'runs' with the land

Both the benefit and the burden of easements run with the land, irrespective of the owners. Thus anyone who buys the dominant property will enjoy an easement, such as a right of way; the owner of the servient property, on the other hand, has to put up with having someone else use his property by walking across it, driving his car on it, or driving animals along it – depending on the nature of the easement.

Even if he sells his property, such rights of way or other easements can be enforced against any new owner.

(d) Enforcing easements

It is important to realize that an easement is an interest in land. It is not a mere agreement to use land in a particular way, which is called a licence. A licence is an agreement which can be revoked at any time. Easements, on the other hand, are rights that are registered to ensure that they are enforced in all subsequent conveyances.

(e) Limiting factors

Because of the nature of an easement – i.e. that it is a right enforceable, theoretically, in perpetuity – either for the benefit of, or against, someone else's land, the law circumscribes the operation of easements. For example, no one can acquire an easement to a fine view. The law regards such a right as too vague to bind someone else's property. If you wish to have a fine view, you must be in a position to impose a restrictive covenant on adjacent land that it should not be built on.

(f) Scope for dispute

Neighbours can find cause for quarrels over easements. For example, you can have a right of way which is a registered easement and not a licence. Nonetheless there can be a dispute over its nature. Is it meant for cars? Or lorries? Can you drive sheep along it?

Many easements date back for a century or more so their present scope has to be determined against today's very different environment from that prevailing at the time of the original deeds.

7.2.2 Right to light

A striking example of an easement is the right to light. It is also a frequent source of vexation – not to speak of litigation – between neighbours.

The problem usually arises when one of the neighbours builds an extension to his house. Can you do more than say 'I don't like your extension – it makes my house darker'?

The law on the subject is very complicated and you would always be well advised to consult a solicitor or chartered surveyor who has experience in property law. The position depends in part on an Act, called the Prescription Act, which was passed in 1832. It is still binding law on the issue of the right to light.

In principle, your only right is that your neighbour should not 'unreasonably' obstruct light from your windows, since your property has benefited from that light from your neighbour's property for 20 years without interruption.

In fact neighbours can reach an agreement which would preserve the existing light; such an agreement might be by means of a restrictive covenant against building on neighbouring land or by some other form of registered charge.

However

(a) there has to be existing light to a window of your house;
(b) the light must have been uninterrupted for 20 years.

◆ **Note:** Acquiring a right to light applies to buildings only. It does not apply to open land, such as a garden. In view of the current enthusiasm for conservatories, it would be interesting to know whether one can acquire a prescriptive right to light for them. It would appear to apply to a greenhouse.

7.2.3 Obstructions to light – when you can act

If there is an obstruction to light, caused, for example, by additional building at the next door house, you can only take action if the obstruction to that light is 'unreasonable'. In other words, the question is now whether you have sufficient light left at your window, not how much light has been taken away.

◆ **Note:** you must object effectively to the changes. If you do nothing about it for a year, the law regards you as having 'acquiesced' to the loss of light.

You have recently bought an old cottage. You use one of the upstairs bedrooms as a studio where you pursue your hobby of engraving. You have chosen this room because of the amount of light it receives throughout the day. Your neighbour had spoken to you several times concerning his plans for a garage but you were unaware that he intended to build a floor above the garage comprising a bedroom and ensuite bathroom. The building has since gone up and your bedroom is now very dark. You have protested to your neighbour about it, as well as to your local planning authority. The planning authority insists that the former owner was sent written notice of the planning application which was also advertised in the local press. You put the matter in the hands of your solicitors but have not heard from them for some while. What is your position?

The test is concerned with how much light has remained rather than how much has been taken away. In this case, there clearly has been such a loss of light that your bedroom can no longer be used for its former purpose. So you may have a good case against your neighbour on the face of it.

On the other hand, the court may decide that you only need enough light 'for ordinary purposes' and to use a bedroom as a studio is to use it for other than ordinary purposes. The question is one of fact and degree – how much light is left? Would it be dark even for an ordinary bedroom?

The fact that you have recently acquired the property does not affect your right to object to the extension provided there has been 20 years' uninterrupted light to your property – no matter who owned it before you.

However, the fact that nothing has happened for a while since you handed the matter over to your solicitors could be seriously damaging to your legal position. If one year elapses and you would appear not to have taken really effective action, the law holds that you have 'acquiesced' in the obstruction to your light.

7.2.4 Preventing a right to light arising in the first place

You can also stop your neighbour from acquiring a right to light!

Action can be taken under the Rights to Lights Act 1959 by registering a notice with your local authority. The notice is called a 'local land charge'. It has the effect of preventing the 20-year period from running in favour of a neighbouring house and has the same effect as if you built an obstruction which barred the light to your neighbour's windows.

Conveyances of property can also state that the building for sale cannot acquire a right to light against neighbouring property.

7.2.5. Right to support

In general, there is a natural right to support for your land. In other words, your neighbour cannot start excavating on his side of the fence in order to build a swimming pool which will cause the land on your side of the fence to subside.

This right of support extends to buildings where damage is caused to them as a result of the land subsidence and not because of the weight of the buildings themselves.

Buildings can, however, acquire their own easement of support from adjoining buildings provided they have been standing together for 20 years or more. So, if you carry out major works to your property which cause damage to the next door property through removal of support, you will be liable for the cost of repairing the damage.

Of course, these problems are usually minimized if people take care and sensible precautions. Surveyors and architects are at hand to give advice and to ensure – as far as possible – that no damage should occur to adjoining property from major works to one's own land or buildings.

7.2.6 Questions of privacy?

A property owner has no inherent right to privacy, neither can a house-holder claim the right to a view, as we have seen.

In general, therefore, you cannot stop someone building next door even if it means that your neighbours will then be able to overlook your grounds or look through your windows.

You can only prevent them where you can show that

- there is a restrictive covenant against building which you can enforce against your neighbours (see above) or

- a right to light and the building would unreasonably interfere with that right or
- planning permission has taken into account the need to ensure privacy for neighbouring property.

7.2.7 Planning laws and privacy

Planning laws can assist you in an endeavour to ensure privacy. Such control may be even more effective if your neighbours plan to build in a conservation area, a green belt area, or an area designated as one of natural beauty (see *Planning controls* immediately below).

> *Your neighbour has applied for planning permission to knock down his house and build a block of flats on his property which immediately adjoins your house. At the moment you are not overlooked but you fear that one of the flats, on the top floor, will overlook your garden thus interfering with the privacy which you now enjoy. You wonder what you can do.*

> You can endeavour to ensure that the planning permission contains a condition that no windows should be put into that part of the wall of the flat which will overlook your garden.

In a recent case, privacy was protected in this way. Indeed the block of flats was put up with an unauthorized dormer window which overlooked a neighbour's garden. An enforcement notice was issued against the man who bought the flat that the dormer window should be removed. He appealed to the High Court and the Court of Appeal, to no avail. The court held that the house next door should not suffer from 'an impression of overlooking'.

7.3 Planning controls

In this section, we have seen that the rights of ownership of property are hedged about with qualifications. It becomes most apparent, however, that 'an Englishman's home is *not* his castle' in the sphere of planning legislation. Controls govern what you can and cannot do with your property if you want to build on to it, make fundamental alterations to it, or change the way you intend to use it.

Many planning applications involve a public inquiry which is when neighbours can most forcefully put their objections to the proposed change to their neighbourhood or neighbouring property. They may form themselves into groups – some such groups are long-standing organizations dedicated to preserving their neighbourhood; other groups may be formed *ad hoc* to prevent or oppose a particular development in their immediate vicinity.

◆ **Note:** many developers have the resources to fight a sustained legal action against such groups. In general voluntary bodies – by their very nature – cannot fund such disputes.

7.3.1 Development and presumption against development

The local authorities draw up structure plans for their area as well as local plans. Any development must take place within these guidelines.

There is a presumption against development in certain areas – in particular, within green belt and conservation areas. That does not mean that all development is automatically barred; it does mean, though, that anyone who wants to build or change the use of an existing building in say, a conservation area, has a much harder job in persuading the local authorities that they ought to give the go-ahead.

(a) Change of use

Under the Town and Country Planning Act 1990, you must apply for planning permission where you intend 'developing' your property or where you intend to change the use of your property in a material way. An example would be change of use of purely residential property into part-business use (such as for a dental surgery) which could generate disturbance and parking problems for the neighbours.

7.3.2 When there is no development

In fact, the law does not specify the meaning of a 'development' and it does not define a material change of use. However, it does state that there is no development, if

- you carry out repairs to the interior of a building
- the building works would not materially affect the outside appearance of your house
- the building is within the grounds of your existing house and is intended to be used for its benefit; the new building might, for example, be a garage. In the words of the statute, the building must be 'ancillary' to the main dwelling house.

Even if there is no development so that you do not require planning permission, you still need to conform to local authority building regulations. A booklet is issued by the Department of the Environment which provides an introduction to building regulations. It also issues a planning guide for householders, available from the Planning Inspectorate (see DIRECTORY).

8. Trespass on or access to neighbouring land

8.1 Access to neighbouring land

The laws of trespass apply to people, animals and things, such as an overhanging eave, or a bulging fence. It also applies, as we have seen, to plants and trees (see above, section 6).

The chapter on *Accidents* deals with trespass in relation to occupier's liability (see section 4.3.2) and the chapter on the *Countryside* considers trespass and straying animals (see section 3.1.1(f)). In this section, we deal with the question of trespass on, and access to, neighbouring land.

8.1.1 Unlawful access

In general, unless you are invited on to land, or are there on business (for example to lay gas pipes), you are a trespasser. (For rights acquired through persistent trespass, see section 8.2 below.)

> *In order to repair your roof, you place a section of your ladder in your neighbour's garden without permission. You then go indoors to fetch your tools. Your irate neighbour shouts across the fence that your actions amount to 'trespass'. Is he correct?*

The answer is 'yes'. You are committing a continuing trespass by leaving the ladder in his garden just as much as you have committed trespass by walking on to your neighbour's land with your ladder in the first place. It is not a defence for you to tell your neighbour that your roof is in urgent need of repairs.

(However, see immediately below.)

8.1.2 Lawful access

A new Act has been introduced into Parliament to get round this problem of a householder/'trespasser' who has to go on to adjacent property in order to carry out repairs to his own property. It is called the Access to Neighbouring Land Act 1992, and is intended to give a temporary right of access, **by court order**, on to neighbouring property to carry out *reasonably necessary* operations which must be 'basic preservation works'.

Thus the Act does not cover alterations or improvements for their own sake but covers maintenance, repair and renewal. It would allow for an inspection visit. You must also show that you could not carry out the works unless you have access to neighbouring land.

(a) Can your neighbour object?

The person living next door to you wants to do some major remedial work to his roof and, as you live in a terrace, he requires that some of the scaffolding is placed against your wall. You feel that it will be a major inconvenience and have strongly objected. He has now applied to court for an access order on to your land. You wonder what you can do.

First, your neighbour must show the court that the works to his roof are 'basic preservation works'. Second, he must show the court that he would not be able to carry out those works without coming on to your property. If he satisfies those terms, you cannot object, strictly speaking. However, you can insist on certain protection for yourself. The access order must be drafted in very specific terms and you can ask for conditions to be attached which would protect – insofar as possible – your privacy and would minimize inconvenience. You could also insist on knowing who will be coming on to your land and when.

♦ **Note:** You cannot ask for payment in a case where there are two residential properties involved.

(b) Trees

An access order can be made where 'basic preservation works' are necessary to deal with trees or shrubs which are in danger of becoming 'damaged, diseased, dangerous, insecurely rooted or dead'. (see also *Problems with gardens* above, section 6).

8.2 Acquiring title to someone else's land – adverse possession

Can the law give you rights of ownership over someone else's land or property? If so, when?

The acquisition of rights over someone else's land in certain clearly defined circumstances is known as 'adverse possession'. Indeed, if you use someone else's land for 12 years without interruption and without permission from the owner, you become the owner of it.

For years you have been parking your car on a piece of wasteland next to your country cottage. You do not know who owns the land. One day you find a fence around the land. Have you any rights?

The fence around the land is definitely an assertion of ownership on the part of someone else.

If you want to challenge that assertion, you must show that

(a) you have used the land as though you owned it;

(b) that use has been uninterrupted for 12 years;

(c) there has been no challenge to that use from the owner of the land.

If you can prove these three essential characteristics of adverse possession, you will have acquired title to it.

♦ **Note:** you are well advised to take advice if you are in dispute over boundaries, restrictive covenants, easements or other property matters. Land law is very technical and full of pitfalls for the unwary.

8.3 Vacant premises

Two problems can arise when you live next to vacant or repossessed premises. The first concerns dereliction through lack of habitation; the second concerns squatters.

Both problems are of particular concern in the present economic climate in view of the numbers of homeless people, as well as the unprecedented numbers of persons defaulting on their mortgages.

8.3.1 Repossessed homes

It is self-evident that if a next-door property is empty, it can cause problems to your own home, such as damp or dry rot. It can be difficult to establish who owns the property and how to take remedial action. As we have seen too (*Access to neighbouring land* section 8.1 above) sometimes you can only take remedial action for basic preservation works by access on to the land next door.

In such a situation, you should try to establish the identity of the owner. Quite often it will be a bank or a building society that has repossessed the property. Where the problem is causing a statutory nuisance (see section 4.3 above), you can ask the local authority to invoke its powers under the Environmental Protection Act 1990.

8.3.2 Squatters

People squat in properties ranging from mansions to empty shop premises, although about 90 per cent of squatters are found in council premises. They may be assisted by squatters' organizations.

As a neighbour, there is nothing you can do about squatters next door unless they cause problems to you of the kind already dealt with – for example, nuisance. Under the Criminal Justice Act 1994 squatters can be guilty of a criminal offence if they fail to leave residential premises after the owner has asked them to do so.

DIRECTORY

Neighbours

Association of Noise Consultants
6 Trap Road
Guilden Morden
Nr Royston
Herts SG8 0JE
Tel. 0763 852958

Boundary Skills Panel
Royal Institute of Chartered Surveyors
12 Great George Street
Parliament Square
London SW1P 3AD
Tel. 071 222 7000

Cleanair
33 Stillness Road
London SE23 1NG
Tel. 081 690 4649

Department of the Environment
2 Marsham Street
London SW1P 3EB
Tel. 071 276 3000

Environmental & Consumer Services
Contact your local council

Federation of Heathrow Anti-Noise Groups
95a Walton Road
East Molesey
Surrey KT8 0DR
Tel. 081 941 2344

Mediation UK
82a Gloucester Road
Bishopston
Bristol BS7 8BN
Tel. 0272 241234

National Association of Councils for Voluntary Service (NACVS)
3rd Floor
Arundel Court
177 Arundel Street
Sheffield S1 2NU
Tel. 0742 786636

Noise Abatement Society
PO Box 8
Bromley
Kent BR2 0UH
Tel. 081 460 3146

National Network in Alternative Dispute Resolution (IDR)
Three Quays
Tower Hill
London EC3R 6DS
Tel. 071 929 1790

Planning Inspectorate
Room 1011
Tollgate House
Houlton Street
Bristol BS2 9DJ
Tel. 0272 218754

Right to Peace and Quiet Campaign
PO Box 968
London SE2 9RL
Tel. 081 312 9997

See also organizations listed in the **Countryside** chapter.

9. COUNTRYSIDE

For those who live in cities and towns, a trip to the countryside provides the means of escape from urban living – from buildings, traffic, noise, pollution and the pressure of people. Estimates are that about 10 million people from the towns visit the countryside every day during the summer months.

Of course, this poses an immediate problem: is it possible to prevent the inundation of our open spaces by the very things from which many citydwellers seek to escape – cars, noise, pollution, and overcrowding?

The law, as we shall see, tries to strike a balance between preservation and necessary development; between conservation of our natural environment and opportunities to enjoy it; between the needs of citydwellers and those of landowners; between those who work on the land and those who want to use it for fun.

At present, as never before, there is a particular focus on, and anxiety about, protecting our environment. This is just as much a local and national issue as it is a global one. Indeed, the intensity of the debate on environmental issues has made us all very aware indeed of just how important it is to strike the right balance between competing needs for our available natural resources.

Many of us think of 'the countryside' in terms of our recreation and enjoyment; indeed it is this aspect on which this chapter concentrates. However, above all, the countryside is a working, living environment and the source of our food. In the most literal sense, we all live off the land.

Much attention is given to the conflict of interest between landowner or farmer and visitor. But there are common interests as well. Not all visitors are necessarily unwelcome! Because of over-production of crops, farmers today are being urged to diversify. Tourists, far from being viewed as undesirable interlopers, may often help to sustain a dwindling income from farming. Summer visitors, too, can help to sustain the economy of many of the fishing villages along our coasts.

As much as possible, therefore, the laws governing access to the countryside must be devised in such a way as to serve the interests of us all, while protecting those things which we most seek from our rural environment.

The authorities involved in 'managing' the countryside span central government; specialized governmental agencies; local authorities; private authorities; voluntary bodies; and, increasingly, EC bodies as well.

The number of pressure groups involved in countryside activities is very striking. Many are active in trying to preserve rural tranquillity, others are concerned with the protection of our flora and fauna; others again wish to assert the right of greater access to what they feel is our natural heritage (see the end of the chapter, for a DIRECTORY of organizations involved in countryside pursuits).

In this chapter we look at

- rights of way
- open spaces

- liability for animals
- sporting rights
- trespass
- protection of flora and fauna

1. Rights of way

The basis of the law concerning access to the countryside in England and Wales is that *all* land is under ownership. There simply is no land available that belongs to the public at large. For every tract of land there is a landowner – whether that landowner is a private individual, a private body (such as the National Trust) a public body (such as the Ministry of Defence), or the Crown. Therefore we have to establish a right to go on to that land – either a right of way or a right to roam. Rights to roam are severely circumscribed (see section 2). So generally we can only go on to land with permission – in other words, we must have a right of way.

The first aspect which we shall consider is the question of rights of way. How do we get to, or through, the countryside?

1.1 Public rights of way

A right of way is a peculiar legal hybrid. It is tangible: i.e. the actual path that you tread on; it is also intangible, i.e. a 'right' in law which you can acquire and which, once acquired, you – or someone else on your behalf – can enforce.

1.1.2 How do we acquire a public right of way?

As all land is under ownership, we need to have a 'right' to go on to land.

How is such a right acquired?

It is acquired by either

- dedication and acceptance

or

- statute – in particular the Highways Act.

(a) By dedication and acceptance

The legal concept called 'dedication and acceptance' stems from the fact that all land in this country is owned.

Where there is a right of way for the general public, that right is regarded as having been 'dedicated' to the public for public use by the landowner. The public, in turn, by using the right of way has, in the eyes of the law, 'accepted' that dedication. The right of way must have been in use for 20 years for the right to be established, unless the landowner has entered into an agreement by deed with the local authority.

(b) Under the Highways Act

The Highways Act 1980 has taken over the common law concept of dedication and acceptance and states that

'Where a way over land . . . has been actually enjoyed by the public as of right and without interruption for a full period of 20 years, the way is . . . deemed to have been dedicated as a highway . . .'

Once a right of way has actually been used by the public 'as of right and without interruption' for the 20 year period, it is then 'deemed' dedicated [i.e. taken to have been dedicated] as a right of way unless there is sufficient evidence of a contrary intention.

(c) Must be uninterrupted use

Thus continuous use for 20 years is conclusive evidence of existence of a public highway or footpath *unless* there is evidence to the contrary, i.e. evidence that there was no intention on the landowner's part during that period to dedicate it. See section 1.3.2(a) below for ways in which a landowner can show that he has not intended to dedicate a right of way and has, for example, interrupted its use by closing it for one day per year.

To sum up:

Public rights of way come into existence in two ways:

- through continuous use, and dedication under the common law;
- through legislation.

(d) Maintenance and upkeep

Once there is an established public right of way, responsibility for its maintenance and upkeep is placed either on the

- local highway authority

or in the case of major roads

- the Department of Transport on behalf of the Crown.

1.1.3 What does a right of way give the public?

As we have seen, a right of way is a hybrid: both a tangible and an intangible right. In particular we are given the right to use it.

(a) The right to pass and repass

The public are allowed to *pass and repass* along a highway for their lawful business without permission from anyone – in other words, members of the public use a highway 'as of right'.

However, although we use the highway as of right, not all highways can be used in the same way. In fact, as we shall see, highways are defined according to their use (see below, section 1.1.5).

(b) For how long does a right of way last?

The phrase is 'once a highway, always a highway'. This means that it should be there for the public use forever. However, loss does occur – particularly of footpaths – and roads can be stopped up under the Highways Act.

1.1.4 What is the distinction between a public and a private right of way?

Private rights of way exist for private use and for limited classes of people – a private access road for individual owners to a common car park is an example. Private rights of way are known as *easements*. (See also below section 1.3.1.)

1.1.5 What limits are there on the right to pass and repass?

Obviously, not all rights of way can be used in the same way. A footpath through a field may be unsuitable for wheeled traffic while pedestrians would be most unwelcome on a motorway.

Public rights of way are classified into

- footpaths
- bridleways

- carriageways
- byways open to all traffic (BOATS)
- roads used as public paths (RUPPS).

(a) Footpaths

You can only use a footpath on foot. You can push a pram along it and you can be accompanied by a dog which does not have to be on a lead but must be kept under control.

> *You are seeking out a picnic spot and see a track marked 'footpath'. It looks wide enough to take your car so you drive down the footpath for about 100 yards and then park. An irate passer-by approaches you and says you have committed a criminal offence; you reply, that at the most, you might have trespassed by driving your car down the footpath. Which of you is correct?*

You are a trespasser because it is trespass to bring a wheeled vehicle – even a bicycle – on to a footpath. You have also committed an offence.

It is a criminal offence to drive a car down a footpath under the Road Traffic Act 1972 unless you have 'lawful' authority, i.e. you are allowed to use the footpath for your car by consent of the owner of the land, or some other authority has given you leave to do so. For example, if you are a disabled driver, you might be given leave by a landowner to use a footpath to drive to a scenic spot.

In theory once a footpath has been established, it belongs to the public for its use forever.

> *Your local footpath has not been used for years; in fact it has become quite overgrown. When you tried to go along it recently, the landowner said that as the footpath was no longer in use, its use had lapsed. Can he be correct?*

A right of way, once established, remains such even if not used for any length of time.

In practice, footpaths can become unusable or lead to nowhere through neglect, desuetude or wilful obstruction (see below section 1.2.1).

(b) Bridleways

In the case of *bridleways*, you can go

- by foot
- on horseback
- by cycle (but cyclists must give priority to walkers and riders).

(c) Carriageways

These are in fact roads which can be used for all purposes and are intended for motor traffic.

1.1.6 Other rights of way

There are two other forms of highway which constitute rights of way.

(a) BOATS

Byways open to all traffic (BOATS): although use is allowed for motor traffic, in fact these are used mainly on foot or by those on horseback.

(b) RUPPS

Roads used as public paths (RUPPS): these are being reclassified as footpaths, bridleways or byways.

(c) Long distance trails

National trails have been created by the joining together of footpaths, bridleways and byways for long distances.

Since 1980, rights of way can be compulsorily imposed by law under the Highways Act 1980. In fact, this power has been very sparingly used for making *new* rights of way. The purpose of this provision has rather been served by linking existing rights of way into long-distance trails over several counties – the Pennine Way is an example.

(d) Cycle paths

Cyclists take note: County councils can designate particular paths and bridleways as *cycle tracks*. These are generally marked (check with your local authority and refer to a definitive map). See section 1.2.2(a) below.

Otherwise there is no right to cycle on a footpath. There is a code of conduct for mountain-bike riding and off-road cycling available from the Countryside Commission and cycling organizations (see the DIRECTORY at the end of this chapter).

1.2 Problems with rights of way

1.2.1 Rights of way can be lost

Although rights of way, once used for 20 years without interruption, are taken to be dedicated to the public forever, in fact they are quite often lost to the public for their use.

In general it is an offence for a landowner to disturb the surface of any footpath, bridleway or unsurfaced carriageway so as to

- interfere with a right of way or
- make it inconvenient to use.

Rights of way can however be lost through

- ploughing and cropping
- physical obstructions
- non-physical obstructions.

(The procedures under which rights of way can be diverted or extinguished under the Highways Act 1980 and the Town and Country Planning Act 1990 are outside the scope of this chapter.)

(a) Ploughing and cropping

The difficulties of securing acceptance of a voluntary code of practice by farmers who plough their fields over rights of way led to the passing of the Rights of Way Act 1990.

▶ **Remember:** There is no right to plough a path which runs along the edge of a field.

After ploughing over a right of way which runs across a field

- the footpath must be made apparent again and kept visible despite the growing crops
- the surface must be restored within two weeks after ploughing.

◆ **Note:** 'Crops' do not include grass grown for pasture.

(b) Physical obstructions

The law in relation to obstructions on footpaths and bridleways has been considerably tightened up under the Rights of Way Act 1990. This Act came into force on August 13 1990 and deals in particular with the problems which have arisen because of ploughing of fields over which public paths run (see section 1.2.1(a) above).

You have been enjoying a walk along a certain footpath for years. You have been told that the land adjoining it has recently changed hands. The last time you tried to walk your way was barred by the new owner who was threatening and abusive. The dog which was with him looked particularly fierce too. What can you do?

Do not attempt to take the law into your hands – no matter what the provocation. Instead inform the Rights of Way Officer of your highway authority which is under a duty to ensure that public rights of way are kept open and free of obstruction. It will then write to the new landowner, probably informally at first, explaining the position and asking him to desist from harassing people who use a public footpath as of right. If he is uncooperative, the highway authority can prosecute. Moreover, private individuals can also prosecute landowners who bar their rights of way. (See section 1.2.2(d) below, on Law enforcement.)

You find your local footpath is blocked by a fallen tree. What can you do?

Reasonably enough, the law suggests that you always try to walk round an obstruction. If that is not possible, you are entitled to try to remove it. You can also inform your local highway authority which is under a duty to maintain the footpath, including the removal of any obstruction. Moreover, where an authority has tried unsuccessfully to get the landowner to remove an obstruction, it can enter on his or her land and remove the obstruction itself. Costs can be reclaimed from the landowner.

(c) Non-physical obstructions

Footpaths can be obstructed in a number of ways. Not all of them may be something as clear to establish as a log of wood blocking your way.

A public footpath runs through a field which its new landowner uses for practising his golf shots. You were narrowly missed by a golf ball while crossing the field on the path.

The procedures for complaint are

(a) to approach the landowner personally;
(b) if this is to no avail, to follow up with a complaint to the highway authority.

(d) Rivers

The question of whether a public right of way could be established on navigable rivers was recently aired in the House of Lords.

A dispute had arisen between Malton town council and four nearby landowners whose land adjoined the river Derwent. The town council wished to protect the public rights of navigation of the Derwent for recreational purposes while the owners said that that would damage plant and river life.

The Law Lords emphatically stated that a right of navigation was not a right of way. It was wrong in law to regard a right of way over water as similar to a right of way over land. The physical feature of a path or road was the land over which it ran. On the other hand, in the case of a river its physical feature was the flowing water which made navigation possible.

No one could 'own' flowing water so it could not be 'dedicated' to the public for its use so as to establish a right of way.

1.2.2 What can be done to stop paths disappearing?

In order to preserve rights of way, certain duties have been imposed on local authorities. These include the duties to

- produce definitive maps
- signpost rights of way
- maintain rights of way
- enforce the public's rights against offenders.

(a) Definitive maps

To safeguard against the number of usable footpaths diminishing because they were not being used or were obstructed, overgrown or forgotten, local authorities are under a duty to survey their areas and to produce definitive maps and written statements of all footpaths and bridleways in their area.

These maps are conclusive evidence that a public right of way exists. Ordnance survey maps show rights of way which have been recorded on these definitive maps.

However, even when a public right of way has been recorded in a definitive map, its *status* is not defined forever.

> *A public right of way through your land was marked on the definitive map as a footpath. The local council made an order to change it to that of a bridleway. You objected and a public enquiry was held. You maintain that once a path has been designated, its designation remains fixed for all time. Evidence was brought to show at the enquiry that there had been long-standing use of the path for riding on horseback.*

An entry on a definitive map is not conclusive evidence forever. A path's status is liable to change so that rights of passage could be enlarged. For example a footpath could become a bridleway in the light of fresh evidence.

If a change is to be made, it must be done according to a statutory procedure which involves a modification order. Such an order can be challenged in court.

> *Your local county council has recently included in a modification order a footpath over your land on the grounds that it was omitted from the definitive map in error. You wish to challenge the modification order. What steps can you take?*

The county council is under a duty to publish the order. You have six weeks from the date of receiving notice of the order in which to object to the council.

The matter will then be referred to the Secretary of State for the Environment who can hold a local inquiry. If he decides to confirm the order you can apply to the High Court to appeal against his decision – again within six weeks of the confirmation.

(b) Signposting

Signposting or waymarking is often undertaken by groups of local volunteers.

The colours are

- blue for bridleways
- red for byways
- yellow for footpaths.

A highway authority is under a duty to signpost all

- footpaths
- bridleways and
- byways

where they leave a metalled road.

◆ **Note:** the landowner's consent is necessary if signs are erected along a route on stiles or gateposts.

Ownership

The surface of a footpath or other right of way is owned by the local highway authority. A landowner still retains ownership of gates and stiles.

(c) Maintaining footpath widths

The widths to be kept clear *across fields* are

- one metre for footpaths
- two metres for bridleways
- three metres for carriageways.

The widths to be kept clear *around the edge* of a field are

- one and a half metres for footpaths
- three metres for both bridleways and carriageways.

(d) Law enforcement

Under the Highways Act 1980, it is an offence for someone who – without lawful authority or excuse – in any way wilfully obstructs free passage along a highway. If found guilty he or she can be fined.

A direct approach to the landowner concerned would always be the best approach. If that fails, or if it is difficult to establish who owns the land, you can report an obstruction to your local highway authority. You must back up your report with evidence – such as a map, a description of the nature of the obstruction and the date on which you encountered it. Proceedings are heard in a magistrates' court.

If you, as an individual or an organization, decide to take legal action, always remember to seek professional advice.

(e) Maintenance

A highway authority is under a duty to maintain a footpath so that it is fit for ordinary passage. However, the maintenance of stiles and gates falls on the landowner.

1.3 Other rights on land

Apart from public rights of way, other rights can exist on someone else's land. These are generally known as *easements* (see also the chapter on *Neighbours*). In this section we deal with private rights of way.

1.3.1 Private rights of way

Public rights of way are dedicated to the public at large. A distinction must be drawn therefore with private rights of way. These are only intended for a limited number of people.

> *Your neighbour has been allowing his own children, together with their school friends, to cut a path through his land on their way to school for many years. Recently some farmers have attempted to use the path to get to their neighbouring fields, claiming that the path is now a public right of way. Your neighbour has objected strongly. What is his position?*

If use of a path has been restricted to a limited group of people with whom your neighbour has connections, he has not created a right of way by dedication.

1.3.2 Landowners and rights of way

Not every landowner intends to allow the public – or even private groups of people – to acquire a footpath across his land by dedication and acceptance. He can show that he has no such intention even if people cross his land on a regular basis.

(a) Rights of landowner in preventing formation of public and private rights of way

We have seen that uninterrupted use by the public for 20 years can lead to the deemed dedication and acceptance of a footpath – unless a landowner shows an intention to the contrary. How would a landowner show a contrary intention?

- By allowing the public to use the path only with the landowner's express permission.
- By interrupting the public's use of the path by, for example, closing the path on one day per year.
- By putting up a notice giving the public access only by leave of the landowner.
- By informing the local county council that the path has not been dedicated as a public right of way. Appropriate maps should be submitted. (For rights of a landowner to prevent trespass, see section 5 below.)

2. Open spaces

2.1 Laws governing open spaces

What is the position if you wish to roam freely in open land?

A right of way gives access to open space only along a defined route, as we have seen. If one deviates from the route, one commits a trespass.

These restrictions were felt to be too great. In 1949, a change was introduced to allow greater access to areas of natural beauty in this country. Certain land is covered by access agreements and is designated as open country (see section 2.1(b) below). The public can also enter private land if the landowner allows them to.

(a) Permission of landowner

Landowners can expressly allow free access on their land. They can lay down certain conditions: e.g. that the public cannot enter the land during the breeding season for animals or wild birds.

◆ **Note:** They can withdraw their permission at any time. Obviously, therefore, it is much in the public's interest to have access to land on a more secure basis. This is done by designation.

(b) Designating open spaces

Under the National Parks and Access to the Countryside Act 1949, local planning authorities could conclude agreements with landowners so that 'open country' should be open to access by the public. (See section 2.3 below.) In the Act 'open country' is defined as meaning mountain, moor, heath, down, cliff or foreshore.

Again such access is subject to certain conditions. The most common are not lighting fires, not damaging trees or paths, and keeping a dog under proper control.

(c) Designation against landowner's wishes

If a landowner does not wish an access agreement to be made over his land, the local planning authority can make an access order. The landowner must then appeal to the Secretary of State for the Environment who can order a public enquiry to be held before reaching a final decision.

A landowner against whom an access order is made is entitled to compensation.

2.2 Guarding open spaces

If we intend to preserve what we have got in the way of open spaces, historic buildings and beautiful landscapes, we must consider planning controls. For protection of natural habitats see section 6.

(a) Town and country planning

Planning legislation was introduced on a comprehensive basis in 1947 at a time when much other sweeping legislation, which affected the nation as a whole, was passed.

Since the Town and Country Planning Act 1947, there have been many further Acts dealing specifically with planning: particularly one in 1971 and, since then, a codifying Act, the Town and Country Planning Act 1990, to which this chapter refers.

(b) Structure plans

A *structure plan* is an overall plan for an area, set out by the county council. It encompasses a council's planning objectives for its administrative area – much in line with government circulars which offer generalized planning direction. Structure plans, therefore, will cover factors such as housing, roads, industrial development and recreational needs.

(c) Local plans

At a local level, *local plans* are drawn up by the local authorities to flesh out the structure plan.

This does not mean that all development outside these plans is forbidden. However, an applicant for planning permission who wants to persuade a local planning authority to deviate from its plans might have a more difficult task in justifying his proposals. (For the definition of what constitutes 'development' see section 2.2(e) below.)

(d) Planning controls

In addition there are strict planning controls in areas which have been specially designated as areas of outstanding natural beauty or as conservation areas. Again, permission for development will only be granted if it meets very specific needs and criteria.

Broadly speaking, no one can 'develop' land or property without first obtaining planning permission. The critical factor, therefore, is what constitutes 'development'.

(e) Definition of 'development'

Development is defined as

- building, engineering, mining and other operations or
- a material change of use of property (land or buildings) from one purpose to another.

◆ **Note:** a *building operation* can be widely defined and includes demolition.

> *You have a house on a plot of land which you would like to demolish. You are told that this would constitute a 'building operation' under the planning laws. You want to know if this is correct.*

The answer is 'yes'.

(f) Material change of use

Change of use can involve

- a totally different type of use, e.g. from residential property to commercial use
- intensification of existing use (e.g. from the stationing of one caravan to the stationing of several caravans); or
- from agricultural use to other use; e.g. conversion of a farm barn into a separate dwelling house.

2.3 Types of open spaces

As we have seen in 'designating open spaces' (see section 2.1(b) above), certain areas of the country were felt to be of such intrinsic interest and beauty that they were designated as open spaces. These will be examined in more detail below.

2.3.1 National Parks

Approximately 10 per cent of the land area of England and Wales forms our National Parks. These were set up by the National Parks and Access to the Countryside Act, which was passed in 1949 at a time of major post-war reconstruction in all areas of national life.

The idea of National Parks was first mooted in the 1930s. The impetus behind the idea was that all citizens were not only entitled to, but should be able freely to enjoy some of the most beautiful expanses of landscape of their country. Certain areas of the country were seen as so special that they ought to be made part of the national heritage and that Parliament itself should give them status to that effect.

◆ **Do take note:** 'National' does *not* mean that the parks are publicly owned.

Much of the land is still in private hands as it always was before the designation of National Parks. About 250,000 people live in these areas, many of which are still being farmed.

(a) Land designated for National Parks

The Countryside Commission describes these areas as 'the most beautiful, spectacular and dramatic expanses of country in England and Wales'.

(b) National Parks objectives

These objectives are

- conservation of the landscape
- recreation.

The balance between these two objectives is sometimes difficult to sustain. For example, some people would like to ban waterskiing and powerboating on Windermere in the Lake District and Llangorse Lake in the Beacons National Park, Powys. Bird lovers complain that the bird population has declined as a direct result of the noise and intrusion of powerboats. Water sports enthusiasts, on the other hand, maintain that they bring jobs, money and tourists.

(c) Changing patterns

The fact is that the Parks may be in danger of being loved to death. In 1949, when they were inaugurated, few families owned a car. Now car ownership is so widespread that ever-increasing numbers of people make excursions and visits to the Parks.

(d) List of National Parks

The list of National Parks gives an idea of their varied landscape including coast, moorland, fells, and precipitous mountainside:

Lake District	Dartmoor
Snowdonia	Exmoor
Pembrokeshire Coast	North York Moors
Brecon Beacons	Yorkshire Dales
Northumberland	Peak District

(e) The Norfolk Broads

The Norfolk Broads were given a status akin to that of a National Park in 1988. A Broads Authority, set up by Act of Parliament, took charge of the Broads area from April 1989 with the tasks of

- acting as sole planning authority
- being in charge of conserving and enhancing the natural beauty of the Broads, and
- protecting landscape and navigation over the network of waterways.

(f) Countryside Commission

The National Parks Commission was set up in 1949. It is now called the Countryside Commission and works in an advisory capacity to the government.

(g) Planning controls

Planning controls for the Parks are the responsibility of the county councils of the areas in which the Parks lie. It was increasingly felt that

more autonomy was needed to protect the Parks properly from depreda-
tion of all kinds but in particular from major industry.

(h) New legislation

As a result, the government has promised the introduction of independent
National Park authorities although no date for the legislation has been set.
A private member's Bill is to go before the House of Lords.

The government has also decided that the New Forest in Hampshire
should be given a new status as an 'area of national significance'.

2.3.2 Areas of outstanding natural beauty

Power to designate an area as one of outstanding natural beauty is
enshrined in the National Parks and Access to the Countryside Act 1949.
The Countryside Commission has the power to propose a designation
after it has consulted with the local authorities and advertised its intention in the local press. The Secretary of State for the Environment then
confirms the designation – after public enquiry if need be.

> *You have read in the local paper that the Countryside
> Commission intends to designate an area of land which
> encompasses your own farm as an area of outstanding natural
> beauty. You feel aggrieved that you were not notified individually
> of the intention to designate.*

- (a) There is no requirement to notify individual landowners of an
  intention to designate provided that the proposal is advertised in
  the London Gazette and local newspapers.
- (b) You are able to make objections against the proposal to your local
  authority if you wish; these objections will then be taken into
  account by the Secretary of State.
- (c) He may institute a public enquiry as a result.
- (d) However, if after a public enquiry, it is decided to designate the
  area as one of outstanding natural beauty, the Secretary of State
  will confirm the designation order.

2.3.3 Conservation areas

These are areas of special architectural or historic interest, the character or
appearance of which should be preserved or enhanced. Conservation
areas are usually designated where there is a group or cluster of buildings
which *together* make it an area desirable to preserve (whereas listed
buildings are listed individually). Although often conservation areas
are designated in towns and cities, they are designated in country areas
too.

> *You own a field which adjoins a village which is a designated
> conservation area. You would like to develop the field for a
> housing project. Planning permission is refused and you argue
> that the field has no building on it so that it cannot be of
> architectural interest; the field has no historical associations so
> that there is nothing there to preserve or enhance either.
> Therefore it is only the village itself which could be called a
> conservation area.*

Interesting landscape features, *together with their setting*, can be
regarded as an 'area' for conservation purposes. In cases of old

villages, their settings would include greens and paddocks, trees and fields coming close to the houses. An area should be looked at as an entity giving rise to special historic or architectural interest and not every part of an area need have on it something of interest.

2.3.4 Country parks

These were set up following on from the Countryside Act 1968 and are run by the local authorities. A few are privately owned. Country parks use historical and natural features to enhance their appeal and sometimes include sports areas.

Entrance is free but a charge can be made for other facilities such as water sports or car parking.

2.3.5 Nature reserves

These are primarily designated for the protection of flora and fauna, and public access might be restricted in the interests of protecting natural habitats.

Nature reserves can be set up by

- statutory powers under the 1949 Act; or
- private bodies such as the Royal Society for the Protection of Birds.

2.3.6 Sites of special scientific interest (SSSIs)

These are sites which are designated as being of particular scientific interest. Sites may be designated not only for wild plant and animal life but also for geophysical and other landscape features of importance.

(a) Designation of SSSIs

Designation is made under the Wildlife and Countryside Act 1981 (as amended in 1985).

An owner or occupier is notified by English Nature (formerly the Nature Conservancy Council) of:

- the reasons for the site's designation
- operations likely to damage those features (for example drainage of land, which would damage the habitat of wild duck, or quarrying, which would affect geological sites).

The owner has three months in which to register any objections.

If the designation is confirmed, the owner cannot carry out the operations specified unless

- Consent has been given;
- The work is carried out in accordance with a management agreement;
- The owner has given four months' notice to English Nature, which has raised no objection.

◆ **Note:** Notice must also be given to the local planning authority. In fact, there has been criticism that local planning authorities have given planning permission for development of SSSIs which is detrimental to their protection, and that between 200 and 300 sites are lost or damaged each year.

2.3.7 Environmentally sensitive areas (ESAs)

These are set up by the Ministry of Agriculture and Fisheries to accord with EC law. Funds are available from the Community if an area is environmentally sensitive (a term which includes flora, fauna or features of natural beauty or of geological, archaeological or historical interest). Farmers are then paid to farm in a way which would enhance environmental protection (for example, using organic farming methods rather than pesticides).

Between 1987 and 1993, 16 sites have been designated as ESAs. A further 6 have been proposed.

(a) Sites of Importance for Nature Conservation (SINCs)

Local authorities are entitled – but not obliged – to designate sites in their area for nature conservation.

2.3.8 Common land

Rights to use common land stem from medieval times when tenants of a particular manor were entitled to certain rights on 'waste land' of the manor – generally the land unsuitable for cultivation. These rights were common to them – hence the terms 'common land' and 'commoners'. Such rights included, for example, the right to take peat for fuel or to graze animals.

(a) Keeping common land open

By the mid-nineteenth century, most of this land had been enclosed (appropriated by local landowners). However, a reaction set in to the systematic enclosure of common land and much more strenuous attempts were made to keep it open.

About one-third of common land is open to the public, who may roam freely. Access to other common land is restricted to rights of way. Other rights, such as to graze cattle or take peat, are restricted to certain 'commoners' in each case.

◆ **Note:** Keeping common land as 'open land' does not mean that it is public land.

(b) Metropolitan areas

Common land can be found in metropolitan areas – Hampstead Heath is an example. Generally speaking there is a right of access to all common land in towns and cities.

(c) Rural areas

Common land in rural areas is still often subject to rights of common, such as grazing rights, but this does not mean that there is any general right of access.

(d) Registration

Under the Commons Registration Act 1965, county councils have to keep a register of common land in their areas.

Since then another Act has been passed, the Common Land (Rectification of Registers) Act 1989 which allows a landowner to challenge an incorrect entry into the register of common land.

You own a large house with a garden and extensive grounds. Some of the grounds have been left uncultivated. You discover

*that one of your neighbours has registered part of your
uncultivated ground as 'common land' and you apply to have the
register rectified. A Commons Commissioner has visited the
site and stated in his decision that the land is not really part
of the gardens of your house. You want to know what you
can do next.*

You can appeal to the High Court. It has ruled that to succeed in
an application for rectification, land has to be a 'garden' and
ancillary to a house. However, a 'garden' does not have to be
cultivated for flowers, fruit and vegetables. Frequently parts of a
large garden are left wild and uncultivated but are still ancillary to
a house and part of its garden.

2.3.9 Beaches, rivers and waterways

The area of the foreshore between the low and high tide line belongs to the
Crown. Although in theory there may be no public right of access, there is
no likelihood of access being barred to the general public. Indeed, the
foreshore is often leased or sold by the Crown to local authorities to
develop beaches for popular enjoyment.

Land above the high water mark is usually under local authority control
and bylaws often govern the area in the interests of public safety. Similarly
1,000 metres of water beyond the low water mark is also usually governed
by local authorities which often impose bylaws to protect swimmers.

There is no general right of access over land adjacent to the beach or
foreshore.

*You park your car above a headland below which there is a very
attractive cove. You start clambering down towards the beach
when a man approaches and says that he owns the land and that
there is no right of way for you.*

Owners of land abutting the coast line can exclude members of
the public from using their land for access to beaches unless a
public right of way exists.

There is an absolute right of navigation in tidal waters. 'Navigation'
includes water sports such as water skiing, jetskiing ('wet bikes') and
speedboats.

*You and your children are swimming in the sea at a resort on the
South Coast when a wetbiker speeds past your little girl. She is
not hit but she falls over in the wake. You write to the local
council and ask why such activity is allowed near swimmers,
particularly near small children. The local authority replies that
it has no powers to ban the sport.*

While there are bylaws to control noise and navigation speeds
near the shore, the local authority cannot stop craft entering the
water.

◆ **Note:** There is no public right of way along the foreshore. A right of way
has to have a delineated route but this is impossible in an area of land
washed by daily tides.

(a) Pollution

Standards of cleanliness of beaches and seawater have been laid down by
the EC. A blue flag system is in operation for clean beaches.

Unfortunately, some beaches fail to reach these standards and there are complaints of pollution from sewage, oil slicks and dumping of chemical waste at sea. Discharge from ships at sea causes a great deal of coastal pollution even where the discharge takes place outside territorial waters: sooner or later, their discharge is washed up on beaches. Pesticides and other chemicals which flow into rivers from factories and farms also reach the sea at some stage and in some form.

Standards are being monitored all the time by local authorities in an endeavour to make sure that holidaymakers can swim in the water safely, without fear of ill effects.

2.3.10 Heritage coasts

Certain areas of coastline have been designated as 'heritage' coast. These coastline areas are not nationally owned but are in private hands or owned by the National Trust or local authorities.

Many of the heritage coasts are within the National Parks while others are in areas of outstanding natural beauty.

The purpose of the designation is both

- conservation so that unspoilt coast should be protected by planning controls and
- 'positive management' to
  - protect natural habitats
  - repair footpaths, and
  - try to mitigate the effects of pollution.

2.3.11 Marine nature reserves

These are areas of land covered by tidal water, or sea beds within the UK territorial waters, which have been designated for the protection of marine and bird life by the government.

2.3.12 New protection for beaches?

A recent House of Commons Select Committee has pointed to inadequacies in the legislation governing coastal planning. It recommends more comprehensive and unified legislation to protect our coasts. It criticizes the number of bodies currently involved which often reflect administrative boundaries rather than a national view of coastal management as an issue to be tackled as a whole.

2.3.13 Canals and towpaths

There are about 2,000 miles of inland waterways which are run by British Waterways for commercial and recreational purposes. The canals are artificial waterways created at the time of the industrial revolution and although there is no automatic public right of navigation through the canals, this is generally permitted subject to bylaw.

The towpaths of canals can be dedicated as rights of way and are very popular with walkers – subject to the overriding rights of those who use towpaths for navigational purposes. Even where a towpath is not dedicated as a right of way, the public is generally allowed to use it. However, if in doubt, the definitive map of your area should have the information you need.

3. Encounters with animals

3.1 Liability: Who is responsible

Incidents involving animals, such as someone being bitten by a dog, can occur anywhere. However, it is in the countryside that we are most likely to encounter animals and where our own animals can do harm.

If an animal causes damage or injury, its 'keeper' i.e. its possessor or owner, is generally responsible.

◆ **Take note:** if an animal is owned or possessed by a child under 16, its keeper for legal purposes is the head of the household to which the child belongs (Animals Act 1971).

3.1.1 Domestic and other animals

The law draws a clear distinction between the keeping of domestic animals and of other animals which are considered 'wild' by nature. It imposes far greater liability on the owner of the latter (see section 3.1.1(g) below).

The first section deals with domestic animals.

(a) Dogs

As a general rule, a dog owner is liable if he or she knew (or should have known) that their dog was likely to be dangerous and attack someone or that it could be dangerous at a particular time, for example when a female is with its young.

> *You own four Jack Russell terriers which escaped from your land. They attacked a neighbour's child in his garden. Your dogs have not attacked people before.*

The owner of the dogs is liable to compensate an injured child on the basis of evidence that Jack Russell terriers are dangerous when left free to run in a pack.

◆ **Pay heed:** It can be seen from this that an owner need not have had detailed evidence of a dangerous characteristic of his or her dog to have 'knowledge' in the legal sense. The popular saying that 'a dog is allowed his first bite' is therefore inaccurate.

(b) Dangerous dogs

In response to some horrifying attacks on people by imported species of fighting dogs, a new Act was passed in 1991.

The Dangerous Dogs Act 1991 requires the owners of pit bull terriers to notify the police, have the dog neutered and permanently marked by tattoo or implant to prove ownership. Liability insurance is compulsory. There are also criminal penalties for, among other things, abandoning such a dog, or for allowing it to be in a public place without a muzzle or leash.

Apart from criminal penalties against owners who fail to obey these laws, anyone who is attacked by a pit bull can sue the owners for damages.

One of the main criticisms levelled against the Act is that it refers to dogs bred for fighting and to 'a type known as a pit bull terrier' without further definition. However, the Act may be extended to other breeds of dog.

Another offence under the 1991 Act is to allow *any breed* of dog to be dangerously out of control in a public place. An offence will also be committed if there is 'reasonable apprehension' that an animal, out of control in a public place, might cause injury – even if it does not actually do so. In other words, people should not be put in fear of dogs.

The courts have the power to order a dog which has injured someone to be put down, and can disqualify its owner from keeping other dogs.

▶ **Enforcement:** The difficulties of enforcing legislation of this kind are obvious and there are estimated to be about 2,000 pit bull terriers of which the police have not been notified.

(c) Dogs and livestock

Liability has always been imposed on the keeper of a dog which 'worries' livestock. Indeed, until the passing of the 1991 Act, it could reasonably have been argued that livestock were better protected by the law on dogs than were people.

Under the Animals Act 1971, *livestock* is widely defined to include cattle, sheep, pigs, goats, poultry, pheasants etc.

> *You are walking along a footpath across a field accompanied by your dog. It is always docile and well behaved and is not on a lead. All of a sudden, it spies some sheep in a corner of the field and starts to chase one of the lambs. In terror a lamb hurls itself against a fence, and injures itself. You are accosted by the farmer who says you are liable to compensate him. You explain that your dog has never done anything like chasing sheep before and – in any event – there was no negligence on your part.*

As owner, you are liable even if you had no previous knowledge of your dog's propensity to worry livestock, nor need negligence be proved. Dogs are to be kept under 'proper control' on footpaths – thus while they do not necessarily have to be on a lead, close control is required.

◆ **Beware:** The owner of livestock is even entitled to kill a dog that has been worrying livestock if it is still on his or her premises and not under anyone's control (in such a case the police must be notified within 48 hours).

Finally, there are criminal penalties for keeping a guard dog unless

- a competent handler is present and
- a warning notice is displayed at the entrance to the premises.

(d) Horses

Horseriding is allowed along carriageways and bridleways but not along footpaths except with permission of the owner of the land. A person taking a horse along a footpath, without express permission to do so, therefore commits trespass and must get off the land if ordered to do so.

There is growing pressure to extend the number of bridleways into a nationwide network to facilitate long-distance riding.

The current Highway Code gives instructions to horseriders as to how to take care of themselves and their horses on the road. It is estimated that there are several accidents each day involving riders and horses and that the numbers of such accidents are increasing all the time. So indeed are the numbers of people who ride horses for sport – there are estimated to be about three million people who ride regularly.

As with dogs, so with horses: a keeper is liable if he or she knew or ought to have known of a horse's propensity to kick or bolt or otherwise be unruly.

> You have recently joined a riding school and have been taken out on a ride with a group of others along a bridleway. Your horse tends to hang back from the others to crop grass and you have not got the expertise to keep it firmly under your control. From a nearby road there is a sudden sound of a car backfiring and your horse turns, injuring a passerby.

> If you had been an experienced rider, you might have been liable in negligence for failing to control your horse. However, in this case, the school itself will probably be found negligent as it should not have handed that particular horse to a novice rider and then failed to ensure proper supervision.

There are compulsory insurance requirements for businesses keeping animals, such as riding schools.

(e) Bulls

Under the Wildlife and Countryside Act 1981, a bull is not allowed to be at large in a field if it is over 10 months old and of a recognized breed. If it is not of a recognized breed, it may be at large in a field but it must be accompanied by cows or heifers.

The recognized breeds are Ayrshire, British Friesian, British Holstein, Dairy Shorthorn, Guernsey, Jersey, and Kerry.

Thus, for those who cannot readily assess the age of a bull, or its breed, the law does not make things too easy but in any event there is liability if a bull's keeper knew or ought to have known that it posed a danger to passers-by.

(f) Straying animals

If a trespassing dog damages your garden plants, or a neighbour's cat kills your poultry, their owners are not normally liable to compensate you for the damage. But an owner of a dog runs the risk of the animal being lawfully killed if it goes on to someone else's land and worries livestock (see section 3.1.1(c) above).

Apart from this, there is no other right to destroy animals which stray on to your property. If straying livestock cause damage to your own animals, crops or other property, their owners will be liable to pay compensation. Moreover, they cannot insist that you should have your land fenced from their animals unless you are under a duty to fence your land (such a duty would be stipulated in, for example, leases or title deeds).

> Some sheep from the nearby farm stray off the land, wander into your orchard, and destroy some very expensive young trees which you have planted there. You ask to be compensated, and the farmer replies that you should have fenced in your land.

> It is not a defence for him to say that the damage could have been prevented if your land were fenced. He must compensate you for the damage his sheep have caused.

> Of course, if damage of this kind were to occur regularly, it would always be better to fence to protect one's property than stand on one's legal rights!

Surprisingly enough, the owner of the land on to which the animals have strayed, far from venting spleen on them, is under a legal duty to feed and water them adequately. He or she must also give notice within 48 hours to the police and their owner (if known). If within 14 days their owner fails to reclaim them or offer compensation for the damage caused, the victim is entitled to sell them at auction to recoup his losses.

◆ **Note that** the owner of straying livestock is entitled to go on to someone else's land in order to recapture his animals.

This is not trespass.

The owner of an animal, whether dangerous or not, is under a duty to prevent it straying on to the highway (except in areas where land is customarily unfenced – as in the North of England, or on village greens). If an accident results from a driver attempting to avoid an animal which has strayed on to the road, therefore, its owner will be liable, at least if s/he knows of its habit of wandering.

(g) Wild animals

Where injury or damage is caused by an animal classed as dangerous (e.g. dangerous species which are in captivity, such as birds of prey, or poisonous snakes or spiders) their keepers can be held responsible without anything else having to be proved – precautions or lack of them make no difference. A keeper of a dangerous animal is obliged to have a local authority licence authorizing him or her to keep the animal.

Liability insurance cover is a condition of all such licences.

An animal is classed as dangerous if it is not commonly domesticated in the UK (even though such animals may be domesticated abroad), or if it is likely to cause severe damage if unrestrained. For example, an elephant's size alone means that any damage it causes will be serious, even if it does not do so viciously. Its keeper is liable even if the only danger posed by the animal is to property (which of course includes other animals), and even if the particular animal is unusually mild or docile.

3.2 Other liabilities of animal owners

The above are the special legislative measures applying to animal owners.

They may in addition fall foul of the law on negligence, and become liable for failing to take reasonable care to prevent their animals causing damage to others.

You may also be able to claim if a neighbour keeps noxious animals which escape on to your property, e.g. if he has unreasonable numbers of bees which swarm in to your garden and sting you.

If an animal's owner purposely causes you harm, e.g. by setting his dog to attack you, you could bring an action for trespass to the person. If he sets his large dog to attack your smaller one, the action will be for trespass to goods.

3.3 When there is non-liability for damage

Neighbours are not liable, however, if the animals coming on to your land are 'naturally' there on their land.

Your family's pet rabbit is killed by foxes living on a neighbour's land.

The neighbour has no responsibility for preventing the foxes making such forays.

3.3.1 When a keeper of an animal may not be liable

As with all potential civil wrongs, a keeper of an animal can set up certain defences to a claim for injury caused by his or her animal.

(a) Contributory negligence

An animal's keeper can claim that injury or damage was partly the result of the victim's own lack of care. For example, if you, as an inexperienced rider, ask to ride a particular horse even though you suspect that it tends to be unruly, you are partly responsible for the injury it causes. As with all cases of contributory negligence, it is a matter of fact and degree.

Liability for damages can be avoided altogether if the victim consented to run the risk of injury knowing of the dangers, for example by intervening in a fight between fierce dogs.

◆ **Note well:** Under the Animals Act, however, the mere fact that a person took up employment with an animal owner does not mean he or she consented to run any risk of injury, so that a stable girl who is kicked by a horse is not prevented from claiming compensation for the injury (assuming, or course that she had not herself provoked the horse by teasing it).

(b) Private land

If you go on to private land without permission, you become a trespasser. A landowner has a duty to persons who come on to his land (see below, section 5, and chapter on *Accidents*). This is known as Occupier's Liability. This duty diminishes according to who comes on to the land, but there is still a duty towards a trespasser, and a landowner cannot allow a dangerous dog to roam freely without a warning sign. However, if you are bitten by a dog when you have no business on the land in the first place, and there is a warning sign which you ignored, the landowner will have a defence to your claim.

3.4 Cruelty to animals

Animals must not be mistreated and it is generally a criminal offence to do so. This area of the law is dealt with in section 6 below.

4. Sporting rights

Sporting rights are a form of property rights.

4.1 Exercising your rights

Landowners own very valuable rights to hunt, shoot or fish on their land.

4.1.1 Similarity with other forms of property rights

Like other property rights, landowners can keep these rights for their own use and enjoyment. Alternatively, sporting rights can be leased, sold, or licensed to other people, or to groups of people, e.g. sporting clubs.

So, like other property rights, sporting rights can generate considerable income to those who own them. In terms of the economy as a whole, about twice the amount of money is spent on hunting, shooting and fishing as is spent on the live arts and cinema admissions. In the region of £1.4 billion was estimated to have been directly spent on country sports in 1990 (see *The Daily Telegraph* 28 February 1992, quoting from the chairman of the Standing Conference on Countryside Sports).

Points to note:

(a) Like all other forms of property, sporting rights are protected by law – in particular by the Game Acts, the Poaching Acts and the civil law of trespass.

(b) Like other forms of property, sporting rights are subject to controls – even for those who own them.

For example, it is generally no excuse for a landowner who kills or injures a protected species of animal to say that he did so on his own land.

4.1.2 Laws governing sporting rights

Many of the laws governing hunting, shooting and fishing date from the early nineteenth century. There is overlap and confusion between the provisions of the various Game Acts. Certainly the language in which they are couched and some of their prohibitions appear archaic. For example, it is an offence to kill certain game on a Sunday or on Christmas Day.

Under the Criminal Justice Act 1994, an offence of *aggravated trespass* has been created. It applies where a trespasser intends to disrupt a lawful activity such as hunting or to intimidate the participants.

4.2 Hunting

(a) Firearms certificate

You cannot keep a gun in a house or outbuilding without a certificate.

You cannot hire a gun without a certificate – or even borrow one – except under stringent limitations.

> *Your neighbouring landowner has offered to take you out for a day's shoot. He has two guns with him and offers to hire one of them to you. You wonder if you need a certificate.*

> Guns cannot be hired except to someone who has a valid certificate. However, you can *borrow* a rifle from your neighbour for use provided you use it for shooting on his own land in his actual presence. Otherwise you will need a certificate even to borrow it.

In general, shotguns need a shotgun certificate and airguns, rifles or pistols need a firearms certificate. Forms for these certificates are available from police stations. An application form must be countersigned by a reputable person. You will have to satisfy the police, who will visit you in your home, that

- you are of good character;
- you have good reasons to apply for a certificate;
- you will not be a danger to the public safety or to the peace;
- you are above the age limit – which varies for young persons between 14 and 17 depending on the firearm;
- you have secure storage for the firearm.

(b) What happens if you are refused a certificate?

There are limited avenues of appeal against a refusal by the police to issue a firearms certificate.

You can appeal to a Crown Court against the police's refusal to issue you with a licence. However, if the Crown Court turns down your appeal, you can take the matter no further.

(c) Game licence

A game licence is needed in order to hunt certain game. 'Game' is variously defined as including hares, rabbits and deer ('Ground Game'); and pheasants, partridges, grouse, heath or moor game, as well as woodcock and snipe ('Game Birds').

Licences are available from main post offices and are issued on payment of the fee, which varies according to season (£6 *per annum* expiring on 31 July; reduced price after 1 November for a limited period).

It is a criminal offence to hunt without a valid game licence.

▶ **Never forget:** a game licence does not give you a *right* to hunt on someone else's land. The landowner's permission to hunt on his or her land is also *always* required.

◆ **Note:** There is no need for a game licence if you are

- hunting deer with hounds (again with permission of the landowner!)
- a beater and are not carrying a gun
- an owner or occupier killing rabbits or deer on your own enclosed land
- acting under the orders of the Ministry of Agriculture.

You must show your licence, if you are on land with a gun or dog, if asked to by

- a landowner
- the police
- someone else with a licence
- a gamekeeper.

You have a valid game licence, as well as permission of the landowner to hunt on his land. You are challenged by his gamekeeper when you are out on a shooting expedition with a dog and gun. You discover that you have not remembered to bring the licence with you.

You can explain the position to the gamekeeper and give him your name and address. If he asks you to leave the land, however, you must do so.

(d) Poaching

The laws against poaching date mainly from the 19th century. Poaching is banned by day or night (the latter is the more serious offence); and it is a separate offence to be on land (whether open or enclosed) with a gun or any other instrument for taking game.

(e) Close season
(See also section 6 below)

There are four close seasons for deer depending on whether they are red deer (stags and hinds) or fallow and roe deer (bucks). The Deer Act 1963 lays down the weapons which cannot be used against deer as well as outlawing other means to kill them (for example, traps or snares). See also section 6 below.

4.3 Fishing

(a) Rights on rivers

The owner of land adjoining one side of a natural river or stream owns the exclusive fishing rights on his or her side of the bank. These rights extend up to the middle of the water and can be sold or leased as separate and valuable property rights – quite apart from ownership of the land itself. These are known as 'riparian rights'.

An owner whose land adjoins a pond or lake has similar rights which extend only as far as the middle of the water unless his land encircles the pond or lake.

Although s/he owns the fishing rights, a riparian owner is still subject to the general laws protecting close seasons for fish. These are laid down in the Salmon and Freshwater Fisheries Act 1975.

> *You own land on both banks of the river and you use a speedboat to make your crossings from one side to the other. You do this throughout the year. You are charged with an offence of wilfully disturbing spawning fish during the close season. You protest that as owner you cannot be charged.*

It is no defence to the charge to say that you are the riparian owner.

(b) Licensing

If you want to fish by the riverside and you are not a member of an angling club, you will need a licence to fish. The National Rivers Authority has 2,500 agents throughout England and Wales who can issue you with a national rod fishing licence. The cost of a standard licence is £13.25 *per annum* with reduced rates for senior citizens, the disabled and juniors (12–16). Seven-day licences are also available. The Authority has recently advertised an increase in the rates to £45 (full rate) and £22.50 (concession).

(c) Permission from the owner of the fishing rights

While the National Rod Licence gives you a licence to fish anywhere in England and Wales, you will still need permission from a riparian owner where necessary to fish from his or her stretch of the river bank.

> *You park your car by a gentle stream and take out your fishing rods. You are asked by another angler to explain your presence. After a bit of discussion, it transpires that the person who is challenging you is a member of an angling club out for the day – fishing there under licence. You tell him that as a member of a club, he is not the owner of the fishing rights and so is in no position to mount a challenge to your presence there.*

You are in the wrong. Whenever fishing rights have been leased or licensed to others, they exercise those rights on behalf of the owner and are entitled to ask trespassers to leave.

(d) Enforcement

A National Rivers Authority bailiff can ask you to produce your licence. If you fail to do so you can be prosecuted. The maximum fine is £2,500.

(e) Fishing rights at sea

Members of the public have a right to fish in the sea up to the highwater mark of ordinary tides. In general the public also has a right to fish in the tidal waters of all rivers and estuaries up to – but *not beyond* – the highwater mark.

♦ **Note:** Fishing – even at sea – is subject to controls over the manner in which fish can be caught, the minimum size of the fish, and the size of the mesh in nets. These controls are to protect against indiscriminate catches. In addition, EC quotas are applicable to commercial fishing.

There are annual close seasons for fish to spawn in as well as weekly close times in certain cases.

(f) Poaching

Poachers can be fined up to £1,000, face imprisonment and have their boats, rods or nets forfeited. The Court of Appeal stated that it was 'easy to suggest that a bit of salmon poaching was not a matter of great consequence. Easy but entirely wrong. Such illicit activity had a real and damaging effect on the community at large'. (*The Times* Law Reports 4 July 1991.)

5. Trespass

5.1 Nature of trespass

At common law, all landowners are entitled to enjoy their land free from the intrusion of others. Indeed, if you do go on to the land of another without the permission of the landowner, you become a trespasser in the eyes of the law. Certain people (such as postmen) are on land by licence and so are not trespassers even though they may not have the landowner's express permission to be there.

♦ **Note:** Trespass is not normally a crime. However, under the Criminal Justice Act 1994, *collective trespass*, committed by two or more people or involving six vehicles, can be a crime, as is *disruptive trespass*, i.e. trespass committed with an intention to disrupt a lawful activity or intimidate persons taking part in lawful activities such as hunting.

♦ **Take heed:** Even if you go along a public right of way, if you wander off it, you can commit a trespass. Similarly, you commit trespass if you use the highway in a way for which it was not intended – for example, by cycling on a footpath (see *Rights of way* in section 1 above).

> *You are a journalist working for a magazine devoted to field sports. You leave the road and walk up and down a field alongside the road, noting the horses which are practising there. One of the stewards tells you that you are a trespasser. You deny that you are a trespasser or had any wrongful intention.*

> The steward is right in this instance; you are a trespasser because you left the highway and came on to private ground. But even if you had used only the highway for making notes of the horses, you would have been a trespasser. You are only allowed to use a highway for 'passing and repassing'.

▶ **Remember:** There is no need to have wrongful intent to order to trespass; you can do so quite unwittingly.

5.2 How to stop trespass

Landowners were increasingly angered by what they saw as the law's inability to protect their land from trespassers. In particular, the phenomenon of New Age travellers in the countryside has led to increasing calls for reform, now enacted in the Criminal Justice Act 1994.

5.3 New Age travellers and problems of enforcement

5.3.1 Travellers in convoys

The laws of access and trespass were not intended to manage large, well-organized groups of people, numbering up to tens of thousands, who travel together at certain times and then gather in pre-selected areas of the countryside for several days at a time – for example, for pop festivals.

5.3.2 Legislation governing travellers

Legislation to deal with travellers was passed under the Public Order Act 1986.

At the time, it was made clear that trespass was *not* to be made into a crime. Thus for travellers to commit an offence, several conditions are imposed:

(a) that they must have come on to private land to camp
(b) that they must have come in a group of at least two
(c) that they have been threatening and abusive
(e) that they must have been asked to leave by the landowner and the police
(e) that they must have refused to leave when asked.

5.3.3 New legislation

Since then, further changes have been enacted to deal with convoys:

- criminal offences for unauthorized parking on land
- confiscation by the police of caravans breaching the law.

This legislation has created a sharp conflict of interest between those who view them as a breach of civil liberty and those who see them as necessary to protect their own properties from unwarranted intrusion.

5.3.4 Laws applicable to gypsies

Special laws are applicable for gypsies, who have 'a nomadic way of life'.

Local authorities are under a statutory duty to provide gypsies with sites although target numbers of sites have not been met in many cases. New Age travellers have failed in the courts to have these duties extended to them.

5.4 Occupier's liability to trespassers

An occupier of premises will not be liable to a trespasser injured by a guard dog if a warning notice is displayed.

However, an owner who uses unreasonable force against a trespasser who refuses to leave when asked, is himself guilty of an offence. He would also be guilty of an offence if he left a guard dog to roam freely over his property – without any warning notice – and the dog savaged the trespasser.

◆ **Note that** the owner of straying livestock is entitled to go on to someone else's land in order to recapture his animals. He is not a trespasser in that case (for trespass by animals generally, see section 3 above).

6. Protection of flora and fauna

6.1 How protection works

Criminal sanctions have been imposed in order to protect certain species of wild birds, animals, reptiles, amphibians and insects. Certain plants are also protected.

6.1.1 Protected species

The present law was passed in 1981 (the Wildlife and Countryside Act). Its focus was on protecting *rare* species. Since then, there has been increasing emphasis on bio-diversity and the need to protect other forms of wildlife, including *common* species of plant, animal and insect life. Common habitats such as hedgerows and meadows are also in need of protection.

The schedule of protected animals and insects has been revised and updated to some extent to reflect these changing criteria. Britain is a signatory to an international treaty on maintaining bio-diversity.

(a) Wild birds

Under the Wildlife and Countryside Act 1981, it is a criminal offence intentionally

- to kill, injure or take any wild bird
- to take, damage or destroy the nest of any wild bird while that nest is in use or is being built
- to take or destroy an egg of any wild bird.

◆ **Note:** to 'destroy' means to do anything calculated to prevent an egg from hatching.

A 'wild bird' is 'any bird of a kind which is ordinarily resident in or is a visitor to Great Britain in a wild state'.

So wild birds are those that

- have not been bred in captivity
- are not included as 'poultry'
- are not generally included as 'game birds'.

As with all criminal offences, intention must be shown; it would not be an offence to disturb a nest inadvertently.

(b) Special protection

With regard to certain species it is an offence intentionally

- to disturb any wild bird while it is building a nest or is in, on, or near a nest containing eggs or young; or
- to disturb dependent young of such a bird.

This special protection exists throughout the year.

(c) Close season

Certain birds are protected during their close season only. The dates of close seasons vary but in general they last from early February to the middle or end of August, i.e. the breeding season.

◆ **Note:** The government can make orders altering the close season dates for any species and add the names of additional species to the lists.

(d) Game birds

It is not an offence to kill or take a game bird, or injure it in the course of killing and taking it, or destroying or damaging its nest or eggs, provided this is done *outside the close season*.

6.1.2 Protected areas

The Secretary of State for the Environment can designate certain areas as areas of special protection for birds. This would apply where, for example, a rare species has built a nest in an unusual location and it is thought best that people in general should be kept away. The landowner and those who come on to the land with his permission are exempt.

A list of bird sanctuaries is available from the Royal Society for the Protection of Birds (see DIRECTORY).

6.1.3 Prohibited ways of killing or taking wild birds

The Wildlife and Countryside Act 1981 also prohibits certain ways of killing or taking wild birds. These prohibited means are

- snares
- traps
- nets
- poisoned baits.

A live mammal or bird cannot be used as a decoy for the purpose of killing or taking any animal.

Self-locking snares which are 'calculated to cause bodily injury to any wild animal' coming into contact with them are forbidden.

The Act also protects certain species from sound decoys, sighting devices for night-shooting, automatic or semi-automatic weapons and dazzling lights.

These measures are obviously intended to minimize pain and suffering, as well as to prevent indiscriminate killing.

6.2 When you are allowed to kill protected species (outside close season)

Rules are in force which allow for the killing of protected species in particular circumstances. The rules relate to matters such as pests, public health and the pain and suffering of an animal.

(a) Pests

Certain birds are generally regarded as pests. These birds can be killed at any time of the year but only by authorized persons.

'Authorized persons' are

- the owner or
- the occupier of land or
- persons acting with their authority or
- persons authorized in writing by the county or district council for the area or
- persons authorized in writing by English Nature or a water authority.

These persons will *not* be guilty of killing or injuring such birds, or destroying their nests or eggs.

So even birds commonly regarded, and indeed, legally categorized as pests still have certain protection in that they can only be dealt with by a clearly defined group of people.

(b) Public health

Killing or taking birds is not an offence if it is done in the interests of public health or to prevent plant or animal disease.

(c) Pain and suffering

Birds which have been injured can be killed to be put out of their misery, or tended if recovery is likely.

> *You take into your care a wild eaglet which has fallen out of its nest. The bird is injured and you tend it carefully. It thrives under your care and you now want to return it to the wild.*

You obviously have not committed a criminal offence in 'taking' the bird from its natural habitat. You would be advised to contact the Royal Society for the Protection of Birds regarding its return to its own habitat (see DIRECTORY).

(d) Works on the land

The killing of birds or disturbing of a nest may be lawful if it is the incidental result of a lawful operation.

> *You have a diseased elm at the far end of your extensive garden. You have to fell the tree for fear it may fall and damage the adjacent highway. You know that there is a family of owls which has set up home in the tree.*

In this case, the operation is not only lawful but necessary under the Highways Act.

A person shall not be guilty of any of the offences of killing, injuring or disturbing protected birds if he or she can show that it happened as an 'incidental result of a lawful operation and could not reasonably have been avoided'. This is a defence of very wide scope. Most people carry out lawful operations on their own land, the 'incidental result' of which can be harmful to wild life. Examples of lawful operations include activities such as ploughing or draining land.

In addition, authorized persons can show that their actions were necessary for public health, or to prevent serious damage to livestock, foodstuffs for livestock, crops, vegetables, fruit, growing timber or fisheries.

6.3 Protection of animals

Criminal sanctions have been imposed to protect certain wild animals.

6.3.1 Offences

The offences are

(a) Intentionally to kill, injure or take any wild animal; and to have in one's possession any live or dead wild animal under protection as specified in the Wildlife and Countryside Act.
(b) To damage or destroy, or obstruct access to, any structure or place which any wild animal uses for shelter or protection. See above, section 6.2 for when it is not a crime to kill a protected animal.

6.3.2 Cruelty to domestic animals by their owners or keepers

Criminal sanctions also exist against owners and others who have charge of a domestic animal and who cause it suffering. A prosecution can be brought against anyone who is cruel to an animal under the Protection of Animals Act 1911.

Under the Abandonment of Animals Act 1960, a person who abandons an animal whether permanently or temporarily in circumstances likely to cause the animal suffering, is guilty of an offence of cruelty.

It is not merely a question of measuring time from when an animal has been left unattended. It has to be proved that the defendant has totally disregarded his duty to care for the animal.

6.4 Protection of wild plants

(a) Offences

It is an offence intentionally to pick, uproot or destroy any protected wild plant. The term 'pick' is defined to include the gathering or plucking of any part of a plant without uprooting it, so it includes the collecting of seeds.

Acts which are 'an incidental result of a lawful operation and could not reasonably have been avoided' are exempt. This, of course, covers farming operations. Concern is mounting for the loss of distinctive wild flowers through agriculture, for example by use of certain fertilizers. A survey was published in November 1993 which gives detail of the loss by species.

(d) Licences

For scientific or educational purposes, for protecting a collection of wild birds or animals, or for conservation purposes, a licence can be issued for ringing or marking or for other appropriate measures to be taken. The licence might be general or specific or granted to a class of persons – say at an agricultural college.

DIRECTORY
Countryside

Airfields Environment Federation
Sir John Lyon House
5 High Timber Street
London EC4V 3NS
Tel. 071 329 8159

Anglers' Co-operative Association
23 Castlegate
Grantham
Lincolnshire NG31 6SW
Tel. 0476 61008

Association of County Councils
Eaton House
66a Eaton Square
London SW1W 9BH
Tel. 071 235 1200

Association of Metropolitan Authorities
35 Great Smith Street
London SW1P 3BJ
Tel. 071 222 8100

Bicycle Association of Great Britain
Starley House
Eaton Road
Coventry
West Midlands CV1 2FH
Tel. 0203 553838

Botanical Society of the British Isles
c/o Department of Botany
Natural History Museum
Cromwell Road
London SW7 5BD

British Association for Shooting & Conservation
Marford Mill
Rossett
Wrexham
Clwyd LL12 0HL
Tel. 0244 570881

British Cycling Federation
36 Rockingham Road
Kettering
Northamptonshire NN16 8HG
Tel. 0536 412211

British Field Sports Society
59 Kennington Road
London SE1 7PZ
Tel. 071 928 4742

The British Horse Society
British Equestrian Centre
Stoneleigh
Kenilworth
Warwickshire CV8 2LR
Tel. 0203 696697

British Mountaineering Council
Crawford House
Precinct Centre
Booth Street East
Manchester M13 9RZ
Tel. 061 273 5835

British Naturalists' Association
48 Russell Way
Higham Ferrers
Northamptonshire NN9 8EJ

British Orienteering Federation
Riversdale
Dale Road North
Darley Dale
Matlock
Derbyshire DE4 2HX
Tel. 0629 734042

British Railways Board
Euston House
24 Eversholt Street
London NW1 1DZ
Tel. 071 928 5151

British Trust for Conservation Volunteers (BTCV)
36 St Mary's Street
Wallingford
Oxfordshire OX10 0EU
Tel. 0491 39766

British Trust for Ornithology
The Nunnery
Thetford
Norfolk IP24 2PU
Tel. 0842 750050

British Waterways
Willow Grange
Church Road
Watford WD1 3QA
Tel. 0923 226422

Butterfly Conservation
PO Box 222
Dedham
Colchester
Essex CO7 6EY
Tel. 0206 322342

Byways & Bridleways Trust
The Granary
Charlcutt
Calne
Wiltshire SN11 9HL
Tel. 024 974 273

Cadw – Welsh Historic Monuments
Brunel House
2 Fitzalan Road
Cardiff CF2 1UY
Tel. 0222 465511

Campaign for the Protection of Rural Wales
31 High Street
Welshpool
Powys SY21 7JP
Tel. 0938 552525

The Camping and Caravanning Club of Great Britain
Greenfields House
Westwood Way
Coventry CV4 8JH
Tel. 0203 694995

Care for the Wild
1 Ashfords
Horsham Road
Rusper
West Sussex RH12 4QX
Tel. 0293 871596

Centre for Accessible Environments
35 Great Smith Street
London SW1P 3BJ
Tel. 071 222 7980

Cleanair
33 Stillness Road
London SE23 1NG
Tel. 081 690 4649

Council for British Archaeology
112 Kennington Road
London SE11 6RE
Tel. 071 582 0494
or
The King's Manor
York YO1 2EP
Tel. 0904 433925

Council for National Parks
246 Lavender Hill
London SW11 1LJ
Tel. 071 924 4077

Council for the Protection of Rural England
25 Buckingham Palace Road
London SW1W 0PP
Tel. 071 976 6433

County Surveyors' Society
Transportation & Engineering
Department
County Hall
Dorchester
Dorset DT1 1XJ
Tel. 0305 224741

Country Landowners Association
16 Belgrave Square
London SW1X 8PQ
Tel. 071 235 0511

Countryside Commission
John Dower House
Crescent Place
Cheltenham
Gloucestershire GL50 3RA
Tel. 0242 521381

Department of the Environment
2 Marsham Street
London SW1P 3EB
Tel. 071 276 3000

English Heritage
Fortress House
23 Saville Row
London W1X 1AB
Tel. 071 973 3000

English Nature
Northminster House
Peterborough PE1 1UA
Tel. 0733 340345

DIRECTORY

The Forestry Trust for Conservation & Education
The Old Estate Office
Englefield Road
Theale
Reading
Berkshire RG7 5DZ
Tel. 0734 323523

Friends of the Earth
377 City Road
London EC1V 1NA
Tel. 071 837 0731

The Game Conservancy
Fordingbridge
Hampshire SP6 1EF
Tel. 0425 652381

Greenpeace Environmental Trust
36 Graham Street
London N1 8LL
Tel. 071 608 1461

Health & Safety Executive
Public Enquiry Point & Information
Centre
Broad Lane
Sheffield S3 7HQ
Tel. 0742 892345

Her Majesty's Inspectorate of Pollution
Romney House
43 Marsham Street
London SW1P 3PY
Tel. 071 276 8061

Inland Waterways Association
114 Regent's Park Road
London NW1 8UQ
Tel. 071 586 2510

International Tree Foundation
Sandy Lane
Crawley Down
West Sussex RH10 4HS
Tel. 0342 712 536

Landscape Institute
12 Carlton House Terrace
London SW1Y 5AH
Tel. 071 839 4044

League Against Cruel Sports Ltd.
Sparling House
83–87 Union Street
London SE1 1SG
Tel. 071 407 0979

Local Ombudsman (England)
21 Queen Anne's Gate
London SW1H 9BU

Local Ombudsman (Wales)
Derwent House
Court Road
Bridgend
Mid Glamorgan CF31 1BN

Long Distance Walkers' Association
29 Marway Road
Brotton
Saltburn-by-Sea
Cleveland TS12 2RH

Ministry of Agriculture, Fisheries & Food
3 Whitehall Place
London SW1A 2HH
Tel. 071 270 3000

The National Association of UK River Protection Societies
The Old House Cottage
Carters Lane
Old Woking
Surrey GU22 8JQ
Tel. 0483 765462

National Association for Outdoor Education
36 Richborough
Bancroft
Milton Keynes, Buckinghamshire
Tel. 0908 320961

National Council for Metal Detecting
61 Newton Road
Newbury
Berkshire
Tel. 0635 522578

National Rivers Authority
Rivers House
Waterside Drive
Aztec West
Almondsbury
Bristol BS12 4UD
Tel. 0454 624400

The National Trust
36 Queen Anne's Gate
London SW1H 9AS
Tel. 071 222 9251

Nature Conservancy Council for England
Northminster House
Peterborough PE1 1UA
Tel. 0733 340345

The Open Spaces Society
25a Bell Street
Henley-on-Thames
Oxon RG9 2BA
Tel. 0491 573535

Ordnance Survey
Romsey Road
Maybush
Southampton SO9 4DH
Tel. 0703 792000

The Pedestrians Association & the **Walkways Service**
126 Aldersgate Street
London EC1A 4JQ
Tel. 071 490 0750

Ramblers' Association
1/5 Wandsworth Road
London SW8 2XX
Tel. 071 582 6878

Royal Commission on the Historical Monuments of England
Fortress House
23 Savile Row
London W1X 2JQ
Tel. 071 973 3351

Royal Forestry Society of England, Wales and Northern Ireland
102 High Street
Tring
Herts HP23 4AF
Tel. 0442 822028

Royal Society for Nature Conservation
The Green
Witham Park
Waterside South
Lincoln LN5 7JR
Tel. 0522 544400

Royal Society for the Prevention of Cruelty to Animals
Causeway
Horsham
Sussex RH12 1HG
Tel. 0403 64181

Royal Society for the Protection of Birds
The Lodge
Sandy
Bedfordshire SG12 2DL
Tel. 0767 680551

Rural Development Commission
141 Castle Street
Salisbury
Wiltshire SP1 3TP
Tel. 0722 336255

Save Britain's Heritage
68 Battersea High Street
London SW11 3HX
Tel. 071 228 3336

The Sports Council
16 Upper Woburn Place
London WC1H 0QP
Tel. 071 388 1277

Sports Council for Wales
Sophia Gardens
Cardiff
South Glamorgan CF1 9SW
Tel. 0222 397571

Tidy Britain Group
Public Affairs Department
The Pier
Wigan WN3 4EX
Tel. 0942 824620

The United Kingdom Environmental Law Association (UKELA)
61 Charterhouse Street
London EC1M 6HA

The Woodland Trust
Autumn Park
Dysart Road
Grantham
Lincolnshire NG31 6LL
Tel. 0476 74297

Worldwide Fund for Nature (WWF)
Panda House
Weyside Park
Godalming
Surrey GU7 1XR
Tel. 0483 426444

Youth Hostels' Association (YHA)
Trevelyan House
8 St Stephen's Hill
St Albans
Hertfordshire AL1 2DY
Tel. 0727 55215

10. MOTORING

For most people, any brush with the criminal law is most likely to be in connection with their motor car. There are 24 million vehicles in Great Britain. Traffic has to be kept moving while, at the same time all road users – whether pedestrians or drivers – must be protected, and accidents prevented. In addition to traffic movement and safety, other matters have to be regulated; for example, the impact of traffic on our environment. Traffic not only produces congestion in towns and countryside but affects the very air that we breathe. Not surprisingly, then, the laws, rules and regulations that govern the motorist are very numerous and complicated; in addition, road use is an area where conformity with European law is becoming increasingly important.

Above all, the law relies on all of us to obey the traffic rules in our own interests. A moment's carelessness can have disastrous consequences for ourselves as well as for others.

In this chapter we look at

- what must be done before you go on the road
- vehicle checks
- buying a car
- company cars
- other motor vehicles
- disabled drivers
- accidents
- car theft
- offences and penalties – general overview
- dangerous driving offences
- careless driving offences
- drink and drug related offences
- speeding offences
- general offences.

1. Before you go on the road

1.1 You must be licensed to drive

It is an offence to drive a car without a driving licence. You can obtain a driving licence once you are 17 or over and have passed the driving test (see section 1.1.1). You can apply to the DVLC for a provisional licence, with a completed application form and the fee, from six months before your 17th birthday. On this form you must declare any disability.

If you hold a provisional licence, you must

(a) Drive only with a driver who has been qualified for three years. The driver must be over 21;
(b) Put 'L' plates on your car;
(c) Inform your insurers;
(d) Not go on a motorway.

Licences are regulated by the type of vehicle that you intend to drive; for example, cars with automatic transmission are in a separate category from manual-transmission cars.

1.1.1 A 'driver' is someone in control of a vehicle

The law takes a broad view in defining the 'driver' of a car. It depends on who has 'substantial control' of a vehicle.

> *You are a provisionally licensed driver. You are being driven by a friend in his car which breaks down. He gets out and asks you to steer while he pushes the car. A policeman comes up to you and asks to see your licence. Have you committed an offence?*

The answer is 'yes'. You are a learner driver and there is no qualified driver in the car with you.

It is even possible for two people to 'drive' a car at the same time – for example a learner driver and his instructor in a dual-control car.

1.1.2 You must take a driving test

Form DL 26 (available from post offices) must be completed and sent to the Clerk to the Traffic Commissioners for your area in order to arrange a test. If the examiner is satisfied that you

- have passed the sight test
- are competent to drive and
- know and understand the Highway Code (see immediately below)

you will be able to obtain a driver's licence from the DVLC.

Once you receive a full licence, it is usually valid until your 70th year, unless a disability intervenes (see section 8 below). Since 1989, in conformity with Europe, a counterpart is issued with your new licence. The counterpart details the category of car that you can drive, as well as all details of convictions, penalty points and disqualifications, if any. When ordered to produce this type of licence, you will have to produce the counterpart as well.

1.1.3 Renewing your licence when aged 70 and over

When the age of 70 is approaching, you will be sent a computer-generated reminder to your last-known address, together with a form for renewal. This form includes a medical declaration but it is not necessary for a doctor to complete it – merely you, the driver. This form is to be returned to the DVLC plus licence fee (£6). Your licence is then renewed for three years. This renewal process will be repeated at three-year intervals.

1.1.4 If you fail the test

The pass rate is about 50 per cent. If you fail you must wait one month before applying for another test. If you feel that the examiner did not conduct the test properly, you can appeal to a magistrates' court.

(a) Approved driving instructors

A register is kept under the Transport Act 1988 of approved driving instructors who must display a certificate in the car. There are also driving instructors' organizations which foster road safety and teaching standards.

1.1.5 The Highway Code

This Code is issued by the Department of Transport.

Breach of the Code is not a criminal offence. However, if you are being prosecuted by the police, for example, for careless driving, and you have not followed the Code, your breach of the Code may be used as evidence against you in any civil or criminal proceedings.

1.2 Your car must be licensed too

There is an annual fee for the car licence that has to be obtained for any car used or even kept on a public road. The licence (the 'tax disc') must be displayed unless the car is kept wholly on private land.

> *You have an old car that you do not drive stored on your land until such time as you decide how to get rid of it. Are you liable for road tax?*

> The answer is 'no'. However, you would be liable if the car were parked outside your house on a public road even if you had no intention of using it.

Disabled drivers can be exempt from paying the car licence fee. However, they are still under an obligation to display the disc (see *Disabled drivers*, section 6 below).

1.2.1 Number plates

Every car has a unique registration number. An initial letter now defines the year of registration and this letter changes each August. It is possible to apply in advance to the DVLC special registration scheme for a particular mark. Number plates can also be transferred on payment of a fee of £80. Concern is being expressed that the ease with which number plates can be transferred facilitates car theft.

1.2.2 Car registration and transfers

A purchase of a new car is accompanied by a registration document giving particulars of the vehicle and the name and address of the registered keeper. This document accompanies any subsequent transfer of the car. Details of the transfer must be filled in on the registration document by you and sent on to the DVLC (see below (b)). The newly named person then becomes the car's registered keeper.

(a) Distinction between keeper and owner of vehicle

The keeper and the owner of a vehicle may not necessarily be the same person. The keeper is the person whose name is on the registration document – this is often also the name of the owner but the distinction must be borne in mind, particularly if you are buying a second-hand vehicle from someone who is unknown to you (see *Buying a car*, section 3 below).

(b) Safeguarding the registration document

If you sell your car privately, do not part with the document until you have been paid in full and the DVLC has been informed. If you sell to a dealer, you must also make sure that you follow the correct procedure for transfer as detailed on the document itself.

If you carelessly hand over your registration document with your car to a new owner without registering the change and informing the DVLC, you may find yourself liable for someone else's traffic offences!

If the car is to be scrapped make sure that the registration document is returned to the DVLC and not handed over to the person taking it away as scrap.

◆ **Note of warning:** Do not retain the registration document in your car (see also section 2.4 below).

> *You have been tempted by a 'snip' of a second hand car, advertised in your local newsagents' and, on inspection, the car looks well worth the asking price. It is a private sale and the owner says that he has mislaid the registration document temporarily. What do you do?*

Do not be too tempted – it may well be that you are looking at a stolen car. If you wish to pursue the matter, write to the DVLC explaining your interest and asking if it can help with registration details. Only buy the car if the details of name and address match those which the seller gives to you.

All these procedures serve more than one function: the DVLC is under a legal duty to supply the licensing particulars of any car on its register to a local authority or to the police in investigating offences.

1.2.3 Insuring your car

It is an offence to drive a car, or to let others use it when you are responsible for the car, without insurance cover. Insurance is thus compulsory by law. Insurance can be negotiated either directly with the insurance company or through a broker. It is worth enquiring for competitive premiums.

You must fill in a proposal form which will require personal and vehicle details. There are two major categories of insurance – *comprehensive* and *third party*.

(a) Comprehensive insurance

Comprehensive insurance covers injury to other persons or damage to their property as well as damage to your own car. It may cover other risks such as legal fees or theft of your belongings in the car and certain personal injury claims.

(b) Third party

Third party insurance is the minimum cover under the law and will cover damage to other drivers and/or their cars if you are involved in an accident for which your driving is responsible. It will also cover passengers in your car – again provided that your driving was responsible for the accident. It will not cover damage to your car or personal injury to yourself, however.

For exclusion from third party cover under the most stringent conditions see below, section 14.5.

(c) 'No claims' bonuses

The insurance companies are safety-conscious in their own interests and try to promote good driving standards through financial incentives, in particular through the 'no claims' bonus. There are disincentives too – for example, a driver convicted of a drink-drive offence may not be able to claim for damage to his own vehicle under his particular policy.

(d) Legal expenses

Some insurers offer to cover legal expenses for an extra premium. In view of the restrictions on legal aid availability (see chapter on the *Legal*

System) and the inherent dangers of driving a car, the premium may be well worth it.

(e) Scrutinizing the small print

Always scrutinize the details of your policy, particularly if someone else uses your car.

> *Your car is insured for your social and business use and for 'any named driver'. One of those named drivers happens to be your son, who asks if he can borrow the car while his own is out of action. He uses the car to pick up a client and take him to his office but on the way has a minor collision with another car. Will you be covered?*

It is most unlikely that you will be able to claim on your insurance. 'Business use' is usually restricted to the policyholder and you could be prosecuted in the circumstances.

(f) Full and frank disclosure

As with all other insurance policies, you are under a duty to make a full and frank disclosure to your insurers. Full disclosure covers among other matters

- named drivers
- previous convictions
- type of use
- involvement in an accident.

(See also chapter on *Goods and Services*.)

◆ **Note:** the Press Office of the Association of British Insurers (51 Gresham Street, London EC2V 7HQ) has free leaflets available for information on car insurance and other insurance generally (see also DIRECTORY).

(g) Disqualification

Any insurance is automatically invalidated for anyone who drives while disqualified.

> *You have been knocked over by a driver who was disqualified from driving after a series of drink/driving offences. What do you do?*

You apply immediately to the Motor Insurers' Bureau (see below).

1.2.4 The Motor Insurers' Bureau (MIB)

The Motor Insurers' Bureau was set up to provide cover against drivers who have caused an accident and have no insurance cover or who cannot be traced (the 'hit and run' driver).

All the motor insurance companies must belong to the MIB by law. It pays out the compensation which the court decides should go to an accident victim who would otherwise be deprived because of the driver's lack of effective insurance. The sum is limited to a quarter of a million pounds.

(a) Hit and run

Whether or not a driver had relevant insurance against which a claim for compensation might be made is clearly irrelevant where the victim is hurt by a driver who is unable to be traced having fled the scene of the accident.

> *While crossing the road at night in an otherwise deserted street, you are knocked over by a driver who makes off at high speed. How can you seek recompense?*

Again, the MIB provides assistance: the Untraced Drivers' Agreement operates where there can be no judgment because the person responsible for the accident cannot be traced.

The MIB investigates the circumstances and decides how much compensation is to be given. You can appeal against the award.

(b) Joy-riders

Joy-riding offences have become increasingly common in recent years (see also *Car theft*, section 8 below). In such cases there may be no recompense for an accident victim from the joyrider who has caused the accident. The MIB can be approached by an innocent victim of an accident. What is the position if the victim is not 'innocent'?

> *You accompany your friend on a joyride and there is an accident. Can you turn to the MIB?*

The answer is 'no': no payment will be made where the victim knows that the vehicle was stolen or the driver was uninsured (see also chapter on *Accidents* 'Voluntary Assumption of Risk').

▶ **Remember:** if you are hurt in any accident, it is always advisable to go to a solicitor who specializes in personal injury cases. The Law Society has a list of solicitors who participate in their Accident Legal Advice Scheme (ALAS).

2. Vehicle checks

2.1 Maintaining your car

There are numerous regulations that require you to maintain your car in working and efficient order; they are vitally necessary in the interests of your own safety, as well as the safety of others.

> *Your car is parked outside your house but you have not driven it for a while; the battery is flat and you have no intention of driving it in the immediate future. A policeman on the beat looks at it and decides that it appears defective. He asks to test it. What do you do?*

He has the authority to test any vehicle on demand if it (a) appears defective or (b) has been involved in an accident.

2.1.1 Offences

It is an offence to drive a car unless the following are in good working order:

- seat belts
- brakes and steering gear
- lights
- windscreen, windscreen wipers and washers
- demisters
- mirrors
- tyres (including spare)
- silencer
- exhaust system.

2.2 Car telephones and alarms

As you must exercise proper control of your vehicle at all times, you should not use a hand-held telephone or microphone while driving. Use of a hands-free microphone is permissible while driving but not if it takes your mind off the road. Only in an emergency may you stop on the hard shoulder of a motorway to answer or make a call.

Car alarms must not sound continuously for more than five minutes. The mechanism must be in good repair.

Under the Noise and Statutory Nuisance Act 1993, which came into effect in January 1994, noise from car alarms of cars parked in the street can be a statutory nuisance (see also chapter on *Neighbours*). If the vehicle is unattended, an environmental health officer can fix an abatement notice on the car. He or she can then either have the vehicle removed or open the vehicle, 'if necessary by force', in order to stop the noise. However, the EHO is obliged by law to leave the vehicle 'secured against interference or theft . . . as effectually as he found it'.

2.3 The 'MOT' test

If a vehicle has been registered for more than three years, it is an offence to use it on a road without a current test certificate. The tests are carried out by examiners authorized under the Act at specified vehicle testing stations.

You should note that the holding of a current MOT certificate does not in any way excuse you if you are charged with a failure to maintain any of the parts specified in section 2.1.1 above. You should always keep wind-screens, windows, lights, indicators, reflectors, mirrors and number plates clean and clear. Ensure too that your seat, seat belts, head restraints and mirrors are adjusted correctly before you drive.

2.4 Checklist summary

In order to drive and to take your car on the road you must have the following documents:

(a) driving licence;
(b) car insurance;
(c) registration document;
(d) current tax disc;
(e) MOT certificate (if your car is more than three years old).

◆ **Note of warning:** do not retain your registration document with your car. Should your car be stolen together with that document, the car might be sold and resold many times with ease without the original thief ever attracting suspicion.

2.5 Seat belts

It is an offence to be a driver or front seat passenger without wearing a seat belt unless a special exemption applies. Similarly, a rear seat passenger must wear a seat belt (if fitted). Exemptions include the holders of medical exemption certificates, people making local deliveries in a vehicle designed or adapted for that purpose, and children in the rear of taxis with partitions. It is the responsibility of an adult passenger to wear any seat belt fitted.

> *You are a front seat passenger and have not been wearing a seat belt. Your driver is involved in a collision, which is entirely the fault of another motorist, and you suffer whiplash injuries.*

Two consequences follow:

(a) You could be prosecuted for breach of the law.
(b) You will certainly receive reduced damages from the other driver's insurance company because you are guilty of 'contributory negligence'. The degree of contributory negligence is usually assessed on a percentage basis, so you could lose half or more of the damages you might otherwise have obtained.

2.6 Seat belts and children

The following table sets out the legal requirements for the wearing of seat belts or appropriate child restraints. (The classification of what is an 'appropriate child restraint' is currently under question, but it is not expected that any new rules will do anything other than modify the present specifications and strengthen the current requirements.)

	front seat	rear seat	whole responsibility
child under 3 years of age	Appropriate child restraint must be worn	Appropriate child restraint must be worn if available	Driver
child aged 3 to 11 and under 1.5 metres (about 5 feet) in height	Appropriate child restraint must be worn if available. If not, an adult seat belt must be worn	Appropriate child restraint must be worn if available. If not, an adult seat belt must be worn if available	Driver
child aged 12 to 13 or younger child 1.5 metres or more in height	Adult seat belt must be worn if available	Adult seat belt must be worn if available	Driver

An appropriate child restraint is a baby carrier, child seat, harness or booster seat appropriate to the child's weight.

The Department of Transport advises that you should not let children sit behind the rear seats in an estate car or hatchback, and suggests that child safety locks, where fitted, are used when children are in the car. (See the Highway Code.)

3. Buying a car

For most people, the money they spend on their car is their biggest single investment after buying their house. The legal rule of *caveat emptor* (buyer beware) particularly applies. Because of the sums involved, if you are not sure about your position it should be considered a money-saver – and not an expense – to consult a lawyer if things go wrong.

3.1 Buying from a dealer

A dealer is someone who sells 'in the course of business'. If you buy a car from a dealer, either new or secondhand, you have certain basic protections under the Sale of Goods Act and other consumer legislation (see also chapter on *Goods and Services*).

3.1.1 Dealer's legal requirements

A dealer cannot get out of the legal requirements that

(a) the car will be fit for its normal purpose;
(b) it is of 'merchantable quality';
(c) it conforms to his description given to you;
(d) he has the right to sell it.

◆ **Note:** a private seller is not bound to you under the Sale of Goods Act (see below, section 3.2).

3.1.2 New cars

New cars are usually bought from a dealer who is franchized by the manufacturer. There are generally manufacturers' warranties that go with the car which can extend your legal rights but cannot replace them or curtail them.

> *You have bought a new car but are not happy with it. The car has broken down after only a short distance. What do you do?*

- Do not delay in contacting the dealer.
- Put your complaint in writing.
- Make no attempt to accept a car repair.
- Do not drive it again in the hope that the fault will 'sort itself out'.
- Return the car and ask for a replacement vehicle. Your contract is with the dealer so do not be fobbed off by being told to contact the manufacturer. You would be advised to send all correspondence to the relevant trade association, if the dealer belongs to one (see chapter on *Goods and Services*).

(a) Delay: a note of warning

Acting fast is the critical factor – any delay can be taken in law to mean that you have 'accepted' the car under the contract. Thereafter you can rely only on damages for repair. In one case the judge held it was too late to return a new car after it had been driven for 142 miles and been kept for three weeks.

3.1.3 Second-hand car purchases

Second-hand car deals can present particular problem areas:

- meeting consumer law standards (for example, 'fitness of purpose' and 'merchantable quality' are not easy to prove in the best of circumstances. Such proof becomes much more difficult to assess in second-hand car deals);
- 'clocking' i.e. turning back the mileage clock;
- stolen cars;
- insurance writeoffs that have been 'repaired' to look as good as new.

> *You have bought a second hand car which looks absolutely perfect on the outside but the steering wheel comes apart the first time you take it out on the road. It transpires that the 'car' comprises two insurance write-offs welded together. What do you do?*

(a) Follow all the steps outlined for the buyer of a new car above (i.e. do not delay in contacting the dealer; and put your complaint in writing).

(b) Insist on your money back rather than a replacement vehicle.

(c) Inform the Trading Standards Department of your local authority which can launch a prosecution under the Trading Standards Act. The dealer has also committed a criminal offence under the Road Traffic Act 1988 so you should also inform the police (see section 3.1.4 below).

(a) Conforming to dealer's description

As noted in section 3.1.1 above, a vehicle must conform to a dealer's description. This is particularly crucial where a second-hand car is concerned. For example, if you make a purchase having been told of a specific defect you will have no redress should subsequent trouble arise out of that defect. However, that defence will not be available should the car subsequently reveal a fault unrelated to the defect told to you by the dealer.

> *You have purchased a car having been told by the dealer that the brake lights may be defective. You drive the car away only to find that the fuel injection system is faulty, as well as the brake lights. What can you do?*

You will be entitled to claim damages in respect of the faulty fuel injection system, but not in respect of the brake light failure.

A dealer may attempt a defence that any defect in a vehicle should have been noticed by you on inspection. That defence may be upheld in the case of an obvious defect, e.g. a dented wing, but will not necessarily be upheld where the defect is one which would not be likely to have been spotted by a lay person. However, to avoid complications of that nature, it is suggested that a person buying a second-hand car (whether from a dealer or privately) should seek an independent inspection/valuation from a body such as the AA or the RAC. As an alternative to incurring the cost of such an inspection, it is advisable to have another person with you at the time of purchase. That person will then be available as a witness to any specific descriptions made by the dealer. (It is unlikely that the dealer will be willing to provide a written declaration of his descriptions – and there may be all sorts of back-of-form conditions which restrict his right to make such statements.)

(b) Waiver of customer's rights

It is common practice for a dealer to request a customer to sign a receipt for the vehicle on which there may be a provision stating that the car has been inspected and that the customer is satisfied as to its condition. That receipt will not secure the position of the dealer against a complaint about a non-obvious defect, but, if you must sign, it is wise to add a proviso to the effect that no defects are observable to you as a lay person.

(c) Buying a car under an existing HP agreement

It is not uncommon for a person to purchase a car which is the subject of a hire purchase agreement.

> *You have bought a second-hand car. A hire purchase company writes to you to say that it is a repossessed vehicle under an existing HP agreement and asks for the car back. What do you do?*

> You should be protected by law. Provided you bought the car in good faith, for value, and quite innocently, without knowing it was on hire purchase, you should be entitled to keep it. However, you would be well advised to seek legal advice immediately. See also chapter on *Goods and Services*.

♦ **Note:** the above protection does not apply to a *dealer* who has innocently purchased a car subject to a hire purchase agreement. Dealers generally have their own recourse in that they can check on a nationwide database network whether a car is on HP or not. The protection also does not extend to you if you purchased the car from somebody who stole it. In such a case the only redress will be against the thief who stole it – which may be poor redress indeed (see below, section 3.1.5).

3.1.4 Dealer's offences

A dealer can be prosecuted

(a) if he makes false statements about the vehicle;
(b) if he sells a car that is not roadworthy, for example, the brakes or steering are in a dangerous condition. Under the Road Traffic Act 1988, authorized examiners can enter a dealer's premises and test whether the used cars offered for sale are roadworthy.

3.1.5 Stolen cars

A vehicle cannot be purchased without the consent of the owner regardless of the buyer's knowledge or intent.

> *You have bought a car that was in fact stolen. You have now been contacted by the police on behalf of its true owner. Again you bought the car in good faith and quite innocently. What do you do?*

You may have no option but to hand the car over to the police. The insurers of the car may have paid out the owner and may therefore settle with you for cash. But it still appears very unfair, as you then find yourself paying twice over. It is a question of which of two innocent parties should bear the loss – you, the buyer, or the true owner. At present the law favours the owner.

◆ **Note:** the question of title to goods is currently under review (see also chapter on *Goods and Services*).

3.1.6 Summary checklist

(a) It is perhaps better to buy from a dealer who is a member of a trade association with a Code of Practice. Such a Code has been drawn up by the Retail Motor Industry Federation. The Office of Fair Trading also has a leaflet on buying a used car (see DIRECTORY).
(b) Have a second-hand car checked by a professional.
(c) Take down in writing the seller's description of the car.

3.2 Buying privately

The buying and selling of cars on the private market is commonplace but it is important for a purchaser to realize that, in such transactions, he does not get the same legal rights as he would when buying from a dealer.

3.2.1 Seller's obligations

The only obligation on a private seller is that any particular specified by him must be true. There is no obligation on a private seller to make any particular specifications about the car, and a buyer has no promise that the car is of proper quality in relation to its price.

3.2.2 Contrast with dealer's position

The legal requirements on a dealer (set out in section 3.1.1 above) are not applicable in relation to a private seller.

3.2.3 Complaints against a private seller

A complaint may be lodged against a private seller where evidence (of a witness or in writing) is available to show that the seller made a false statement about the car and that false statement is relevant to the buyer's complaint. In truth, a buyer's best line of defence is to protect himself prior to purchase by having an independent body carry out a vehicle check and valuation. It is possible to sue in respect of a false promise made by the seller, but in practice such an action is unlikely to prove rewarding.

3.2.4 Dealer posing as a private seller

A dealer – often one operating part-time – may sell a car pretending to be a private seller. In some instances it may be possible to spot that the individual is in fact a dealer by noting separate advertisements showing the same name or telephone number. Should you purchase a vehicle from someone who is in fact a dealer the normal dealer's promises are applicable (see section 3.1.1 above), and your buyer's privileges are not affected by the fact that the sale was represented to you as being of a private nature.

A dealer acting in this way is guilty of a criminal offence.

3.2.5 Car under existing HP agreement

The unwitting purchaser of a car subject to a hire purchase agreement where the sale is of a private nature may be protected in the same way as if the car had been purchased from a dealer. See the resultant position as outlined in section 3.1.3(c) above. (For misrepresentations in connection with HP transactions, see chapter on *Goods and Services*.)

3.2.6 Stolen cars

The purchase in a private sale of a stolen vehicle affords no protection to the purchaser. The same position applies as when the car was purchased from a dealer (see section 3.1.5 above).

3.3 Buying at auction

Buying a car at an auction may enable one to save a good deal of money. However, the following practical considerations apply to restrict your ability to make a claim for legal remedy if the car proves to be defective:

- the auctioneer will almost inevitably exclude both himself and the person selling from liability for any defects. A dealer is not able to sell and to exclude his legal promises but there is no such restriction on an auctioneer
- generally, an auctioneer will not reveal the name of the seller – usually a dealer. In such a case the dealer might be traced only by applying to the person last named on the registration document to try to find out to whom the vehicle was sold. Often it will be the case that a purchaser of a defective vehicle at auction will be unable to find any person to sue.

4. The company car

It is estimated that more than two million people in this country drive company cars. The employer acquires the car (usually on a three-year lease) and pays the cost of repairs, road tax and insurance. Naturally the issues that most often arise concern the tax advantages and/or disadvantages to the employee of such an arrangement. By and large there has been a steady increase in tax on company cars.

4.1 The benefits

The general rule is that, from 6 April 1994, where a car is placed at the disposal of an employee or a director earning more than £8,500, it is taxable on a sliding scale. The scale is based on the original price of the car, its age and level of business mileage. While petrol and portable telephones are also taxed, car parking facilities at the place of work are not.

4.2 Insurance

This is usually effected by 'block fleet' policies taken out by the employer (see also section 14.5 below). It is also the employer's duty to ensure that the car is insured.

You are driving a company car on company business and have a collision with another car. It transpires that the car you are driving is not insured. What can you do?

There is a special defence for employees using vehicles in the course of their employment if they are quite unaware that the car lacks cover. In such a case, their employer could be prosecuted.

5. Other motor vehicles

In general, the rules outlined in this chapter relating to motor cars are equally applicable to other vehicles which are used on-road or in public places. Accordingly, this section does no more than draw attention to particular requirements placed on drivers of vehicles which are outside the legal definition of a motor car.

5.1 Heavy goods vehicles

HGVs are subject to special rules concerning, among other things, laden and unladen weight, the fitting of tachometers (devices recording speed, mileage and hours driven) and speed limitations. It is not practicable to detail these rules except to note that vehicles weighing over 7.5 tonnes, and all articulated vehicles, are subject to a maximum speed limit of 60 mph on motorways. Additionally, you must be aged 18 to obtain a licence to drive a medium-sized goods vehicle and aged 21 for entitlement to a HGV licence.

5.2 Mopeds

A moped is a vehicle of not over 50 cc with a maximum design speed of not over 30 mph. The kerbside weight is not to be in excess of 250 kilograms.

A licence may be obtained from the age of 16.

If you ride a moped you, and any pillion passenger, must wear an approved safety helmet which must be fastened securely. Helmets are 'approved' if passed by the British Safety Standards Institute and thus carry a BSI seal of approval. It is advisable to acquire a new helmet to ensure a correct fit. In any case, it is not possible to be certain that a second-hand helmet has not been weakened in a collision or by having been dropped. Your pillion passenger must sit astride the machine on a proper seat and keep both feet on footrests.

It is an offence to ride a moped on any motorway.

5.3 Motorcycles

You may obtain a provisional licence to ride a motorcycle from the age of 17. While riding under a provisional licence, approved 'L' plates must be displayed at both front and rear and the cycle must not exceed 125 cc. To qualify for a full licence you must complete successfully a two-part test. The first is on an off-the-road circuit designed to show whether you can control your vehicle properly. A certificate of having passed that test must be produced before application can be made to take the second part of the test.

If you have held a motorcycle provisional licence for two years, it cannot be automatically renewed. You will have to wait a period of one year before reapplication can be made.

The rules regarding the wearing of helmets and carrying a pillion passenger are as for moped riders (see section 5.2 above). Note that it is illegal to carry more than one pillion passenger.

5.4 Passenger service vehicles

Special rules apply in relation to passenger service vehicles (including minibuses designed to carry eight or more passengers) and it is not appropriate to detail them here. However, following a series of coach and minibus fatalities, there exists the possibility of the introduction of seat belt legislation.

Minibuses, PSVs and taxis require an MOT certificate as soon as they are one year old (not three years, as is the norm).

5.5 Tractors

You must be aged 17 or over to drive a tractor on the road. Road tax is payable if the vehicle is ever on a public road – even if doing no more than crossing it, e.g. from one field to another.

5.6 Electrically assisted pedal cycles

These cycles, having a speed not in excess of 15 mph, are not classified as motor vehicles and no licence is required.

6. The disabled driver

6.1 Declaration of disability

You must declare your disability to the licensing authorities when making your application for a driving licence or if there has been the onset of a disability since receiving your full licence.

6.2 Entitlements

Persons who are chronically sick or disabled qualify for certain benefits, including parking concessions.

6.2.1 State benefits

Certain very severe illnesses may render you unfit to drive at all. You can receive driver-potential advice and assessment from the Mobility Information Service for a small fee (see DIRECTORY). If you are able to drive, you must find out about your various entitlements. These include an invalid carriage (these are being phased out), exemption from excise duty and VAT, a mobility allowance, and parking facilities.

> *You sustained a serious leg injury in a sporting accident. You are dependent on your car for getting about, as a result. You have a full driving licence. What do you do?*

(a) Inform the DVLC and your insurers.
(b) Establish which kind of car you are able to drive – for example a car with automatic transmission. Advice of all kinds is available. For example under the MAVIS scheme in Crowthorne in Berkshire, there is a facility to try out various models of car

and/or adaptations. Other organizations, such as Motability, give assistance on car purchase, as well as HP and leasing facilities (see DIRECTORY).

(c) The DVLC will ask for further details of your medical condition. It will also ask for permission to consult your doctor and specialist, who must certify that you can still drive.

(d) You will then receive a restricted licence, possibly limited to three-year revisions – that states specifically that you must drive a car with 'controls which can all be correctly and conveniently operated'. If you feel that the licence is too restrictive, you are entitled to appeal.

(e) You can apply for a mobility allowance, and car tax and road tax exemptions. The mobility allowance can go towards the cost of leasing or buying your car.

(f) You can apply for an orange badge if you are left with 'a permanent and substantial disability' in walking. This enables you to park on single yellow lines and in metered parking bays in certain circumstances. It can be withdrawn if it is abused (see below, section 6.3).

6.3 Use of disabled person's badge

It is an offence to display a disabled person's badge when driving a motor vehicle on the road, except where the badge is issued and displayed in accordance with the regulations.

An able-bodied person may display such a badge on his vehicle and avail himself of the parking concessions if he is transporting a disabled person provided that the disabled person's badge concession would be available for use on his or her own vehicle. These badges are also available for the transportation of disabled non-drivers. Parents may have one if they have a disabled child, for example.

> *You are transporting your disabled wife in your own car to do the shopping. She is registered disabled and generally displays a disabled person's badge on her invalid car. Today you want to purchase some large items which would not easily fit in her car and which she could not carry on her own. You both set out to do the shopping. Are you guilty of an offence when you park on the line outside the store you intend to visit and display her badge?*

The answer is 'no', you are not in breach of any legal provisions. However, should you take your wife home and then drive alone to do some private business, using the badge to park in an otherwise illegal position, you are guilty of an offence and are liable on summary conviction to a fine not exceeding level 3 on the standard scale. (See section 9 below.)

6.4 Temporary disability

The above concessions are not applicable where you are suffering from a temporary disability, in particular if you are taking prescribed drugs or medicines. It is an offence to drive when so influenced. When taking prescribed medicines, ask your doctor if it is safe to drive. Similarly, ask your pharmacist if you are purchasing over-the-counter medicines.

7. Accidents

The cardinal rule is that you must report an accident to the police where it involves injury to another person, damage to another vehicle or to an animal (but not a cat!), property adjoining a street, or 'street furniture' which usually means a lamppost, bollard etc. You must also stop after an accident. See also the chapter on *Accidents*, section 1.1.

7.1 Obligation to report an accident

If someone else is injured (including a passenger of yours) in an accident you are required to stop and to produce your insurance details. If you cannot produce insurance details at the time of the accident, a report must be made to the police within 24 hours and insurance details must be produced to them within five days.

If someone else's property or animal is injured you are required to stop. If at that time you do not exchange your name and address, a report of the accident must be made to the police within 24 hours.

> *You are driving along a rather dark, narrow country road, with the car radio turned up, and you pass a car on your right. You think you might have heard a scraping noise but cannot be sure because of the noise of the music. The next day you notice a substantial dent to your car and realize that there was a collision with the other car. What do you do?*

You are under a duty to report the accident to the police within 24 hours.

Failure to report an accident thus arises once you become aware that it has happened. It also applies whether or not there was somebody else at the scene. For the penalties for failing to report an accident, see section 14.3 below.

7.2 No obligation to report an accident

However, you are not under an obligation to report to the police if

(a) You have a collision with another car and no one is hurt, and you stop to exchange your name and address with the other driver, as well as registration and insurance details.
(b) Only your own car is damaged.

7.3 The immediate tasks after an accident

Irrespective of the legal liability to stop and exchange your name and address and/or insurance details (see sections 7.1 and 7.2 above) you should stop and check whether anyone has been injured and to take the precautions outlined below.

> *You are driving along a quiet suburban street well within the speed limit. You notice out of the corner of your eye that some boys are kicking a football on the pavement. All of a sudden, one of them races after the ball into the road just in front of you. You swerve to avoid him and hit a car coming from the opposite direction. The boy is unhurt but the other driver appears quite dazed and both cars have been badly damaged. What do you do?*

(a) Call an ambulance as you have no way of ascertaining whether the other driver is suffering from shock and/or concussion.
(b) Call the police.
(c) Keep a cool head – the most difficult task of all!

(d) .Make no admission as to any liability.

(e) Endeavour to take down witness details, as once the crowd which gathers at the scene drift off, you are unlikely to be able to trace them again.

(f) Try to make a preliminary sketch of the position of the cars.

7.4 After the event

(a) Write down all the details as you remember them.

(b) Inform your insurers whether or not you expect a claim.

(c) Give in all the relevant documents at your nearest police station: licence (plus counterpart, if any), insurance, and MOT, within five days. If you could not give them to the police present at the time of the accident you must specify then which police station you intend to go to.

(d) Go back to the scene to take measurements, and even photographs.

(e) If the police inform you of any prosecution, possibly for careless driving (remember you did notice the boys out of the corner of your eye), you should contact a solicitor who specializes in road traffic offences, or seek other legal advice (see chapter on *The Legal System*).

7.5 Insurance certificate and driving licence

It is advisable to retain your insurance certificate in your car at all times and not to drive without your driving licence. These precautions can reduce the inconvenience of having to attend at a police station to produce either document.

8. Car theft

Car theft continues to grow and the Home Office has issued a list of the makes and models of cars most likely to be stolen. It is estimated that one in four drivers leaves his or her car unlocked. There are two separate offences that concern the taking away of vehicles under the Theft Act 1968.

8.1 Theft

This involves an intention – as with all theft – to deprive the owner permanently of his possession. Car theft is usually perpetrated by well-organized, professional thieves and the cars are made to 'disappear' quickly – either literally by being transported out of the country, or by 'laundering' through other means. Stolen cars are often then used to carry out other crimes, or other car thefts.

The rule is that a thief can never become the 'owner' of the car, and so he cannot pass on title to the car to another person – even one who buys in good faith. Thus anyone buying a stolen car is liable to its true owner – if the owner can trace it.

The owner of a Mercedes Benz handed over his car and the log book in the course of an armed robbery when he was held up at gun point. He was also forced to write a 'receipt' for an alleged £46,000 so that it could look like a sale. The robbers then threatened to kill his family if he told the police. The Mercedes thereafter changed hands three times before the owner approached the police a month later.

The court held that the successive new 'owners' had no title to the car.

8.2 Taking a vehicle without consent, or 'joy-riding'

This is usually carried out by juveniles. It is defined under section 12 of the Theft Act 1968. Because there is no intention to deprive the owner permanently of his car but to dump it at some point, it is categorized as a separate offence from theft. The large numbers of joyriders occupy a great amount of police and court time and teenage joyriders are an increasing hazard on the road.

8.2.1 'Aggravated Vehicle-Taking' Act

In March 1992, the above Act became law to meet the increasing danger from joyriders.

It lays down an aggravated form of the offence of taking, driving, or being a passenger in a vehicle without the owner's consent. On indictment there can be a maximum penalty of an unlimited fine or two years' imprisonment. It is also subject to compulsory disqualification from driving.

An aggravated offence occurs if one of the following conditions is present:

(a) that the vehicle was driven dangerously on a road or public place;
(b) that an accident took place in which someone was injured;
(c) that an accident occurred in which there was damage to the vehicle or to other property.

8.3 Insurance notification

Should your car be stolen or taken without consent, it is important that you notify your insurer without delay. If the car is not recovered or is found smashed by joy-riders, your insurance company will provide your only form of redress.

The courts now have extended powers to convict persons on these charges. Powers relate only to conviction on criminal charges. No provision is made for the convicted person to make restitution to the aggrieved owner for damage to his car. (For the position on personal injury, see section 1.2.4 above.)

9. Offences and penalties – general overview

The Road Traffic Act 1991 introduced stiffer new penalties for a wide range of offences. The toughening up on the effective enforcement of traffic laws is well illustrated by the fact that no fewer than seven offences may attract a period of imprisonment. Additionally, many of the provisions have been redrafted to make it clearer when an action constitutes an offence.

The principal particular offences will be considered in some detail in subsequent sections.

9.1 Alternative verdicts

It is possible in certain cases for a person charged with an offence to be convicted of a lesser one. This route will presumably be taken where the outcome of prosecution for the more serious offence is uncertain. The following Table sets out the 'offence charged' and the lesser alternative available.

Offence charged	Alternative
Causing death by dangerous driving	Dangerous driving. Careless and inconsiderate driving
Dangerous driving	Careless and inconsiderate driving
Causing death by careless driving when under influence of drink or drugs	Careless and inconsiderate driving
	Driving when unfit through drink or drugs
	Driving with excess alcohol in breath etc.
	Failing to provide specimen
Driving or attempting to drive while unfit through drink or drugs	Being in charge of vehicle while unfit to drive through drink or drugs
Driving or attempting to drive with excess alcohol in breath etc.	Being in charge of vehicle with excess alcohol in breath etc.

No doubt if you are charged with one of the offences in Column 1, your legal adviser will be pressing for a reduction to the lesser, alternative charge.

9.2 Enforcement and technology

The prosecution may obtain a conviction by producing in evidence photographs taken from speed cameras and cameras situated at traffic lights. It is not necessary for such photographs to be backed up by eyewitness evidence. Where photographic evidence is not available you cannot be convicted of a speeding offence solely on the opinion evidence of one witness.

9.3 Driver identity

The owner of a vehicle will himself be guilty of an offence if he refuses to divulge the identity of the driver of his vehicle if that driver is suspected of having been involved in a serious offence. An owner will not be convicted, however, if he can establish that he did not know and could not reasonably have been expected to know the identity of the driver. A company and its directors may also be found guilty of failure to disclose unless it can be demonstrated that failure to keep records of drivers was reasonable in the circumstances.

9.4 Interim disqualification

Where a magistrates' court refers an offender to the Crown Court for sentence or defers sentence for social inquiry etc., the court may disqualify that person pending his ultimate sentence. This power is exercisable only in cases where the offence is one which attracts a discretionary or mandatory disqualification from driving. In practice, it seems likely that an interim disqualification is more likely to occur where the offence is subject to a mandatory disqualification.

Credit will be given for the period of interim disqualification when it comes to the imposition of the sentence.

You are convicted on 1 March 1993 and placed under interim disqualification for an excess-alcohol offence. You appear for sentence on 31 March and are disqualified for 12 months. When will your disqualification order end?

At midnight on 28 February 1994.

9.5 Newly qualified drivers

It was announced in February 1994 that a new package of measures is to be introduced in an effort to cut down on casualties caused by newly qualified drivers. These measures are

- retesting of new drivers convicted of serious driving offences
- post-driving-test driver training
- road safety education for the under-16s
- separate theory testing as part of the driving test.

9.6 Classification of penalties

Road traffic offences may lead to

- imprisonment
- fines
- penalty points endorsed on your licence.

9.6.1 Penalty points

The penalty-point system is intended to deter drivers from unsafe driving since the accumulation of 12 or more points over a three year period will result in a disqualification for a minimum period of six months, and for a longer period if the driver has previously been disqualified. Indeed you may lose your licence simply through committing a number of very trivial offences under the totting-up procedure.

If your disqualification results from an accumulation of 12 penalty points on your licence those penalty points will be removed from your licence.

However, if you are disqualified for a specific offence, e.g. dangerous driving, those previous unrelated penalty points will not be removed from your licence.

You have 6 penalty points, dating from January 1994, on your licence and on 1 June 1994 are disqualified from driving for a period of 12 months, having been convicted of careless driving. On 30 June 1995 you are convicted of driving without insurance and 8 penalty points are awarded against you. Will you again be disqualified from driving?

Yes. The court will take account of your original 6 points. You now have 14 penalty points awarded within a three year period and disqualification is applicable.

◆ **Note:** The courts are most unlikely to hear favourably any pleas to the effect that your business interests will be adversely affected by any disqualification imposed.

9.7 Penalty table

Offence	Maximum penalties			
	imprisonment	fine	disqualification	penalty points
Causing death by dangerous driving	5 years	Unlimited	Obligatory – 2 years minimum	3–11 (if exceptionally not disqualified)
Dangerous driving	2 years	Unlimited	Obligatory	3–11 (if exceptionally not disqualified)
Causing death by careless driving under the influence of drink or drugs	5 years	Unlimited	Obligatory – 2 years minimum	3–11 (if exceptionally not disqualified)
Careless and inconsiderate driving	–	£2,500	Discretionary	3–9
Driving while unfit through drink or drugs or with excess alcohol; or failing to provide a specimen for analysis	6 months	£5,000	Obligatory	3–11 (if exceptionally not disqualified)
Failing to stop after an accident or failing to report an accident	6 months	£5,000	Discretionary	5–10
Driving when disqualified	6 months (12 months in Scotland)	£5,000	Discretionary	6
Driving after refusal or revocation of licence on medical grounds	6 months	£5,000	Discretionary	3–6
Driving without insurance	–	£5,000	Discretionary	6–8
Driving otherwise than in accordance with a licence	–	£1,000	Discretionary	3–6
Speeding	–	£1,000 (£2,500 for motorway offences)	Discretionary	3–6 or 3 (fixed penalty)
Traffic light offences	–	£1,000	Discretionary	3
No MOT certificate	–	£1,000	–	–
Seat belt offences	–	£500	–	–
Failing to identify driver of a vehicle	–	£1,000	Discretionary	3

10. Dangerous driving offences

The offence of driving recklessly has been replaced by two offences:

- driving dangerously
- causing death by dangerous driving – or, as the Act puts it, causing death 'by driving a mechanically propelled vehicle dangerously on a road or other public place'. This attracts the most serious penalties.

The meaning of 'dangerous driving' is the same for both offences.

10.1 Meaning of dangerous driving

A person is regarded as driving dangerously if

- the way he drives falls far below what would be expected of a competent and careful driver, and
- it would be obvious to a competent and careful driver that driving in that way would be dangerous.

'Dangerous', in this context, means likely to cause either injury to a person or serious damage to property.

10.1.1 Dangerous driving covers state of vehicle

Driving will also be regarded as dangerous in circumstances where it would be obvious to a careful and competent driver that driving the vehicle in its current state would be dangerous. This extends to anything attached to or carried on or in the vehicle and the manner in which it is attached or carried.

> *A load of hay carried on your open-backed truck falls off and causes an accident to the vehicle behind you. The load was large but you had not tied it down in any way. You had given no particular thought as to whether the bales were likely to be stable. Could you be found guilty of dangerous driving?*

> Yes. The jury could find that it would have been obvious to a careful and competent driver that there was a clear risk that the load might fall and cause death or injury. It does not matter that you did not consider that possibility.

10.2 The meaning of 'mechanically propelled vehicles' and 'public place'

10.2.1 Type of vehicle

Dangerous driving offences extend to any mechanically propelled vehicle rather than being restricted to a 'motor vehicle'. So the offence could extend, for example, to dangerous driving of stock cars, scramble bikes and even a mechanical sit-on lawnmower. It would also extend to a vehicle which is being towed and could not be driven under its own motive power.

10.2.2 Type of place

The extension of the offence to driving not only on a road but also in a public place means that an offence may be committed in, say, a public car park or in a pub car park to which the public have access.

10.2.3 Exclusion: motor-sports events

There is an exclusion covering areas in which the driving occurs in accordance with an authorization for a motoring event given under regulations made by the Secretary of State.

You are taking part in an authorized rallying event and take risks which could very well result in damage to a fellow competitor or his vehicle. You collide with another vehicle causing damage to it. Can you be found guilty of an offence of dangerous driving?

The answer is 'no'. The driving was undertaken in the course of an authorized motoring event.

10.3 Penalty for causing death by dangerous driving

The maximum sentence for causing death by dangerous driving is ten years' imprisonment and/or an unlimited fine. The offence is triable only on indictment [i.e. in a Crown court]. The offence carries an obligatory disqualification period of not less than two years.

Alternatively, a charge could be laid for manslaughter caused by driving. However this step is likely to be limited to only the most serious of cases since, should there be an acquittal on that charge, an alternative verdict of committing the statutory offence would not be possible. In contrast, if there is an acquittal on a charge of causing death by dangerous driving, an alternative verdict of dangerous driving or of careless and inconsiderate driving may be reached. Should an offender have been convicted of causing death by dangerous driving within ten years preceding the current offence, the obligatory minimum disqualification period is three years.

10.4 Penalty for dangerous driving

The maximum penalty for dangerous driving is

- on indictment (Crown court proceedings): two years' imprisonment and/or an unlimited fine
- on summary trial (Magistrates' court proceedings): six months' imprisonment and/or a fine subject to the statutory maximum.

The offender must be disqualified for not less than 12 months.

If a person is found not guilty of dangerous driving an alternative verdict of careless and inconsiderate driving may be brought.

10.5 Mandatory retesting

Where a person is disqualified for

- manslaughter by driving
- causing death by dangerous driving or
- dangerous driving

the court must order that person to be disqualified until the appropriate driving test has been passed. In such cases the test will be an extended driving test – not the standard 'L' test. The extended test will be approximately double the length of the standard test and will, in general, require the candidate to drive for an unspecified period on an unrestricted dual carriageway. Fees for the retest must be met by the offender and are approximately double those charged for a standard test. (For the definition of a 'restricted road', see section 13.1 below.)

11. Careless driving offences

It is an offence to drive a mechanically propelled vehicle on a road or other public place without due care and attention, or without reasonable consideration for other persons using the road or place. It is also an offence if death is caused by such careless driving when under the influence of drink or drugs.

The meaning of 'mechanically propelled vehicle' and 'public place' is discussed in section 10.2 above.

11.1 What constitutes careless driving?

There are no hard and fast rules of law and each case depends on its particular circumstances.

> *You signal that you intend to turn left and then turn right. Can you be convicted of careless driving?*

The answer is 'yes', if you have taken no precautions to look behind you to see if any other vehicle was coming from behind. However, if you made certain that no other driver was to be inconvenienced or endangered by your action, you could escape conviction.

Other examples of careless driving include

- crossing a white line
- failing to stop and look at a T junction
- edging on to a road when the view is obstructed
- reading a newspaper in the car.

11.2 Penalties for careless or inconsiderate driving

An offence of this nature may only be tried summarily and, if convicted, the offender may be fined up to £2,500. Endorsement of one's licence is obligatory with penalty points in the range of 3 to 9. Disqualification is discretionary.

11.3 Death caused by careless driving when unfit through drink or drugs

For this offence to be founded it must be established

(a) that a death has been caused as a result of the defendant's having driven without due care and attention or without reasonable consideration for other persons using the road or place, and

(b) (i) at the time of driving the defendant was unfit to drive through drink or drugs, or

(ii) the defendant had consumed so much alcohol that the proportion of it in his breath, blood or urine at the time exceeded the prescribed limit, or

(iii) the defendant, within 18 hours after the driving, failed without reasonable excuse to provide a specimen as required.

It is not necessary for the prosecution to show that the intoxicant caused the careless driving resulting in death. It is sufficient that there was careless driving resulting in that consequence and that the defendant transgressed one of the three provisions outlined above. If a person fails, without reasonable excuse, to provide a specimen, he is liable to be convicted as if he had provided a specimen which was over the limit. The prescribed legal limits are set out in section 12.2.1 below.

11.4 Penalty for careless driving when unfit causing death

The maximum sentence for this offence is five years' imprisonment and/or an unlimited fine. There is an obligatory disqualification period of not less than two years. That minimum period is to be increased to three years where there has been a conviction for another such offence within 10 years of the commission of the current offence. Rehabilitation courses for drink-drive offenders are considered at section 12.7.

In two recent cases where the defendants, whose drunken driving caused three deaths, received very lenient sentences, the Lord Chief Justice issued new guidance on sentencing policy. He stated that sentences should reflect society's abhorrence of these crimes and that sentences should punish the driver and deter others. In the worst cases, sentences up to the statutory maximum of ten years should be imposed (see *The Daily Telegraph* and *The Times*, 18 December 1993).

A person found not guilty of careless driving causing death may nevertheless be found guilty of an offence of

- careless, and inconsiderate, driving
- driving when unfit through alcohol and drugs
- driving with excess alcohol in breath, blood or urine, or
- failing to provide a specimen.

12. Drink driving offences

The best advice is never to drink and drive. A drunken driver can be as dangerous to himself and others as someone out of control with a loaded gun.

▶ **Never forget** for the safety of yourself and others:

(a) The police can easily check the alcohol limits laid down by law, with simple tests.

(b) It is a serious offence to refuse a test without reasonable excuse.

There are a number of offences which can be grouped under different categories, and these are outlined below.

12.1 Being under the influence

This offence covers driving, attempting to drive, or being in charge of a vehicle while under the influence of drink or drugs. In effect, it applies whenever you are unfit to drive, i.e. when your ability is impaired through drink or drugs.

The courts take a very broad view of 'being in charge' of a vehicle; at all times someone is generally assumed to have charge of a vehicle. You would have to show that you had handed over the vehicle to someone else's charge, or were so far from the car (e.g. at home in bed) that you had ceased to be responsible for it.

> *You know that you have had a great deal to drink so do not intend to drive. But you are walking with a slightly swaying gait to your car with your ignition keys in your hand when you are stopped by the police and asked to take a breath test. Have you committed an offence?*

The answer is 'yes', usually having ignition keys on you is sufficient proof that you are 'in charge' of your vehicle if you are also under the influence of alcohol.

12.2 Being over the limit

Being over the limit is an offence that entails driving, attempting to drive, or being in charge of a vehicle with excess alcohol in breath, blood or urine.

The alcohol in a pint of draught beer could bring you over the limit, depending on factors such as your sex, size, degree of fatigue etc., as well as the time that you have taken over your drink. There is no 'safe' amount of alcohol that you can drink!

12.2.1 Legal limits

- 35 microgrammes of alcohol in 100 millilitres of breath
- 80 milligrammes of alcohol in 100 millilitres of blood
- 107 milligrammes of alcohol in 100 millilitres of urine

12.2.2 Asking to see a solicitor

It is advisable to request the presence of a solicitor in any circumstances where you have been asked to attend at a police station to give a specimen.

12.3 Refusing the tests

This offence covers failing to provide a specimen of breath, without reasonable excuse, for a breath test (at a roadside test), and failing to provide a specimen without reasonable excuse for analysis or laboratory test (following the preliminary roadside screening).

Your roadside test has proved positive and you have been taken to the police station where there was no breath analysis machine. You are asked to provide a sample of blood but say you have a phobia about needles because of AIDS. Can you be found guilty of 'failure to provide' a specimen?

The answer can be 'yes', if the police can show that you have received injections in the past. Fear of AIDS may be considered a reasonable excuse provided you can show medical evidence of genuine phobia (see below, section 12.5 (8)).

12.4 The motorist's safeguards

All the drink/driving offences exist to protect you and the public against drunken driving. There are also safeguards to protect the motorist – for example, the police cannot go in for random breath testing (see section 12.4.1 below). Whether the correct balance has been struck in the public interest between the police and the motorist arouses much controversy.

12.4.1 Random breath testing

Random breath testing is not allowed. You must have given the police 'reasonable cause to suspect' that you are over the limit, for example by driving erratically or by committing some motoring offence. You can also be asked to take the test if you have been involved in an accident.

12.5 Other safeguards

(a) Only a uniformed policeman can ask you to take a roadside test.
(b) You can only be asked to take another test if the first one is positive, i.e. the first test is taken purely as a screening device.
(c) Any further tests can only be done at certain police stations by an officer specially trained for the purpose, or at a hospital.
(d) You can ask to be told of your rights and ask to see the pro-forma police form. You can ask to see your solicitor or the duty solicitor.
(e) You must give two specimens of breath and only the lower one is used. You will receive a signed printout of the result. If you are on the borderline the police must tell you that they can ask for the sample to be replaced by blood or urine. In the last resort, the final decision is that of the police unless there are medical reasons why you cannot give blood.
(f) A specimen of blood must be taken by a doctor.
(g) You must also receive a sample of either the blood or urine, clearly labelled, for your own private analysis.

(h) If you are a sick person, specimens can only be taken with the doctor's permission.

◆ **Take note:** The police have the right to detain you until it appears that you would not recommit the offence, i.e. until you have sobered up.

12.6 Penalties

A person convicted of a drink-driving offence is liable to a maximum term of imprisonment of six months and/or a fine of £5,000. An obligatory disqualification period of 12 months is also applicable. If found not guilty of an alcohol- or drug-related offence involving driving or attempting to drive, you may be found guilty of an alternative offence of being in charge of a vehicle when unfit to drive through drink or drugs or with excess alcohol in breath, blood or urine.

12.7 Courses for drink-drive offenders

Rehabilitation courses are available in selected areas for an experimental period. The continuance and extension of such courses will presumably depend on their success. An offender cannot be compelled to attend such a course but, if he does so successfully, his period of disqualification will be reduced. A court will not make an order for such a course unless it is satisfied that a placement will be available for the offender. A qualifying offender must be at least 17 years old and he must meet the costs of the course. Further, the latest date for completion of a course must be at least two months before the last day of the reduced period of disqualification (e.g. in the case of a two-year disqualification which is reduced by six months, the specified date for completion must be within 16 months).

Rules are laid down regarding certificates of completion necessary to satisfy a court that the disqualification period may be terminated. The rehabilitation courses scheme is for an experimental period to the end of 1997 unless extended by an order of the Secretary of State. A convicted person may also be required to resit a driving test before his period of disqualification is terminated.

12.8 Defences

It has been consistently held that a defence against a drink/driving charge will not stand unless the driver was under reasonable immediate fear of his life or of serious injury. Thus, a man who claimed he had driven while over the limit to escape unwelcome homosexual advances was found to have no viable defence.

Similarly, a woman who claimed she feared violence from her boyfriend following an argument about another man did not have a good defence. However, she might have been considered to have a reasonable defence if she had driven the car to avoid violence if there was reliable evidence of his violent behaviour towards her.

13. Speeding offences

You must not exceed the various speed limits laid down for motorways and all other public roads. Only in exceptional circumstances will a defence be available.

> *Your daughter has been unemployed but has at last found a job. She sets off in the morning only to return 30 minutes later to say that she has missed the bus and will be late for work. You drive her to work – racing to get there on time. You are stopped by the police for speeding and given a fixed penalty notice. Will the prosecuting authorities make an exception in your case?*

You could write a letter setting out the circumstances and it would then depend on the view that they take of the circumstances. In a case of genuine emergency, such as the need to rush someone to hospital, you would be more likely to get a sympathetic hearing.

13.1 Restricted roads

The general rule is that you cannot drive on a 'restricted' road at a speed exceeding 30 miles per hour. Restricted roads are defined as those where lamps are placed not more than 200 yards apart.

13.2 Who imposes limits

Other national speed limits are imposed by the Minister of Transport while local limits are imposed by the local authorities. The motorway limit of 70 miles per hour is regulated separately, but all roads, without exception, are subject to speed limits.

13.3 Regulation of classes of vehicle

Different classes of vehicle are also regulated: for example a motor car drawing a trailer on the motorway should not exceed 60 miles per hour.

13.4 Specified speed limits

Type of vehicle	Built-up areas	Single carriageways	Dual carriageways	Motorways
	mph	mph	mph	mph
Cars – including car-derived vans and motorcycles	30	60	70	70
Cars towing caravans or trailers	30	50	60	60
Buses and coaches	30	50	60	70
Goods vehicles not exceeding 7.5 tonnes laden	30	50	60	70*
Other goods vehicles	30	40	50	60

*Limit is 60 mph if articulated or towing a trailer

◆ **Note:** The 30 mph limit applies to all traffic on all roads with street lighting unless signs show otherwise. Local authorities have the power to vary speed limits within their areas. The authorities may impose speed restrictions on particular local roads permanently or temporarily, which may be effective in respect of only certain hours of the day; for example, speed restrictions near schools during recognized hours of school-related traffic.

13.5 Photographic evidence of speeding

Cameras have been installed for the detection of speeding. Photographic evidence from these cameras may be relied on by the prosecution without there being any corroboration by a witness to the offence. In some instances cameras which do not actually provide photographic evidence have been installed but, as the police move working cameras from site to site, it would be unwise to assume that at any time one particular camera is not functioning.

13.6 Penalties

A person found guilty of a speeding offence is liable to a possible fine of £1,000 (£2,500 for motorway infringements) and may have his licence endorsed by between 3 and 6 penalty points (maximum 3 in cases of fixed penalty offences). Furthermore, the court has a discretion to disqualify the driver.

14. General offences

There are a great number of offences which might be committed by a motorist other than those referred to in previous sections of this chapter. An overview of the more important of these is given below.

14.1 Causing danger to other road users

A person is guilty of an offence if he intentionally and without lawful authority or reasonable cause

(a) causes anything to be on or over a road, or
(b) interferes with a motor vehicle, trailer or cycle, or
(c) interferes (directly or indirectly) with traffic equipment in such circumstances that it would be obvious to a reasonable person that to do so would be dangerous.

'Dangerous', in this context, has the same meaning as in the offence of dangerous driving (see section 10.1 above).

> *You are fed up with heavy goods vehicles constantly taking the route past your home instead of using the nearby alternative dual carriageway. You presume this is being done to avoid traffic congestion problems on the dual carriageway. In desperation, after a sleepless night because of the roar of juggernauts, you build a temporary barrier at the nearby crossroads, hoping this will deter vehicles from turning into your road. You don't think this will be dangerous – merely a deterrent. Can you be charged with an offence of causing danger to other road users?*

Yes. You intentionally placed an obstacle on the road without lawful authority and it would be obvious to a reasonable person that this would constitute a danger. It is not necessary for you to have considered it dangerous.

14.1.1 Penalties

The maximum penalties for an offence of causing danger to other road users are

on summary trial, six months' imprisonment and/or a fine subject to the statutory maximum;

on indictment, seven years' imprisonment and/or an unlimited fine.

14.2 Vehicle construction and use offences

It is an offence to use, or cause or permit another person to use a motor vehicle or trailer on a road where such use involves a danger of injury because of

- the condition of the vehicle
- the purpose for which the vehicle is used
- the number of passengers carried or the manner in which those passengers are carried
- the load of the vehicle.

It is also an offence to contravene construction and use requirements as to brakes, steering or tyres or weight requirements. These offences lead to a mandatory licence endorsement of 3 penalty points. The offender is also liable for discretionary disqualification, unless he can establish that he did not know, and had no reasonable cause to suspect, the existence of a defect.

An authorized constable or a vehicle examiner may prohibit the driving of any vehicle considered unfit. Generally, such a prohibition will continue in force until the vehicle has passed a test showing that the defects have been rectified.

14.3 Accidents

The requirements to stop at the scene of an accident and to report an accident are dealt with at section 7 above. A failure on either count can result in a maximum of six months' imprisonment and/or a fine of £5,000. Disqualification is discretionary but the offender's licence is to be endorsed with between 5 and 10 penalty points.

14.4 Licence violations

It is an offence to drive otherwise than in accordance with a licence. This is applicable regardless of whether the offender has no licence at all (possibly because he is under age and could not qualify for a licence) or whether the holder is driving a vehicle not covered by his licence or in a manner not permitted by his licence. For example, the holder of a provisional licence driving without 'L' plates or without an accompanying approved licensed driver would be committing an offence. An offence of this nature attracts a maximum fine of £1,000, discretionary disqualification and penalty points in the range from 3 to 6. Driving when disqualified or when not permitted to drive by reason of physical disability are more serious offences and are subject to a maximum period of 6 months' imprisonment and/or a fine of up to £5,000, with a discretion as to further disqualification; a licence may also be endorsed with up to 6 penalty points.

14.5 No insurance

It is possible to gain an exemption from third-party insurance but as this requires a deposit of not less than £500,000 with the Accountant-General, this is an option unlikely to be invoked except by a body running a very substantial fleet of vehicles. The majority of road users will have no such exemption and commit an offence if driving without at least third-party insurance cover. An offence may result in a fine of up to £5,000, possible disqualification and endorsement of one's licence with penalty points ranging between 6 and 8.

14.6 No MOT certificate

You must have a current MOT certificate for any vehicle on a public road where one is required, e.g. when a motor car is three years old or more. Such a certificate is not needed for a vehicle held solely in a private place but must be available where, for example, the vehicle is parked on a public road – even if you have no intention of driving it. An offence can lead to a maximum fine of £1,000 but does not involve endorsement of your licence. Of course higher penalties may be attracted if, for example, use of the vehicle is considered to have constituted dangerous driving (see section 10.1).

14.7 Traffic signals

If you fail to stop at a red traffic light or at a stop sign, or ignore a traffic warden's instructions, etc. it may be that you will find yourself charged with dangerous or careless driving (see sections 10 and 11), but the normal result will be that you will be issued with a fixed fine and have your licence endorsed by up to three penalty points. It should be remembered that photographic evidence of such a failure is sufficient without other witness evidence being supplied.

Temporary traffic lights set up, say, at an area of roadworks, must be obeyed in the same way as permanent lights.

14.8 Seat belts

If you fail to observe the seat belt requirements (see section 2.5), you are guilty of an offence punishable by a fine of up to £500. Penalty points are not incurred.

14.9 Parking restrictions

Apart from parking restrictions on a yellow line, double yellow lines, red route or other designated parking-restricted areas, there are the offences of

(a) Parking in a manner that obstructs other cars.
(b) Leaving your vehicle in a dangerous position.

14.9.1 Local authorities

Local authorities run their own parking schemes although the Minister of Transport has overriding authority, e.g. designating red routes in urban areas.

14.9.2 Taking parking offences out of the hands of the police – 'decriminalization'

The Secretary of State is able to make orders accepting local authority etc. plans for permitted parking and special parking areas. Failure to observe parking provisions in such areas may not be considered criminal, providing the offence relates to a *stationary* vehicle. Usually, a ticket will specify a fixed fine to be paid for the parking infringement.

14.9.3 Parking meters

Where parking meters are provided you are required to comply with the displayed conditions relating to payment and to duration of stay.

You have found an empty metered parking bay in a busy street. It still has one hour of unexpired time on the meter so you leave your car there and return an hour later. You then put in sufficient coins for another two hours. Have you committed an offence?

The answer is 'yes'. You have two legal choices: (a) to remove your car before the end of the hour of 'free' time; or (b) to put in the coins on your arrival that would have brought you within the two-hour limit. You cannot do both.

14.9.4 Parking-ticket adjudicators

In London, local authority adjudicators are available to consider contested parking-offence cases. This is a government-backed effort to remove from police and magistrates' courts and burden of dealing with such cases. Other cities, including York, Coventry and Bristol, are considering the appointment of parking-ticket adjudicators.

14.9.5 Wheelclamping

The police have authority to have vehicles clamped that are in breach of parking restrictions; a fine must be paid for the vehicle's release.

Charges applicable to officially clamped vehicles are

- for release of vehicles following clamping £38
- for release following removal £95

A charge of £12 per day is made for the storage of vehicles left in police custody and £50 for disposal of unclaimed vehicles.

14.9.6 Clamping on private land

Landowners and other authorities have resorted to using private security firms to clamp vehicles on private land. This has led to some abuse in the past with 'cowboy' clampers charging exorbitant fines to drivers to release their vehicles. This whole area is currently under some scrutiny and motorists are generally advised to pay the fine but to seek legal redress if they feel they were wrongly treated. Do take it up with your motoring organization if you are a member of one.

DIRECTORY

Motoring

Association of British Insurers (ABI)
51 Gresham Street
London EC2V 7HQ
Tel. 071 600 3333

Automobile Association Legal Services
Fanum House
Station Road
Cheadle Hulme
Cheshire SK8 7BS
Tel. 061 485 6188

British Parking Association
7 Hillside
Portbury
Bristol BS20 9UD
Tel. 0275 374098

Department of Transport
2 Marsham Street
London SW1P 3EB
Tel. 071 276 3000

Disabled Drivers' Association (DDA)
Ashwellthorpe
Norwich NR16 1EX
Tel. 050 841 449

Disabled Drivers Motor Club
Cottingham Way
Thrapston
Northamptonshire NN14 4PL
Tel. 080 124 724

Disabled Motorists Federation
National Mobility Centre
Unit 2a
Atcham Estate
Shrewsbury
Shropshire SY4 4UG
Tel. 0743 761889

Driving Instructors Association
Safety House
Beddington Farm Road
Croydon CR0 4XZ
Tel. 081 665 5151

DVLC
Licensing Centre
Swansea SA6 7JL
Tel. 0792 772151

Guild of Experienced Motorists
Station Road
Forest Row
East Sussex RH18 5EN
Tel. 0342 825676
(Members only on application)

Institute of Advanced Motorists Ltd
IAM House
359 Chiswick High Road
London W4 4HS
Tel. 081 994 4403

Insurance Ombudsman Bureau
City Gate 1
135 Park Street
London SE1 9EA
Tel. 071 928 4488

Mobility Advice and Vehicle Information Service (MAVIS)
Department of Transport
TRRL
Crowthorne
Berkshire RG11 6AU
Tel. 0344 770456
Information Service: 081 212 5257

Mobility Information Service
National Mobility Centre
Unit 2A
Atcham Estate
Shrewsbury SY4 4UG
Tel. 0743 761889

Motability
Gate House
West Gate
Harlow
Essex CM20 1HR
Tel. 0279 635666

Motor Insurers' Bureau
152 Silbury Boulevard
Central Milton Keynes
MK9 1NB
Tel. 0908 240000

Office of Fair Trading
Field House
15–25 Breams Buildings
London EC4A 1PR
Tel. 071 242 2858

Order of the Road
14 Churchfields
Nutley
Uckfield
East Sussex TN22 3NA
Tel. 082 571 2271

The Pedestrians' Association
incorporating **Walkways**
126 Aldersgate Street
London EC1A 4JQ
Tel. 071 490 0750

Retail Motor Industry Federation
201 Great Portland Street
London W1N 6AB
Tel. 071 580 9122

Royal Society for the Prevention of Accidents (ROSPA)
Cannon House
The Priory
Queensway
Birmingham B4 6BS
Tel. 021 200 2461

Society of Motor Manufacturers and Traders Ltd
Forbes House
Halkin Street
London SW1X 7DS
Tel. 071 235 7000

RAC Legal Service
Spectrum
PO Box 700
Bond Street
Bristol BS99 1RB
Tel. 0272 232444

RAC Motoring Services Ltd.
RAC House
M1 Cross
Brent Terrace
London NW2 1LT
Tel. 081 452 8000

The Vehicle Builders and Repairers Association
Belmont House
Finkle Lane
Gildersome
Leeds LS27 7TW
Tel. 0532 538333

Veteran Car Club of Great Britain
Jessamine Court
15 High Street
Ashwell
Herts SG6 5NL
Tel. 0462 742818

11. ACCIDENTS

In this chapter we look at the legal position where an accident has happened – not only traffic accidents, but any situation where people happen to suffer an injury to themselves or damage to their property. Such things can happen anywhere – for example, at home, in the street, at work or at school.

If you hurt yourself or damage your property through your own carelessness, you will have no redress unless you have taken out insurance to cover this situation. For example, while gardening, you trip over a rake you had earlier forgotten to remove. In falling you injure your wrist, and also break your spectacles.

Clearly your only recompense is to claim on a personal accident policy or household insurance.

If an individual is injured *through someone else's fault*, however, there may be a claim for damages in law. In the example just given, if you have a similar fall due to an implement left lying by a council workman in your local park, you may well have a good claim for compensation.

The general rule is that you may be able to claim damages if

(a) you have been injured by someone's failure to take precautions against causing injury
(b) it was a situation where a reasonable person would have been aware of the risk of your being injured, and
(c) he or she would have taken precautions to avoid the risk.

The same applies if your property or possessions are damaged or destroyed.

In fact, as we shall see, the law provides patchy and not necessarily consistent protection. For example, an accident at work is likely to give more comprehensive rights to compensation than an accident in someone's home, even though both accidents may be equally disruptive and painful.

In this chapter we look at

- when an accident happens
- when you can sue
- defences to a claim of negligence
- occupier's liability
- accidents in the street
- railway, bus or coach accidents
- accidents at work
- accidents involving children
- medical accidents
- accidents and sport
- claiming compensation.

1. When an accident happens

1.1 What to do after an accident

If you think you may be able to lodge a claim for an accident, act promptly. People involved in accidents are hurt, upset, angry and confused. It is difficult to keep a cool head but, if you can, do remember to do the following (or if too injured, ask someone else to help):

(a) Take the names and addresses of any witnesses to the accident. After a traffic accident, call the police if anyone is injured.

(b) Ask your doctor or hospital casualty department to examine your injuries and to keep a detailed record for later use.

(c) Take measurements and photographs of the scene of the accident, of visible injuries and of property damage as soon as possible.

(d) Write out a full narration, recording the date, time and the weather conditions if relevant. Include a sketch plan where appropriate.

(e) Inform your insurers if you think you may be covered for the type of accident.

(f) Make a note of details of torn clothing, broken spectacles, taxi rides, medical expenses, etc. as all these additional losses and expenses can form a claim for 'special' damages (see *Claiming compensation*, section 11 below).

(g) Make enquiries to see if similar accidents have happened at the same site.

Some solicitors give you a first interview free under a scheme known as *Accident Line*. Their names can be obtained by telephoning Freephone 0500 19 29 39, or by writing to Freepost, PO Box 61, London NW1 7QS.

So if you do think that you have a claim, seek advice promptly. Delay may result in your claim lapsing (see section 2.2 below).

2. When can you sue?

The law does not regard a duty to take care as being owed to everyone in the world. The test is a test of 'reasonableness'. Was it reasonably foreseeable that someone else would get hurt by a failure to take care? That is the question to be asked. If the risk of harm to another person is remote it is unreasonable to impose a duty of care on the person who might otherwise be at fault because of careless behaviour. This will depend on the circumstances of the incident.

Thus to prove negligence, the victim must show that

- it was reasonably foreseeable that harm would result from a failure to take care
- there was a duty of care owed to him or her
- the duty was not discharged
- damage or injury resulted.

Even if all these criteria can be established, the person at fault may still have a defence to the claim (see section 3 below). If the injury or damage is pure happenstance or 'Act of God', of course no remedy is available – it is for this type of incident that insurance must have been obtained in advance if compensation is to be available. See also section 3.3 below.

You are a spectator at a car rally which takes place in bad weather conditions over rough terrain. You are standing beside a hairpin bend, near the track, when the driver of the lead car swerves and his car's bumper gives you a glancing blow on your legs. You are treated immediately for a surface wound, but your right leg gives you considerable pain thereafter. You want to know whether you can sue the rally organizers.

Each case always depends on the circumstances.

The rally organizers quite clearly have a duty of care towards spectators who attend their events. The question of whether they failed in their duty in this case depends on the facts: if a judge finds that they employed an inadequate number of stewards to supervise the spectators in bad weather conditions which made driving more hazardous, then you would probably have made out your case.

If, however, you stationed yourself in a dangerous spot by standing too near the track, you might have contributed to your own misfortune; in other words your damages could be considerably reduced because of your own 'contributory negligence'. See *Defences to a claim of negligence*, section 3 below.

If it was the case of a driver who, acting in the heat of the moment, misjudged the distance, there may be no fault on anyone's part.

2.1 Time limits

The law lays down time limits within which you must begin legal proceedings. *Take legal advice on this.*

In cases of personal injuries or death, there is a three-year time limit, which runs from the date of the injury or the date when the victim knew of this (whichever is the later). If you are going to take legal steps to claim damages, you must commence them before this period expires, and should therefore act as soon as you can after the event.

> *A workman was exposed to noxious dust over a period of years. As a result he contracted silicosis.*

This was a case in which he was suffering damage long before he knew of it so the three-year period began to run only from the date on which he became aware of his illness.

There are exceptional circumstances where even shorter periods apply.

Although, the courts have power to extend time limits, they will only do so in exceptional circumstances. Therefore it is in your interests to act promptly, otherwise you may lose your chance of compensation for good.

Children can bring a claim for personal injury in their own right within three years of their 18th birthday. Children under 18 must sue through their parent or guardian, who will bring an action on their behalf.

2.2 Civil and criminal proceedings

The aim of civil proceedings is to compensate the victim. The aim of criminal proceedings is to fix blame and allocate punishment.

However, in recent years the distinction between civil and criminal proceedings has become somewhat less significant in this regard because a criminal court now has the power to order a convicted offender to pay compensation to his victim. For claims over £1,000 which result from criminal injury, a claim can also be made to the Criminal Injuries Compensation Board. The compensation ordered on a criminal case will be on a limited scale. Furthermore, a recent White Paper has indicated a 'fresh approach' to compensation for criminal injury. A tariff scheme is to be introduced with fixed awards for injuries.

Criminal proceedings are often completed much more speedily than civil cases and usually at no financial cost to the victim. Even if you intend to bring civil proceedings for damages as well, the fact that the offender has been convicted in a criminal court will often assist you in proving your claim. For example, if you were involved in a car accident as a result of another driver's dangerous driving, the fact that the driver has been successfully prosecuted for dangerous driving would assist you in bringing a claim for damages where you need to prove that he had been at fault. The amount awarded in the civil courts has no upper limit.

2.3 Alternative sources of compensation

Because of the limitations imposed by the law on claiming damages, as well as the time and the expense involved, the main protection against accidents comes from insurance.

(a) To take care of ourselves, we take out life policies, personal accident insurance, health policies, household and all risks policies, etc.

(b) To take care of others, we take out liability policies (compulsory third party insurance for your car serves the same function).

Before going to court, consider first any speedier route for immediate assistance. For example

- an occupational sick pay scheme or pension scheme that may provide benefits for work accidents
- social security benefits – information can be obtained from your local DSS office or Citizens' Advice Bureau.

3. Defences to a claim of negligence

Even if you can establish that someone else was *legally* at fault in causing you harm, he or she may have a successful defence to your claim. This can have the effect of preventing you from recovering any damages at all or, with less drastic effect, of reducing the amount you can recover. The most common defences are

- contributory negligence
- voluntary assumption of risk
- unavoidable accident.

◆ **Take note:** Only one of these defences need apply.

3.1 When the victim contributes to the accident

The wrongdoer may argue that although the harm was caused partly by his or her fault, your lack of care also contributed to the accident. If that can be proved, your damages will be reduced proportionately.

You are driving your car at night with dipped headlights down a narrow, dark street. You collide with the back of a parked lorry which has no rear lights or reflectors. The owner of the lorry argues that although he was negligent in stationing his unmarked lorry in that way, you were also negligent because you should have made sure that your headlights were properly on. What is the position?

Although the lorry owner was negligent, you are likely to be held partly to blame for the collision and your damages will be reduced accordingly – perhaps by up to 20 per cent.

In other circumstances, although aware of a danger, you may find yourself in a 'no choice' situation. For example, in a recent case, a tenant complained to his landlord that a steep flight of stairs from his flat to the street was badly lit and lacked a handrail. The landlord, who was responsible for maintenance, did nothing to improve the situation. One evening, the tenant fell on the stairs and suffered a broken hip. The landlord was held liable in full for the damages claimed by the tenant, who was not considered contributorily negligent in the circumstances because he could not avoid using the dangerous stairs.

3.2 When the victim took the risk

If you agree to run a risk and then an accident does indeed occur, you may not be able to make a claim.

You and your friend decide to test your 'hot hatch' cars in a race on an open road. The cars collide. What is your position?

Even if your friend was to blame for the collision, it would be unlikely that your claim against him would receive a sympathetic hearing in court!

You persuade your friend to give you a ride on his newly purchased motor bike, although he warns you that he is not yet proficient and that you come on it at your own risk.

You probably could not hold him liable for any resulting accident.

Similarly, you are assuming the risk if you accept a lift from a driver knowing he is probably too drunk to drive safely.

However, when someone is engaging in a business which entails a risk of injury or property damage, they may ask customers to sign a form, or they may put up a notice exempting the organizers from liability. Even if you have seen the notice or signed such a form, the attempted exemption is invalid in law if an accident involving personal injury results from the organizers' negligence.

You decide that you wish to learn horse-riding and approach your local stables. You are asked to sign a form exempting the management from liability. Your horse bolts in the road on your second lesson and you fall off, suffering a broken wrist. Afterwards, you learn that the horse has been unruly before.

You are not prevented from making a claim by having signed the exemption clause.

3.3 Unavoidable accident

Where an accident occurs because of something or some situation which could not have been foreseen and against which precautions could not have been taken, this is a complete answer to a claim for compensation. An example would be a traffic accident which took place because of a driver's sudden heart attack.

4. Occupier's liability

The vast majority of accidents happen in the home. Whether you can sue anyone depends on the cause of the accident and whether or not the accident happened in your own home or in someone else's. This section deals with accidents which result from the actual state of the premises, although, of course, accidents happen in the home for all sorts of other reasons – for example, a faulty cable on a vacuum cleaner could cause a nasty shock (see chapter on *Goods and Services*, section 6).

4.1 Who is an occupier?

The fundamental rule is that persons in control of premises – whom the law calls *occupiers* – must exercise a reasonable degree of care to ensure that their premises are reasonably safe for others to use. Accordingly

- a local authority is responsible for schools, libraries and streets
- shopkeepers, hoteliers, publicans etc. are responsible for their business premises
- other authorities in charge of premises also owe a duty of care, for example, British Rail are responsible for railway stations, the CAA for airports, the Area Health Authority or hospital trust for clinics and hospitals.

Two important points to remember:

(a) Although called an 'occupier', it is the person or body in control or in charge of the premises who is liable; it need not be the person in 'occupation' of the premises in the everyday meaning of the word.
(b) 'Occupier's liability' also means that as a private householder, you are responsible for the safety of those who come into your house or flat. (See section 4.3.1 below.)

4.2 What are premises?

'Premises' has a very extended meaning; it does not just apply to buildings. Even cranes and lorries have been held to be 'premises' for the purposes of occupier's liability.

4.3 Who can claim

Only persons who suffer physical injury or damage to property can claim. For example, *A* and *B* visit a department store. *A* trips on loose carpet, sprains her ankle and tears her coat. *B* has her purse stolen from the fitting room while trying on a dress. The shop owner, as occupier, is responsible for *A*'s loss and injury but not for *B*'s.

The occupier can be liable even if the injury is caused *indirectly* by the dangerous state of the premises. In a recent case a police officer successfully sued Reading Football Club when he was injured by a lump of concrete thrown during violence at a football match. The club, as 'occupier' of the ground, was responsible for the fact that to its knowledge the premises were not in good repair so that the terrace could be broken up to form missiles, and it was known that visiting fans would contain a violent element.

4.3.1 Responsibility towards those you invite

The occupier's primary responsibility is to any person who comes into the premises

- as a guest
- to do a job (e.g. to repair the washing machine)
- or for some other lawful purpose, such as to read the meters.

4.3.2 Responsibility towards those you do not invite

The liability for harm suffered on property even extends to

- authorized ramblers
- children tempted by some attraction (such as a pond or 'conker' tree)

- 'trespassers' – which includes people innocently straying from the highway
- undesirables.

The extent of the duty diminishes with each category. Thus the duty owed to someone who trespasses on to your property has been defined as 'humanitarian' only. In other words, you cannot allow a real danger to exist on your property as a deterrent to others. For example, if you own a vicious dog which you allow to roam loose over your property and it savages someone who strays on to your land, you would still be liable to pay the victim compensation.

If there is a danger on your property you must protect yourself by warning notices and by actively discouraging trespassers.

4.3.3 Problems with children
(See also section 8 below)

As an occupier you may be responsible for children tempted to trespass on your property.

▶ **Do remember** that young children may not be able to see or to read warning signs, and that they may be expected to be less careful of their own safety than adults (see *Children and accidents*, section 8 below).

4.4 Accidents in the home

4.4.1 Accidents involving yourself

If you spill gravy on your kitchen floor and then slip and injure yourself, you can blame no one else. If, however, your neighbour slips on the gravy, you are responsible as occupier of the premises – most household insurance policies do carry an occupiers' liability clause protecting you against such accidents. **You are advised to check your policy on this!**

4.4.2 Accidents involving visitors

You are under a duty to ensure that your premises are safe for those you may invite or permit to enter. Uneven garden paths, for example, could mean you are responsible for resulting falls by your friends, neighbours, postmen or delivery men, etc.

> *Your local horticultural society has asked you to arrange an 'open day' for members of the public to visit your garden on behalf of a charity. A close friend warns you that when she arranged a similar open day, one of the visitors tripped over a bit of loose paving in the garden path. She says that she has been receiving letters from a lawyer threatening legal action as a result of the accident. What should you do?*

If you are planning to have large numbers of strangers on your property, e.g. if you are having a fête or opening your garden for charity to members of the public, first check with your insurers to establish that you are adequately covered against accident. (Under the National Gardens Scheme you would be covered by a group liability policy.)

4.4.3 Accidents in your rented home

You are responsible for the state of the premises whether or not you own your home or live in it as a tenant. However, your landlord is generally responsible for the safety of the common parts, such as lifts and stairs, and is liable not only to you but to your family and other visitors.

Manchester City Council was fined the maximum £25,000 when faultily installed heating in council flats caused the death by carbon monoxide poisoning of one of the tenants. His dependants could also claim compensation from the council.

A business landlord is liable in the same way as a residential one.

4.5 Accidents on someone else's property

4.5.1 Private premises

See sections 4.3 and 4.4 above.

4.5.2 Public premises

You have reserved a book at the local library and have received a card to say that the book is waiting for collection. When you arrive, there are trails of melted snow in the entrance hall of the library from other visitors but no mats have been laid to cover the slippery floor. You fall and injure yourself. A friend advises you that you ought to sue the local authority but you are not sure of the legal position. The library building is generally well looked after. What is the position?

Your friend is right: the local authority is liable even though the condition of the entrance hall was only temporarily unsafe.

The cause of the danger could be a major problem such as a design defect in the building itself or it could be a simple matter of failure to replace light bulbs. In other words, it does not depend on the occupier's personal 'fault'. But as in all these cases, it is a matter of degree. The emphasis is on the word 'reasonable', i.e. the occupier of premises has a duty to take *reasonable* care to see that his or her premises are *reasonably* safe for others to use.

4.5.3 Safety for persons

The primary duty of an occupier is to take care to see that the premises are safe for those who come on to them. But adults are expected to have some care for their own safety, especially in the case of those who could be expected to be aware of special dangers – e.g. an electrician would be more aware of faulty wiring than the householder. (See section 4.6.2 below.)

4.5.4 Safety for property

Moreover, the premises have to be reasonably safe not only for people but also for their property, provided that the loss or damage to property results from the state of the premises and not from some other cause.

While staying in an hotel, you hang your clothes and put your suitcase in the wardrobe. Because of a leaking roof, the cupboard is flooded and your belongings are ruined.

The hotel is liable to pay compensation. (However, this may be limited to a woefully inadequate maximum of £100 in total per guest under the Hotel Proprietors Act 1956, if the hotel has a notice to that effect.) A different rule applies if the loss of your property took place through the negligence of an employee of the hotel. For example, the £100 maximum will not apply if a chambermaid forgets to lock the door behind her and your clothes are stolen.

4.6 Defences to a claim

Apart from showing 'reasonable care', there are other defences to a claim for accidents under occupier's liability. Only one of these defences must be proved:

(a) An independent contractor was responsible.
(b) Special risks were taken.
(c) Adequate warning was given.

4.6.1 The independent contractor

If the hazard was caused by an independent contractor, it is generally the contractor and not the occupier who will be held responsible.

> *After taking recommendations you carefully select a firm of electrical contractors to rewire your house. Unbeknown to you, they do their work negligently. You then call in a carpenter to erect some bookshelves and he suffers a severe shock when he plugs an electric drill into a socket. He threatens to sue you. You want to know whether you are liable.*

Even though you are the occupier, you probably have no liability in this case. In law it is the electrical firm which ought to be sued.

4.6.2 Specialists and special risks

An occupier is not liable for special risks if (s)he employes someone with their own special expertise but who has an accident nonetheless.

> *A window cleaner balances his foot on an ornamental trellis attached to an outside wall of your house. The trellis gives way and he falls.*

You are not liable. It was his job to know that an ornamental trellis would not be strong enough to support his weight. If, however, while going upstairs inside your house, the window cleaner tripped on a loose stair carpet, you would be liable.

4.6.3 Giving adequate warning

An occupier may be able to discharge his duty of care by giving adequate warnings of the danger. For example, a supermarket employee may stand beside a spillage, warning customers away, until the staff can clean it up.

If the danger is exceptional, a mere warning notice will be entirely inadequate so warning lights, notices or fencing off dangers may be appropriate in particular circumstances.

Notices which attempt to exclude a business's liability for death or personal injury are ineffective in law. Even for property damage, a notice may be ineffective if unreasonable. A company which runs a parking garage can protect itself by a notice stating that it will not be responsible for damage to or theft from cars but that will not absolve it from gross negligence.

> *You leave your car in a parking garage where you have to hand over the car keys to the staff who then park the car for you. Your ticket states that your car is left at your own risk. There is a notice to the same effect. A member of staff drives your car so negligently that he rams it against a concrete bollard. The garage proprietor denies liability and points to the clauses on the ticket.*

You should not take 'no' for an answer in these circumstances. Take legal advice as you may have a very good claim for the damage to your car.

5. Accidents in the street

Many of us have tripped on a pavement, got up a bit shaken and a bit bruised, and then walked on. If however, you fall because of a broken, uneven or loose pavingstone or because of a hole in the road, and you have the misfortune to hurt yourself or damage your belongings (e.g. spectacles), the local highway authority may be at fault.

5.1 Highways

5.1.1 What is a highway

◆ **Take note:** A 'highway' comprises the road which you cross (the carriageway) and the pavement which you walk on (the footway).

5.1.2 Highway authorities

Local highway authorities are

- county councils in non-metropolitan areas
- metropolitan borough councils outside London
- London borough councils within London
- district councils or parish councils for unclassified roads, footpaths and bridleways.

(Motorways and trunk roads are the responsibility of the Department of Transport.)

All these authorities maintain highways at public expense and keep a list of the highways in their area. This information is particularly important if you fall far from where you live and you have to ascertain which highway authority is involved. You can write – or inquire in person – and should not be charged for the information.

If the accident was caused by a mains cover or ongoing repairs, the appropriate organization to claim from may be the utility companies (e.g. British Telecom, British Gas or the water authorities).

As always, in circumstances in which you think you have a claim, take legal advice.

5.1.3 Dangers beside the highway

Passers-by can also be endangered by what happens *beside* the highway. A pile of rubble or a trench adjoining a footpath could cause injury to someone who is not keeping strictly to the path, and the contractor responsible will be held liable for such injuries. Liability will depend on how near the danger was to the highway. This depends on the circumstances and is not a simple matter of measurement.

5.1.4 When the local highway authority is liable

The authority is only responsible for dangers arising from the condition of the highway. Not all accidents in the street are attributable to this. (See section 5.1.7 below.)

The liability of a highway authority is based on lack of due care, so that if it could not have known of the danger it would also have a good defence.

Some building work is going on in the next door property and a lorry tips its load of bricks on to the pavement, cracking some flagstones. You have a bad fall as a result. What is the position?

The local highway authority is not expected to be aware of an incident such as this as soon as it happens. Regular inspections and maintenance (of which a register will be kept by the authority) may demonstrate its reasonable care. You would probably have to take the matter up with the building contractor involved as responsible for your accident.

The authority would be liable only for physical damage, not economic loss. A farmer whose economic survival depended on milk tankers having access to his farm could not sue for the road being in such bad condition that the tankers could not get through, as his loss was purely economic.

5.1.5 Maintenance

A local highway authority's duty is to repair the highways in its area and maintain them in a reasonable condition. What is reasonable is a matter of degree. A reasonable person using the highway would expect

- some degree of unevenness in a pavement
- to take some heed of where he or she walks
- more holes in a road than in a pavement.

The extent of the duty also depends on the type of highway; it is reasonable for a highway authority to devote more resources to the repair of a busy shopping street than to an unfrequented footpath.

▶ **Remember:** Although maintenance involves clearing away standing snow or ice and providing extra protection in bad weather, e.g. by gritting or salting roads, again the duty is a matter of degree.

> *You slip because of a puddle of water on the pavement. You feel that you were not at fault and would like to take the matter up with your local highway authority. Have you any case?*

It is unlikely that the highway authority would have a duty to clear purely temporary hazards such as those caused by rainwater puddles, unless the gullies or sewers were permanently blocked because of lack of repair.

A highway authority could be liable if the danger in the street could be limited by the use of warning signs. Where a motorcyclist was injured when he collided with the kerb on an unmarked sharp bend in the road, the court held the authority to be negligent in failing to erect warning signs.

5.1.6 Lighting

The duty to maintain extends to the provision of adequate lighting to be kept in working order.

5.1.7 Objects in the street

Where an accident has been caused by something falling into the street, negligence is usually present. Materials do not normally fall from building sites unless someone has been careless; walls do not collapse unless there has been dangerous neglect of repairs.

> *You are injured by a piece of guttering which falls from the roof edge of a building. You want to take the matter further but do not know whether to approach the highway authority or the building owner.*

The 'occupier' is liable (see *Occupier's liability*, section 4 above) unless there was some other cause for which he is not responsible (e.g. there had been underground subsidence at the foundations, or the guttering had been vandalized by a trespasser).

The same principle applies to trees.

A large beech tree growing in your next door neighbour's garden topples over onto the roadway, damaging your car. Your neighbours deny all responsibility. What is the position?

Your neighbours are liable if they knew or should have known the tree was diseased or otherwise dangerous, but not if they could not have known that fact, e.g. if there was only below-ground damage to the roots. There is no duty to have experts examine trees unless there has been some cause for concern about their safety.

5.1.8 Danger created by others

Danger may have been created by necessary work on underground mains or cables. Gas, electricity or water companies responsible for such excavations must take precautions to prevent danger to passers-by. If the authority responsible has put up warnings, this may be sufficient to discharge its duty to take all reasonable care. The warning must also be adequate.

5.1.9 Handicapped persons

An 'adequate' warning must take into account the fact that certain passers-by can be particularly vulnerable to hazards in the roads.

A trench in the street, excavated by the electricity company, was protected by signs and lights which warned ordinary pedestrians of the danger, but gave inadequate warning for persons with a visual handicap.

A court decided that it was reasonable for the company to have had such people within its consideration. It should have anticipated their presence and done more to protect them against the danger it had created.

6. Railway, bus or coach accidents

6.1 Operator's duties

Whether we travel by bus, coach or train, those in charge of operations are under a duty to use reasonable care and skill to ensure our safety. Their duty of care applies to our possessions too.

6.1.1 Insurance

All carriers have compulsory third party insurance cover for their liability. (If you have accident cover or all risks property insurance you may also be able to claim against your own insurers.)

6.1.2 Exemption clause

Statements on a ticket or on other notices which try to limit or avoid the operator's liability for death or personal injury are ineffective in law. They can, however, reasonably impose limits on their liability for lost or damaged property.

6.1.3 To whom is the duty owed?

The duty is owed to all passengers irrespective of the terms under which they travel.

You and your four-year-old son take a 'Runabout' coach trip from London to Nottingham. The company is privately-run. Your son is allowed to travel free as a special concession. The coach is involved in a collision on the M1 due to the driver's negligence. Your son is thrown forward on to the seat in front of him and breaks his nose. Your hold-all, containing your camera, comes crashing down from the rack above your head and your camera is damaged beyond repair. The company dispute liability on the grounds that your son did not pay for his fare. They also point to a limitation of liability clause on your ticket and state that you can only recover £50 on your camera. What is your position?

The operating company's duty of care is owed to all passengers, even those who have not paid for their journey (e.g. elderly passengers on a free bus pass) or reduced-price passengers (e.g. children). However, you will be bound by the limitation of liability on damage to property.

6.1.4 Scope of the duty

The operators of the service will be liable if the accident results from failure to ensure that the vehicle is in a safe condition and is driven safely.

(a) Safety of vehicle

The vehicle must be *reasonably safe* for its purpose. This means that vehicles must be regularly maintained and inspected.

For example, the operator is liable for brake failure if a proper system of inspection would have prevented such failure. British Rail has been held liable for injuries caused by train doors opening, while the train is in motion, because of faulty locks.

(b) Safe driving

The vehicle must not be driven negligently. Operators are liable for the unsafe driving of their employees. In some cases negligence is obvious (e.g. where there has been a collision between trains).

You sat upstairs on a bus with your elbow projecting from the open window. The driver pulled away from the kerb too close to a pole, and your arm was badly injured.

The operators would be liable for their employee's negligent driving.

In another case a woman was in the process of boarding a train which started with a jolt, so that she fell between the platform and the moving train; she lost both her legs as a result, and recovered full damages from British Rail.

◆ **Note:**
- It is negligent for a driver to jolt the vehicle when starting.
- It is negligent for a driver to move off without checking to see if passengers are attempting to board or alight from the vehicle.
- It is negligent for a driver to disregard the safety of standing as well as of seated passengers.

(c) General safety

A safe system must be in operation. This means, for example, that British Rail is liable for unsafe wiring of signals, or where someone is crushed because of overcrowding on trains or platforms.

6.2 Occupier's liability

Like any other occupier, bus and rail authorities are also responsible for the safety of their premises.

- platforms must be at a reasonable height for train-users
- stations must be kept in a safe condition, e.g. floors must be safe and there must be proper lighting.

Failure entails liability not only to passengers but to other persons on the premises, such as someone meeting a friend off a train or coach, or merely visiting the station to shop or to use a toilet.

6.3 Defences available to operators

Where your own lack of care has contributed to the injury, your damages will be reduced proportionately (see section 3 above). It has been held to be contributory negligence for a passenger to try to board a moving bus, or to try to close an open carriage door while the train is in motion.

6.4 Ships, aircraft, hovercraft

The liability of those who operate other forms of transport such as ships, aircraft or hovercraft, and their premises (hoverports, airports, etc.) is similar to the above. There are international conventions limiting the level of compensation, which may vary according to random variables such as where you embark and disembark, so always insure before you travel.

6.5 Accidents abroad

If you have an accident abroad, your rights and liabilities will depend on the law of the foreign country where the accident occurred. Always advise your travel insurers as soon as possible, and in serious cases contact the nearest British consulate. If you booked through a package offered by a UK travel company you may be able to claim compensation from them for certain kinds of accidents, e.g. unsafe hotels or touring coaches. (See Chapter 6, *Goods and Services*, section 9.)

7. Accidents at work

Liability for the safety of a workforce depends on a complex interaction between employers' liability for negligence and a growing number of statutory regulations which have imposed extra, and in many cases stricter, duties on them.

Accidents at work are extremely common – in fact, nearly 50 per cent of claims for personal injury going through the courts annually concern work accidents. Apart from the misery and pain involved for the victim and his family, work accidents cause other immense and untold costs: firms lose productivity and can even go out of business; insurance premiums go up; the National Health Service, on already stretched resources, has to provide treatment and facilities to cope with those who are hurt; and the DSS has to support employees who can no longer work – either in the short or long-term.

◆ **Take note:**

- small firms have a worse record of accidents than big firms
- retail and service industries are just as accident-prone as heavy industry.

▶ **Employers should always remember** that victims of work accidents, even of quite minor accidents, are increasingly ready to litigate.

7.1 Before an accident occurs

If you are an employer, it is your legal responsibility to assess what potential harm your employees or others might face in the workplace, to decide on the necessary safety precautions, and consistently maintain these to a reasonable standard. Apart from facing claims for damages from injured employees, your business might be shut down and the management fined for breach of safety regulations. If you are an employee, the failure of your employer to take proper care is putting you at risk.

> *You have complained several times to your boss that the lift in the office building seems unsafe. He has taken no notice. While you do not wish to keep bothering him about it, you do not want to run the risk of injury. What do you do?*

> If you believe that you are exposed to an unreasonable risk of injury, you should consult your trade union if you have one. You may also find it useful to get in touch with the Health and Safety Commission who are responsible for safety standards. Its inspectorate not only gives advice but also has enforcement powers (see DIRECTORY at the end of the chapter).

If any danger is so extreme that you leave your job, you could take your case to an industrial tribunal. In a recent case, a tribunal decided that an employer had 'dismissed' his employee when she left her job because she felt that security was still too lax after a robbery. If you are dismissed or otherwise victimized because you have complained about unsafe circumstances at work, you would also have a good case for taking the employer to an industrial tribunal.

7.1.1 Employer's liability insurance

- By law employers must take out insurance to cover themselves against employees' compensation claims.
- An employer is also likely to have taken out a public liability policy. That covers the risks of injury to or damage to property or other persons such as customers, contractors or their employees working on the policy-holder's premises. It may also cover the intake of noxious emissions or pollution.
- If the employer's business involves known risks (for example, it may be concerned with chemicals), the insurance company will inspect and insist on compliance with extensive safety precautions to minimize accidents.

▶ **Employers beware:**

- any failure to observe insurers' precautions can affect the validity of the insurance cover
- any failure to take these precautions is also a factor in assessing an employer's liability to an injured employee
- uninsured costs in most work accidents are four times those of insured costs, in overtime, legal costs, delayed production etc.

Employers are actively encouraged to take preventive action beyond their insurance and statutory obligations. Advice is offered by the Health and Safety Executive in the hope that employers will appreciate that safety measures are very much in their own interests.

▶ **Employees**, you should remember too that you can take out your own accident insurance cover.

7.2 When an accident occurs

In the short term, an injured employee is entitled to statutory sick pay for up to 28 weeks if still employed, and if out of work to some form of sickness benefit. If still unable to work after six months, a claim could be made for long-term invalidity or disablement benefit.

◆ **Take note:** Obtaining these benefits does not disentitle an injured person from also claiming compensation in the form of damages from the employer.

Check your occupational sick pay or pension scheme as well for benefits.

If you have taken out your own insurance policy against accidents, any amount received from your own insurer would not be deducted from damages from your employer – provided you have paid the premiums yourself.

Make sure that your accident is brought to the immediate attention of your employer. This must be done in writing. Even if you appear not seriously hurt at the time, you may suffer long-term harm and may need to make a claim at a later stage. Any firm employing more than ten workers must keep an accident record book.

7.2.1 Scope of employer's liability

The duty of an employer is to take *reasonable* care to prevent injury to people or their property at the workplace. The duty is a duty of care, it is not an absolute duty. The duty of care has various aspects:

- the provision of safe arrangements and working methods
- the provision of safe work premises
- the provision of suitable materials and equipment and training in how to use them
- the provision of competent staff.

7.2.2 Safe arrangements, training and working methods

The employer must plan to ensure that the method of carrying out the work does not expose employees to unreasonable risks. This includes a duty to provide training about hazards and the methods for their prevention. There may need to be a regular educational programme, bringing home to employees the particular steps they should take to reduce the risk of injury.

In one case two youngsters were sent to an engineering firm to gain work experience. They were told to clean a large machine using rags and paraffin and in so doing their overalls became soaked with paraffin. When they stood next to the stove, their overalls burst into flames. The company was held liable for their injuries, as it had failed in its duty to set up a system which ensured supervision of inexperienced workers and kept management informed of workplace practices.

If the use of a safety device or a change in the distribution of the work between employees would avoid known hazards, an employer's inertia in not providing or introducing these might give rise to liability. The general standards and practice of the industry as a whole may be relevant in determining whether the risks were known before the accident.

Particular instructions as to the method of carrying out the work or warnings of the dangers given to the employee may be sufficient to discharge the employer's liability, but it is not enough to issue instructions unless adequate steps are also taken to see that they are observed.

However, as in all cases of negligence, the facts of a particular situation will determine what is reasonable. If an employee has some autonomy in determining how the work is done, an employer may be exonerated from blame, particularly if the employee is skilled or experienced, unless there is reason to believe the dangers are being ignored or they are hidden ones.

> *A librarian was required to stack shelves from a trolley full of books. She could select the number of items to place on the shelves at any one time. While lifting a load she injured her back, and was eventually obliged to give up the job.*

> Her employer was not liable to her for the injury, because practice has shown that where employees have control over the size of their loads and the way they choose to lift them, it should constitute an effective system for avoiding excessive strains.

It is not only the weight of a load, of course, which can affect the risk of injury – the objects may be slippery, sharp or hot; by regulations employers must design systems of work on ergonomic lines when requiring manual operations of all kinds.

7.2.3 Safe work premises

Employers are liable if they fail to provide a safe workplace for staff, including the means of access to the workplace and places to which they are sent out to work. For example, the employers were liable when three workmen died after being sent to clean a dangerous gas-filled sewer with no training or protective equipment. The structure and fittings of the premises must not themselves cause a risk of injury; uneven, greasy or debris-covered floors, inadequate lighting, loose carpets, are obvious examples. Failure to provide fire extinguishers where inflammable chemicals are dealt with would be another example.

Safety standards for the place of work may rise with time, as knowledge accumulates about particular hazards. Employers are expected to be aware of government and HSE publications warning of particular risks.

7.2.4 Suitable materials and equipment

Equipment must be safe and suitable for the job in hand. The employer must ensure that it is regularly inspected and maintained, and that those who use it are adequately trained.

If the job is sedentary, safe seating must be provided. There is a growing awareness of the importance of muscular and other strains involved in today's high-tech offices. Prolonged use of VDU units can involve eye and muscle strain as well as hazards to pregnant women. In all cases, equipment must be checked to see that it is suitable for safe use. There are also regulations requiring guards to be fitted to dangerous parts of machines, protection against equipment overheating, stability of equipment etc.

If the task is hazardous or the machinery, e.g. paper guillotines, dangerous, then training must be given. Protective safety equipment must be made available.

▶ **Remember:** Even when personal protective equipment, e.g. gloves, goggles, safety harnesses has been provided, employers will be liable if they fail to insist on their use.

By regulation, employers are also required to meet certain standards for the comfort and welfare of their employees, such as heating and ventilation, which go beyond pure safety measures.

7.2.5 Competent staff

One of your work colleagues is known to be a practical joker. One day, he pulls away your chair as you are about to sit down – as a result, you land on the floor. You suffer more than mere social embarrassment, as you hurt your back badly. What can you do?

Theoretically, you could sue your colleague but as he is probably not worth suing, you could pursue a claim against your employers. They would be liable in damages if they knew of your colleague's propensity for horseplay and had taken no steps to warn him against silly behaviour.

The same principle applies if you suffer an injury because a fellow-employee is inexpert, given to outbursts of temper, or drinks too much.

A worker in a canteen was injured when struck on the head by a raw potato thrown by a fellow employee. She was awarded substantial compensation by the Criminal Injuries Compensation Board. The employer was also civilly liable in damages.

An employer's liability extends beyond problems posed by fellow-employees and can include dangerous actions of a third party on the work premises.

Your employer engages a firm of heating engineers to instal gas heaters in your office. They do the work negligently, with the result that an appliance explodes, injuring you.

Your employer is liable to you.

7.3 Safety legislation

The negligence liability of an employer is heavily overlaid with statutory duties flowing from Acts of Parliament, statutory regulations, and increasingly, EC Directives. All these have imposed more and more duties on employers to safeguard their employees' health and safety.

The Health and Safety at Work, etc. Act 1974 imposes a general duty on employers to ensure, so far as is reasonably practicable, the health, safety and welfare at work of all employees. There are regulations under the Act which cover particular industries or workplaces, e.g. the use of lead in the potteries industry or the wearing of protective helmets in the construction industry. There are a large number of measures designed to control particular types of hazard, such as the use of computers, electrical dangers, risks of eye injury, hazardous levels of noise. Important among these are controls on substances hazardous to health, including chemicals, dust and micro-organisms. The Health and Safety Commission publishes guides to the regulations to help employers comply. Regulations also came into force in 1993 to give effect to a comprehensive EC Directive on the management of health and safety, providing for risk assessment in the workplace, and which may lead to higher standards of care and precautionary measures.

Offices are also regulated by legislation and regulations, which cover such matters as the provision of adequate lighting, heating, cleaning, sanitary facilities, seating for sedentary work, and safe lifts.

Where office premises are occupied by different firms and companies, it is the owner of the premises who is responsible for the safety of the common parts of the building, including entrance hall, stairs, passages and toilets.

Almost all of these legal duties imposed on employers are enforced either by the Health and Safety Inspectorate or by the local authority environmental health officer (although fire precautions are enforced by the local fire authority). There is the sanction of criminal proceedings against the employer and/or the power to bring work to a halt until safety measures are introduced.

From the point of view of an injured employee's claim for damages, the claim can be based on breach of statutory duty. The victim's task of establishing liability is made simpler in such a case, because negligence need not be shown.

The employer's duty to take the prescribed safety measures is usually absolute – for example, to fence moving parts of machinery in a factory. It would not be any defence for an employer that it was too expensive to take such steps.

◆ **Note:** The statutory duties may be phrased in unqualified terms, or may be expressed as a duty to take all reasonable practicable steps. Each case will have to be considered individually.

7.4 Contributory negligence

Employees have a duty to co-operate with the employer to take care for their own and others' safety.

> *You are sent by your firm of chartered surveyors to survey the roof of a three-storey block of flats. You have telephoned to the main office for additional assistance as you realize, once on site, that the task is too much for a single person. In the meantime, you decide to explore the roof – as far as possible – by examining the loft. You fall through and are injured.*

You may be found by the court to have contributed to your own misfortune in this particular case – even if your employers were also negligent in having sent you to do a task without proper assistance.

Employees who put their colleagues or members of the public at risk by carelessness or by disobeying safety instructions lay themselves open not only to the (possibly theoretical) claim for damages jointly with their employer but also, of course, to disciplinary charges and even dismissal. Criminal charges are also a possibility.

7.5 Staff at risk from the public

A new concern for employers and their employees arises from the fact that staff can be at risk from members of the public – as highlighted by the tragic case of Suzy Lamplugh, an estate agent who kept an appointment with a 'client' and was never seen again.

Employers can be held liable if they fail to take all reasonable steps to prevent and guard against the likelihood of risk to their employees.

They may not be liable for accidents occurring on other premises for which they cannot take responsibility. For example, employees sent to work on a building site in Saudi Arabia who were injured there could not hold the employer in Britain liable as he could not control daily events there. His responsibility was only to take reasonable steps to ensure the safety of the employees on his own or other premises where they were directed to work.

Certain groups of employees are particularly vulnerable in their dealings with the public. Social workers, nurses, DSS staff, bus and van drivers and schoolteachers have been threatened, abused and physically assaulted in the course of their duties. The right to claim civil compensation in these cases works in tandem with the criminal law.

Employees who are victims of criminal assault may be able to receive compensation from the Criminal Injuries Compensation Board.

8. Accidents involving children

The law recognizes that children are vulnerable and unpredictable and that what is an obvious danger to an adult may be an allurement to a child.

Primarily it is the legal responsibility of parents, or of others who have charge of the child – even temporarily, such as a childminder, baby-sitter or teacher – to see that they are safe. Their safety involves both taking precautions at home (having safety gates on stairs and childproof containers for medicines) and taking particular care of children out of doors. Older children are expected to take some care for their own safety, e.g. when crossing the road.

8.1 An accident caused to a child

8.1.1 Precautions and safety measures

Note the safety regulations designed to protect children against accidents – for example, regulations covering the flammability of clothing and the safety of toys or nursery equipment. Check that any toy or equipment you buy carries a BS, BSI or CE mark which mean that safety standards are being complied with. There is no need to wait until an accident actually occurs.

You buy your three-year-old child an expensive boxed doll. On the box it states that it is suitable for a child of 36 months and over but has no other mark. The hand of the doll comes away from its arm and could be easily swallowed – even by a three-year old. You think the toy is not safe and should not be on the market. What can you do?

Inform the safety standards officer of your local authority who will take the matter up with the manufacturers and retailers. Standards officers have enforcement powers in addition to their investigative duties.

(Advice on safety can also be obtained from the Child Accident Prevention Trust and the Royal Society for the Prevention of Accidents, see DIRECTORY.)

8.1.2 Parents and other carers

If other people look after your children while you are at work, it is not always easy to establish whether they are properly qualified to do so.

You leave your toddler with a childminder while you go out to work. The child gets hurt on a swing. You are sure it was an avoidable accident and that the minder was just not taking due care. Have you any redress?

You must complain to your local authority which keeps a register of childminders who have been vetted by its own staff. You can also sue the childminder on the child's behalf.

The Children Act 1989 lays down guidelines for the registration by the local authority of all persons who look after children under eight on domestic premises, for gain, for more than two hours per day (see also chapter on *Children*).

8.1.3 Road accidents

Damages for a child hurt in a road accident will be reduced by the extent to which its own carelessness contributed to any injury.

> You are driving your car during rush-hour in a busy road at about 20 mph. An 11-year-old boy, without looking, runs into the centre of the road to retrieve a ball, and is struck by your car. The child suffers a broken arm. You feel that you were not altogether at fault for the accident.

In a similar incident, the driver was held only 25 per cent to blame for the accident. The court felt that the child's blameworthiness, even taking account of his age, was considerably greater.

Where a four-year old ran quickly into the road into the path of an oncoming car, the driver was held not liable for her injuries. His attempt to avoid her was all that a prudent motorist could have done in the circumstances.

8.2 When a child causes an accident

8.2.1 Parents' liability

In general, parents are not liable for the damage that their children cause, although they may feel moral responsibility, e.g. to pay for the replacement of a neighbour's window broken by their son's cricket ball.

But it does happen that parents are personally negligent in not properly controlling their children. The fault is then theirs in failing to prevent an accident. In the case of a young child accompanied by an adult, it could be that the adult would be held wholly or partly responsible. For example, a driver who sees a little girl walking with her mother might reasonably expect the mother to prevent the child from running into the road. A parent who does not control children in a car, to the detriment of other road users, will also be held responsible.

> You have picked up two of your son's school friends for the school run and the three boys are being very rowdy in the back seat of your estate car. They unwind the car windows and start throwing conkers on to the road. Unfortunately, one hits the windscreen of an oncoming car so that the driver is distracted and has a minor accident. He complains that you were to blame for the accident and that it was your duty to have controlled the children in the car in the interests of other road users. Is he correct?

The answer is 'yes'.

A parent's liability for a child's actions is also related to the danger involved.

> A father allowed his 13-year old to keep an airgun and fire it in the garden, even after the son had damaged a neighbour's window with it. Then another child got hurt in a shooting incident.

The father was held liable in negligence. The result would probably have been the same even if the father had repeatedly warned his son to take care when using the gun, as children cannot be expected to be obedient to instructions 100 per cent of the time.

(To allow a child under 14 to have an air weapon is now a criminal offence.)

8.2.2 Liability of other carers

When a child causes an accident while in the care of others, the same principles apply. In the 'school run' scenario above, the mother is equally responsible for the accident whether the offending conker was thrown by her son or by one of the other children.

8.3 Children at school

8.3.1 Safety of premises and equipment

A local education authority is responsible for taking reasonable care for the safety of a child at a maintained school. The governing body of a fee-paying school owes the same duty of care to its pupils. In the case of opted-out schools, the board of governors is a formally constituted body. As such, it is required to have insurance cover against accidents on school premises. The duty of care requires the school to provide safe premises, just as the occupier of any other premises must.

> *Heavy swing doors with a powerful spring are installed in a primary school. A small girl catches her hand in the door and it is crushed.*

The school (or education authority) is liable, as such doors are unsuitable for a school for this age group.

Playgrounds, sports facilities and school buses are also required to be suitably designed and safely maintained. The child's safety at school must also be safeguarded by the provision of suitable materials and equipment (e.g. round-ended rather than pointed scissors should be provided for younger children), and by a reasonable level of supervision. This does not mean constant supervision, although obviously more supervision is required the younger the child or the more dangerous the activity. It is not unreasonable for the duty to supervise to be delegated in appropriate circumstances to unqualified staff such as dinner ladies, or to prefects or monitors.

8.3.2 Negligent supervision

Schools are responsible for the negligence of the staff in failing to protect pupils' safety. For older children warnings about dangerous substances or practices may be a sufficient discharge of the teacher's responsibility to safeguard his pupils.

> *Where a teacher warned pupils in a chemistry lesson about the dangerous nature of a chemical, he was held not to be negligent when one of the pupils carelessly spilt some of the chemical on another pupil, causing burns. On the other hand, where a teacher had left an unmarked container of the dangerous substance in a position where pupils could get at it, he was held to have been negligent.*

Provided there is a reasonable level of supervision, a school is not liable if a child is hurt during playground games, even if the injury is caused during organized sports activities.

> *A pupil was severely injured by a head-on tackle during a school rugby match. Some degree of instruction had been provided.*

The school was not liable, and was found not negligent in failing to insure the pupil nor in failing to advise his parents to take out such insurance. The Central Council for Physical Recreation arranges bulk insurance through schools to cover this type of accident.

8.3.3 Claims against children

You are a teacher on playground duty. A pupil, with a history of aggressive disruption, throws a cricket ball with all his force at you and fractures a cheekbone. You want to know whom to sue.

You can claim damages from the education authority for failing to protect you from the risk of such an injury.

8.4 Children and occupier's liability

Premises must be reasonably safe for children, and that means taking into account the fact that children are less able to take care of themselves than adults.

Your four-year-old is injured when she slips between the bars of an airvent in a walkway in a shopping centre. It is clear that such an accident could not have happened to an adult or an older child. Would that be a factor in assessing the safety of the premises for the purposes of liability?

The answer is 'no'.

A two-year-old girl, when visiting the zoo, put her hand through the bars of a cage, where a chimpanzee grabbed it and bit off two fingers. The zoo was held at fault and responsible for the width of the cage bars.

A playground manager (such as the local authority) will be liable if a child is injured by

- unsafe or defective equipment
- unsuitable surfaces, or
- hidden dangers.

A toddler is badly cut by pieces of glass concealed in a sandpit in a public park.

The local authority which manages the playground can be held liable to pay her compensation.

A tree has been planted in a public park with attractive but poisonous berries. A child eats the berries and becomes ill.

The local authority which owns the park is liable as its officials should have realized the berries presented a dangerous attraction to children.

8.4.1 Children as 'trespassers'

The question of children who trespass on land and who then get hurt is a vexed problem for the courts. There might be liability to children who trespass in certain circumstances.

(a) If there is a hidden danger on the land, or an allurement which tempts children to use it even without permission (e.g. a ramp suitable for skateboarders to practise stunts), and

(b) if the occupier knows that children trespass on the land and lets them do this,

he may be regarded as having given them 'permission' and will be liable if they are injured.

9. Medical accidents

Under the general rules of negligence, professional persons, such as doctors and dentists, must exercise a *reasonable degree* of skill so as not to cause foreseeable injury to their patients.

◆ **Take note** that

(a) The social climate has changed. Today, in the UK, aggrieved patients are more prone to take doctors to court and to sue them for an alleged failure to treat them properly.

(b) Awards of damages in medical negligence cases can be very large – a single case of a brain-damaged baby can lead to an award of damages of over a million pounds. In addition, these large awards can be made to a number of people who, together, form a 'class' of litigants: for example a group of people who all received transfusions of contaminated blood.

(c) Medical accidents can and do occur without anyone to blame. A simple and routine operation can go disastrously wrong because the patient reacts badly or does not recover properly. Such patients are as much victims of medical accidents and can suffer just as much as in cases where negligence is proven. Yet they cannot recover compensation because they cannot point to a doctor and say 'It is his fault'. There is strong argument that there should be a 'no-fault fund' to meet the needs of such patients. But how will society pay for such a fund when negligence suits are already costing so much?

9.1 Difficulties of proving negligence

In all cases, liability is based on lack of due care. In some cases, this is beyond argument, as when, for example, a dentist pulls out a sound tooth.

In other cases, medical accident victims may have great difficulty in proving negligence.

9.1.1 Standard of care required

▶ **Remember:** a doctor or dentist is not to be judged by the highest professional standards but is required to exercise the skill and care of the average competent practitioner in his or her field.

9.1.2 Establishing cause and effect

It can be very difficult to establish cause and effect, because

- doctors are often loath to testify against fellow-professionals in negligence suits;
- patients have to prove that the doctor failed to practise an acceptable standard of professional skill which it is not easy for a lay person to establish or to judge;
- the courts have tended to be protective towards doctors for fear of 'opening the floodgates' to litigation;
- a victim of a medical accident has the added difficulty of establishing that it was the doctor's or hospital's negligence which resulted in the injury. This is a particular problem where the negligent conduct is said to be a *failure* to treat or to diagnose.

Your 15-year-old son fell off his bike and was taken to casualty, where the doctor in charge diagnosed a knee injury. In fact the boy had also injured his hip, as was discovered when he returned to the hospital some days later. By that time the hip joint had become deformed. You would like to sue on your son's behalf but have taken a second opinion from a consultant orthopaedic surgeon who says that the deformity would have resulted from the original fall even if the damage to the hip had been diagnosed on the first visit to casualty.

The courts would hold that if the same result would have followed, irrespective of the treatment, you could not recover damages in negligence.

A patient who suffered extreme pain and fear because she was awake during an operation sued the anaesthetist's health authority. The court held the anaesthetist had not been negligent because he had used a generally accepted anaesthetic technique which was approved by a responsible body of medical opinion even though it carried a small risk of the patient's awareness during the operation.

◆ **Note:** If you think you have a claim, take legal advice. Medical negligence is a specialized and difficult area. Seek out a solicitor who specializes in medical negligence cases and always act promptly. Time limits may seem ample (three years in the usual cases) but all such matters can taken an inordinately long time to process.

9.2 Defences to negligence

9.2.1 Medical knowledge at time of accident

Practitioners are expected to apply the medical knowledge current at the time of treatment. You would have to show that the treatment was known to have risks or to cause serious side effects at the period when it was actually used on you.

9.2.2 Adequate information provided

The doctor's negligence may consist in failing to provide information to the patient or in failing to obtain the patient's consent to treatment. In the case of a treatment which in itself carries with it some risk of harm or side-effects, it is a good defence for the doctor to show that the patient was informed about the risks and consented to run them. This again is a question of degree.

You underwent pain-relieving surgery on an arthritic joint. The doctor did not warn you that there was a risk that the joint might fuse. What is the legal position?

First, the health authority can argue that the fusion might have taken place in any event.

Secondly, the House of Lords has held that a doctor was not negligent when he did not warn a patient of a one per cent risk of partial paralysis from pain-relieving surgery. However, if there had been a ten per cent risk or more, their Lordships said, a patient should be told of it so that the patient has full knowledge of any unfortunate consequences (i.e. in legal terms, could give 'informed consent'). If a substantial body of doctors would not have regarded it as necessary to warn the patient, failure to do so will not be regarded as negligent in law.

If no information was given, the patient may be able to sue – therefore, for example, pregnant women suffering from epilepsy should be warned about the danger that anti-convulsive drugs prescribed to control the illness may cause serious birth defects.

9.2.3 No consent given

If no consent at all has been given to a particular procedure the doctor is clearly liable, e.g. in cases where women who consented to an abortion or bladder operation found a hysterectomy had been performed on them as well.

9.2.4 Other factors

Doctors have also been held to be negligent for

- failing to investigate the patient's medical history before administering further treatment, or
- failing to provide adequate information so that those responsible for subsequent treatment are duly informed.

You were discharged from hospital after surgery. The surgeon failed to inform your GP that your condition required continued monitoring at home. Your recovery from the operation is greatly prolonged as a result.

The hospital is liable.

9.3 Who is responsible

9.3.1 NHS treatment

For NHS treatment the health authority or self-governing hospital trust is responsible for any proven lapses in skill or care of its employees. It will not matter whose fault or error caused the accident – whether a senior consultant or junior doctor, nursing sister or student nurse. A consultant who works part-time in the hospital is also a member of staff for this purpose.

You were treated by an inexperienced registrar when you attended a casualty station after an accident. In fact he even told you it was his first day on the job. You now feel you were incorrectly treated. Will his inexperience be relevant to establishing liability?

An inexperienced doctor would not be excused from negligence on account of his lack of skill. The health authority is under a duty to ensure adequate staffing so that there is proper supervision for trainees.

In fact, junior doctors in training constitute the largest single group of high-risk doctors as far as claims are concerned. The excessively long working hours of junior doctors and the inadequate conditions under which they often work constitute a special problem over which the trainees themselves have no control, but for which their employers can be held responsible.

9.3.2 Private treatment

In the case of a fee-paying patient, the doctor must be sued personally. If the injury was caused by negligent nursing care the private hospital is sued.

All doctors carry insurance under special schemes (see DIRECTORY).

9.4 General non-medical safety in hospitals

Security is a growing problem in hospital. Numbers of people wander in and out of hospital premises for all sorts of reasons, but there have been some horrific cases of injuries to patients in hospitals from outsiders.

As far as responsibility for the actions of its own staff is concerned, a hospital is liable for a patient's physical safety – even apart from the treatment administered. Cases include a patient who was scalded by being given too hot a bath, and an inadequately supervised child patient who fell out of a window.

Hospitals are also responsible for the safety of their premises, like any other 'occupier' (see section 4.1 above).

9.5 Complementary medicine

There is a growing recognition, even in the medical profession, that practitioners of complementary medicine have a role to play in a patient's wellbeing. Osteopaths, chiropractors, acupuncturists and others are also governed by the general rules of negligence: i.e. they must use a reasonable degree of skill so as not to cause foreseeable injury to their patients.

◆ **Take note:** Practitioners of complementary medicine are not required to be as skilled as qualified doctors. They must be reasonably skilled and use such care as one would expect from an ordinarily competent person in their particular field. Although they are not required by law to be registered, many of them are registered by their own organizations, which lay down training standards to give a level of competence patients should expect.

▶ **Check** to see that a practitioner is registered.

> *You have a trapped nerve in your neck and are in a great deal of pain. A friend recommends you to a masseur. He examines you, looks at your X-rays and agrees that your neck condition is very serious. He then proceeds to give you a strenuous massage. Your condition worsens. Has the masseur breached his duty of care?*

If practitioners of complementary medicine undertake treatment for a serious condition when they knew or should reasonably have known that they were not competent to deal with it, they could be liable for recklessness or negligence.

◆ **Note:** Unlike doctors, alternative therapists are not always obliged by law to obtain insurance cover. Responsible therapists will have done so. Even though many of the techniques used are 'non-invasive' (i.e. are unlikely to do any harm) you should always check with their umbrella organizations with regard to the insurance position.

9.6 Veterinary medicine

A vet owes the same duty as a doctor to discharge his duties with a reasonable level of competence and care. As vets also frequently provide medication, they are responsible if the products are unsafe or unfit for their purpose.

> *You are a farmer who asks the vet to inoculate your herd of cattle against summer mastitis. Unknown to the vet the serum used is defective.*

He is liable to compensate you for losses in the herd (although he will be able to claim reimbursement from the suppliers).

There may be more difficulties about calculating compensation if the animal is not a working animal but a pet. Distress at the loss of a much-loved cat may not be compensable even if due to maltreatment, although damages for inconvenience, refund of expenses etc., will be claimable.

10. Accidents and sport

Public attention, as never before, has been focused on the subject of accidents and sport. Mass disasters, such as those at the football fields of Bradford and Hillsborough, have led to direct government intervention in matters of public safety and crowd control. Far-reaching legal issues have been raised by these events for which the ordinary rules of negligence have seemed inadequate.

◆ **Note** however, that you may have no claim for damages at all if you have consented to run the risk of some degree of injury, as, for example, where the sport is an inherently dangerous activity, such as skiing or hang-gliding. Novices should ensure there is adequate supervision and/or qualified instructors.

If you engage in such sports regularly, personal accident insurance can be arranged through the governing body of the sport, as an ordinary personal accident policy may not cover you. Always tell your insurer before embarking on a dangerous sport.

In all cases it is a matter of degree. You may have consented to run some risk of injury but you will not have consented to negligence on the part of others, such as the employment of an unqualified instructor or failure to maintain a ski lift properly.

10.1 Sports premises

10.1.1 Occupier's liability

The general rule is that of occupier's liability (see section 4.1 above): anyone who is injured by unsafe sports premises can claim compensation from the persons in control of the premises.

So those who offer sports facilities to members of the public must take all reasonable steps to ensure that the facilities provided are reasonably safe for ordinary use.

Your local public swimming baths offer a heated outdoor pool. You take a dive into the pool from the diving board and suffer head injuries as a result. It transpires the diving board has been sited at a part of the swimming pool where the water was insufficiently deep for diving.

The local authority is clearly liable to you in this case.

An aerobics class is held in the hall of an adult education institute. You become a member of the class but you injure your back when you slip on the polished floor of the hall.

The local education authority which runs the institute is liable to compensate you, as although you voluntarily undertook the risks inherent in brisk exercise, you were entitled to assume that the premises were reasonably fit for the purpose of aerobics.

The degree of care which such occupiers or organizers of sports events must show will vary with the circumstances. Dangerous sports or especially vulnerable participants (e.g. children, the disabled) are entitled to expect a greater degree of care, and more steps to be taken for their safety.

10.1.2 Outside the sports facilities

Clubs or other occupiers of sports halls or grounds may be liable for accidents which occur beyond the boundaries of their premises.

You are cycling along a road and are struck on the forehead by a ball which has been hit by a golfer from a golf course which adjoins the road. You learn that the course has been laid out with a hole in such a position that balls are frequently driven into the road.

You can claim damages for injury from the club (and also from the player if he can be identified).

In a recent case a family whose home bordered a village green where cricket matches were customarily played obtained an injunction to prevent such games from taking place, after they proved that they and their property were regularly in danger from cricket balls.

♦ **Note:** If the incident had not been usual, but had been wholly exceptional, the club would not have been liable.

Increasing criminal law controls have also been introduced to curb violence by supporters at sports events, especially soccer hooligans. For example, the 1989 Football Spectators Act allows offenders to be ordered to report at police stations on match days. But an attempt to hold the police responsible in the civil courts for their alleged failure to control the crowd at the Hillsborough Stadium failed.

10.2 Spectators

A spectator at a sporting activity may have a claim against a participant who has injured him, for example a competitor at a motor rally who drives so recklessly that his car leaves the track and plunges into the crowd.

However, misjudgment in the heat of the moment need not be negligence.

You are a competitor in a gymkhana. You gallop your horse so fast round a corner that it swings off the track and injures a spectator. The spectator sues you personally as well as the organizers. What is your position?

In a similar case, the court held that the rider was not liable to the injured spectator.

♦ **Note:** a victim's damages will be reduced if his own lack of care contributed to his injuries.

10.3 Injuries on the sports field

A failure to observe the rules of a sport, even if this causes injury to another player, does not necessarily give rise to liability. There would have to be negligence. As we have seen, a want of judgment in the heat of the game does not necessarily amount to absence of due care. Participants in contact sports will be taken to have consented to run the risk of injuries incidental to the game (see *Foul play*, section 10.3.1 below).

Before an ice hockey match players are warming up on the ice. A player who has not yet put on his safety helmet suffers a head injury when another player's practice shot at the goal ricochets off the goal post.

The court decided that as shots at goal are a normal part of warming-up, the injured player had no claim.

10.3.1 Foul play

Concern has been voiced in many quarters at the increasing levels of deliberate violence on the sports field. Foul play can amount to a criminal assault, as well as giving rise to civil claims for damages, and there are several cases where players have been sent to prison for such incidents. In the criminal law there is no difference, said one judge, between mugging an old lady in the street and mugging an opponent on the playing field.

During a club rugby match your jaw is fractured by an off-the-ball punch from a player from the opposing team.

Apart from criminal liability, you can sue for damages for assault, and can also claim from his club, which may be liable for his conduct.

Many clubs now carry insurance to protect players against injuries.

▶ **Remember:** if you are injured by the deliberate violence of anyone – on or off the field, whether player, referee or spectator – you can also lodge a claim for compensation from the Criminal Injuries Compensation Board.

10.4 Defences to a claim

You may be taken to have voluntarily run the risk of injury (like a spectator at a cricket match who is injured in the course of play when the batsman hits a six) as long as the danger is incidental to the ordinary course of the sport or game. In a decided case this defence was successful even against a six-year-old plaintiff who had been taken to a match by his father.

Contributory negligence may also be raised as a defence e.g. if in order to take action photographs, a spectator positions himself in a spot where injury is foreseeable.

11. Claiming compensation

11.1 A note of warning

The aim of damages is to compensate a victim of an accident, but he may not in fact get as much as he has lost, partly because compensation will always be in money – which cannot compensate for e.g. the loss of a limb – but also because the law limits the type of losses which can be included in the calculation.

Damages are not awarded to punish the person whose fault caused the accident, although there may separately be a criminal prosecution arising out of the same facts.

◆ **Note:** Court actions in the High Court are always lengthy, risky and expensive processes. If other ways of obtaining compensation are available, particularly if the amount claimed is not large, these should always be considered in preference – e.g. settlement out of court, arbitration, etc. See section 2.4 above, and also the chapter on *The Legal System*.

11.2 General damages

11.2.1 Property damage

When property is damaged, the compensation will be the cost of repairs or the amount by which the value of the property is diminished by the accident. If beyond repair, the cost of replacing it or its pre-accident market value will be awarded.

11.2.2 Personal injuries

The damages awarded to compensate the victim will include

- financial loss, e.g. loss of earnings, medical costs
- an amount given to compensate for pain and suffering

- an amount given to compensate for temporary or permanent impairment of the ability to engage in his usual activities before the accident, such as sport.

11.3 Special damages

Expenses actually incurred by a victim are sometimes called special damages, e.g. medical expenses, costs of nursing assistance, costs of disablement aids. These can also be claimed from the wrongdoer.

11.4 Nervous shock

The damages awarded to a victim will include an amount to compensate for psychological suffering. However severe the distress which an accident causes to the victim's family or friends, it is not something for which compensation can be claimed. If the shock of seeing the accident, hearing about it or seeing the victim shortly afterwards causes actual psychiatric illness, however, those in a close relationship to the victim, e.g. spouse or parent, can be awarded damages for their own mental injury.

In one case, after a man and his three children were severely injured in an accident, the wife and mother was told of it and was taken to the hospital, where, on seeing the condition of the family members, she suffered severe shock which made her ill.

She could recover damages from the negligent driver who caused the accident.

11.5 Fatal accidents

Where someone is fatally injured in an accident, his dependants can bring an action against the person who was at fault. The claim is strictly for the loss of the financial support of which they were deprived by the victim's accidental death, and the extent of that support will have to be proved. The legal definition of dependants who can bring such an action includes not only spouse and children, but also close relatives, ex-spouses and cohabitees who lived with the deceased for more than two years.

Only one action can be brought, for the benefit of all the dependants together, and the damages will be divided among them in proportion to the support they have lost. Proceedings must be started within three years from the date of death or from the date of knowledge of the dependants.

Where the dependants include a spouse or child of the deceased, a claim for damages for bereavement can be included. The parents of an unmarried child victim can claim a fixed sum of £7,500 for bereavement.

DIRECTORY

Accidents

Action for Victims of Medical Accidents
(AVMA)
Bank Chambers
1 London Road
Forest Hill
London SE23 3TP
Tel. 081 291 2793

Association of British Insurers (ABI)
51 Gresham Street
London EC2V 7HQ
Tel. 071 600 3333

**British Acupuncture Association &
Registrar**
34 Alderney Street
London SW1V 4EU
Tel. 071 834 1012

**British Association for Accident and
Emergency Medicine**
The Royal College of Surgeons
35–43 Lincoln's Inn Fields
London WC2A 3PN
Tel. 071 831 9405

British Association for Immediate Care
7 Black Horse Lane
Ipswich
Suffolk IP1 2EF
Tel. 0473 218407

British Chiropractic Association
29 Whitley Street
Reading
Berkshire RG2 0EG
Tel. 0734 757557

British College of Optometrists
10 Knaresborough Place
London SW5 0TG
Tel. 071 373 7765

British Homoeopathic Association
27a Devonshire Street
London W1N 1RJ
Tel. 071 935 2163

British Medical Association
BMA House
Tavistock Square
London WC1H 9JP

Centre for Accessible Environments
35 Great Smith Street
London SW1P 3BJ
Tel. 071 222 7980

Child Accident Prevention Trust
4th Floor,
Clerks Court
18–20 Farringdon Lane
London EC1R 3AU
Tel. 071 608 3828

Criminal Injuries Compensation Board
Morley House
26–30 Holborn Viaduct
London EC1A 2JQ
Tel. 071 936 3476

Disabled Information and Advice Line
(Dial UK)
Park Lodge
St Catherine's Hospital
Tickhill Road
Doncaster DN4 8QN
Tel. 0302 310123

**General Council & Registrar of
Osteopaths**
56 London Street
Reading
Berkshire RG1 4SQ
Tel. 0734 576585

General Dental Council
37 Wimpole Street
London W1M 8DQ
Tel. 071 486 2171

General Medical Council
44 Hallam Street
London W1N 6AE
Tel. 071 580 7642

Health & Safety Executive
Public Enquiry Point Information Centre
Broad Lane
Sheffield S3 7HQ
Tel. 0742 892345

**Health Service Commissioner
(Ombudsman) for England, Scotland,
Wales**
Church House
Great Smith Street
London SW1P 3BW
Tel. 071 276 2035

The Medical Protection Society Ltd
50 Hallam Street
London W1N 6DE
Tel. 071 637 0541

National Association for Mental Health (MIND)
22 Harley Street
London W1N 2ED
Tel. 071 637 0741

The Patients Association
18 Victoria Park Square
Bethnal Green
London E2 9PF
Tel. 081 981 5676

Public Concern at Work
Lincoln's Inn House
42 Kingsway
London WC2B 6EN
Tel. 071 404 6609

Royal Pharmaceutical Society of Great Britain
1 Lambeth High Street
London SE1 7JN
Tel. 071 735 9141

Royal Society for the Prevention of Accidents (ROSPA)
Cannon House
The Priory
Queensway
Birmingham B4 6BS
Tel. 021 200 2461

UK Central Council for Nursing, Midwifery and Health Visiting (UKCC)
23 Portland Place
London W1N 3AF
Tel. 071 637 7181

Victim Support
Cranmer House
39 Brixton Road
London SW9 6DZ
Tel. 071 735 9166

12. THE LEGAL SYSTEM

Like all the other aspects of the law which we discuss in this book, the legal system is undergoing profound changes.

Within both branches of the legal profession – the solicitors and the barristers – there is a generalized, if sometimes grudging, acceptance of the need for reform and change. Debate is now over the pace of change and the type of reform – that is to say, the extent, rather than the principle – of solicitors' access to higher courts (see section 5 below).

At the same time, the legal system is under scrutiny by the public as never before. Clients are asserting their rights. They want to know about costs, about efficiency, where and how to complain if they are dissatisfied with the way their case is handled. Restrictive practices within the legal profession, which once may have looked arcane and somewhat endearing, are now often simply seen as unacceptable.

So pressure groups from both within and without the profession keep up the demand for change. Enlightened judges and lawyers realize that yesterday's concepts sometimes have little relevance in today's world. The famous 'reasonable' person in English law is known as 'the man on the Clapham omnibus'. How relevant is such a concept when it may be a woman on the bus? Or a Bosnian refugee? How do we ask for consensus on values and behaviour in a pluralistic society where ethnic groups comprise not only native-born but recent arrivals whose view of the concepts of the common law may not coincide with those of the man on that Clapham bus? However, their expectations from the legal system and their requirements for justice have to be met too.

The government's role in bringing about change also cannot be over-emphasized. A most striking example is in the area of legal aid. The bill for legal aid has grown to £1,100 million a year. Both branches of the profession have tried – in vain – to resist the cuts proposed in the legal aid system (see section 2.2 below). Nonetheless, both branches will have to adjust to leaner times.

The great division of law is into two separate branches – the civil and the criminal. In this book, we have dealt almost exclusively with civil law. This chapter on the legal system maintains the same emphasis. The criminal law is enforced by the State in trials which are initiated by the Crown Prosecution Service. Even with rising crime figures, only a minority of people are involved in the criminal justice system.

However, the civil law involves us all – one way or another – from our births to our deaths. It governs our relationships with our families, our environment, our homes, and even our pets! The more we know about the law, the more we can understand the world around us and how to handle the problems we encounter in our everyday lives.

In this chapter we look at

- seeking advice
- paying for advice
- the trial
- judges

- seeking justice – the courts
- sources of law
- reforming the law.

1. Seeking advice

1.1 Consultations and advice

In England there are basically two kinds of lawyers: solicitors and barristers. There are, however, many sources of advice.

1.1.1 Solicitors

If you have a legal problem, you will usually turn first to a High Street solicitor who deals with a great variety of work. This work includes 'contentious' (related to the word 'contest') and 'non-contentious' business.

However, most of the work never involves the courts, that is, most solicitors' work is non-contentious. This involves such standard legal tasks as, for example, the drawing up of a will or seeing to the conveyancing on a house purchase.

Contentious work – as the name implies – concerns a contest between two parties and involves litigation (going to court). Contentious work can be criminal, matrimonial, or other civil work (for instance a claim for damages for a personal injury or a boundary quarrel between neighbours).

In any event, solicitors do all the preparatory work in a case. They also conduct negotiations which, in many instances, can lead to a settlement out of court.

Solicitors usually practise in partnership although some are sole practitioners. They are all members of the Law Society which looks after their interests.

The Law Society publishes a regional directory of its members. This gives information on the types of work which solicitors' firms offer.

It also gives details of those solicitors who offer a low-fee first interview or a free first interview. These directories are available in local libraries and Citizens' Advice Bureaux. The cost is no longer uniform (it used to be £5) but is fixed at a local level. About 6,000 firms nationwide offer this service (see also section 1.8 below).

Until now, solicitors have not appeared in the higher courts as advocates. Instead they have had to instruct a barrister to appear for their client (see *Barristers* immediately below). However, solicitors are progressively having the right to appear in higher courts after suitable training. Application for this right was made by the Law Society to the Lord Chancellor and approved in December 1993.

Solicitors should inform their clients of how much they will charge (see *Paying for advice* below, section 2). They are also obliged to have a complaints handling procedure within their own firms.

Solicitors, under their professional obligations, should also provide the following information to clients:

- the name of the person who has the routine conduct of the client's affairs
- who to approach in the event of any problem with the service
- how the client's affairs are progressing.

1.1.2 Barristers

Barristers are advocate lawyers who appear in the higher courts (see section 5 on the court structure). When they appear in court, they are briefed by their instructing solicitors.

Barristers are known as Counsel and have no direct dealings with the public – hence someone with a legal problem is not able to consult counsel. However they do advise solicitors in consultation on points of law. Barristers are considering proposals to deal direct with the public on non-contentious work.

Until now, barristers have had a monopoly of the right to represent clients in the higher courts (the 'right of audience'). However, changes are in force which enable solicitors to undertake this also.

Barristers are self-employed but work in offices called *chambers*. Each set of chambers employs a clerk who negotiates the barristers' work and sets their fees. Barristers do take on cases free of charge in the public interest as well (see, for example, section 1.12 below). They have also instituted a 'Century Brief', allowing a junior barrister to represent a client for two days' hearing for £100.

◆ **Note:** litigants can also act for themselves without instructing solicitors or counsel (see section 5).

1.2 Law Centres

Law Centres offer legal advice. Their offices are usually in the local high street. There are about 60 law centres in England and Wales, found in inner city areas in the main, and generally funded by local authorities. They are run by lawyers and advice workers and tend to specialize in a particular area of law, for example housing and immigration. Specialities may vary from one area or centre to another. If a law centre is not able to take on a case itself, it can usually refer you elsewhere (see, for example, *Local referral schemes*, section 1.8 below).

1.3 Legal advice centres

There may be a legal advice centre in your area. These are staffed by volunteer lawyers who offer free advice and assistance, the type of legal advice depending on the particular centre. They can also assist clients in pursuing their claims in tribunals, small claims court, etc. These centres are usually run by church groups, charities. etc.

1.4 Citizens' advice bureaux

You can also obtain advice from a Citizens' Advice Bureau (CAB) – an advice shop run by the National Association of Citizens' Advice Bureaux. These are financed by grants from central and local government. CABs deal with all sorts of queries and they are often the first port of call for the public for free advice. They are frequently in a position to offer help with a range of issues such as consumer queries, debt, repossession, etc.

An advice worker will help you to establish your legal position. If there is a difficult problem, you will probably be referred to a solicitor, law centre or legal advice centre for assistance in sorting it out. There is no charge for advice from a CAB and there are lots of leaflets available. Addresses can be found in the local telephone directory.

1.5 Alternative Dispute Resolution

More and more emphasis is being placed on solutions to conflict outside the courts through mediation rather than confrontation. The generic term is *Alternative Dispute Resolution* (ADR). As we see immediately below, ADR can take many forms.

1.5.1 Arbitration

In some cases, disputes can be resolved by arbitration. For example, a dissatisfied customer may use an arbitration service provided by a trade organization (see chapter on *Goods and Services*).

1.5.2 Conciliation and mediation

Another alternative way of resolving disputes is conciliation. This assists parties to resolve their themselves. Its use in divorce proceedings with regard to the matrimonial home, etc. is a cheaper and less stressful process than a full court case and is being progressively encouraged. See chapter on *Divorce*.

1.5.3 ACAS

The Advisory, Conciliation and Arbitration Service (ACAS) was set up to act as mediator in industrial disputes. It normally deals with large disputes between trade unions and management but also deals with individual employer and employee disputes.

Every application to an industrial tribunal is also first sent to ACAS to determine whether there is any possibility of a negotiated settlement.

1.6 Equal Opportunities Commission and the Commission for Racial Equality

These two Commissions were set up to deal with particular problems, generally involving issues of discrimination, particularly in the work place.

1.6.1 Equal Opportunities Commission

The EOC was set up to work towards the elimination of discrimination against women and to promote equality of opportunity between men and women.

1.6.2 Commission for Racial Equality

The CRE was similarly set up to work towards the elimination of racial discrimination and to promote equality of opportunity and good relations between persons of different racial groups.

Many of these issues are looked at in the chapter on *Employment*.

1.6.3 Functions of the Commissions

The Commissions have power to assist individuals in bringing cases under the Race Relations Act and the Sex Discrimination Act. They can conduct formal investigations into alleged instances of discrimination. They may also apply to the court for a decision on whether certain types of unlawful discrimination have occurred. They can take action on behalf of an alleged victim of discrimination and they handle individual complaints as well as acting on a referral basis, e.g. from a trade union.

1.7 Other legal personnel

1.7.1 Legal executives

Legal executives work in solicitors' offices and deal with routine legal work. They qualify as legal executives after passing examinations set by their own Institute, plus five years' work experience. They sometimes work under the supervision of a solicitor but also carry out many tasks on their own, specializing in a particular area of law, e.g. wills and probate, or conveyancing. They are bound by a strict code of conduct. The Institute of Legal Executives provides an information pack on training requirements (see DIRECTORY).

1.7.2 Licensed Conveyancers

These are persons who are trained to become licensed conveyancers. They are then allowed to compete with solicitors in conveyancing work.

The Council of Licensed Conveyancers oversees disciplinary matters. All licensed conveyancers must be insured so that clients are protected in transactions undertaken on their behalf. The Council publishes a booklet giving details of current training requirements (see DIRECTORY).

1.8 Local referral schemes

In October 1993, the Law Society issued a press release on the introduction of a new local referral scheme. Through their local Law Society, solicitors will act in conjunction with local advice agencies (such as Law Centres and CABs) to set up such a scheme. The public will be given information on firms which offer low-cost or free first interviews. These details are indicated by the Law Society in their regional directories. Each local scheme will decide which areas of law it intends to cover within a broad framework of 'personal matters'.

An initial interview is intended to diagnose the problem and discuss the issue of fees, as well as assessing the client for eligibility for legal aid.

1.8.1 Accident Line

This service offers callers a free advice session on Freephone 0500 19 29 39.

1.9 Duty Solicitor Scheme

If you are arrested – or even if you are just being questioned by the police – you are entitled to the free advice and assistance of a solicitor under the Duty Solicitor Scheme.

Duty solicitors are available on a voluntary rota basis to provide assistance and cover in magistrates courts. They are usually paid out of the legal aid fund.

You can also ask to see your own solicitor or see a solicitor from a list which the police should provide to you.

1.10 Specialist groups and organizations

Certain organizations listed in the Directories at the ends of chapters in this book offer help to their own members. Others (such as Victim Support) may offer advice to members of the general public. These groups and organizations may be in a position to refer problems to their own legal departments (for example, if you are a member of the RAC, you may be able to approach their legal department in the event of an accident).

In certain other cases, an organization may put you in touch with a solicitor in your area who is a specialist in a particular field. For example, the mediators' associations can supply names and addresses of local solicitors who are trained to deal with family disputes through mediation. They also give information about fees payable.

◆ **Do note:** not all the organizations listed are in a position to give help in this way.

1.11 Trade unions

Many employees are members of a trades union which will assist them in the event of a dispute at work or other problems involving the work place, for example, threatened redundancy.

1.12 Free Representation Unit

The Free Representation Unit was set up by members of the Bar. It deals only with cases which are referred to it by other advice agencies, such as a law centre or a CAB. Its representatives, who are qualified barristers, act on a voluntary basis in the various tribunals, for example employment or social security tribunals where legal aid is not available. A representative only takes on a case after representation in a particular case has been authorized by the FRU's committee.

◆ **Note:** the FRU does not accept referrals direct from members of the public.

1.13 Seeking advice – problems to overcome

There are certain major problems to overcome in seeking advice – apart from a psychological reluctance. These are not fanciful – they can be real problems for anyone with an everyday legal concern. They are

- expense
- time
- complexity of the law.

1.13.1 Expense

The question of lawyers' fees and costs in litigation are dealt with below (see section 2).

As we have seen above, there are many avenues to explore in seeking advice on everyday legal problems which need not necessarily lead you to be very much out of pocket.

The fact of the matter is that – in theory – we should all be entitled to access to justice. In fact, it is often only the very rich or the very poor who can afford to pursue their claims. But as with so many of these issues, we have to look at the reverse side of the coin too. If litigation were too readily available and became a matter of course, anyone with a grudge could look to the law to sort out their problem. How would the system cope with such an avalanche of 'justice-seekers'?

At the same time, the Lord Chief Justice tellingly rebuked the legal profession recently. He stated that fees charged by both barristers and solicitors were 'often out of all proportion to the job'. By charging such high fees to their corporate clients, this had a 'trickle down effect' so that even modest civil actions became prohibitively expensive.

The reputation of both branches of the profession would be much improved if the pursuit of higher fees were to be replaced 'by a more modest concept of the rate for the job', he said. (Quotation from the *Law Society Gazette* 90/36 6 October 1993).

1.13.2 Time

There is no question that pursuing a legal remedy – no matter how just your cause – can be very time-consuming. Procedures are unwieldy and slow of their very nature; lawyers are often hard-pressed and can only give their limited time to your case. Of course for every person who approaches a lawyer, his or her problem is the most pressing of all. But multiply this factor by the number of clients and it is not surprising that we sometimes feel we are not getting the attention our problem deserves.

At the same time, court business is also under tremendous pressure. It can take a year to 18 months for a case to be heard in the Queen's Bench Division of the High Court (see below, section 5.9). In the Chancery Division, it can take even longer – up to two years.

1.13.3 Complexity of the law

It is not just the layperson who sometimes finds the law impenetrable. Judges also complain that a body of law which affects us all, for example, in the employment field, will be difficult to interpret because of its complexity.

Sometimes, issues cannot be simplified. Sometimes, however, lawyers are correctly accused of using difficult language and arcane phraseology for its own sake.

It is encouraging that many of the leaflets presently being put out by various departments and organizations bear the 'Crystal Mark' of clarity, approved by the Plain English Campaign. For example, the Legal Aid leaflet 'How to get Free or Low Cost Legal Help' issued by the Legal Aid Head Office in April 1993 bears this mark. The Legal Aid Board also makes its advice leaflets available in many other languages.

1.14 Legal Services Ombudsman

If you are unhappy with the way your legal problem has been handled, you can complain to the Solicitors' Complaints Bureau in the case of a solicitor or to the Bar Council in the case of a barrister. If you feel that the professional body itself has not dealt satisfactorily with your complaint, you can apply to the Legal Services Ombudsman, who will investigate the matter.

Not all cases are dealt with by the Ombudsman and you are advised to study his terms of reference carefully. There is a firm time limit of three months in which to refer your complaint to him. The services are entirely free of charge.

You can contact the Ombudsman's Office either by writing or by telephoning him (see DIRECTORY for details).

2. Paying for advice

2.1 Lawyers' fees

Lawyers are supposed to tell their clients in advance about the possible level of charges and how costs are likely to be calculated.

The best possible approach to avoid future conflict is to ask for the information to be provided in writing. Indeed the solicitors' professional written standards require that solicitors 'give clients the best information possible about the likely level of charges'.

In fairness to the profession, not all legal fees are calculable in advance, however. Unforeseen problems may arise. For example, you may have written to your landlord complaining of dangerous steps in the common parts of a block of flats. He may do nothing about it and you eventually instruct your solicitor to write on your behalf. If your landlord then seeks evidence from other tenants by affidavit [sworn evidence] or an expert's report, you may have to counter by supplying your own evidence from another expert and other tenants. In no time at all, the costs snowball. You can ask for a periodical statement of costs.

Barristers' fees are negotiated between solicitors and the barristers' clerks.

2.1.1 Conditional fees

Until recently English law did not allow lawyers to take on cases on a speculative basis. However, under the Legal Services Act 1991, in a limited number of situations, a lawyer can take on a 'no win, no fee' case. Conditional fees apply to

- Personal injury cases
- Insolvency
- Human rights cases to be heard before the European Court of Human Rights.

The conditional fees system has been introduced at the same time that legal aid eligibility has been cut (see below, section 2.2.2). Thus it is intended to counter-balance a possible denial of access to justice for a broad range of persons.

With a contingency fee, a lawyer takes a cut of the damages if you win and receives nothing if you lose. Under the conditional fees system, however, a lawyer will be able to double his fees if he or she wins the case. However, the loser will still have to pay costs (see below, section 2.3) which should be a great disincentive to spurious litigation. Would-be litigants would be well advised to examine their own case very carefully before risking a 100 per cent increase in loser's costs.

2.1.2 Legal insurance schemes

If you are not entitled to legal aid, another way of paying for legal advice is via legal insurance. It is not unlike private health insurance and is sometimes offered as an extra with household insurance.

2.2 Legal Aid

Legal Aid is help towards legal costs.

Legal Aid solicitors have a characteristic legal aid sign and their names are listed in the Solicitors' Regional Directories at your local library.

Legal Aid is divided into civil and criminal legal aid and help under the green form scheme (see section 2.2.4 below). As a result of rules introduced in April 1993 you are only eligible for completely free legal aid if you are on income support. You may still get some financial assistance depending on your income.

2.2.1 Qualifying for legal aid

2.2.2 Income

Usually the solicitor would be in a position to tell you whether you qualify for legal aid – and if so, to what extent you qualify. All sorts of factors are taken into account in assessing your eligibility:

- your savings
- your income
- your partner's income
- your dependants
- your property
- your possessions.

◆ **Note:** The figures given below are in the process of being revised after protests from the profession that the constraints on income are too stringent.

2.2.3 Merit

You also have to satisfy the Legal Aid Assessment Office that your case has some merit for civil legal aid. In other words you must have reasonable grounds for taking someone to court (in which case you are the plaintiff) or reasonable grounds for defending a court action which someone is pursuing against you (in which case you are the defendant). The value of your claim is also a factor – the amount involved may make it uneconomic to pursue.

2.2.4 Green form scheme

If you can't afford to pay the costs of a solicitor to advise you, it is possible that you may qualify for legal advice and assistance under the green form scheme which offers up to two hours' work by a solicitor at no charge, and three hours' on matrimonial matters.

You qualify for help under the green form scheme if your savings are below £1,000 and your income is no more than £61 per week or you are receiving income support, family credit or disablement allowance.

2.2.5 Civil legal aid

The amount of legal aid you can claim depends on your income and savings.

(a) Income

If your annual disposable income is £2,294 or less you will be entitled to full legal aid. If it is more than £6,800 you will not qualify for legal aid at all. In between those two figures you will be entitled to some legal aid but will be required to make a contribution.

(b) Capital

Your savings and items of substantial value (but not the house you live in) must be added up. The difference is your disposable capital. If this amounts to less than £6,750, you will qualify for Legal Aid. If it is less than £3,000 you will not have to pay a contribution.

2.2.6 A note of warning

▶ **Remember** that if you are successful in legal proceedings, you may be asked to make a contribution to your solicitor's bill. Therefore it would be wise to check with your solicitor whether it is worth going ahead with your case. The importance of this note of warning cannot be overstressed. In such circumstances, legal aid acts as a loan – many people forget that they may have to pay towards their solicitors' bill even in the event of a positive outcome to their claim. Legal aid may put the client in the same position as a fee-paying client (see also section 2.3.1 below).

For example, you are a married woman and do not work. You petition your husband, who has moved in with another woman, for divorce. As you are living apart from him, his income does not count towards your financial qualifications for legal aid, which you obtain. You seek a cash settlement against him and are successful. You then have to pay your solicitor's bill out of that settlement.

◆ **Note** that you will not be eligible for legal aid for matters coming before industrial, social security or immigration tribunals. Legal aid is not available for all matters before the courts; for example, road traffic offences are excluded.

2.2.7 Criminal legal aid

The amount of legal aid to which you are entitled is calculated by looking at your weekly disposable income and your savings.

Disposable income is the amount left after deducting sums for income tax, national insurance, mortgage, council tax and providing for any dependants you may have.

You will qualify for full legal aid if your weekly disposable income is £45 or less. For every £3 over that amount you will have to pay £1 towards your legal costs.

2.3 Costs

The legal expenses payable for the services of a solicitor and barrister in court are known as costs. In a court action the losing party usually has to pay the costs of the successful party. The court controls the amount of these costs by way of a procedure called 'taxation of costs'.

2.3.1 Another note of warning

Even if you win a case, and your opponent is ordered to pay your costs, do not necessarily expect to be paid in full. Even as a winner, you can end up out of pocket. For example, the taxing master of the court might think that your solicitors overcharged on their hourly rate, or that they took too many hours to prepare the case. After taxation of costs, you will then have to pay the shortfall between what your solicitors charged you and what has been allowed by the taxing master.

If an unsuccessful litigant is legally aided and his opponent is not legally aided, the successful party will not normally be able to recover costs from the legally aided party.

3. The trial

3.1 The adversarial system

If a matter cannot be resolved out of court the matter goes to trial and is supervised by a judge. The parties and their lawyers present the two sides of the story and the judge ensures that the rules are adhered to. He or she decides who wins the case on the evidence and arguments presented by each party.

This system is known as the 'adversarial' system.

3.2 Litigation as a last resort

All litigation is a gamble. There is never any certainty as to the outcome. No matter how convinced you are of your own case, you must never forget your opponent is equally convinced of the rightness of his or her own cause.

You must not forget, either, that the role of the judge is to stand back and take an impartial and objective view of the case. Even if you feel that justice is on your side, the judge's view of the dispute may not be the same as yours – for example, the judge's interpretation of a tiny provision in a statute may be fatal to your case.

4. Judges

There are several levels of judges.

4.1 Magistrate

A magistrate sits in the local magistrates' court (see section 5.4) and hears minor criminal cases. Magistrates are chosen by the Lord Chancellor from applicants within the local community. They are also known as Justices of the Peace. Three magistrates usually sit together to hear cases and they are advised on the law by a magistrates' clerk who is a qualified lawyer.

There are also some full time magistrates who are known as stipendiaries. These are legally qualified people who sit alone to hear cases. They are found mainly in the big cities.

4.2 District judge

District judges sit in the county court and hear 'minor' cases such as small claims (see section 5.1). They also decide on some preliminary questions which might arise in other cases.

4.3 Circuit judges

These sit in both the county courts and the Crown Courts in the six areas around England and Wales known as circuits. They are mostly former barristers although a few are former solicitors.

4.4 Official referees

These are circuit judges nominated to sit as High Court judges to deal with cases which need a detailed examination of documents and accounts or scientific investigation. They deal particularly with cases involving the construction industry.

4.5 Masters

These are senior judicial officers who hear minor cases and rule on preliminary issues in the Chancery Division and the Queen's Bench Division of the High Court.

4.6 High Court judges

These sit in the High Court in London and in centres around England and Wales and hear the more serious cases.

Once appointed as a High Court judge a person might be selected as one of the judges who sit in the Court of Appeal and hear appeals from the lower courts on points of law only.

The Lord Chief Justice is the senior judge in England who sits in the Criminal Division of the Court of Appeal and presides over the Queen's Bench Division of the High Court.

The Master of the Rolls is the senior civil law judge who presides over the Civil Division of the Court of Appeal.

4.7 House of Lords

The Law Lords are the most senior appeal judges. They sit in the House of Lords. There are ten of them and they sit in groups of five to hear appeals.

5. Seeking justice – the courts

The truth is that the general public do not find the courts user-friendly. In a very real sense, of course, the formality is there to serve a purpose. We are meant to be in awe of the law. Furthermore, certain technical rules which govern court proceedings, for example, the laws of evidence, are intended to be a genuine safeguard to litigants.

But given that people's liberty, property, or even their own children, can be removed from them by court proceedings, the public are entitled to a greater degree of consideration and understanding than they sometimes presently receive. Alas, certain judges and court administrators all too often seem to forget that they are there to serve the public and not vice versa!

Procedures in the civil courts have been described as 'cumbersome, inflexible and archaic'. These are harsh terms indeed – used in a joint report issued by the Bar and the Law Society in September 1993.

A Court Charter is available and should be read by all would-be litigants and witnesses. There is also a Supreme Court Check-list for those who wish to be litigants in person at the Royal Court of Justice, rather than instructing a solicitor or barrister to act for them.

5.1 Bringing a small claim – arbitration proceedings

The small claims court is part of the general court system. It enables you to take your own case to court by using a simple straightforward procedure. If your claim is £1,000 or less it will automatically be treated as a small claim. Claims over that amount may also be dealt with as a small claim but then the court has to agree to this.

Small claims are heard by a district judge.

To bring a claim in the small claims court you have to go through the following procedure.

(a) Fill in the court form stating the amount claimed, why it is being claimed and who the claim is against. Many legal centres and other bodies will help with form-filling.

(b) Take the completed form to your local county court. The staff there will go through the form and ensure that it is properly completed. You will have to pay a filing fee and they will retain the form to start your case moving.

(c) Within two weeks or so the court will send a summons to the person against whom you are claiming (the defendant). The defendant must send back a defence within 14 days. If he or she fails to do so you may be entitled to a ruling in your favour without the matter going any further. The court will be able to tell you if that is the case.

(d) If the defendant does send in a defence the court will set a date for a pre-trial review which will be some months later. Then the district judge will review the case and order each party to exchange any documents such as invoices or letters on which you rely to prove your claim.

(e) If the case has to go to court it will probably do so within six months from the time you fill in the form.

The hearing is in private. The judge will supervise the proceedings and each party will tell his or her side of the story. The judge then usually makes a ruling at once having heard all that you have to say.

(f) If you win, you will be entitled to claim any expenses you have incurred in bringing the claim and you will be able to claim back the court fee. There should be no other costs involved.

A leaflet giving information on how to go about bringing a claim in the small claims court is available from the CAB free of charge.

◆ **Note of warning:** you may find that the other side has legal representation even though you yourself are pursuing a claim in person. However, if you lose, you are not obliged to pay their costs.

5.1.1 Extension of the small claims procedure

There are current proposals to institute a small claims procedure for personal injuries where the amount of damages is not expected to exceed £1,000.

5.2 Tribunals

Tribunals are informal courts within the civil legal system which deal with cases in specialized areas. They consist of a lawyer, sometimes sitting with lay members, who will probably have experience in the field in which the dispute has arisen.

They include industrial tribunals dealing with disputes between employers and employees, especially concerning unfair dismissal or discrimination (see sections 1.6.1 and 1.6.2 on the Equal Opportunities Commission and the Commission for Racial Equality, see also chapter on *Employment*).

Tribunals are intended to be simple and easy to use but they often involve complicated areas of law. It is thus becoming more common for lawyers to be engaged to argue points of law.

However legal aid is not available for such cases. The layperson acting for him or herself against a lawyer briefed by an employer can be severely disadvantaged (see *Free Representation Unit* above, section 1.12).

Other tribunals cover such areas as immigration, rent and other land assessment, social security, immigration and mental health. The Medical Appeal Tribunal hears appeals against refusal of claims for mobility allowance and other injury-related benefits.

5.3 Employment Appeals Tribunal (EAT)

The EAT hears appeals from industrial tribunals. It comprises a High Court judge and two lay members with knowledge of industrial relations, e.g. trades union officials etc. Legal aid is available for those who qualify for it to bring an appeal before the EAT.

5.4 Magistrates' Courts

Magistrates' Courts are the lowest courts in the criminal justice system. They also have a civil jurisdiction in family matters dealing with, for example, maintenance and adoption. They are also responsible for granting liquor licences for restaurants, betting shops and casinos etc.

5.5 Crown Courts

The Crown Court is a more senior court which deals with criminal cases heard by a judge and jury. It also acts as an appeal court where the judge sits with some lay magistrates to hear the appeals.

5.6 County Courts

County courts are situated all over England and Wales; they are presided over by a circuit judge and have the power to hear all but the most important civil cases. They deal with money claims, building society house repossession cases, landlord and tenant disputes, disputes over wills and the winding up of companies, as well as bankruptcy.

They also have jurisdiction over family matters with power to grant divorces and make orders concerning property and children.

They are presided over by a circuit judge.

Cases may be transferred from the county courts to the High Court if a complex issue arises which needs a ruling by a High Court judge. A case may also be transferred back again to the county court as necessary.

5.7 Court of Protection

Relatives can apply to the court for a receiver to be appointed where there is a patient incapable of taking care of his or her own property. The Court issues a Guidance Note with notes for personal applicants, as well as notes for solicitors. The forms include medical certificate and a certificate listing family and property. The patient is generally informed and observations and representations can be made at the hearing. The court also registers enduring powers of attorney. (See also chapter on *Death – Before and After*).

5.8 Coroners' Courts

A coroner must hold an inquest if a death is not due to natural causes.

An inquest is not strictly speaking a trial – it is an investigative procedure. However, there may be witnesses who are called and, in certain circumstances, a jury. Juries are usually summoned if someone has died in custody or in connection with an arrest.

Although relatives may be represented by a lawyer, no legal aid is available.

Coroners' courts also investigate treasure trove in order to decide whether the treasure belongs to the Crown. A jury is always present.

5.9 The High Court

The High Court sits at the Royal Courts of Justice in London and at other centres throughout England and Wales. It is divided into three sections: Queen's Bench, Chancery and Family.

5.9.1 Queen's Bench Division

This is the biggest of the three divisions. Its work covers general civil claims for damages in tort (breach of duty) and contract.

Within the QBD there are specialist courts:

- the Commercial Court, which deals with commercial matters
- the Admiralty Court, which deals with shipping disputes
- The Divisional Court, which deals with judicial reviews and appeals from the magistrates' courts on points of law.

Judicial review is the process for reviewing administrative decisions, e.g. by government departments, local authorities etc. The court can examine the legal and procedural elements of such a decision but is not entitled to rule on its merits.

5.9.2 Chancery Division

This division deals with disputes concerning matters such as tax, land, mortgages, property, trusts etc. It also deals with wills.

There are 14 judges sitting in this division.

There are specialist courts within the Chancery Division:

- the Companies Court, which deals with company matters, e.g. winding up, directors' disqualifications, administrations etc.
- The Patents Court, which deals with disputes concerning copyright, passing off etc.

5.9.3 Family Division

The Family Division as the name suggests deals with family matters, particularly disputes in divorce proceedings. It also has jurisdiction over wards of court and deals with adoption. (See chapter on *Children*).

5.10 Court of Appeal

This court hears appeals from the county court, High Court and Crown Courts. It is divided into the criminal and civil divisions and is situated at the Royal Courts of Justice in London. The Lord Chief Justice presides over the Criminal Division. An appeal is usually heard by three judges known as Lords Justices. However some appeals are heard by two judges if the case is considered appropriate.

5.11 House of Lords

The Lords of Appeal in Ordinary (The Law Lords) are the legal members of the House of Lords, and form the highest court in England. The House of Lords hears not only English appeals but also Scottish civil, though not criminal, appeals. Generally the House of Lords hears only appeals on points of law of general public importance. Permission has to be obtained to pursue such an appeal, either from the Court of Appeal or from the House of Lords itself.

5.12 Privy Council

The Judicial Committee of the Privy Council hears appeals from what remains of the Colonies, the most important being Hong Kong, and from those former British territories which have chosen to keep it as their final Court of Appeal, including New Zealand, Trinidad and Singapore.

The Privy Council is made up mainly of those Law Lords who sit in the House of Lords. However, sometimes a judge from one of the Commonwealth countries is also invited to sit.

5.13 Court of Justice of the European Union

The European Court of Justice (ECJ) is the court of the European Union sitting in Luxembourg. It has jurisdiction over Member States on matters concerning Community law. Its judgements on the interpretation of this law are final and take precedence even over House of Lords' decisions.

A national court may refer a question to the ECJ where it considers that interpretation of EU law is necessary before it can make a decision on a case before it. However a court is *required* to refer a question to which there is no answer under national law.

The ECJ gives general guidance in its rulings but it is for the national courts to apply its interpretation of EU law to the specific case giving rise to the reference.

5.14 European Court of Human Rights

The European Court of Human Rights sits at Strasbourg and hears disputes between individual litigants and any country which has signed the European Convention on Human Rights and Fundamental Freedoms, to which the United Kingdom is a party.

A prospective litigant has no direct access to the court. The Commission set up by the Council of Europe first vets it to ensure that there is no further assistance to be had from the national courts and that the issue relates to a right guaranteed by the Convention.

The court is made up of a judge from each Member State and each judge gives a separate decision.

6. Sources of law

6.1 Common law

The basis of English law is known as the 'common law'. This means that it is a system of law which has been built up over the centuries by decisions of judges in particular cases. Reports of these cases are published in the Law Reports. Cases decided in the higher courts are more influential than those in the lower courts. Where decisions differ, decisions in the higher courts overrule those from the lower courts.

6.2 Equity

The strict rules of law are influenced by a discretion which the courts have, to ensure that the rules are applied fairly. This is called the 'equitable jurisdiction' or 'equity'. Over the years rules have also evolved to lay down when the discretion can be exercised. Just because a rule works unfairly in a particular case does not mean the courts can modify its operation, however.

Certain court procedures are known as 'equitable remedies' – the most common instance being an injunction. For example, a court may make an order (or grant an injunction) to stop you from using a footpath in a dispute with your neighbour over a right of way.

6.3 Statute

Statute law is made up of Acts of Parliament. The Government normally introduces a Bill suggesting new rules to be followed on a particular topic, which has to pass through both Houses of Parliament. It then receives the Royal Assent and becomes law.

6.4 Precedent

This is the system whereby decisions made by a court in one case are applied to cases where similar issues arise. The House of Lords has the final word on any point of law and the decisions of the Court of Appeal overrule decisions of the lower courts etc.

6.5 European Community Law

The European Court of Justice was set up under the EC Treaty to interpret European Community law which applies to all the Member States of the EC (now the European Union). There are 13 Judges, one from each Member State. There are also six Advocates General who assist the judges of the court by delivering an opinion in open court after written and oral submissions. The Court of Justice, when giving its ruling, usually follows the outcome suggested by the Advocate General although the court is free to disagree with the opinion. There is also the Court of First Instance established to relieve the Court of Justice of some of its heavy case load.

European law is contained in Regulations, Directives and Decisions. A Regulation is binding on all Member States directly. A Directive affects all the member States but it is for the individual Members to achieve the aim of the Directive by taking whatever measures are necessary.

7. Reforming the law

Contrary to popular impression, the law is not static. It moves with the times as we have seen again and again throughout this book.

However, it needs certainty too. We cannot have our legal system in a continual state of flux. We must know – as far as possible – that our actions which are legal today will not be made illegal tomorrow. This should be kept in mind when charges of 'being out of date' are levelled at the law. As always a line must be drawn between certainty and reform. As always, too, the position of the line will have proponents and opponents.

Change comes from many sources as we will see below.

7.1 Parliament

In the UK, there is no written constitution. Parliament has the right to make or change any law and the courts must then enforce it. In theory this right is unfettered except by international obligation.

In practice, of course, MPs are answerable to their own constituents and so they endeavour to ensure that the legislation which they pass will reflect a broad consensus. Sometimes they may fail to gauge public opinion correctly, such as with the Poll Tax, and the law may become unworkable. Sometimes, there may be an overhasty reaction to public opinion, and the law may not be as carefully considered as it might have been. An example, in some eyes, is the Dangerous Dogs Act which was passed in response to attacks on children by pit bull terriers (see chapter on the *Countryside*). Ultimately, though, it is to Parliament that we must all turn – whether judge or layman – for reform of those areas of the law that are in the most pressing need of change.

7.2 The precedents

Again contrary to popular impression, judges themselves continually keep the law under review. The whole system of common law and precedent depends on judge-made law although judges will say that their task is only to interpret the law and not to 'make' it.

Once a definitive decision has been given in the House of Lords, it then binds all the other courts – unless reference is made to the European Court of Justice or the Court of Human Rights. A striking example of judge-made law is the recent House of Lords' decision that a man can be guilty of marital rape (see Chapter 1). This single decision overturned a very different, centuries-old, judicial perception of the laws governing the relationship between husbands and wives.

7.3 Law Commission

The Law Commission advises the Government on law reform. It is headed by a High Court Judge seconded from his duties for the purpose, usually for a period of three years. Scotland has a separate Law Commission.

The Commission's function is to make proposals for updating and reforming the law. Throughout the book, we have mentioned proposals put forward by the Law Commission, for example, on changes to the marriage laws (see Chapter 1).

7.4 Royal Commissions

The government will appoint a Royal Commission to examine a particular area of law in the light of a pressing need for such an investigation. After a series of miscarriages of justice in the criminal justice system for example, a Royal Commission on Criminal Justice was appointed under Lord Runciman with wide terms of reference.

7.5 Pressure groups

The importance of groups keeping up pressure on the government for change in the law cannot be overemphasized. Such groups can be formed by concerned members of the public or can come from within the legal system itself.

7.5.1 Within the legal profession

In a sense, of course, no one is more likely to be aware of anomalies in the legal system than those who deal with it as part of their everyday business.

There are many groups within the profession, both solicitors and barristers, who have a fundamental concern with changing the law. Official bodies such as the Law Society and the Bar Council may reflect this concern to a greater or lesser degree. Other groups are formed by members of the professions, such as the organization called *Justice*, which investigates complaints of wrongful conviction.

7.5.2 The public at large

Pressure groups within the public at large can spring up to meet an immediate need. Their voices can be heard quickly and effectively. A recent example is the fathers' response to their perceived view of the injustices of the Child Support Agency (see chapter on *Children*).

However, there are many long-standing groups which work consistently towards changes in the law in their particular sphere of interest. An example is an organization such as the Ramblers Association which has consistently campaigned for the proper enforcement of the laws concerning rights of way (see chapter on *Countryside*).

DIRECTORY
Legal System

The Court Service Secretariat
Lord Chancellor's Department
Southside
105 Victoria Street
London SW1E 6QT
Tel. 071 210 2059

Council for Licensed Conveyancers
16 Glebe Road
Chelmsford
Essex CM1 1QG
Tel. 0245 349599

Crown Prosecution Service
50 Ludgate Hill
London EC4M 7EX
Tel. 071 273 8152

The Free Representation Unit
49–51 Bedford Row
London WC1R 4LR
Tel. 071 831 0692

General Council of the Bar
3 Bedford Row
London WC1R 4DB
Tel. 071 831 4209

The Institute of Legal Executives
Kempston Manor
Kempston
Bedford MK42 7AB
Tel. 0234 841000

Law Centres Federation
Duchess House
18–19 Warren Street
London W1P 5DB
Tel. 071 387 8570

Litigants in Person Society
11 Eastgate Street
Winchester SO23 8EB
Tel. 0962 854 003

The Law Society
113 Chancery Lane
London WC2A 1PL
Tel. 071 242 1222

Legal Action Group
242 Pentonville Road
London N1 9UN
Tel. 071 833 3931

Liberty
21 Tabard Street
London SE1 4LA
Tel. 071 403 3888

National Association of Citizens' Advice Bureaux
115–23 Pentonville Road
London N1 9LZ
Tel. 071 833 2181

Office of the Legal Services Ombudsman
22 Oxford Court
Oxford Street
Manchester M2 3WQ
Tel. 061 236 9532

The Society of Licensed Conveyancers
55 Church Road
Croydon CR9 1PF
Tel. 081 681 1001

Solicitors Complaints Bureau
Portland House
Stag Place
London SW1E 5BL

Supreme Court Accounts Office
Room EO1
Royal Courts of Justice
Strand
London WC2A 2LL

INDEX